Governance Series

Governance is the process of effective coordination whereby an organization or a system guides itself when resources, power, and information are widely distributed. Studying governance means probing the pattern of rights and obligations that underpins organizations and social systems, understanding how they coordinate their parallel activities and maintain their coherence, exploring the sources of dysfunction, and suggesting ways to redesign organizations whose governance is in need of repair.

The series welcomes a range of contributions—from conceptual and theoretical reflections, ethnographic and case studies, and proceedings of conferences and symposia, to works of a very practical nature—that deal with problems or issues on the governance front. The series publishes works both in French and in English.

The Governance Series is part of the publications division of the Centre on Governance and of the Graduate School of Public and International Affairs at the University of Ottawa. This is the 24th volume published in the series. The Centre on Governance and the Graduate School of Public and International Affairs also publish a quarterly electronic journal, www.optimumonline.ca.

Editorial Committee

Caroline Andrew
Linda Cardinal
Monica Gattinger
Luc Juillet
Daniel Lane
Gilles Paquet (Director)

The published titles in the series are listed at the end of this book.

THE BLACK HOLE OF PUBLIC ADMINISTRATION

RUTH HUBBARD & GILLES PAQUET

UNIVERSITY OF OTTAWA PRESS
OTTAWA

University of Ottawa Press
542 King Edward Avenue
Ottawa, ON K1N 6N5
www.press.uottawa.ca

University of
Ottawa Press

The University of Ottawa Press acknowledges with gratitude the support extended to its publishing list by Heritage Canada through its Book Publishing Industry Development Program, by the Canada Council for the Arts, by the Canadian Federation for the Humanities and Social Sciences through its Aid to Scholarly Publications Program, by the Social Sciences and Humanities Research Council, and by the University of Ottawa.

We also gratefully acknowledge the Centre on Governance at the University of Ottawa and Invenire4 Ltd., whose financial support has contributed to the publication of this book.

LIBRARY AND ARCHIVES CANADA CATALOGUING IN PUBLICATION

Hubbard, Ruth, 1942-
The black hole of public administration / Ruth
Hubbard & Gilles Paquet.

(Governance series, 1487-3052 ; 24)
Includes bibliographical references and index.
ISBN 978-0-7766-0742-9

1. Public administration—Canada. 2. Civil service—Canada.
3. Canada—Politics and government. I. Paquet, Gilles, 1936-
II. Series: Governance series (Ottawa, Ont.) ; 24.

JL108.H83 2010   351.71   C2010-902837-6

Table of contents

THE BLACK HOLE OF
PUBLIC ADMINISTRATION

RUTH HUBBARD & GILLES PAQUET

UNIVERSITY OF OTTAWA PRESS
OTTAWA

University of Ottawa Press
542 King Edward Avenue
Ottawa, ON K1N 6N5
www.press.uottawa.ca

University of
Ottawa Press

The University of Ottawa Press acknowledges with gratitude the support
extended to its publishing list by Heritage Canada through its Book
Publishing Industry Development Program, by the Canada Council for the
Arts, by the Canadian Federation for the Humanities and Social Sciences
through its Aid to Scholarly Publications Program, by the Social Sciences
and Humanities Research Council, and by the University of Ottawa.

We also gratefully acknowledge the Centre on Governance at the University
of Ottawa and Invenire4 Ltd., whose financial support has contributed to the
publication of this book.

© University of Ottawa Press 2010

LIBRARY AND ARCHIVES CANADA CATALOGUING IN PUBLICATION

Hubbard, Ruth, 1942-
The black hole of public administration / Ruth
Hubbard & Gilles Paquet.

(Governance series, 1487-3052 ; 24)
Includes bibliographical references and index.
ISBN 978-0-7766-0742-9

1. Public administration—Canada. 2. Civil service—Canada.
3. Canada—Politics and government. I. Paquet, Gilles, 1936-
II. Series: Governance series (Ottawa, Ont.) ; 24.

JL108.H83 2010   351.71   C2010-902837-6

Table of contents

LIST OF TABLES

LIST OF FIGURES

The effort to be more 'scientific' than the underlying subject matter permits carries a real cost in blinding us to the real complexities of public administration as it is practiced in different societies.

—Francis Fukuyama

If you fall in a black hole, what will happen?
You will be able to see images of far away objects distorted in strange ways, since the black hole gravity bends light.
However, no one can see you since light can't escape the hole.
What will happen to you is that you will be moving fast towards the center and depending on the size of the hole,
you will eventually hit the center (the singularity) sooner or later.

—Kamel M. Refaey

Public Administration in Distress

...new tools...create opportunities
to achieve new goals
or to do things in new ways.

—Emmanuel G. Mesthene

Some voices have denounced the poverty of public administration and the unduly generous representations of it being taught and propagandized by naive academics and self-serving bureaucrats (Laliberté 2009). These criticisms have been starkly ignored by the tribe of aficionados (academics and practitioners *en postes*) of traditional public administration: this tribe has remained unabashedly uncritical and has propagandized a fictionalized vision of an efficient and effective arrangement.

There had been hopes in the 1980s that the new public management initiatives triggered by politicians (however primitive their perspectives might have been at times) would succeed in shaking the traditional arrangements, built on the state-centric view of the world borne out of the 1930s Depression and of World War II. This was not to be. The phenomenal dynamic conservatism of the public administration tribe has been successful in stunting any genuine renaissance.

The Hegelian notion of the transcendent state and the Westminster fantasies about the neat structure of cascading power (from the citizenry to Parliament to government to the non-partisan public service) remained the basic references. Political parties and politicians have been uncritical about the nature of the game they are playing, the uppermost bureaucracy has been placid and self-centred *grosso modo*, and the di Lampedusa principle has prevailed—to change everything (or seem to do so) in order that nothing change (although it seems to) (Wallerstein 1998: 85).

Much inefficiency and ineffectiveness ensued, and, as a result, there has been "a loss of belief in the ability of the state structures to achieve this primary objective of improving the common weal. It resulted in a widespread and amorphous antistatism, of a kind totally unknown in the long period between 1789 and 1968" (Ibid., 31–32). This amorphous 'antistatism' has led to an implosion of the moral contracts of the politicians and the bureaucrats with society. A new clerisy of columnists, single-issue activists, and other extra-state actors has taken over the pulpit and provided the opinion-molding.

In parallel, over the last twenty years there has been a new learning generated by the literature on governance, and to the lessons learned from the experiments carried out in the private and social sectors or in the public sector elsewhere. Yet Canadian federal public administration has been somewhat deaf to the new learning.

Indeed, it has vehemently fought that new learning and staunchly defended the canon in good currency in the mid-third of the 20th century, by taking refuge behind both the so-called 'great successes' of public sector governing during that period, and a bizarre claim about the foundational singularity of the state sector.

In its defence of traditional public administration, the tribe has indeed taken much comfort in the gospel according to Jane Jacobs—stating that public and private management could not learn from each other because they were ontologically different

(Jacobs 1992). This fallacy has been denounced by the governance literature, but public administrators and public administration scholars have been clinging to this foundational dogma. This proved to be a major impediment to social learning.

How else can one explain that virtually all recent federal clerks of the Privy Council, beginning with Paul Tellier's PS2000 in 1989, have failed (despite their bombastic declarations about public service reform) to 'fix the culture' or improve aspects of the human resource system for the core public service, and that today—twenty years later—the 2009 Report of the Advisory Committee appointed by Prime Minister Harper could state bluntly:

> [w]e were appalled to see that many of the systems within the Public Service are seriously outdated. For example, the pay system is built on a forty year old platform that costs 15 times more per employee to operate than the industry standard (Mazankowski and Tellier et al. 2009)?

Or that, a report of the Public Policy Forum in 2008 could observe that their:

> examination revealed…a growing worry that the public service is becoming isolated from other segments of Canadian society; [t]he existence of mistrust and strained relationships between public servants and citizens, politicians and stakeholders, between Ottawa and the rest of the country and between public service leadership and its workforce… (Public Policy Forum 2008: 12–13)?

Or that another recent report could suggest that:

> [t]he *[Accountability] Act* increases both the machinery and bureaucracy of accountability and in so doing may reinforce an already marked tendency within Parliament and the media to focus on hindsight, blame and compliance rather than getting results and high quality outcomes that matter to Canadians (Green 2007: 23)?

This book challenges the Panglossian view, in the Canadian public administration community, that critical problems do not exist in Canada's public governance, and builds on the presumption that:

> a new order will emerge out of this chaos over a period of fifty years, and that this new order will be shaped as [a] function of what everyone does in the interval—those with power in the present system, and those without it (Wallerstein 1998: 90).

Moreover, it suggests not only what might be done in the interval to correct governance failures and to facilitate the emergence of the new order, but also a general philosophy that should guide these efforts—a philosophy of open sourcing.

Open sourcing as fata morgana

To our way of thinking, 'open sourcing' (involving a much larger number of much more active interested parties as producers of governance) as a model of governance is slowly and painfully emerging in Canada's private, public and social sectors, but in ways that are often not recognized as fully as they should be. Open sourcing, like decentralization, is not a panacea. But this radically participative way of collaboratively governing corresponds (under the right conditions) to the most effective way to deal with a fast paced, globalized, interconnected world (transfixed by complex issues, wicked policy problems, value conflicts, and where social learning is the imperative) (Paquet 1999a).

Some say that open sourcing is a mirage. Maybe, but it is an inspiring mirage:

> a Fata Morgana which makes beautiful lands arise before the eyes of the members of a caravan and thus increases their efforts to the point where, in spite of all their sufferings, they reach the next tiny waterhole. Had such tempting mirages not appeared, the exhausted caravan would inevitably have perished in the sandstorm, bereft of hope (Leszek Kolakowski quoted in Hirschman 1967: 32).

Open-source 'small g' governance is a promising reference point because it promises innovation; innovation presumes social learning; and social learning is rooted in participation, conversation, dissent and deliberation. Innovation in governance is rooted in the dissent of the governed about the way the system is run. If it is undeniable that dissent can be destructive, it is equally true that it need not be (Carter 1998; Sunstein 2003). Deliberation may be the source of polarization and amplification of error, when individual participants are more likely to be wrong than right, but it may also be the source of significant social learning when participants have the sort of knowledge and competence that leads one to presume that participants are more likely to be right than wrong (Sunstein 2006).

The sort of generalized conversation likely to foster the integration of modern society, unbeknownst to its citizens and other agents, is a result of passing through and somehow managing a variety of conflicts, and thereby learning the hard way, through dissent and deliberation, to trust one another and to cooperate (Hirschman 1995: 235). Some call it "the democratic miracle". Stewardship through dissent is at the core of the innovative culture (Horibe 2001).

Innovation requires imagination and improvisation, playing with the prototypical organizations and institutions in place, not following the rules but rigorously challenging and revising them. Serious play with these prototypes is the essence of innovation: it often starts with promising but barely satisfactory prototypes, emerging from a system that promotes and encourages their being put forward, and creatively extends and imaginatively redevelops them.

An intriguing example of a vague prototype that has triggered an interesting though short-lived conversation in Canada is the idea of 'open federalism'—*fédéralisme d'ouverture*—proposed by Stephen Harper in December 2005. However vague and ill defined the concept may have been, it has generated some modicum of serious play (Montpetit 2007; Banting et al. 2007). While it is unlikely to lead to what we call open-source experimentalist governance in Canada—the model we regard as the most promising—it is nevertheless a very good illustration of the potentialities of an experimentalist process if it can gain momentum (Sabel 2001, 2004).

Central to our perspective is the fact that there is no reason why such serious play around an interesting idea should need to be triggered by an utterance from a professional politician or a senior bureaucrat or a public administration scholar. It can as well emerge from the uttering of any citizen, if appropriate access to meaningful forums were ensured so that informed or expert citizens could actively and creatively partake in conversations about issues of significance (Blattberg 2004).

However, we are not there yet. Even such a cautious idea as 'open federalism' has quickly succeeded in lighting up the forces of dynamic conservatism, both in the media and the branches of academe enamored with state centricity. Defenders of the *status quo* have quickly thrown discredit on the idea and caricatured it as mere 'open cheque book' federalism.

The reason why progress is so slow on the road to what we will call 'small g' governance is that the ethos of the federal public administration in Canada these days has reached new heights of risk-aversion and self-absorption. This is such that even the new wave of young, bright and entrepreneurial public servants finds itself too often quickly tamed and demoralized, and its imagination and creativity neutered—however crucial these features might be for effective governance (Paquet 2008a). The black hole metaphor is apt.

Structure of the book

Our intent in this book is not to present *un tableau des horreurs* of all the dysfunctions of Canadian federal public governance—even though it is tempting to believe that this sort of tableau might be necessary, given the cognitive dissonance of politicians, senior officials in the Canadian public service, and the clutch of public administration academics. The challenge is one of balance: to say enough about the dysfunctions to mobilize the needed response, and yet not to wallow in highlighting the pathologies, thereby generating despair.

One may presume that there have been a sufficiently large number of precise indictments of parts of the Canadian public administration apparatus to constitute a wake-up call (Laliberté 2009; Paquet 2009b). Our *point de départ* is that reasonable observers should by now have been persuaded that the Canadian federal public administration is in need of repairs. What this book is trying to accomplish is nothing more than to initiate the discussion leading to the reparative process.

The introduction sets the stage for our inquiry by identifying two powerful and complex underlying processes: first, the dual process of change in the governing of modern democracies: the shift from 'Big G' government (top down and authoritarian) to 'small g' governance (more horizontal and participative), and the concomitant shift of public governing itself from 'G$_1$' emphasizing mainly reliability to 'G$_2$' attempting to respond innovatively to the evolving environment (Paquet 2009d); and second, the extraordinary process of fictionalization of public administration: sanitized and inaccurate stylizations of what is really going on by actors and experts, and the bizarre attempts to impose these surreal stylizations on the operations of the real world of public administration.

Part I sets the stage for an examination of the real world of Canadian federal public governance by looking first at the historical evolution of the broad features of the Canadian federal apparatus as a social learning system through the lens of the role of the Clerk as a *révélateur* of the way in which the public governance system functions. Second, it provides a broad-brush picture of the evolution and prospects for the political-bureaucratic interface in the Canadian federal public administration, sets the context for an evaluation of the extent to which the operations of the public administration system have been failing, examines the recent evolution of Canadian public governance, and sketches some of the plausible scenarios that may unfold.

Part II identifies and documents certain areas of concern in greater detail. It does not deal with a comprehensive catalogue of pathologies revealed through safe-space discussions with senior public servants between 2006 and 2009. Such conversations provided bits of evidence of many serious dysfunctionalities of the Canadian federal public administration (in the political and bureaucratic realms, and also in their interfaces), and illustrations of the ways these pathological traits have led to governance failures.[1] A few of these traits deserved particular attention, so we have focused on the toxicity of quantophrenia and disloyalty on the public administration apparatus. Finally, we have felt it useful to illustrate how serious governance failures have materialized by looking at two particular cases: the neurotic state and the fiscal imbalance files.

Part III is an invitation to creative subversion in order to tame the 'black hole': an invitation to critical thinking and to a first round of transformation in the federal public administration process. It suggests five types of repairs that would appear to be warranted as a first stage in the revamping and refurbishment of the federal public governance system in Canada.

These repairs are only a sample of initiatives that could easily be launched since they would only extend, more robustly, some experiments that have already been under discussion for a fair amount of time in Canada. Some, like alternative service delivery, have been meekly pursued since the 1970s, others, like public-private partnerships and refurbished organization design, have shown their potential more recently, and the highest and best use of ombudsmanship (an ancient institution that may have extraordinary promise as producer of governance in our complex world where mediation and organizational innovation are the new imperative) would appear to be a promising road.

The conclusion indulges in some prospection of what the contours of Canadian federal public administration might look like once the system has been modified and redesigned to make it truly autopoietic. It probes what lies beyond the short run for Canadian public governance.

The postface sketches in broad terms the sort of transformation strategy that might usefully be initiated in the shorter term to trigger the sort of systemic adjustment necessary to plug the 'black hole'.

This work owes much to the stimulating environment provided by the Centre on Governance at the University of Ottawa, to the spirit that has underpinned the travails of its adventurous outgrowth, Invenire, and to the hospitality of the Graduate School of Public and International Affairs at the University of Ottawa and of the Public Ethics Centre at Saint Paul University in Ottawa. We must extend our gratitude to Robin Higham, Jeffrey Roy and Christopher Wilson for robust intellectual exchanges over the years, and to a small number of colleagues and friends (acknowledged at different places throughout the book) for assistance and help.

Special gratitude is due to Luc Juillet for allowing us to use a paper he co-authored with one of us in preparing chapter 5 of this book.

None of these persons should be presumed to be guilty of anything by association.

Allow us to close this preface with a pre-emptive warning.

One cannot synthesize work done over some ten years into a syncretic and integrated whole without ironing out unfortunate infelicitous phrases, seeming inconsistencies, and without putting flats and sharps on arguments that, with the benefit of hindsight, would appear to require them. This we have been careful to do in this volume.

But the reader will find that there have been some *leitmotivs*, some crucial phrases required to hammer down arguments, some process advices, and some key references (somewhat counter-intuitive and not yet culturally ingrained) we have refused to iron out because, though they may sound ever so slightly repetitive (and they are in a certain sense), they have proved necessary both to bolster our arguments at various places in the volume, and to build meaningful guideposts for our ongoing discussions. These very few instances may irk some minimalist readers, and we apologize for it.

This shotgun approach may prove, however, useful in ensuring that even casual readers will not be spared having to confront such fixtures. For those whom these very few recurrent motifs might annoy ever so slightly, allow us to invoke in our defence, Gertrude Stein, who used to say that "there is no such thing as repetition. Only insistence." For insistence, we do not apologize because, in our estimation, too many observers of the Canadian scene have not been insistent enough on those issues.

Endnote

1   The conversations were carried out under the auspices of the Association of the Professional Executives of the Public Service of Canada (APEX) between the fall of 2006 and the fall of 2009. Unfortunately this ongoing experiment allowing discussions of wicked problems with senior bureaucrats under Chatham House rules has now been terminated. We have been informed that it did not fit "with the new business plan of APEX". Jean Laliberté (2009), given his caustic evaluation of the scene, would not have been surprised. We were.

From 'Big G' Government to 'small g' governance

> *None of the absolute advantages of institutions*
> *like businesses or schools or governments have disappeared.*
> *Instead, what has happened is that most of the relative advantages*
> *of those institutions have disappeared—relative, that is,*
> *to the direct effort of the people they represent.*

> —Clay Shirky

This book is the result of years of ruminations by a practitioner and an academic on the pathologies of public governance in Canada. These reflections, inspired mainly by real crises in various sectors, but also fuelled by social imaginings in reaction to them, have led both of us to commit a variety of diagnoses, commentaries and suggestions to paper over the last ten years. Not all of them have been well received or necessarily regarded as wise at the time. As a result, many of these modest general propositions we have put forward have been merrily swept under the carpet by friend and foe. But some of these propositions have survived ordeal and contestation, and have become a set of organizing ideas that have informed our conversations and scribbling more or less explicitly.

These organizing ideas have found their way into various solo or joint papers. Many were outbursts at particularly annoying acts of provocation; others were stimulated by consultancy work for a variety of clients; still others emerged from extensive free-wheeling conversations at Bistro 115 or Lapointe's over many lunches.

These pieces have coalesced into a broad approach to the governing problems of Canada (as a socio-technical system) that runs counter to the prevailing view.

The prevailing view is one best echoed by Iain Gow's model of Canadian public administration: a neat and tidy Westminster model (hierarchical, accountable, transparent, oversight-heavy) in which elected officials are purported to be in charge, and the state plays a transcendent role in defining the public interest on the basis of shared values. Gow suggests that this model has been operating in Canada as an echo of a vibrant tradition of moderation and pragmatism, with a strong tolerance for ambiguity (Gow 2004).

Our view is that this is fiction. In fact, the Canadian public administration is painfully trying to meet the new challenges of coping with a turbulent, more complex and diverse environment by slowly and with great difficulty transforming itself into a less state-centric, more decentralized, more participative governance apparatus. The slow progress on this road has left the Canadian federal public administration in a state of strain and stress that has been made all the more acute because of the cognitive dissonance of both practitioners and academics intent on clinging to a Panglossian view that everything is as good as it can be in the best of all worlds (Paquet 2009a). As a result, there is an implicit collusion of most of those concerned to occlude the challenges generated by the sweeping changes in the environment: signs of distress of Canadian public administration are ignored, governance failures are denied, and required repairs are declared unnecessary.

A tectonic change

At least since the Great Depression of the 1930s, conventional wisdom in Canada has claimed that Canada needs to be firmly governed from the state centre to ensure the requisite degree of guidance, coherence and redistribution to meet the imperatives of development, stability and equality. 'From the centre' in this context means 'top-down', with 'Big G' government firmly in control, with the federal voice being the strongest one in the government choir, and with much more coercion or competition than collaboration among the different levels of government.

We believe that this view is antiquated.

Increasingly over recent decades, improving Canada's stewardship in the face of accelerated change and increasingly wicked problems has entailed the need to mobilize the collective intelligence of the whole country through the fostering of more participation and of a scintilla of open-source culture, the encouragement of dissent and participation, the instituting of multiple deliberative private, public and social forums, and what Michael Schrage famously dubbed 'serious play' (much exploratory work with new tools and perspectives, rapid prototyping as a vehicle for innovation in all sorts of domains, much experimentation and social learning as the new imperative).

All the while, government has continued to play an important role in the broad process of societal governance. But in Canada, as in other advanced democracies, it no longer occupies the front of the societal boat, and it has had to transform itself accordingly. In fact, by the 1970s, state centricity had already come to be regarded as somewhat ineffective. But the requisite re-arrangement has not materialized organically or quickly or always in as felicitous a manner as might have been hoped for (Paquet 1999b).

There has been much denial about both the reality and the irreversibility of the drift from 'Big G' government to 'small g' governance since we first proposed the hypothesis in the 1990s. Much energy has been expended in active efforts to manufacture the illusion that top-down control could continue to be made viable by all sorts of subterfuges. Some of these subterfuges have injected in the body politic a certain coefficient of *gouvernementalité à la Foucault*—working at persuading the citizen to rationalize his/her own voluntary servitude in the name of self-realization (Paquet 2008a).

The central theme of this book is that the Canadian small g governance regime—an evolving nexus of private/public/civic and formal/informal arrangements designed to ensure effective and robust coordination when power, information, and resources are widely distributed and value pluralism runs deep (Paquet 2005a)—is a work in progress. Governing can no longer be reduced to a set of rules imposed top-down by some state actors who presume (or are presumed) to be in charge, and it cannot be assumed that the new governance apparatus will emerge organically and in a timely manner.

In the recent past, it has become clear that nobody is fully in charge. So instead of focusing hopes on top-down solutions engineered by public sector luminaries as the source of the rules in good currency, one has been led to inquire about the various forces, agents and groups that have collectively become the producers of governance, that are, wittingly or not, generating those rules or conventions, or are engaged in the process of modifying them, and about the ways in which they have contributed, and are contributing, to the stewardship of the country through registering support or dissent creatively and innovatively.

The emerging dynamics at work are analogous to what lies behind any open-source system like Linux and Wikipedia, where whoever wants to, and is able to do so, contributes to the final product. It belongs to everyone and is produced by all. Obviously, in the case of a country or a vast social system, the processes are immensely more complex than those that underpin Linux or Wikipedia, but this does not mean that these processes cannot be understood and reconstructed. Consequently, while we concede to Francis Fukuyama that public organizations and institutions have come to resemble not only 'black boxes' but 'black holes', we suggest that the problems they pose remain tractable (Fukuyama 2004).

Two mega-processes and more

Two major propositions underpin our reconstructive and reparative approach (Paquet 2009d).

The first proposition suggests that the governing of our complex socio–politico–economic systems has drifted clearly if slowly over time from a dominance of 'Big G' government (hierarchical, authoritarian and coercive) to a dominance of 'small g' governance (more horizontal, pluralistic, participative, experimentalist and based on voluntary agreements). This has led Canada's governance to become somewhat less state-centric and more network-based, to accommodate more diversity through greater variety.

The second proposition suggests that not only has 'Big G' been reduced in scope, but that it has also been significantly transubstantiated as government and public governing have been forced by turbulent and hostile environments to shift from G_1 (processes mainly emphasizing reliability) to G_2 (processes largely attempting to develop new and innovative responses to the evolving environment, new ways to seize emerging opportunities: working iteratively, building prototypes, eliciting feedback, refining them, and repeating the cycle).

It is our view that, through prototyping and serious-play interventions at both levels (the drift from G to g and the changing mix of $G_1 + G_2$), that Canada is evolving. These two mega-processes are clearly intermingled: both are a response to the turbulence in the environment. As the 'Big G' to 'small g' drift is accelerating, traditional government is forced more and more to abandon its focus on reliability in order to innovate, to invent new valid ways in order to cope with new challenges: to do different things and to do them differently. This, in turn, has generated new challenges at the political–bureaucratic interface.

Quite different experiments have emerged in different regions and sectors as a result of these transformations. But such experiences have often been prevented from unfolding successfully by interventions of interest groups and state actors whose dynamic conservatism has worked at sustaining the old institutional order against all the forces pressing for a more participative, inclusive and collaborative order. We have shown the toxic nature of such efforts in a recent book (Hubbard and Paquet 2007a).

These two mega-processes are still a work in progress, but we suggest that, for the time being, the Canadian federal public administration shows signs of distress: this is ascribable to many factors of which one is that the political-bureaucratic interface has become dysfunctional.

Part of the responsibility for the present critical dysfunction has to be shouldered by elected officials whose unfortunate rush to follow the ill-conceived advice of Justice Gomery to placate the foul mood of the citizenry (in response to the so-called sponsorship scandal) led them to put into law (*Accountability Act*) a pre-emptive indictment of the motives, intentions and competence of all public office holders, elected or appointed.

Another part is ascribable to a natural suspicion of the old guard public service (selected, trained and promoted by the former government) when the new government came to power. Usually, such distrust evaporates over a short period when a majority government succeeds another one. In the case of a succession of minority governments that may or may not last (in a country that is not used to the challenges of minority governments), it has obviously not disappeared and is an impediment to good governance.

Yet another part of the responsibility clearly rests with the broader public service for its failure to support the agenda of the new government and to experiment as creatively as it could and should in its implementation; and for its permitting rearguard action by fundamentalists within its ranks (who consider the upper bureaucracy as a superior and more reliable interpreter of the public interest and of the common will than the elected officials) to sabotage the political-bureaucratic interface actively or passively.

This may be said to have contributed to preventing government from governing *selon son esprit* in some issue domains. This rearguard action, tolerated at the highest level, has contributed significantly to the current toxic distrust prevailing at the political-bureaucratic interface. This is not a unique Canadian phenomenon. It has been observed elsewhere, and that has led to *Magna-Carta* type actions in the United Kingdom where ministerial and civil service codes have been required (with enforcement at the highest level) to ensure a sounder and more effective political-bureaucratic interface (Rosanvallon 2006; Thomas 2009a).

Government as nebula of facts and fictions

Government (and by this we mean politicians and bureaucrats, and their circumstances) is a complex adaptive system. It is akin to an eco-system. It is made up of a large number of actors, relationships, routines, norms and mindsets that are in a constant process of evolution in the face of the challenges of the day. It is a set of ongoing relationships between people and organizations, governed by reactions to the environment and by mutual expectations. It has become differentiated, integrated and instituted in a particular manner over time, and its governing has had to evolve accordingly. To enable the system to maintain itself, to grow and to innovate, the governing apparatus must be as varied and changing as the environment and the interactions it is trying to deal with.

This complex world of government is most often represented and synthetically stylized into static hierarchical organization charts—schematic pictures with job descriptions and lines of command to which are attached rules and protocols—by both practitioners and scholars for convenience sake. Of necessity, these schematic pictures can only represent a pale shadow of the real living organism. The actual organism has a neural quality: formal hierarchical relations are routinely circumvented for a variety of reasons (some 'good' and some 'not-so-good' from the different perspectives of politicians, citizens, clients, bosses, employees, etc.) and supplemented by all sorts of informal, lateral and transversal connections.

Consequently, there is an important difference between the neural reality of government, state and public administration (again expressions used to include politicians and bureaucrats and their circumstances) and the *fictionalized* versions of it that one finds in official charts and textbooks: the former is messy while the latter are neat and tidy.

These stylizations and fictions in good currency cohabit somewhat uneasily in daily life. As long as the fiction did not contaminate the real thing too much, damage was limited. Of late however, this fictionalization of public administration has become more grotesque, has gained some credibility and legitimacy in higher circles, and has even served as a guide in the repair work that has come to be regarded as necessary as a result of multiplicities of governance failures and scandals of all sorts.

Indeed, as a result of this drift, reality is being made to look more like what the fiction suggests it should be like.

The impact of this sequence of distortions—reality giving rise to fiction, fiction taking an ever-greater distance from reality, and then reality tending to be shaped to look more like fiction—may be said to be particularly acute at the federal level in Canada, but it has been observed in many democracies. This has led to an ever-greater incapacity of public administration to cope with wicked problems generated by a more complex and turbulent environment.

We argue that nothing less than a re-foundation of the very notion and 'machinery' of public administration is called for.

Fictionalization

This sort of development has been, in part, an unintended consequence of the emergence of the transparency mania and of the growth of the whimsical and unaccountable power of media, columnists, academics and celebrities, who have all claimed entitlement to the role of opinion-molders, and made a career of making misinformed and misguided pronouncements about what public administration should be like.

In a world of growing mistrust of democratic institutions, rock stars, *chansonniers*, starlets, and TV news readers have elevated themselves to the role of guardians of the public interest, and, basing their utterances on minimal knowledge, an immense intellectual arrogance, and a complete licence to deceive, have become the new chiromancers. The main message of those chiromancers has been a call for total transparency and a form of simplistic and unintelligent accountability (Paquet 2009b).

The impact of these *"magistrats de l'immédiat"* (Lacouture 2005) has been immense in the downgrading of public discourse, in the feeding of primitive and simplistic hypotheses about the workings of modern society, in the propagation of cartoonesque views of social problems, and in the propagandizing of misguided policies. Such has been their power that politicians and bureaucrats have been led to respond to such pressures by taking their ill-inspired fiction seriously rather than by exposing the deceptions on which these misguided pronouncements are based. The policy debates have therefore quickly been brought to the lowest common denominator. As Onora O'Neill puts it "if we want to restore trust, we need to reduce deception and lies rather than secrecy" (O'Neill 2002: 70).

In the face of chiromancy, politicians and bureaucrats are willing to go through any contrived maneuvers to maintain their semblance of legitimacy, and their hold on centralized power, here and elsewhere (Sue 2003; Rosanvallon 2006).

Reality and fiction

Simplifying is a strategy of survival for practitioners and a strategy of prehension for academics. As long as the process does not introduce undue focalization and distortion, it provides a convenient map that may ease traffic and facilitate effective operations.

But when the mental maps in good currency become very distant cousins of the daily activities in the real world they claim to depict, a true chasm is created between reality and fiction, and the canonical fictions become toxic. The canonical fictions that are among the most toxic today are the Westminster model, the policy process as hyper-Cartesian, and the Kafkaesque representations of financial accountability and human resources management.

The mythical Westminster system purports to describe our governing system as a somewhat linear line of command: citizens creating a Parliament in charge that imposes its will through the government responsible to it, and the top bureaucracy, accountable to the government, thereby guiding the policy and administrative operations. This cascade of accountabilities is mythical but regarded as sacrosanct. In fact, citizens have become disinterested, and most of the elected officials they put in place have little to say about anything. Bureaucrats are usually given only vague directions to guide them in serving the population. Moreover, the dual legitimacy of parliamentarians and bureaucrats (through election and through expertise respectively) is far from being anything as asymmetric as is presumed. In fact, the most important unresolved problem in a system of parliamentary democracy is the ambiguous, complex and inter-creative relationship between elected officials and bureaucrats (Thomas 2008).

The stark choice manufactured by centralizers is that the only choice is 'centralization or chaos'. It excludes by definition anything but the hierarchical and paternalistic governing mode, and it constitutes an ideological stance on the part of those in power who wish their position not to be challenged.

As Donald Lenihan and others put it: "While governments have responded (to new outside forces) with talk of greater openness, collaboration, partnerships, democratic renewal and so on, unlike businesses, they have not gone through anything that could fairly be described as a paradigm shift of their own. On the contrary, they remain bound by the hierarchical, controlling... culture of the past." (Lenihan et al. 2007: 21) Such a stance is in sharp contrast with the forces that have driven some more enlightened governments elsewhere toward devolution and a philosophy of subsidiarity as a result of a better appreciation of the necessity to do so to respond well to the differentiated needs of a more diverse citizenry.

Another fiction is the stylized view of the policy formation process in the form of the mythical policy cycle, rooted in ritualized rationality: goals, alternative means, choice of instruments, implementation, evaluation, etc. Anyone familiar with the real-life system of policy making knows that it is a process that is anything but linear (Carl A. Taylor 1997; Paquet 2009b).

The fictional pictures of the financial and human resources management systems have also been denounced by frustrated practitioners. The lack of realism of the stylizations proposed for what are quite chaotic and ineffective systems at the federal level has been denounced.

In an Institute of Public Administrators of Canada (IPAC) interview of David Good, a former federal assistant deputy minister, Good bemoans the idea in good currency that:

> idealized management frameworks associated with performance
> management, performance audit management controllership,
> and human resources development assume that these conditions
> (bringing up and in timely information through performance
> reporting and auditing) can be obtained across government
> when in fact they tend to be specific only to a particular range of
> government activity (Dutil 2003).

In the same spirit, the human resources management system celebrated as superbly efficient and effective by so many from the previous Clerk of the Privy Council down through the whole hierarchy has little to do with reality.

Fictions trumping reality

Noting that such fictional accounts of what is going on are very poor and distorted stylizations of the real world of public administration would be less consequential:

(1) if it were simply the reflection of souped-up public relations caricatures prepared by zealous bureaucrats or of cartoons etched by simple-minded academics;

(2) if such stylizations had not become more unrealistic of late than they were in yesteryear; and

(3) if they had not been thrust ever more readily on unsuspecting public managers as templates to be implemented and to serve as guideposts.

As the complex public administration system has become even more complex, the gap between the stylizations in good currency and the real world has increased: these stylizations have become more and more inaccurate. But more importantly, there has been an extraordinary attempt by senior officials in public administration to use these bizarre and surreal stylizations, and to impose them on the operations of the real world. Utopian management frameworks have been thrust onto public administrators by sorcerers' apprentices.

Two former senior bureaucrats (Ian D. Clark and Harry Swain) sounded the alarm in 2005:

> There is a fundamental tension between actually getting the job done and trying to demonstrate adherence to the precepts of utopian management frameworks. These frameworks can be helpful as long as they remain explanatory, exhortatory, and voluntary ...(but w)e advance the following general hypothesis: once a utopian management framework is formalized for application across the government, its mandated requirements

become surreal for departmental managers...mandated
requirements emanating from...utopian frameworks will
inevitably be surreal and unhelpful...We would categorize as
surreal all the externally imposed management requirements that
are derived from management improvement frameworks"(Clark
and Swain 2005: 456, 466).

Such utopian frameworks have been foisted on the public
administration world unrelentingly over the last decade or
two to make reality look like the cartoonesque and Kafkaesque
chromos–proposed by internal dreamers and naive academics.
While it is difficult to explain why this was done, there are
interesting hypotheses.

Lenihan et al. have suggested one:

The deeper story behind Savoie's book [Savoie 1999] is...
that it uncovers a trend, not an aberration....[Eddie Goldenberg
said that "There is no substitute for governing from the Centre"
in November 2003] Goldenberg...either underestimates it
or ignores it....Centralization is a logical consequence of the
belief of leaders that they must do what they can to ensure their
plans and decisions are carried out in an increasingly complex,
changing and uncertain environment. It is a last-ditch effort to
continue governing from within an increasingly creaky 19th
century command-and-control structure" [Italics removed]
(Lenihan et al. 2007: 25).

Indeed, there is evidence, in many areas of public
administration, that fiction trumps reality: in the post-Gomery
era, the new accountability arrangements have succeeded in
preventing bureaucrats from doing their work, in generating
waste and inefficiency, and in killing innovation, while pretending
to have put in place a new and improved public management
system.

The dean of Canadian public administration experts, J. E.
Hodgetts (recently deceased) had compared much of what
followed as a result of the Gomery report as:

akin to rearranging the deck chairs on the Titanic. The real issues are to be found in the engine room of the ship of state… (it is said that) the excessively partisan performance of the public accounts committee makes it a dubious contributor to accountability. Yet this is true only because it has to live with the government's interpretation of accountability, an interpretation that has produced the supreme contradiction of ministerial responsibility…the doctrine of mutual deniability whereby no one claims to be accountable at the end (Hodgetts 2007: 538).

It must be conceded that, in certain cases, reality has succeeded in trumping fiction. For instance, there is selective blindness in following through with Kafkaesque frameworks of rules (like the management accountability framework). This means that much that is happening in the real world can often materialize only as long as one stays under the radar screen or far from the scrutiny of Ottawa 'watchdogism'.

Indeed, formal rules have come, in certain loci, to be mercifully regarded as nothing more than useful markers that have to be kept in mind but are negotiable. Such capacity for scheming virtuously and for learning to navigate around the fiction is obviously welcome. However, living concurrently in both a real and make-believe world is costly: it often leaves the fake image in good currency of a textbook-perfect public administration apparatus, unchallenged because of its irrelevance. As a matter of consequence, the imperfect real public administration remains also unchallenged because of its claimed non-existence.

Envoi

The rest of this book proposes to exorcize the 'malefits' generated by this process of fictionalization to a significant degree.

In Part I, we proceed with re-establishing the factual basis required to be able to describe the present state of affairs more accurately, and to suggest a line of inquiry capable of revealing the causes and sources of noted deficiencies.

In Parts II and III, we document the seriousness of the observed pathologies and dysfunctionalities, and we explore some of the obvious corrective measures that might be envisaged in certain issue domains.

Finally, in closing, we underline the importance of adopting a two-tracked strategy to plug the black hole of public administration. This is necessary because eliminating the sources of harm is not the same thing as effecting innovative repairs to promote the good. One needs to address both sources of difficulties: find ways to sabotage the dynamics of harm at play that prevent clinical modifications to be carried out, and use all available means to ensure that needed innovative repairs are carried out.

PART I

The Dynamics of the Broader Context

It is not possible to gauge the efficiency, effectiveness, value-adding capability, the innovativeness and capacity to learn and transform the Canadian federal public administration, and to imagine ways to improve it without first gaining an appreciation of the broader context within which it has been operating, of the historical mortgage that has shaped this context, and of the challenges that this public governance regime is facing in modern times. Ideally, one would need a sense of the whole Canadian social system and its circumstances, of what the Canadian federal system has lived through, and of the forces that have got the public administration apparatus to crystallize in its present form—with its strengths and weaknesses. This is too much to expect from two relatively short chapters.

A more modest and somewhat idiosyncratic introduction to the Canadian public governance regime has been developed through two anamorphoses—systematically distorted and partial representations—of the dynamics of Canadian public administration: one through the lens of the Clerk of the Privy Council; the other through an analysis of the more recent drift of the Canadian federal system.

The first one has a retrospective flavour. It etches the dynamics of the evolution of Canadian federalism in historical perspective with a view to presenting the tapestry of forces at work in shaping the governing of the federal public sector. This is done through the lens of the role of the Clerk of the Privy Council, the most senior and the most powerful bureaucrat in Ottawa. Through an analysis of the evolving context of the Clerk, and of the ways in which the Clerk's role has itself evolved, it is possible to gain an appreciation of the dynamics of the Canadian federal public administration from the time of Confederation to the present.

The second one has a more prospective flavour. It zooms in on Canadian federal public governance in the more recent past to show how its fabric has evolved, and how the two drifts from 'Big G' to 'small g' and toward a new mix of $G_1 + G_2$ have changed the ways in which social learning has proceeded. Some scenarios for the future evolution of the Canadian system are presented, and the broad levers likely to be used to effect a general transformation of the system are identified.

This macroscopic overview is meant to equip the reader with an appreciation both of the rich fabric and of the evolution of the Canadian federal public administration system. Like any such synthetic sketch, it is not a totally aseptic picture. Indeed, our sketch is boldly idiosyncratic: it is as accurate and as complete as possible, but we have underlined some drifts that have appeared important to us in this historical process, and we have most certainly framed the differential probabilities of potential futures on the basis of certain parameters that have appeared to us to be of critical importance.

Some may not agree with our observations about the long trend toward decentralization, subsidiarity, and the dominance of social learning, and even less with our suggestion that this trend is indeed a desirable outcome. But whether our hypotheses are welcome or damned by the reader, the basic compendium of information presented and the material on which we base our observations of the past and our conjectures about the future, should help in gaining a good sense of the challenges faced by the Canadian federal public administration apparatus over the last 150 years or so. This compendium also supports our concerns about the particularly difficult choices it now faces and allows the reader to develop alternative hypotheses.

If our canvas is, as we expect, sufficiently rich, it should provide the reader with enough information to deal critically with our provisional conjectures but also to contextualize the pathologies we denounce in Part II. This canvas, we hope, will also allow the reader to develop a sufficiently sophisticated understanding of the challenges ahead to gauge the extent to which the repairs we propose in Part III may suffice or not in initiating the sort of systemic overhaul of Canadian public administration required to trigger an 'open-source-inspired' renaissance.

CHAPTER 1

The Clerk as *Révélateur*

...he was born poor, died rich,
begat a new form of art
and hurt no one along the way.

—Duke Ellington at Louis Armstrong's funeral

The way a socio-economy governs itself is defined by a composite of private, public and civic mechanisms, practices, norms, organizations, institutions and regimes. This amalgam constitutes an ecology of governance: "many different systems and different kinds of systems interacting with one another, like the multiple organisms in an ecosystem." (Hubbard and Paquet 2002: 27). As Anderson suggests, such arrangements are not necessarily "neat, peaceful, stable or efficient...but in a continual process of learning and changing and responding to feedback" (Anderson 2001: 252).

From the time it became a country in 1867, Canada has had a variety of ecologies of governance. The relative importance of the public sector (the machinery of government, organization, processes and personnel) within it, and its architecture, have evolved both as a result of external and contextual circumstances and of the transformation of the guiding principles and norms in good currency at any particular time. In general, the public sector (federal, provincial, local) has acquired an increasingly significant weight over this period. Some have argued that it was because the public sector could do most things better than other sectors (H. Hardin 1974). In the recent past, this sort of assumption about the superiority of the public sector has been questioned, but the public sector remains a significant factor in the governing of the country.

The last three decades have brought new, and even more daunting, challenges for the public sector: the need to accommodate deep diversity, globalization, and the citizens' rising desires to be 'kept in the loop' have increased the pressure to adjust both more substantially and more rapidly (Hubbard and Paquet 2005). This has led to public sector reforms throughout the world.

The Clerk of the Privy Council (hereafter, the Clerk), who is also the Secretary to Cabinet and head of the (federal) public service in Canada, is a central figure in the federal government-cum-state governance apparatus. The incumbent sits at the heart of 'federal government' and holds many of the key levers that can redefine the 'shape' of the public sector.

The current duties of the Clerk are wide ranging and are described as follows by the Privy Council Office:

> …the most senior non-political official in the Government of
> Canada,…[that] provides professional, non-partisan support to
> the Prime Minister on all policy and operational issues that may
> affect the government…[and] also has particular responsibilities
> with respect to: ensuring the continuity of government between
> successive administrations; keeping custody of the records of
> previous administrations; and enabling the government of the
> day to understand and recognize the established conventions
> of Canada's constitutional monarchy…[comprises roles as]
> Deputy Minister to the Prime Minister…[including] advice
> on appointing senior office holders in the public service and
> organizing the government…Secretary to the Cabinet…[and]
> Head of the Public Service (Canada 2010a).

In a Westminster-type system, the Prime Minister, as leader of the political party that forms the government (the executive), is quite powerful. The executive formally 'governs' with the consent of Parliament, and many key positions (including those of deputy ministers and many heads of Crown corporations) are filled *de facto* by the prime minister. The power carried by the position is especially great if the distribution of seats in Parliament is based on a 'first past the post' system of election (as is the case in Canada). Such a system tends to produce a majority for one political party in the legislature. In such situations, the Clerk also can carry enormous power and influence within the formal machinations of government.

Following the evolution of the role of Clerk through history can provide interesting insights into the ways in which Canada has coped with the challenges of change. The Clerk is obviously neither the sole site of power, nor necessarily the most important in a federal system that leaves much of the public sector under provincial and local dominion, but the incumbent has a privileged vantage point.

He/she can observe the interactions among the different forces at play (private, public and social; federal, provincial, local), as well as the strains that they impose on the existing governing architecture, and the incumbent has a vast array of direct and indirect levers of power with which to influence the strategies that have been designed by all these actors to cope with these strains.

These levers are dependent—for their weight, usefulness, and scope—upon the goals and nature of the Prime Minister that the Clerk serves, as well as upon his/her own. Like a seismograph, the Clerk registers much of what happens in the environment, and perceives and acts on, both challenges and opportunities with varying degrees of effectiveness.

Our strategy is to look at the Clerk as *révélateur* (i.e., as a syncretic character that reveals, through its pattern of activities and more or less explicitly stated priorities, the way in which the existing forces in the broader socio–political terrain are aligned, somehow kept in balance and harnessed to allow progress). Some of this pattern is ascribable to external pressures; much of it is an echo of an internal reconciliation of different principles and power sources at play, but some part of it is ascribable to the process of fictionalization that was mentioned in the introduction.

What the Clerk does may be at variance with what bureaucrats, academics and politicians are expecting this person to do. Judgments may therefore vary as to the performance of a Clerk at any point in time. Moreover, these expectations may tend to alter dramatically the effective work of the Clerk. Fiction and reality will interplay.

Whatever the outcome, the Clerk is likely to be more fully aware than most other actors of the tensions at work, and since his/her job is to ensure that they remain under control, his/her statements and action plans (even when they are somewhat cryptic and revealed in oblique ways) may be regarded as indicative of the main zones of friction in the ecology of governance and of the strategies to deal with them.

We use this approach to provide a panoramic view of the evolution of the Clerk's role at the federal level, in Canada, since Confederation. The first section sketches some key aspects of the evolving context; section two identifies the different clerks and prime ministers who worked in tandem, highlighting some markers for the different periods. In the third section, we put forward hypotheses about the contextual forces at work, and the demands that they impose on societal governance, and suggest ways in which these forces have shaped the evolution of the core role of the Clerk. The fourth section provides a 'windshield survey' of the different periods in support of the plausibility of our hypotheses. Finally, we speculate on the future of the Clerk's function, and the governance it underpins.

An evolving context

Before exploring the evolution of the role of the Clerk, it is crucial to identify a number of interdependent sets of forces that have shaped the social architecture of governance in Canada over the last century or more.

First, external forces have rocked the country: two world wars, the Depression of the 30s, the internationalization of production, decolonisation, etc. These have commanded a number of important transformations in the governance system. Moreover, the frames of reference have evolved and gradually transformed Canada's very notion of its capacity to govern itself. The emergence of Keynesian economics turned economic thinking on its head with the notion that government could and should manage 'aggregate demand'. This has underpinned the rise of the welfare state in the developed world. Later, as governance failures came to be ascribed to the failures of the public sector, 'new public management' swept the Western world and modified the very notion of the public sector.

Second, the various shocks that hit the Canadian socio-economy revealed that the federal governing arrangements hammered out in the 19th century were not satisfactory for coping with 20th century crises. A long series of commissions—from the one on the relationship between capital and labour in the 19th century, to the Rowell-Sirois Commission established in 1937, to a variety of task forces and working groups—have suggested ways to respond to the need to take better account of significant imbalances and major dysfunctions.

Third, the role of the state itself has changed as a consequence of these developments: from being an important player operating in a relatively narrow range of the governance terrain to one that occupied more of the center stage in the 1950s and 60s. It has actively (and some would say intrusively) set up programs to give expression to the welfare state, and has presumed itself to be the premier spokesperson and guardian of the public interest.

More recently, concerns about government overload, legitimacy deficit, and social limits to growth imposed by the welfare state have given rise to experimentation with new ways of governing strategically (Paquet 1996-97). After almost a century when the idea of the centrality of the state seemed to grow boundlessly, there has recently been a reversal of the trend: one can observe an underlying drift from 'Big G' government to 'small g' governance. Table 1.1 illustrates some important characteristics of this drift (Hubbard and Paquet 2007a).

Table 1.1   The drift from G to g

	DRIFT	
	G ———————————————→ g	
Key Characteristics	Public sector ≥ (better than) private	Private sector ≥ (better than) public
	Redistribution on the basis of rights	Redistribution on the basis of needs
	Soft egalitarianism	Subsidiarity
	Centralization	Decentralization

The old assumption that the public sector could always outperform the private sector has been challenged. In lieu of a top-down, state-engineered soft egalitarism, based on rights and predicated on centralization (i.e., in order to be able to redistribute resources, one must first bring them to the centre), a new bottom-up governance framework has emerged, in response to weakening east-west economic ties and rising deep diversity among segments of the country. This new framework of governance has been woven around the notion of needs and the principle of subsidiarity (Paquet 1999a).

These strands of experience suggest a provisional partitioning of the Canadian experience into four distinct periods characterized by particular patterns of challenges and responses.

To use a very crude architectural metaphor, one might say that the first period (1867–1940) can be seen as one of basic construction of the federated house; the second (1940–1975) as one of dramatic expansion of the house with key rooms being added; the third (1975–1994) as one during which the house becomes more and more ill-suited to the family's needs; and the more recent, fourth period, as one in which the federal house is gradually restructured into condos, but *dans le désordre*.

Some key events for these four periods are highlighted in table 1.2 to provide a basic background for our discussion.

Table 1.2   *Three interdependent threads*

Period	External forces	Strains on the federation	Role of the State
I (1867–1940) Building the house	• Gaining the authority to govern itself: WW I, Charnak (1922), Imperial Conference (1923) • Westminster Act (1931) • Social programs sweep Europe • Keynesian economics (1936)	• Early wounds: Manitoba schools (1880), Riel Rebellion (1885), conscription (1917), residential schools • Rowell–Sirois Commission on fiscal imbalance begins work (1937)	• Activist government: last half of the 19th century •infrastructure (1920s) (railways, harbours, navigation) and tariffs • Maritime subsidies and special freight rates (1926)
II (1940–1975) Expanding the house and finishing key rooms	• WW II • Canadian Supreme Court final arbiter (1949)	• Rowell–Sirois rejected (1940) except for UI • Tax powers borrowed WW II, took decades to return • Conscription (1944) • Status Indians get the right to vote (1960) • White paper on Status Indians rejected (1969) • Peter Lougheed, Alberta (1971)	• Rise of welfare state: UI (1940), Family Allowances (1945), OAS/GIS (1951), modern equalization (1957), Medicare (1966), CPP 1966), the DREE (1969) • Rise of individual rights: Bill of Rights in federal jurisdiction (1960), OLA (1970)

Period	External forces	Strains on the federation	Role of the State
III (1975–1994) House ill-suited to the family's needs	•Thatcher (1979–1989) • Reagan (1981–1989) • New Zealand reform (IMF driver) • UK executive agencies • Australia, 5 yr. terms for deputies	• Regional maturity: René Lévesque, Que (1976); Frank McKenna, NB (1988); Ralph Klein, Alberta (1992) • Aboriginal aspirations acknowledged (1991) • Quebec opposes patriation (1982) • Quebec referenda: getting closer to 'yes' • Meech Lake (1987) Charlottetown (1992)	• Belt tightening begins: late 70s • NEP (1980) • Charter of Rights & Freedoms (1982)
IV (1994–2006) Condos?	• Blair devolution • North American economic integration accelerates	• Provinces/ territories start saying no (Gun Registry (1995) and Kyoto (1998)) • Nunavut (1999) • Council of Federation (2003) • BC Citizens' assembly on electoral reform (2003)	• Program review (1994) • Deficit eliminated (1995–96), not to return • Big, centralized government with differences: - innovative funding - restructuring, retooling, reframing - infrastructure

Period	External forces	Strains on the federation	Role of the State
IV continued			• Fiscal imbalance again (three levels) • Federal money flows to problems: health, cities, 'have not' provinces
V (2006– ?) Renovations	• Global recession (2008)	• BC climate change agreements Washington and California (2007) • Internal trade: labour mobility and dispute resolution	• Fiscal imbalance acknowledged • GST cut to 5% from 7% • Fiscal stimulus (CA$ 50B federal deficit in 2009)

This commingling of forces has given rise to two 'meta-phenomena'.

The first is the evolution of the relative importance of the federal government within the public sector apparatus in Canada. As major infrastructure projects proved essential, and world wars and economic crises unfolded after Confederation, the federal government had to shoulder an ever-greater portion of state action. Indeed, by the end of the 1930s, a need was felt for fiscal transfers from the provinces to the federal government to enable it to do its job. The valence of the federal government within the public household sector in Canada grew steadily until the 1960s.

Since then, as social issues (such as health, education and quality of life) have come to dominate the state agenda, provinces and local communities have faced increasing strains, and have demanded and received a growing portion of the fiscal pie. Moreover, as provinces/territories have acquired new capabilities, the relative importance of the federal portion of the public sector has declined. Recent discussions about the problems of fiscal imbalance call for yet more fiscal transfers from the federal to the provincial and local governments, so that they can perform their legitimate jobs adequately.

The second meta-phenomenon is the slow and silent revolution that has seen the executive branch acquire more and more real power and control over the public sector. One might legitimately speak of a drift from a 'parliamentary democracy' to a 'governmental democracy'. This drift is not unique to Canada, but, in this country, the executive branch has absorbed the power of the legislature to a greater extent than elsewhere; Parliament has become more and more a spectator to the government's operations. Importantly, as well, within the executive in Canada, power is increasingly seen as concentrated around the prime minister's office.

These two meta-phenomena have had a significant impact on the role of the Clerk.

On the one hand, the slippage in the valence of the federal government has reduced the scope of the Clerk's power, and it has transformed his/her role into one calling for a greater capacity to cooperate (a shift from power 'over' to power 'with'). On the other hand, the growing authority of the executive, and the centralization of power around the prime minister's office, has significantly increased the Clerk's power and relative influence.

On balance, the potential for the Clerk influencing the federal public sector's architecture and operations (and therefore the whole Canadian public governance system) have probably grown. This does not mean, however, that the political masters of the day have allowed the clerks to employ the full sweep of their potential powers, nor does it mean that their usable powers have been exploited as well as possible, or to the fullest extent that they might have been.

Le tableau d'honneur

In the period from 1867 to 2009, twenty-one clerks (twenty men and one woman) have occupied the position of Clerk of the Canadian Privy Council, and have served governments led by twenty-two different prime ministers. To help keep the names, relationships and challenges of the time in mind, table 1.3 (A-D) co-relates the clerk-prime minister tandems for this long historical stretch, partitioned into four periods, with a sample of the challenges faced by the governance apparatus of Canada in each time period.

The Clerk has been called upon to play quite different roles in each of these four eras. We shall attempt, in the next two sections, to identify the dynamics underpinning this broad evolution, and to probe each of these periods provisionally to gain an appreciation of the *vraie nature* of each period, as well as the ways in which the Clerk can serve as a useful *révélateur* of the constellation of forces at work, of the *habitus* of the period, and of the propensity to deal with issues in a particular way.

Table 1.3a   Canadian clerks through history, Period I (1867–1940)

Year	Clerk	Prime Minister	Key Events
1867–1872	W. H. Lee	J.A. Macdonald (C) (1867–1873)	British North America (BNA) Act. Power split: UK parliament, fed. and prov. governments
1872–80	W. A. Himsworth*	A. Mackenzie (L) (1873–1878) J.A. Macdonald (C) (1878–1891)	Activist state last half 19th century, first two decades of 20th. Federal focus infrastructure (railways, harbours, navigation) and tariffs.
1880–82	J. O. Côté		

* Note: The PCO website incorrectly spells his name "Hinsworth".

Year	Clerk	Prime Minister	Key Events
1882–1907	J. J. McGee		
		Abbott (C) (1891–1892)	
		Thompson (C) (1892–1894)	
		Bowell (C) (1894–1896) Tupper (C) (May–Jul 1896)	
1907–23	R. Boudreau	Laurier (L) (1896–1911)	External affairs established (1909)
		R. L. Borden (C,U) (1911–1920)	WW1 (1914–18). Canada full partner at Paris Peace Conference. Conservative–Liberal coalition (begins 1917) Civil service reform (1918–19) modern Civil Service Commission (PSC) begins
		Meighan (U) (1920–1921)	Coalition formally ends
		King (L) (1921–1926)	Charnak crisis (1922) First crown corporation: CNR (1922) Imperial War Conference (1923). Another step to independence
1923–40	E. J. Lemaire		King/Byng affair (1926)
		Meighan (C) (Jun–Sep 1926) King (L) (1926–1930)	Brief minority government Great Depression (1929–1939)
		Bennet (C) (1930–1935)	Westminster Act (1931) cuts apron strings Bank of Canada and public broadcasting (1935)
		King (L) (1935–1948)	Rowell– Sirois established 1937 WW II (1939–1945)

Table 1.3b   Canadian clerks through history, Period II (1940–1975)

Year	Clerk	Prime Minister	Key Events
1940–49	A. D. P. Heeney	(King continues)	Provinces relinquish tax room for WWII Rowell–Sirois reports 1940 (QC, ON and AB boycott it) Rise of the welfare state: UI (1940), Family allowances begin (1944)
		St Laurent (L) (1948–1957)	
1949–52	N. A. Robertson		Supreme Court becomes final arbiter (1949) OAS/GIS begins (1951)
1952–53	J. W. Pickersgill		
1954–63	R. B. Bryce		Modern equalization program begins (1957)
		Diefenbaker (PC) (1957–1963)	Height of Cold War, Cuban Missile crisis Glassco (1962) 'let managers manage'
1963–75	R. G. Robertson	Pearson (L) (1963–1968)	CPP begins mid 60s (QPP analogue) Medicare begins 60s Constitutional reform efforts begin 60s
		Trudeau (L) (1968–1975)	DREE established (1969) OLA (1970) Alberta starts asserting itself (Lougheed 1971)

Table 1.3c Canadian clerks through history, Period III (1975–1994)

Year	Clerk	Prime Minister	Key Events
1975–79	P. M. Pitfield	Trudeau continues	PQ first elected in Quebec (1976)
1979–80	M. Massé	J. Clark (PC) (1979–1980)	Minority government
1980–82	P. M. Pitfield	Trudeau (L) (1980–1984)	NEP (1980) Quebec referendum defeated (1980) Constitution patriated effective1982: last ribbons of empire, no Quebec support, Charter, symbolic recognition of aboriginals
1982–85	G. F. Osbaldeston	Turner (L) Jun–Sep 1984)	Canada Health Act (1984)
1985–92	P. M. Tellier	Mulroney (PC) (1984–93)	FTA implemented (1989) Frank McKenna NB premier (1988–98) PS 2000 TF's (1989) Nielsen TF Meech Lake reform failed (1990) RCAP (1991)
1992–94	G. S. Shortliffe		Quebec ref defeated (1992) (smaller percent) Ralph Klein (1992–present) Charlottetown Accord defeated (1992) Aboriginal as third order of government End of constitutional reform attempts
		Campbell (PC) (Jun–Nov 1993) Chrétien (L) (1993–2003)	Radical structural change, 32 departments to 23

Table 1.3d   Canadian clerks through history, Period IV (1994–2010)

Year	Clerk	Prime Minister	Key Events
1994–99	J. Bourgon	Chrétien continues	2nd Quebec referendum efeated (1995) 50.4% to 49.6% response to RCAP (1996) Post Kyoto process approved (1997) Canada signs Kyoto (1998) Program review to eliminate deficit, renewal of policy capacity, La relève
1999–2002	M. Cappe		Alberta opposes fed./prov. communiqué on climate change Nunavut established (1999) Romanow and Kirby on health care (2001)
2002–06	A. Himelfarb		BC Citizens' assembly electoral reform begins (2003) Council of the Federation (2003)
		Martin (L) 2003–06	Sponsorship scandal, strengthening public management, democratic deficit, cities agenda
2006–09	K. Lynch	Harper (C) 2006–	Minority government Feb. 2006
2009–	W. Wouters		Minority government Oct. 2008

Through an iconoscope…a guiding hypothesis

To explore the evolution that has taken place, we would like to use an instrument similar to a 19th century iconoscope: a crude optical instrument that accentuated differences the better to appreciate them. The design of our iconoscope is inspired by the work of Emery and Trist (1965), McCann and Selsky (1984) and Metcalfe (1998). It borrows some elements of their neo-institutional approach and uses them to correlate some of the central activities connected with the different governing and management functions of the Clerk with the texture of the environment.

Our basic hypothesis is that, as a society moves from a placid to a clustered—or disturbed—reactive, and then to a turbulent and even an hyper-turbulent environment, the nature of its governance changes, and the role of the Clerk (with the predictable leads and lags) registers and reflects, with varying degrees of accuracy, the way in which the environment has been transformed, the extent to which the governing apparatus has evolved, and the extent to which it has kept up with the challenges to be met.

In a relatively placid environment, self-conservation and preservation prevail and tactical moves suffice; when the environment is placid-clustered, strategic adjustments are required; when the environment is disturbed-reactive, governing entails some adjustments in the functioning and operations of the organization. When the environment becomes turbulent however and the ground is in motion, more fundamental modifications are in order: social learning is necessary. It is not any longer sufficient to tinker with tactics, strategies and operations. One must adjust the very structure and mission of the organization in order to ensure that it responds adequately to the changes in circumstances. Social learning entails not only a modification of the means and ways used in the pursuit of the general objectives of the organization, but also a reframing of the notion of the business the organization is in, an adjustment of its very mission, objectives, ends (Paquet 1999a).

In the language of Argyris and Schön (1978), social learning is truly double-looped learning: in its efforts to adapt to new circumstances and to cope, the organization must first learn new ways to reach its objectives, but it must also be ready to reframe those very objectives and invent new ones when the circumstances come to show that the old ones are no longer useful. For it is only through social learning leading to an overhauling of the structure and mission of the concern that it may hope to survive.

In the face of a turbulent environment, double–looped social learning therefore leads to fundamental innovation as a surviving strategy—through a morphological transformation in the structure of the organization—but also through the very redefinition of what business the organization is in. In addition, such modifications normally lead to building on collaborative strategies with groups that might have been competitors in normal times but now become partners because they see that collaboration is required for survival (Paquet 2009a).

If and when hyper-turbulence threatens to become endemic, collaborative strategies may fail to harmonize member goals around shared principles and appreciative skills; collaboration may be too expensive, too threatening, ineffective, or counterintuitive to such a degree that only social triage will do, that is, a partitioning of the environment and of the system into domains varying radically in terms of turbulence and adaptive capacity in an attempt to better allocate and protect the limited adaptive capacity (Emery and Trist 1965; McCann and Selsky 1984; Paquet 2005a).

In a relatively placid environment, with state power clearly allocated to multi-level governments that can operate in relatively airtight compartments, the Clerk can be a simple note taker and recorder of decisions taken by his/her federal political masters. As the environment becomes more complex, though, it requires different governance capabilities and interventions. To meet this need, the Clerk (and his/her entourage) become the co-leaders (with the prime minister of the day) of the architectural team, and is also a key member of the strategic team. While the compartments of different levels of government can still operate relatively effectively, some overhaul is essential.

In turbulent environments, the ground is in motion and the reference can no longer be inflexible goals and means because they require substantial revision as the environment changes. The reference becomes some shared focal points that serve as the basis for orientation maps. These focal points are principles not shared values. The reference to shared values is an echo effect of folk sociology. It is quite difficult to find such shared values in a pluralistic society. One may reasonably state, as Joseph Heath has done in the 2003 John L. Manion Lecture, that this is a myth based on the false presumption that "social integration is achieved through value-consensus", that shared values are what make people cohesive as a group, and that the state exists to promote these values (Heath 2003).

While most sociologists have by now abandoned the theory of shared values, 'shared values theorists' continue to thrive. Indeed, one of the main problems with the way in which the Canadian Charter of Rights and Freedoms has been interpreted is that it has been regarded as a system of values rather than some principles (efficiency, autonomy, subsidiarity, etc.) deemed to help maintain a neutrality of the state and other institutions *vis à vis* different notions of the good.

In a world in which hyper-turbulence lurks just around the corner, even agreement on principles and efforts at collaborating fail. The only survival strategy then is to collect and protect the available resources and skills in the hands of those best able to utilize them, and to sacrifice those portions of the concern less likely to survive. It is tantamount to the sacrifice of a limb to save the rest of the body. Such partitioning is always agonistic, and the allocation of resources gives rise to some disaggregation of the organization. In the language of McCann and Selsky, certain segments (social enclaves) with better adaptive capacity are strengthened by being provided with additional resources, while other segments (social vortices) with less adaptive capacity are literally sacrificed and allowed to disintegrate (McCann and Selsky 1984).

This sort of partitioning may not be desirable for ethical reasons, but as members become aware that, by selective decoupling, they can create a defensible space and that they create a shared identity for defending scarce resources and skills from both real and perceived threats, social enclaves will materialize, if only to avoid catastrophic collapses.

Stewardship in turbulent environments amounts to identifying principles likely to provide the requisite coordination and integration: an agreement on a few guideposts likely to permit the conversation to proceed, to facilitate the double-looped learning, and to ease the required structural changes.

In high-risk environments, combining uncertain threats with unimaginable ones (Dror 1999), hyper-turbulence may become common place and major transformations are in order. The shift from G to g becomes not just useful but necessary. However, it is not always easy to effect: major forces of dynamic conservatism (by persons and groups who would be badly served by the changes) may effectively slow down the process of reform for quite a while.

As the degree of turbulence in the environment increases (type 4, in the language of Emery and Trist), operational, tactical, and strategic management reforms are no longer sufficient (Emery and Trist 1965). Required is the development of capacities for collaborative action in managing large-scale reorganizations and structural changes at the macro level (Metcalfe 1998). In such environments, the ground is in motion. The private, public and social sectors and the multiple levels of government acting independently not only cannot ensure effectiveness, but they may make things worse and amplify tendencies toward disintegration.

What is required is collective action by "dissimilar organizations whose fates are, basically, positively correlated" (Emery and Trist 1965: 29).

If such collaboration were to fail, the emergence of great strain would lead to partitioning—the emergence of social enclaves and vortices—and eventually to the collapse of the system. In a catastrophe theory-type graph, Metcalfe has synthesized the predicament that a shift to a truly turbulent environment raises for organizations, and he depicts the major aspects of the issue in three dimensions: the degree of complexity of the environment, the degree of sophistication of management/governance capacities, and the level of governance effectiveness (figure 1.1).

Figure 1.1   Les Metcalfe's catastrophe theory framework

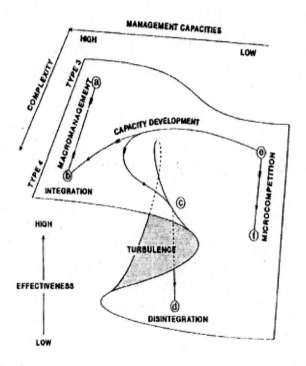

Source: L. Metcalfe 1998: 28.

He shows that, as complexity increases, management capacities must improve to avoid disintegration. If these capacities already exist, they must be brought into use (a–b); if they do not exist, they must be developed (e–b). If they do not exist and no development effort is made (e–f), or if the capacity building is inadequate (e–c–d), then disintegration ensues. A type 4 environment requires innovations that strengthen 'collaborative' relationships (Metcalfe 1998).

This framework shows how the dual task of group mobilization and building capabilities are integrally related. The architectural team and the strategic team charged to make use of the new structures are profoundly different: different in make-up (broader), in leverage (more indirect), and in scope (wider). It is not so much a team as 'an ecology of teams' that gradually, circuitously and experimentally, by trial and error, feel their way along (learning well or poorly along the way). The emphasis is on the need for creative politics, for innovative institutions and for new modes of coordination (Paquet 2005a, b).

The Clerk, who stands at the interface between the environment and the political process, will 'register' the tremors in the environment, and should/will be called upon to 'respond' by playing a key role (directly or indirectly) in 'shaping' the governance capabilities (and safeguarding the integrity of key state processes). It is possible that in disturbed environments the response may be made sharply and effectively at the operational level and the appropriate stewardship may ensue. Turbulent environments, however, are a different matter. What is called for is a new form of stewardship that is likely to require much more than simple retooling and restructuring. Collaboration may require a whole reframing of the situation, an enlightened capacity to eliminate the significant obstacles to collaboration, and much imagination in mobilizing reluctant partners through getting them to visualize both the benefits from collaboration and the costs of disintegration, and to buy into the proposed network governance.

As different environments materialized, the Clerk's burden of office has obviously had to evolve. But it would be naive to expect that the adaptation has always been perfect. A mix of differences of opinions about the state of the environment, together with problems of personalities and crises, has generated a greater or lesser goodness of fit between clerks and circumstances materializing with shorter or longer lags. Indeed, one may even be bold enough to hypothesize that a pattern of evolution may be detectable in a two-dimensional tableau stylizing the mix of roles played by the Clerk horizontally, and the sort of persona or dominant focus it generated for clerks diachronically as one proceeds through the four periods identified above and beyond (table 1.4).

On the horizontal axis, one may broadly identify the different forms of challenges faced by all clerks, from concerns about information, to a need for coordination, to forms of integration and required stewardship (including safeguarding the integrity of processes, and guarding the political/policy boundary), to involvement in management on an *ad hoc* basis in times of crisis, to continuous monitoring and management.

On the vertical axis, one may venture to label what might appear to be a characterization of the Clerk's function through time: from an officer simple recording decisions and preserving collective memory, to more ambitious functions involving the shaping of cognition as secretary to Cabinet, an active intermediary role at the federal-provincial interface, shaping enabling institutions, acting as policy advisor and shaping policy directions, becoming involved in crisis management as the overseer of the management of the public household, involvement in operations proper, and shaping the emotions and affects of the public service.

The centre of gravity of the role of the Clerk has drifted significantly from the role of registrar and recorder of information, in period I, to the role of partner in shaping institutions and organizations in period II. In period III, the federal fortress came under attack. As a result, there was a blunter use of command and

Table 1.4 *The clerk as rélévateur of the evolution of governance*

FUNCTION OF CLERK	ROLES OF CLERKS					
	Information	Coordination	Integration	Stewardship	Meddling	Management
Discontinuities		Secretary to Cabinet (shaping cognition)	Inter-provincial coordinator (shaping institutions)	Social architect & engineer (shaping organizations)	Managing crises	Systems/ processes/ public service reform (shaping culture)
I Clerk as registrar	CLERK AS REGISTRAR					
II Clerk as partner		CLERK AS COORDIN-ATOR	CLERK AS INTEG-RATOR	CLERK AS STEWARD	CLERK AS CRISIS MANAGER	CLERK AS MANAGER
III Clerk as mercenary						
IV Clerk as fixer			NETWORKED (provinces, territories, big cities)			
V Clerk as network						

Secretary to Cabinet

Deputy to PM

Spin matters

G ——————————————————————→ g

Note: Degree of emphasis in role increases with intensity of colour. | little | some | heavy |

42

control. This translated into even stronger links between the prime minister of the day and the clerk, emphasizing the dimension of 'personal deputy minister', as opposed to the others.

The shift in focus during this period allowed the Clerk to indulge directly or indirectly in a mix of coordination and meddling. The coordination role revealed the new difficulty in orchestrating the collaboration among the different levels of government and among the private, public and social sectors, while the meddling in operations became more and more prevalent as the search for mechanisms likely to help in meeting these challenges seemed to lead more and more often to stalemates.

This drift in the centre of gravity in period III has been ascribable both to the failure to fully develop a sound diagnosis of the *malaises* generated by the new environment, and to the growing lack of capacity for a renewed macro-management/governance of issues. As a consequence, towards the end of that period, the federal government was led to piecemeal experimentation with management instruments at the micro level, such as alternate service delivery (ASD) vehicles.

The recent period (IV) has been as chaotic as period III, but in a less obvious way. By period IV, the shift from 'Big G' government to 'small g' governance had become a fact of life. The state in advanced democracies everywhere had begun slowly and painfully to move away from centre stage, towards the smaller (but absolutely crucial) role of nurturing, supporting, enabling, catalyzing, and acting as societal failsafe.

Political leaders in Canada have been in denial both about the inevitable decline in the role of the state, and about the lessening of federal influence within the federation. Even had the Clerk understood what was happening, he/she would have been discouraged from speaking up (even privately), prevented from stimulating and encouraging the overhaul of governance of the country as much as was required, and forced into a good deal of social work as the public service and the provincial/territorial and local governments were savaged in the name of deficit and debt reduction.

This, in turn, led to the involvement of the Clerk in human resources management to a greater degree than heretofore, helping to put out brush fires, and emphasizing process over substance. Indeed, to some extent, in period III, and most importantly in period IV, the Clerk developed a bifocal approach to his/her burden of office: on the one hand, putting an emphasis on shaping cognition as secretary to Cabinet and deputy minister for the Prime Minister, and, on the other hand, meddling in detailed files as crisis manager and person responsible for the public service. This has meant a relative retrenchment from the core function of integration and stewardship.

If this reasoning holds, the Clerk of the future may have to refocus his/her burden of office on the central functions of integration and stewardship, and to recognize that, in any event, such a burden of office can no longer be carried out in one place. The Clerk may have to move to a post-modern version of the network governance of period II.

A windshield survey

A serious review of the last 140 years of Canada's life-world experience, through the lens of the Clerk, would require a book length exposé. A more detailed analysis will have to await a more extensive examination of the historical files.

What we can present in these few pages is a 'through the windshield' view of this experience that seems to support our hypotheses. We are quite conscious that this broad brush survey may appear cavalier to some and as not providing a full scale and rigorous test of the broad hypothesis sketched in table 1.4. Its purpose is to provide a plausibility test. While the body of ethnographic evidence marshalled may not satisfy or please many, it is quite substantial and we feel confident that subsequent work will support our provisional assessment of the extent to which any Clerk's work may have been less than adequate and why.[1]

The world of the Clerk

According to Gordon Robertson, who held the office from 1963–1975, a good clerk must have "…apart from a sound record and knowledge of the public service,…good judgment, a temperament compatible with the prime minister's, and complete reliability". To be successful, Robertson explains, it is necessary to have "…the sure confidence of…the prime minister [and] of ministers and heads of departments" (Robertson 2001: 215, 305).

This point of view is unduly limiting. It speaks only about a portion of the Clerk's world. It does not throw much light on the role of the Clerk as *révélateur*.

Our view of the Clerk's world is more complex. In our reading of the evolution of the function, we take into account a fuller perspective that recognizes the centrality of the Clerk's role as a mix of maven, connector and salesman (Gladwell 2000), and as a person in need of a sextant that takes into account the three sets of constraints imposed by the environment, the governance capabilities available, and the character of the prime minister.

To the extent that his/her knowledge base is incomplete and the learning stunted, to the extent that the community of practice of which he/she is a part is limited, and to the extent that the ability for contagion and charisma are inadequate, the Clerk is less than ideal: he/she will have a lesser grasp of the richness of the environment, will be less able to tap fully into a larger community of practice, and will be less able to communicate effectively with all those who are meant to carry out the various stewardship functions, and to inspire them.

In a world of learning, connection and persuasion, the Clerk has to balance three sets of forces in defining viable strategies.

First, the environment (external forces, strains on the federation and the role of the state) imposes its diktats. The Clerk will have to be well informed about its changing parameters. Not all clerks have been equally adept at this capacity for profound appreciation of context. Furthermore, as the complexity of the environment has grown, more and more sophistication has been required for there to be any reasonable degree of understanding.

Second, the capabilities and kinds of instrumentation that are available to cope with the environmental challenges have to be appreciated. At first, much of the apparatus (and the community of practice underpinning it) was informal, fluid and highly personalized. As the country matured though, and the environment became more complex and more turbulent, there was a gradual crystallization of these capacities. They were instituted in organizations that gradually acquired lives of their own. Eventually, rigidity set in, and loyalty to the broader underlying purpose gave way to loyalty to the organization/institution itself. As a result, over time, change came to be experienced by the apparatus as an attack on its vested interests, and the Clerk had to gain an appreciation of the extent to which he/she might or might not be able to make use of it.

Third, the continuing tension between the prime minister of the day and the Clerk, but also between the politicians and the bureaucrats, is omnipresent. Depending on personalities and on the fit between their personal values and plans, the tension might be greater or lesser, but it is never absent. Over the last 140 years, the Prime Minister has not always been at one with the Clerk: in some cases, it led to the Clerk leaving the post entirely. Also, as the public sector expanded, additional sources of expertise arose within, and prospered outside government, so that politicians could and did benefit from advice from many sources other than the Clerk.

Thus, the Clerk requires a great deal of environmental intelligence, a mental agility that enables him/her to make the highest and best use of existing capabilities, and a large reserve of wisdom to dovetail his/her work with the priorities, predilections, and style of the prime minister of the day. When broad changes in any of these contexts are registered, the Clerk has to re-triangulate his/her own position, and redefine what is likely to succeed.

The first two periods

During the first period (1867–1940), internal and external pressures forced the Canadian state to adjust rapidly. Canada was continuously gaining authority and independence from Britain throughout this period, and building internal capacity (e.g., income tax on the occasion of the World War I, Civil Service Commission 1918–19). The federal government's intentions to be pro-active in the fight against poverty, social injustice and inequalities, were on the agenda even by 1919. It was, though, mainly the need to react to the ravages of the Great Depression that triggered a new kind of activism.

In the pre-1940 era, the basic social architecture that had existed since before Confederation was periodically 'tweaked' on an *ad hoc* basis. The Clerk does not seem to have played any role of great significance—other than the traditional one of registrar that he had played since before Confederation. Politicians had their hands firmly on the rudder, and the degree of complexity neither was, nor appeared to be, such that it required a particularly elaborate governance apparatus. Crises were handled by special committees of inquiry, and there were pieces of legislation in which the Clerk must have had a hand, but only to the extent of rigorous and careful processing.

There appears to have been little overwhelming accumulation of knowledge having an impact, little intermediation, and little in the form of leadership. Indeed, some holders of the office seem to have taken pride in their lack of interest in policy. In short, the clerks were not called upon to be the mix of maven, connector and salesman, or even helpmate to the prime minister of the day until the role of secretary to Cabinet was added to their functions at the beginning of period II.

Faced with external and internal challenges, Mackenzie King reached for a few people to help, calling on those persons (like the father of A. D. Heeney, the person who was to become the first Clerk who cumulated the role of secretary to Cabinet, and O. D. Skelton) who had impressed him, This led over time to the arrival on the scene of 'social architects' such as Skelton

(Under-Secretary of State for External Affairs, 1925–1941), and then later Clifford Clark (Deputy Minister of Finance, beginning in 1932), and Graham Towers (first governor of the Bank of Canada, beginning in 1935). In this way, the seeds were planted for the development of the network of intelligent generalists who helped make period II's effectiveness possible.

The activism triggered by the Great Depression, and the challenges created by World War II, dramatically changed the terrain of operations. Momentous challenges like these could not be handled by 'gifted amateurs'. Something needed to be done to address King's notorious lack of organization in the face of the need to take decisions and execute them quickly. The dual mandate of Clerk and secretary to Cabinet that King gave to Heeney in 1940 meant that the Clerk, and a network of mandarins around him, were able to significantly redesign the House between 1940 and 1975.

There were important weaknesses in capabilities and instrumentation. Heeney found Cabinet operations inadequate when he arrived in 1940.

> There was no agenda, no secretariat, no official present at meetings to record what went on, no minute of decisions taken, and no system to communicate the decisions to the departments responsible to implement them....It was obviously a system that could operate only where the pace of events was relatively slow and where matters requiring decision were not overly intricate or complex. Even so, it was a singularly inefficient and unfair way for a collective executive to reach decisions for which all would share responsibility (Robertson 2001: 76).

Granatstein describes Heeney's contribution:

> Almost single-handedly Heeney had carried the Canadian government into the modern era....In the process of doing this...[he] had converted the Privy Council Office from a minor functionary's post into an executive secretaryship that handled the whole range of government business. He made the Clerk of the Privy Council and the Secretary to the Cabinet the invaluable

servant of Prime Ministers, ministers, and the government, as well as an official with significant power in his own right. And Heeney established the non-partisan nature of the joint post, making its incumbent a civil servant like the others (Granatstein 1998: 207).

In the East block itself, the mandarins created the mechanisms – notably in the Privy Council Office and the Prime Minister's Office – through which the Prime Minister and Cabinet could shape, direct, and control the course of events in Canada to the extent they chose or were able. In the process they also created a central government structure and system in which great power flowed to them as well – a necessary, and probably not entirely unwelcome or unplanned, concomitant (Ibid., xxii).

Heeney had an enormous impact on both organization and policy, but other senior players (part of the network around him) were crucial as well: among them Lester Pearson, Jack Pickersgill, Norman Robertson, Clifford Clark, Gordon Towers, W. A. Mackintosh, and a bit later, Bob Bryce. The dimension of guardian of the political/policy boundary in dealings with the government and the prime minister of the day, as well as of classical 'guardian' values, were natural consequences. In effect, the public service as an institution, with the Clerk as its head, became a part of the checks and balances of the formal governance system.[2]

It was an era of collective leadership, based on friendship and trust by a group constituting an old boys' network, which was well connected nationally and internationally. They wielded enormous power. The network of partners is a mirror image of the clustered world of politics. The very fact that one clerk could become a minister of the Crown is a good indication of the closeness of the partnership, although, at the same time, they stood their ground as 'keepers of the integrity of the system'. More importantly, this collection of people (along with some ministers) seems to have been imbued with a strong sense of the need to construct a propulsive state. In that sense, they reflected the Keynesian spirit of the times and the confidence that institutions could be built to manage the political economy.

It was only with the Rt. Hon. John Diefenbaker's arrival in 1957 that signs of diffraction began to appear. The then-Clerk, Bob Bryce, earned Diefenbaker's trust, but was reportedly the "universal joint" for virtually all of the other mandarins, who were never able to overcome the Prime Minister's mistrust (Ibid., 270–271).

Gordon Robertson, Bryce's successor, was the last Clerk of this era. He was like the mandarins in terms of education (law at Oxford on a Rhodes scholarship), entry to the public service (External Affairs in 1941), entry to the 'corridors of power' as secretary to King, in 1945, in the form of a public service secondment to the Prime Minister's Office (PMO) (headed by Pickersgill), and later as advisor in the Privy Council Office (PCO) to St. Laurent. (Robertson 2001).

But the times were different, and the period was drawing to a close. The grand era of the mandarins, and of the 'clerk as network and partner', was coming to an end. Robertson's contributions included adding more formality and structure to the functions of the PCO and the PMO.

The 1972 election, which Pierre Trudeau nearly lost, seems to have played a very important role in determining the shape of government at the very end of this period and the beginning of the next. The authors were told that when Gordon Robertson left the position in 1975, it was for two reasons: first, because Pierre Trudeau had lost interest in domestic politics. This is consistent with what Bliss reports "[the] crass, highly political, lavish, desperate side of Trudeau Liberalism emerged after [the nearly lost election of] 1972" (Bliss 2004: 260). Secondly, Robertson disagreed profoundly with Trudeau about Quebec. His departure heralded a shift in the role of the Clerk towards that of helpmate that has only deepened with time.

The next two periods

The underlying drift from G to g was beginning to be fully felt during period III. As early as the late 1960s and early 1970s, broad worldwide forces (inflationary pressures, the oil crisis) disrupted the environment and revealed the inadequacy of both traditional understanding of the context, and of the capabilities and instrumentations to cope with these new challenges.

The mid-1970s was a time of major upheaval. The environment was quite turbulent. International integration, urbanization on the national scene and pro-active Keynesian policies had served Canada well until the 1950s. By the 1960s, though, a Canada-made recession (*à la* James Coyne) and world inflationary pressure, along with the demographic destabilization generated by the baby-boomers, the oil crisis, and an exuberant and dangerous monetary policy in the early 1970s, were ushering in a period of hyper–turbulence on many fronts.

Instability on the international front, a misguided pursuit of aggregate demand policies in the face of aggregate supply crises, a consequent decline of credibility in government, and in the public service, led to much chaos at the centre.

Period III was dominated by two strong and determined prime ministers, the Rt. Hon. Pierre Trudeau and the Rt. Hon. Brian Mulroney.

Trudeau was in power until 1984, with the brief *inter-regnum* of a minority Clark government in 1979, and another, even briefer, period when he handed the reins to the Rt. Hon. John Turner in 1984. He has been described as a "fighting intellectual [and] a man with an extraordinarily clear vision of the structure of the Canada he wanted to mould..." (Bliss 2004: 246). This was a man who told the Canadian Bar Association, in 1967, that "...the power of both the federal and the provincial governments would be restrained in favour of the Canadian citizen..." (Ibid., 253), and who would have Ottawa "...patriate Canada's Constitution, with an amending formula and a Charter of Rights and Freedoms, whether the provinces liked it or not" (Ibid., 266). He chose Michael Pitfield as his Clerk; this appointment has long been viewed as significantly shifting the balance towards greater valence for the role of deputy minister to the prime minister. Indeed, "Pitfield came to speak more (and more), whether to ministers or to departments, in the name of the prime minister" (Robertson 2001: 310).

Trudeau's appointment of Pitfield was contentious among politicians (Robertson 2001: 309) and, the authors were told, many senior bureaucrats left as a result. The reality was that there was no longer a network of expertise in Ottawa working as a knowledge-accumulation machine. As a result, every segment of the House was building its own partial and feeble information base. This was the time when, in the face of impending economic disaster, an array of different economic forecasts based on incomplete information, was leading to actions that were both disconnected from one another and disconnected from the broad economic realities.

Not only was the diffracted knowledge not generating cumulative and effective learning, but in addition, despite its claim to be in charge, the centre seemed to be becoming more and more disconnected from its environment. Disasters on the national and international fronts were papered over by a good deal of rhetoric, but the role of the Clerk was no longer one that included acting as connector, as it had before. As for persuasion, it no longer seemed to be seen as necessary: the leader knew best.

At the same time, the expansion of the federal public sector, especially towards the end of the former period, had raised important management challenges. The 1976 Auditor-General's report advised that 'Parliament had lost control of the public purse'. There was a clear need to manage this sprawling 'empire' better. In its 1979 report, the Lambert Commission highlighted weak accountability and extolled meta management, eventually giving rise to the program and expenditure management system (PEMS). Numbers of experienced professional managers were brought into the public service to help the government to get a better grip on controlling and managing public expenditures.

Trudeau was a fan of these new managerial methods (Robertson 2001: 256), and Pitfield reached for the imposition of a rational system of setting objectives and making adjustments. He was responsible for introducing the heavy PEMS (envelope) system in 1977 during the brief minority government of the Rt. Hon. Joe Clark, and then embellished it when Trudeau returned and reappointed him.

Pitfield's successor was Gordon Osbaldeston. He was the epitome of 'professional manager', and he tried more practical managerial improvements, including dismantling the worst excesses of the PEMS system, during the Rt. Hon. John Turner's brief *inter-regnum* as Prime Minister. Unfortunately, his low-key, and somewhat laid-back, temperament did not match that of the Rt. Hon. Brian Mulroney, and he did not survive beyond the transition to the majority Progressive Conservative government that arrived in 1984.

Mulroney's choice as his first Clerk was Paul Tellier: a bright, quick, and experienced manager, whose effectiveness was ascribable to his singular understanding of people, rather than relying on the lens of ideas or systems. Like his predecessors, Tellier saw it as important for the Clerk to continue to safeguard key processes, but he also saw the importance of acting as backstop for the deputy minister cadre, so that he could (and did) delegate a good deal to them.

Tellier was not a person likely to wait for cumulative social knowledge to come forth, nor to scan the environment, looking for ways to enhance and enable it. The co-leader role stayed submerged (not to reappear to this day). He valued networking, and, thus, adapted well to the style of the person for (or with) whom he worked. Yet his network was not as wide-ranging as it had been in period II. It also tended to focus on internal issues.

By this time, as 'new public management' swept over most advanced democracies, the political leadership in Canada (as well as citizens generally) were pushing for change in the 'culture' of the public service. Tellier, and then Glen Shortliffe, tried to effect change by acting on the public service or through organizational reform. Tellier's approach was to institute a series of deputy-led task forces (PS 2000), but he neglected to take into account the fiscal difficulties that would swamp other efforts, including a six-year wage freeze, and he failed to understand the profound effect that the Al Mashat affair of 1991, and other events, would have in undermining the unwritten contract between the senior public service—its political masters and the country. He also failed to realize to what extent the public service had become resistant to change.

Shortliffe, who succeeded Tellier, kept the focus on internal state reorganization, and created the de Cotret Task Force. This initiative, with support from the 'machinery of government' portion of the PCO (possibly at the behest of Mulroney), was intent on accomplishing organizational change that would improve decision making through a 'quick and dirty' reform of the public sector.

The frame of mind in place during most of this period was a focus on internal reorganization of the state and attempts to impose a rational regime of control on the state as a way to cope with a new world where the state was no longer in charge. The relative failure of this period may be ascribed, to a great extent, to the role of Clerk having lost much of its capacity for social learning, its broad connections through sectors and social groups, and its interest in or sense of responsibility for persuasion (e.g., the exhortation of elites, including its political masters). The Clerk's function became more and more personalized and high profile. As a result, while not playing the role of maven, connector and salesman well, the Clerk became less of a steward.

Period III was an era in which the Clerk had ceased to be at the core of a brain trust advising the politicians; the Clerk was often charged with implementing ideologically-inspired and ill-informed policies, imbued by a state-centric view of the world and immune to social learning. The Clerk was no longer the architect and designer of Canadian governance: he was the engineer, charged with implanting the wishes of the political masters.

By the end of this period, and the beginning of the next, the breadth of what was expected of the Clerk was no longer 'a part of the oral tradition of the senior public service'. One might even say that the guidance to ministers and bureaucrats on fundamentals like accountability began to reflect an increasingly distorted version of some basic principles (Franks 2005).

The Rt. Hon. Jean Chrétien swept into office with a majority in 1993, having defeated Paul Martin for the leadership, and was re-elected twice. His first choice for Clerk was Jocelyne Bourgon. At the end of his ten-year tenure, he turned over the leadership of the Liberal Party to the Rt. Hon. Paul Martin, in late 2003.

Period IV (and the Chrétien-Bourgon tandem) began with the mortgage of momentous public deficits at the federal level that could no longer be ignored. Expediency trumped rationality: Canada's program review in the mid-1990s was the occasion to devolve responsibilities both to non-state actors and to junior levels of government in the name of deficit fighting and fiscal expediency. It was done *dans le désordre* but it generated a large number of loose collaborative regimes where separate facilities and rigid organizational forms had previously prevailed.

Bourgon was a superb personal deputy minister to the Prime Minister. Not one who had learned to be effective either by networking or delegating, she nevertheless acted decisively to institute the necessary repairs, and was remarkably successful on a number of internal fronts. For example, she recognized the dramatic weakening of policy capacity, and worked on rebuilding it. She saw the need to recruit new talent at all levels to replace managers about to retire, and identified the deficit on the values and ethics front.

Nevertheless, her tenure was in strict continuity with the philosophy of carrying out only internal repairs and refurbishment as a response to the need for a transformation of governance more broadly. This internal focus, and the refusal or inability to recognize the mammoth changes in the environment, led to the Clerk being confirmed as a 'fixer'.

The growing turbulence of this period may have included accusations of waste, mismanagement and corruption, but it also gave rise to significant instances of retooling (e.g., the Canadian Food Inspection Agency in 1997), restructuring (e.g., airport devolution-framework in 1994), and reframing (e.g., Nunavut in 1999) (Paquet 1999b). Nevertheless, these initiatives did not seem to echo (except in an accidental way) the emergence of a new philosophy of governance.

Experts have observed that public sector reform should proceed in three stages: first, a systematic review of government programs to retain only those which are necessary and appropriate; second, an organizational review to determine how best to organize to get that work done; and finally, a service delivery review to determine the most efficient and effective ways to deliver services.

Unfortunately, the federal government carried out these stages in exactly the reverse order of what would appear to be called for. First, in 1989, came Tellier's PS 2000 with its several deputy-led task forces to tackle key systems and 'service to the public'; then came Shortliffe's organizational reform, likely stemming from the de Cotret Task Force work of 1992–99; and finally came program review in Period IV, with the appointment of Bourgon.

Bourgon was replaced in 1999 by Mel Cappe, who limited his sights to one area of change for the public service—human resource (HR) management—and gave the other deputies room to devise other improvements as they thought best. He succeeded, where many had hitherto failed before in changing the HR management system, although some argue that the change did not go far enough (Hubbard 2003).

Alex Himelfarb replaced Cappe in 2002, and served for the remainder of this period, as well as the transition that resulted from the winter 2006 election, which brought the Conservatives to power with a minority government. He seems to have performed as a kind of 'universal joint' role for handling crises à la Bryce, despite his ability to do more.

The Himelfarb years were not only a rather tragically-gripping illustration of the centrality of the Clerk's role, but also of the fragility of the function in the absence of strong political leadership. He was appointed at the end of a Chrétien era explicitly to breathe a new policy soul into a tired government. But political infighting, national fractiousness and a blind commitment to a centralized mindset crippled the Prime Minister. Survival became the dominant underlying theme of the latter days of the Liberal Chrétien-Martin governments, and the Clerk, despite a strong interest in policy development and great skill at mediation, was reduced to the role of 'fixer' and *bricoleur*.

Whatever the pace and structure of the interventions by the Clerks of these two periods, they have all proved to be internally focused on overhauling the state, and may be said to have generally failed to meet the challenges of their maven, connector and salesman function. As a result, the job of Clerk has lost its crucial place, and has failed to mount the sort of network of expertise that would help to shape the new Canadian governance. During all these years, the PMO trumped the PCO, and the Clerk's role has been fundamentally eroded.

Yet, there was a significant discontinuity between periods III and IV. In period III, there was a denial on the part of both politicians and bureaucrats that a new world was emerging, and much of the bafflement and frustration came from futile internal efforts to cope in a *Quixotic* way with forces denied. In period IV, the Clerks were conscious of their elusive powers in this new environment, and conscious of the need to govern differently, but, given the fact that federal politicians were still in denial about the need to do so, they were to be satisfied with coping—with the hope that they might do some good by *bricolage* here and there.

The dawn of period V

This section is, of necessity, speculative. While the revealed performance of past Clerks has shown that there has been considerable erosion of their functions in the recent decades, only time will tell if the role of the Clerk is going to be refurbished.

With the election of the Stephen Harper government in early 2006, and the nomination of Kevin Lynch, hopes were high that Canadian public governance would change. This was the case both because of the different mindset of the new government (more prone to defend decentralization) and because of Kevin Lynch's reputation of a strong intellect, and a demonstrated focus on ingenious and effective execution in the face of increasing environmental turbulence.

A significant number of federal politicians were by that time no longer in denial about the need to govern differently. Emphasizing the importance of the real collaboration that has become essential in today's world, the Harper government's first throne speech set out a commitment "to building a better federation in which governments come together...[to] respond to concerns about the fiscal imbalance...[and to] an open federalism" (Canada 2006a: 4).

The conjunction of a Prime Minister with a policy vision with a Clerk who is also policy-driven appeared to provide an ideal moment to bring back the sort of joint venture that Canada lived through in the post-1940 years of period II—of Clerk as partner—that could again provide Canada with the momentum to redesign the House to meet the emerging new challenges.

What made Period II a success was an alignment of ideas and principles, combined with a capacity for grand design, and the necessary execution skills. If the current opportunity were to be used well, the Harper government had to emulate the best of that period. But it had to do it in a different way and in a more difficult environment. It had to find new and creative ways to harness the energies of many more players (across levels of government and sectors) using an alignment of ideas and principles that resonates with much more diverse Canadians. It had also to execute well despite much greater complexity and diffusion of responsibility than ever before. Moreover, it had to employ a new kind of stewardship—one that is mostly based on meaning making rather than trying to control from the top since the context has changed.

Over the decades, the adaptive capacity of the senior bureaucracy to an increasingly dynamic environment has diminished—constrained by an increasingly sclerotic centralized infrastructure and a mindset focused to a growing degree on pursuit of its own interests. Decades of a centralized mindset would have to be overcome as well as the well-entrenched culture of risk aversion on the part of the senior bureaucracy, and its growing degree of political correctness. All these factors have dramatically reduced the capacity to transform the public governance apparatus at a time when what is needed is a better alignment with the evolving context.

It is fair to say that the tenure of Kevin Lynch has proved to be a major disappointment perhaps because the expectations were unduly high. Lynch proved unable to overcome and transcend the distrust that was to be expected between a Conservative government expected to partner with a senior public service that had been recruited and promoted by the former Liberal governments that had been in power for more than a decade.

There were likely several contributing factors for this lack of success.

For one thing, the Clerk ignored instances of blatant disloyalty to the new government in the upper ranks of the bureaucracy and allowed a chasm to develop between the upper bureaucracy and a new government that could be said to be 'rationally paranoid'. Even if only five percent of the senior bureaucrats might be said to be determined to pursue their own version of the public interest in active or passive opposition to the new government agenda, if one does not know who they are in the upper structure, it is sufficient for paranoia to flourish.

The minority government situation did not help. The blindly partisan legislature, as revealed by the work of parliamentary committees, could not but help to sustain the old loyalties in the public service. So there was a high cost in not ensuring a minimally effective communication system at the interface of the political and the bureaucratic, and in not ensuring both parties at this interface would be summoned not to dismiss out of hand messages coming from the other partner. This allowed outright statements about the blinding ideological mindset of the elected officials to be aired by senior bureaucrats, and about the reluctance of the bureaucracy to embrace the general directions chosen by the elected official to be tolerated, without both parties being reminded of their burden of office and of their responsibilities to each other.

The Gomery roadshow and its aftermath (in addition to the higher degree of risk aversion and political correctness) contributed also significantly to a formalization of administrative processes and to an ossification of the rapport between politicians and bureaucrats at a time when a new covenant would appear to be required (Thomas 2008; Paquet 2009a).

As a result, the anticipated refurbishment of the federal public governance required by the new environment and promised by the new government did not materialize. This cannot be ascribed only to the Clerk, but the fact that it did not materialize under the guidance of a very Cartesian clerk revealed that the sort of social architecture work required was beyond the reach of a Cartesian clerk living in an age of distrust. As George Lakoff would suggest, empathy may be required to complement reason and rationality, but the need for re-foundation had also to be recognized by the Clerk (Lakoff 2009). It was not.

Networks and covenants of the sort that existed in period II were built on empathy and trust, and the clerks of period II were first and foremost producers of empathy and trust. But there was also an unusual capacity for creative design in the period II teams. This creative ingredient—extremely crucial in hyper-turbulent times—was blatantly absent in period IV and has remained absent in period V.

The arrival of Wayne Wouters on the scene, a person trusted by the upper ranks of the bureaucracy and known to be a pragmatist, might mark a return to a minimalist clerk as fixer for the time being but with a view to building a transition to a regime built on empathy and trust—*reculer pour mieux sauter*!

Any progress beyond that minimalist position will require that Wouters gets the existing system of distrust unstuck. This is an Herculean task because the present mindset has been allowed to crystallize for quite a moment: it will require breaking the cycle of distrust through mandating:

(1) tact, civility and respect for the public service on the part of elected officials and their cohort;

(2) attentive listening and creative collaboration of the public servants to the broad travails of the elected masters;

(3) a new brand of constructive critical thinking on both sides in the name of better serving the citizenry; and

(4) nothing less that the restatement of the dual legitimacy of the elected and of the experts, both with responsibilities in the pursuit of the public interest, but within the broad understanding of a new code of conduct of the sort recently introduced in the United Kingdom that reminds both parties of their duties. Like the Magna Carta that reiterated some key principles that had been forgotten in the heat of action, such codes are absolutely necessary if a new covenant is to be forged between the political and the bureaucracy (Thomas 2009a).

It may mean the end of the Clerk as the kingpin of a top-down governing enterprise, and the full realization that, in the world of 'small g' governance, what is required is not an *homo manipulator* like Richelieu, but a person like Gildardo Magana. Of Magana (who took over the Mexican revolution after the assassination of Zapata) it was said by John Womack that:

> …what he had learned was to mediate: not to compromise, to surrender principle and to trade concession, but to detect reason in all claims in conflict, to recognize the particular legitimacy of each, to sense where the grounds of concord were, and to bring contestants into harmony there. Instinctively, he thrived on arguments, which he entered not to win but to conciliate (Womack 1969).

It remains to be seen if Wayne Wouters can be a Gildardo Magana, and whether he will be able to break the cycle of distrust, to generate a re-foundation of the political-bureaucratic covenant along the lines of some form of collaborative stewardship based on renewed trust, and to launch a process of social architecture capable of generating the sort of infrastructure required for collaborative public governance to emerge and to thrive. At the present time, the generalized trust deficit is the major hurdle (Sibley 2009).

Conclusion

It is difficult to do justice in a few pages to a phenomenon as complex as the evolution of the Clerk of the Privy Council as an institution that has echoed the evolution of Canadian society, while helping to change it. Our purpose has been to provide a broad overview of the phenomenon, and to suggest a hypothesis about both the evolution of Canada, and of the role of the Clerk.

The elusiveness of the Clerk's role and the fact that it is the locus of no *imperium* (absolute power), nor *potestas* (real power), but simply of *auctoritas* (authority, but not power) makes it difficult to pin down. *Auctoritas* is based on an impersonal capacity to augment, safeguard, and add value to what exists, which is embodied in the person charged with that role.

This elusiveness explains why each clerk has had to re-invent the role in different contexts and circumstances, and why whatever has been invested in the role at a given time has not carried on to his or her successor. *Auctoritas* comes from the person: whatever emanates from such a person is less than an order but more than simple advice (Agamben 2003).

The evolution of the role of the Clerk, and the variety of forms taken by its *auctoritas,* has revealed much about the times. The role reached a pinnacle in period II, when a network of mandarins exercised it fully: the Great Depression, Word War II and the great leap forward of the postwar era made it possible for such authority to be very effective.

With the decline of the power of the state (and of the federal government within it), and the emergence of a polycentric governance, such *auctoritas* has proved more difficult to exercise. The role of integrator and steward has been first diffracted, and then largely submerged. The elusive authority of the Clerk has ceased to have a determinant impact, and has come to be overshadowed by the role of helpmate to the party in power.

It may well be that the only way to give the Clerk more robust roots in the new context is through the recognition that the law of requisite variety has wide applicability. As Ashby's law put it, the variety in the control system must be equal to or larger than the variety of the perturbations in order to achieve control (Ashby 1956). So, in a tumultuous world, marred by diffraction, it may well be that any form of *auctoritas* designed to augment, safeguard and add value will require governance (effective coordination when power, resources and information are widely distributed) by a network.

In that sense, the experience of network governance in period II may deserve some in-depth examination and suggest some directions for the future. It should also be clear, though, that the new network governance will bring together a new array of actors that transcends the confines of the federal-level, state-centric apparatus.

Whether the arrival on the scene of a new prime minister and a very new clerk will trigger a move toward a 'clerk as network *auctoritas*' and lead to a transformation of the institutional and organizational architecture of Canada—a real *perestroika*—remains to be seen. (Paquet 2005b, c)

But if it were not to materialize, and if such network governance were not to assure the requisite degree of collaboration, hyper-turbulence might be around the corner and social enclaves and vortices may ensue.

Some (more cynical than we are) already see signs of such social triage and even catastrophic disintegration on the horizon. But our hopes are greater than their fears at this time. Decentralization, polycentric governance, social learning and moral contracts may still provide the basis for effective governance.

However one cannot easily see how this could materialize without a good deal of adaptive capacity development and without 'clerk as network *auctoritas*'.

Endnotes

[1] Much of the work done to gain a good ethnographic sense of the world of the Clerk is based not only on the limited written works on this subject that we quote, but also and most importantly on interviews carried out with a variety of persons who have had the opportunity to work closely with different Clerks. Information obtained in this latter manner was supplemented by a number of safe-space discussions with authoritative persons in order to ascertain whether our reading of the different situations was accurate. *In toto*, the views of some twenty 'witnesses' have been sought.

[2] For example, on one occasion, in period III, the authors were told, the secretary of the Treasury Board intervened when political advisors wanted the president of the Treasury Board to issue a public report on expenditures in a way that downplayed or obscured 'bad news' and set things out in the most flattering light for the government. He advised the president that this overstepped the political-public interest boundary and would not be an acceptable action for the latter to take. Thus, it could not be supported by the secretary. The president agreed and the credibility of the office was preserved.

CHAPTER 2

Toward an Autopoietic Federalism

A system is autopoietic when its function is primarily geared to self-renewal.

—Erich Jantsch

Introduction

The term *eunomics* has been defined by Lon Fuller as "the science, theory or study of good order and workable social arrangements" (L. L. Fuller 2001: 62). This chapter is an exercise in eunomics to the extent that it is attempting to determine which one of two types of order—centralized or decentralized—is likely to be preferable in democratic confederal systems.

The debate about centralization and decentralization is a debate about means. In the case of federalism, it points to different ways in which a particular governance regime might crystallize structurally, and it argues in favour of one form over the other. But such discussion makes little sense unless one can identify, ever so loosely, the long-run purpose being pursued. By purpose, one does not mean the precise end products that are sought, but the process that one wishes to sustain.

In this chapter, federalism is assumed to be a collaborative governance regime attempting to respond to the heterogeneous challenges of pluralistic internal and external environments, through experiments with structures, processes and mechanisms that are capable of generating the requisite amount of coordination to deal effectively with the variety of citizens' demands, as well as to ensure a timely capacity to transform through social learning in the face of changing environments or evolving values (Paquet 1977, 2005a: chapter 13).

In the public sector governance world, a slight centralization–to–decentralization drift has been observed in the last half century. Some have bemoaned it; others have celebrated it. There has been a parallel evolution in private sector governance with the emergence of the H-form firm—an horizontal organizational form pioneered by organizations like Benetton that have transformed their production process away from a focus on vertical control and economies of scale (the V-form) toward one (the H-form) geared to horizontal and transversal networking, generating flexibility and variety at low costs while maintaining and even improving quality and self-renewal.

Our hypothesis is that this drift is to be welcomed because of two broad sets of considerations. First, only by devolving decision making to local arenas is there any likelihood that a differentiated population (with diverse views about the nature of the good) can hope to receive public goods and services in keeping with its diverse preferences. Second, decentralized arrangements are more likely to generate necessary experimentation and quick learning of new means and ends because of the polycentric nature of their governance.

But this argument is unlikely to be persuasive unless one can also show that a strategy aimed at reinforcing this drift is technically feasible, socially acceptable, implementable, and not too politically destabilizing (Carl A. Taylor 1997). Indeed, it has been the main counterargument of the phalanx of centralizers that decentralization may be theoretically desirable but unworkable in practice. For most centralizers, the only choice is between centralization and chaos.

We proceed in five stages. First we examine the general organizational drift from 'Big G' to 'small g' triggered by the need to provide variety, flexibility and fast social learning at low cost. Second, we identify major blockages that have slowed the process of social learning underpinning this evolution, and some ways in which they can be overcome. Third, we succinctly take notice of the attacks on decentralization as unworkable, overly costly, and inequitable (among other things), and show these criticisms to be ill founded. Fourth, we sketch four plausible scenarios for the future of Canadian federalism and argue for open-source federalism (i.e., less state centricity, more collaboration and generalized inclusion) as the most promising possible future. Fifth, we identify some prerequisites for this vibrantly decentralized federalism scenario to become regarded as a preferred alternative, and some of the virtuous scheming that will be necessary to launch such a Canadian *perestroika*.

From G to g

It has been suggested by Daniel Innerarity (quoting an apocryphal Sigmund Freud) that there are three impossible professions (to educate, to cure and to govern): success in these tasks require some sort of collaboration of the parties who, at first sight, would appear to be simple beneficiaries (Innerarity 2006: 193). This is certainly true about governance. Public governance and its circumstances in most democracies is a complex adaptive system like the human central nervous system or immune system, or an eco-system, and operates the same way. The human immune system includes a brigade of antibodies that fight and destroy an ever-changing cast of invading bacteria and viruses of such variety that the system must continually learn, adapt, improvise and overcome. The central nervous system contains hundreds of millions of neurons, interacting, combining and recombining in different patterns to deal with a complex and ever-changing context; it has a continually renewed ability to cope, anticipate, adapt and learn (Holland 1995).

Similarly, public governance and its circumstances is made up of a large number of actors, relationships, routines, norms and mindsets that are in a constant process of evolution in the face of the challenges of the day.

Such a system has certain characteristics.

First, it is *open*, that is, it receives material and non-material resources from the external environment, and it is shaped to a degree by its environment. As a whole, it is like a living organism capable of scanning the context and of managing its interdependence with its environment.

Second, because it is open, the system must *adapt* to its environment, that is, modify its social and technical texture in response to the changes in the environment, if it wishes to maintain a certain 'goodness of fit' with the context and be *adopted* by the environment in turn. Adoption means that the environment bestows a higher probability of survival and prosperity on the organism as long as a higher degree of goodness of fit prevails. In the case of a public socio-technical system, a higher degree of goodness of fit with its context generates high performance, while misfits produce lower performance levels.

Third, it must be sensitive to what is occurring in the world beyond in terms both of space and time, and modify its technologies, its processes and its structures in an effort to respond strategically and effectively to the environment. This entails a process of *differentiation* of the system to respond to the different challenges posed by the environment.

Fourth, it is a complex system in which the *interactions* among the individuals and their organizations generate a dynamic of their own. Every agent is forced to define strategies to react to the actions of other agents. Agents must adapt and discover new rules and new behaviors that generate the requisite 'coordination and integration' for high performances to ensue for the system as a system.

The public sector as a 'complex adaptive system' is therefore a set of ongoing relationships between people and organizations, governed by reactions to the environment and by mutual expectations. It has become differentiated and integrated in a particular manner over time, and its governance has had to evolve accordingly: to enable the system to maintain itself—to grow and to innovate—governance must be as varied and diverse as the environment and the interactions it is trying to deal with. This is the 'law of requisite variety': the capacity of a system to evolve and learn effectively (i.e., to govern itself in an effective manner) depends on its capacity to move to more complex forms of differentiation and integration, to be able to deal with the variety of challenges and opportunities in novel ways, and to maintain its coherence through time while retaining or shedding some characteristics that are sources of good fits or misfits.

The drift from state-centric governing

Over the last few decades, there has been a shift from state-centric governing towards arrangements that give greater valence not only to the private and social sectors but also to junior levels of government and smaller units in general. The situation is best captured by John Naisbitt's *Global Paradox*: the bigger the world economy, the more powerful its smallest players. The idea that the central government is the most important part of governance is becoming obsolete. In addition, new forms of polycentric governance are emerging as more important because they are more effective in generating timely responses (Naisbitt 1994: 51).

In Canada, this drift from 'Big G' government to 'small g' governance was not the result of a deliberate change in philosophy (even though such a shift has materialized over time), but of chronic public deficits that forced the central government to restructure its operations.

Beginning with the creation of Canada in the late 19th century, it was assumed that the public sector was able to perform better than the private sector (and the central 'headquarters' better than the local ones in all sectors) in tackling the challenges of the country. From the late 1970s on, doubts began to creep in about it (Paquet 1997). As a result, it was not until the 1990s, when the fiscal situation of the Canadian economy had deteriorated sufficiently for it to become thinkable that the IMF (International

Monetary Fund) might be forced to discipline the Canadian government, that Prime Minister Jean Chrétien's government was forced to review, systematically, what the citizens could legitimately expect from the state. This exercise is often referred to as 'Program Review', and led to a significant drift from 'Big G' government to 'small g' governance (Paquet 1999b).

Although this action was mainly inspired by fiscal pressures, a philosophy of subsidiarity became the guidepost calling both for a new division of labour among sectors (private, public, social) and a drive towards devolution of responsibility (within the public sector and across sector boundaries). Wealth creation concerns came to carry more weight than its distribution, so the case for state-centrism and centralization (because massive redistribution requires bringing the loot to the centre first) weakened. In Canada, soft egalitarianism, enforced as a matter of right, gave way to a new consensus on 'equability': on redistribution only to the extent that needs required it, and that politically unacceptable inequality called for correctives.

The new division of labour among sectors entailed the abandonment of the old sharp division between the public and the private sectors as many new forms of mixed organizations proved more efficient. Indeed, one might regard the Jane Jacobs book of the early 1990s (Jacobs 1992) as the last stand of those for whom any mixing of the private and public sectors could only lead to "monstrous hybrids". *De facto*, it became the new norm that various forms of partnership between sectors could better achieve the efficiency and equity goals that were jointly sought (Goldsmith and Eggers 2004).

Government also gradually realized that, in order to be effective, meso-level actions were required. This has led to a corresponding deconstruction of the public sector into new units that are more local (city–regions) and more clearly aligned with communities of practice (that crystallize within and around issue domains or arenas). These units of analysis emerged as basic building blocks where individual practitioners (the professional realm), domains (skills, practices, rules), fields (kinds of expertise), and the interest of other stakeholders (consumers, citizens, business executives, etc.) were more likely to be well aligned. In certain arenas, the appropriate level for aggregating communities of practice proved to be at the federal or provincial levels, but there was a growing likelihood in many sectors that smaller or more-diffuse building blocks, arranged in baroque ways, could produce better results (Gardner et al. 2001; Wenger et al. 2002).

The centrality of mechanisms and ligatures

The system of governance in good currency in Canada is a complex and fuzzy palimpsest of layers of formal and informal arrangements accumulated over time as new rules have come to be written over old ones. Any intervention in this script always disturbs delicate and fragile equilibria in the mix of structure–theory–technology that makes up this social system: the structure of roles and relations among individuals, the theory/views held within the system about its purposes, operations, environment and future, and the prevailing technology of the system all hang together, so that any change in one produces change in the others (Schön 1971:33). Poor performance is often ascribable to a poor alignment between the perspectives of the different stakeholders or between theory/structure/technology.

Given that the structures and roles of a system, and the 'theory–in–use' are much more deeply embedded sub-systems than technology, effective interventions may work better through engineering new mechanisms that may help it achieve its social learning potential, rather than by trying to change structure or theory. The vested interests in the technologies are less likely to unleash the full force of strong dynamic conservatism.

There is also a need for inter-domain coherence to be ensured by adequate ligatures that reinforce the underlying institutional order. The multiple logics at play in different issue domains or arenas generate spill over effects onto others. The degree to which taboos might exist in one sector is bound to limit what can be done in another. But the emergence of new mechanisms in one domain (like users' fees) is bound not only to affect the structure of roles and the theory of what business one is in within that domain, but also to have some reverberation on related issue domains.

Ligatures are also quite important at the cognitive level. They establish a corridor within which one may experiment safely. This is the sense in which the reference points constituted by 'the welfare state' for instance (with its focus on security and entitlements as a matter of right but also with its priority to redistribution over wealth-creation and its anti-growth and anti-efficiency bias) has served as a key nexus of ligatures for the old institutional order.

Mechanisms and ligatures are in the process of changing in democracies around the world including in Canada. They are crystallizing around the new reference point we have called 'the strategic state' at the core of 'small g' governance (Paquet 1996–97). This has dramatically changed the valence of the public sector, implying significant change in the structure and functioning of public administration.

Major social learning blockages

Canadian well-being is the result of the success or lack of success in organizing, instituting and governing in ways that have a high yield in economic, political and social terms. Such coordination and governance may take many forms and shapes—mixing top-down hierarchical coercion, horizontal exchange relations, relationships based on solidarity, and bottom-up self-organizing processes, generating a sense of direction from below. Federalism as a mind-set allows for this fluidity and variability and, as a result, fosters the design of a public sector and its circumstances that are likely to promote more effective social learning.

To catalyze social learning in complex organizations, one must have some view about the ways in which collective intelligence works. Elsewhere, we have very profitably used an approach suggested by Max Boisot (Boisot 1995).

The information space

In an effort to identify the major obstacles to social learning (and therefore to guide corrective interventions), Max Boisot has mapped the social learning cycle in a three-dimensional space—the information space—which identifies an organizational system in terms of the degree of 'abstraction, codification and diffusion' of the information flows within it. This three-dimensional space (see figure 2.1) defines three continua: the farther away from the origin on the vertical axis, the more the information is codified (i.e., the more its form is clarified, stylized and simplified); the farther away from the origin laterally eastward, the more widely the information is diffused and shared; and the farther away from the origin laterally westward, the more abstract the information is (i.e., the more general the categories in use).

The social learning cycle is presented in two phases with three steps in each phase: phase I emphasizes the cognitive dimensions of the cycle, while phase II deals with the diffusion of the new information.

In phase I, learning begins with some scanning of the environment, and of the concrete information widely diffused and known, in order to detect anomalies and paradoxes. Following this first step (s), one is led in step 2 to stylize the problem (p) posed by the anomalies and paradoxes in a language of problem solution. The third step of phase I purports to generalize the solution found to the more specific issue to a broader family of problems through a process of abstraction (at). In phase II, the new knowledge is diffused (d) to a larger community of persons or groups in step 4. There is then a process of absorption (ar) of this new knowledge by the population, and its assimilation so as to become part of the tacit stock of knowledge in step 5. In step 6, the new knowledge is not only absorbed, but has an impact (i) on the concrete practices and artifacts of the group or community.

Figure 2.1   *Learning cycle and potential blockages*

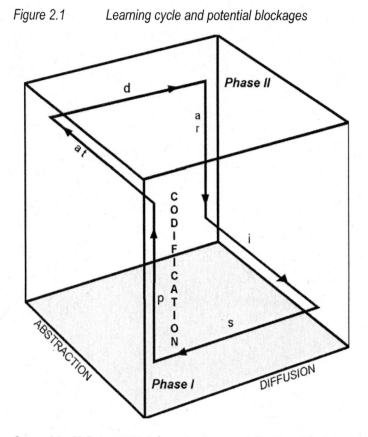

Source: Max H. Boisot 1995. *Information Space — A Framework for Learning in Organizations, Institutions and Culture.* London, UK: Routledge.

In figure 2.1, one may identify the different blockages through the learning cycle: in phase I, cognitive dissonance in (s) may prevent the anomalies from being noted; epistemic inhibitions of all sorts in (p) may stop the process of translation into a language of problem solution; blockages preventing the generalization of the new knowledge because of the problem definition being encapsulated within the *hic et nunc* (at) may keep the new knowledge from acquiring the most effective degree of generality. In phase II, the new knowledge may not get the appropriate diffusion because of property rights (d), or because of certain values or very strong dynamic conservatism which may generate a refusal to listen by those most likely to profit from the new knowledge (ar), or because of difficulties in finding ways to incorporate the new knowledge (i).

Interventions to remove or attenuate the negative effects of such blockages always entail some degree of interference with the mechanisms of collective intelligence. In some cases, such as the modification of property rights, the changes in the rules appear relatively innocuous, even though government interferes significantly in the affairs of the mind: correcting social learning blockages modifies relational transactions and, therefore, the psycho-social fabric of the organization.

Learning blockages

In the case of liberal democratic societies, and in the case of federal systems in particular, there are inherent blockages in each of the two phases.

The first kind of blockage is at the epistemic level.

Citizens have increasingly ceased to regard the state as omnipotent and benign. As a result, they have asked to be more involved in both policy development and program design, as well as to have access to the levers required to change organizational or institutional behavior. This has rendered the process of collective learning considerably more cacophonous. This, in turn, has meant a greater difficulty in creating the requisite forums and agoras for deliberation, significantly slowing down the process of aggregation of preferences, and mitigating the capacity to distil a dominant view about many of the anomalies. In this way, both the processes of codification and abstraction have been greatly impaired in recent times in these societies. To this must be added the obfuscation and confusion that is often sewn by irresponsible and ideologically anchored media.

For federal states, there is an additional complexity because two or more orders of government share 'sovereign' authority—something that adds to the numbers of players and consequently generates somewhat greater coordination challenges to overcome. A further impediment can stem in the case of Canadian federalism from a mix of cultural factors (a certain trust in authority and dislike of conflict), the congenital arrogance of the federal government, and the often unenlightened competitiveness of other orders of government. This has led to both a heightening of natural tensions and to some cognitive dissonance and ambivalence on the part of citizens bombarded by contradictory messages.

For example, the federal government, in Canada (and elsewhere), has been often described as

> [using its power]…in a way that creates a single, nation-wide community with shared values and shared, enforceable understandings of how local communities of all descriptions should be organized (Carter 1998: 19).

This 'anti-democratic' and 'anti-communitarian', top-down approach has led to much cognitive dissonance: the whole debate about fiscal imbalance in Canada is a good illustration of this cognitive blockage (Paquet 2004a).

The second kind of blockage is at the diffusion level, where collaboration is again mandatory for effectiveness.

While by definition, federalism as a formal system should be better able to serve a pluralistic and deeply diverse citizenry more appropriately than in a unitary one (which is why it was invented), in today's world the multiplication of levels of government and governance, the extent of local patriotism, and the existence of a wide variety of different interests and values can make the diffusion of particularly helpful responses to generic problems more difficult than might otherwise be the case.

Canada's brand of competitive formal federalism has proved capable of generating confusion and action overlap, and of allowing counterproductive adversarialism to inhibit collaboration in a significant way. The collaboration and partnering that are needed entail power sharing, and are often regarded as unacceptable in principle by the very organizations claiming to want to partner

(Paquet 2001b). The relatively recent antics of Newfoundland's Premier Danny Williams and of federalist leaders in Quebec have shown how inflammatory populist rhetoric can easily trump political rationality. So in difficult times, when the amount and kind of collaboration required are deeper and richer than before—and there is a need for a greater variety of forums, reporting standards and collaborative structures of a more permanent sort—these essential elements are often simply not there or not used.

It is clear that some '*bricolage*' is in order: the social learning apparatus needs to be repaired and enriched if decentralized governance is to be as effective as it can be. But it does not mean in any way that the decentralization strategy is unworkable or ineffective because the existing institutional basis is deficient in certain ways and requires some institutional makeover.

The case for *bricolage*

One may divide the array of mechanisms through which one may intervene in the social learning cycle into four broad families corresponding to the portion of the system to be catalyzed. On the cognitive side, forums and reporting mechanisms are meant to ginger up phase I of the social learning cycle; on the diffusion/dissemination side, one is looking at mechanisms to generate trust and fail-safe mechanisms in order to strengthen phase II. While these mechanisms may not be sufficient to ensure optimal functioning, they would appear to be at least necessary to make decentralized arrangements workable.

Getting rid of inhibitions in the cognitive sub-cycle

Collective intelligence is based on a capacity for all the stakeholders to work cooperatively in detecting anomalies, codifying them and generalizing the findings to a broader family of issues. It requires three things:

    (1) a modicum of timely and credible information on which the different parties or groups may base their provisional judgment about the state of affairs;

(2) a locus (real or virtual) for stakeholders to work at reconciling their viewpoints, working through their relations with each other, and learning from each other (Yankelovich and Rosell 2001); and

(3) the basic conditions for sustainable partnerships: ensuring that all parties gain from the arrangement, and that each party is likely to honour its obligations even when that is not necessarily the preferred option (Sacconi 2000).

An uninformed or a misinformed agent is unable to develop an appreciation of the situation and can be easily manipulated into taking a stand that can only lead to his/her not achieving the best possible level of knowledge and well-being. And it cannot be presumed that the required information will materialize by 'immaculate conception'. Consequently, it is crucial to ensure that the modicum of timely and credible information is available and accessible for agents to be able to make reasonable decisions. This is the rationale for the existence of public agencies like Statistics Canada, but there are also private and non–profit agencies that have emerged to perform similar functions.

In many sectors and domains, like health, the relevant comparable indicators have not been available until very recently, and are still far from completely satisfactory. In education, opacity remains the rule. It is therefore of prime importance to ensure that, in issue domains where intervention would appear to be required, the basic usable facts are not only recorded but made available to the citizenry. Nothing destroys the effectiveness of nonsensical rants or toxic lies more effectively than a modicum of information appropriately explained to the citizens (Paquet 2009a, b).

Another key family of missing mechanisms has to do with 'forums' for dialogue and multi-logue. Even though there may be a fair understanding of the rationale for partnering, and an appreciation of the different structures and roles that would be useful, in many cases, the barriers to partnering are often ascribable to the lack of a locus where the different parties can meet, deliberate and negotiate.

A good example is the issue of fiscal imbalance between the federal, provincial and local governments. This calls for fiscal 'concertation', but there is no place where the three parties can meaningfully meet and negotiate. While it might have been expected that the Council of the Federation (where provincial and territorial leaders meet) could serve this purpose, the fact that the federal government and the big municipalities have been explicitly excluded is bound to have a stunting effect on the whole process of deliberation.

For collective intelligence to develop, effective feedback is crucial. Consequently, there must be feedback if there is to be accountability, learning and behavior adjustment in response to context and other stakeholders. In a game without a master, agents face constant tradeoffs among a multitude of *de facto* vertical, horizontal and transversal accountabilities, and not just the traditional financial one. Such accountabilities are embodied in moral contracts with all other meaningful stakeholders that can only be couched in the most general terms, but they need to be binding in order to be meaningful.

Therefore, another key family of missing mechanisms is 'reporting'. The lack of quick and clear feedback reports means that there is no strong learning loop. While adding a reporting mechanism in no way pre-directs the outcome, it ensures that there will be learning and heightened collective intelligence. New techniques of collective reporting may not only generate a heightened degree of collective intelligence but may also have a significant impact on dissemination of effective responses and trigger new modes of collaboration. Indeed it may lead to the crystallization of an issue domain that serves as a focal point for multiple stakeholders.

Getting rid of blockages in the diffusion sub-cycle
The diffusion sub-cycle depends first and foremost on stewardship and trust. It requires a capacity for listening and the open-mindedness of all parties to overcome the rivalry and envy that threaten cooperation (O'Toole 1995).

First, we need to think differently about stewardship. Traditionally, there has been a tendency to count on super–bureaucrats or "delta bureaucrats" *à la* Dror or the judiciary to provide the lead when the different stakeholders appear unable to come to terms about a general direction for action (Dror 1997). This is potentially dangerous in today's world because presuming the 'necessity' of top-down and centralized decision making undercuts the possibility of any stewardship emerging from the creativity of partners. It is a holdover from the outmoded state–centric view of the world.

James O'Toole has proposed a different view. For him, the leader's ability to lead is a by-product of the trust he has earned by serving his followers. The burden of office of the leader is to "refine the public views in a way that transcends the surface noise of pettiness, contradiction and self interest" (O'Toole 1995: 10-12). This view of leadership suggests that impasses may indeed be overcome by the stakeholders themselves.

The key family of mechanisms to refurbish trust is not, as usually assumed, strictly focused on stratagems to reduce secrecy or increase transparency. "Demands for universal transparency are likely to encourage the evasions, hypocrisies and half-truths that we usually refer to as 'political correctness,' but which might more forthrightly be called 'self-censorship' or 'deception'" (O'Neill 2002: 73).

One should therefore focus on deception—the real culprit in reducing trust—and transparency does little to reduce deception. What is needed is a family of 'mechanisms to reduce deception, evasion and outright lies'. This can be done by rejecting politically correct vocabulary, by refusing to endorse slogans, half-truths and complicity with them, and by insisting on an active view of citizenship based on duties, not rights (Ibid., 37–38).

But most importantly, this will emerge from the development of 'trust systems' that are made of mechanisms to help transfer trust from individuals to the system as a whole (Thuderoz et al. 1999). This has proved to be immensely easier to accomplish at the meso-level where issue domains are broad but limited enough to ensure that communities of practice can conveniently meet, meaningfully deliberate and generate workable arrangements or promising experiments. While it may be impossible to create a trust system about the whole of the health field, it may be thinkable to develop one in dealing with mental health. In such a more circumscribed world, domain, field, community of practice and stakeholders interests are likely to be better aligned, a steady diet of conflicts happily resolved, and elements of trust allowed to emerge.

However, it would be naive to assume that there will be no opportunism. As a result, a residual threat is required: the threat that, if cooperation does not prevail, an outcome that no one desires might ensue. This is why the family of 'fail-safe or default mechanisms' is so powerful: in effect a knife is being put to the throat of the negotiators, thus creating the right incentive reward system to act in good faith. When fail-safe mechanisms or default mechanisms are in place, inaction is not an option and sabotage is discouraged: when parties fail to come up with a collaborative answer, every one is aware that the fail-safe mechanism kicks in.

These fail-safe mechanisms might be 'quasi-markets', binding referenda, earmarked taxes, or other devices that empower the citizenry and the users, and reduce the margin of arbitrariness that officials (in the private, public and social sectors, governors and managers) may enjoy: citizens are not pawns in the hands of knights in this new world of 'small g' governance, but queens attempting to deal effectively with knaves. The fail-safe mechanisms induce elected and non-elected officials to act more like knights than knaves (Le Grand 2003).

Decentralized federalism and its enemies

Despite the plausibility of the decentralization strategy being the preferable option (if the major blockages are removed or attenuated), it has been sufficient for those in denial *vis-à-vis* the drift from the welfare state to the strategic state (Hubbard and Paquet 2007a) to simply claim that whatever may be argued at the conceptual level in favour of decentralization is unlikely to work in practice. This tactic is often based on anecdotal evidence and has been used very widely to infer, without further consideration, that centralization is mandatory.

In this section, we propose to deal succinctly with a few of those attacks on decentralized federalism that are purported to be deadly.

Lack of capacity and competence of the citizenry

This first attack is based on the presumed expertise at the centre and the presumed incompetence of the citizenry, but also of lower order governments and of private and social concerns. It is tantamount to an epistemological *coup d'état* by senior governments: the claimed technical expertise at the centre is said to be sufficient to banish all other parties to the role of lobbies of all sorts—agents that have opinions and preferences but no moral authority or adequate expertise to legitimately and properly assess the situation and to decide on the 'called for' action. This is a form of cognitive despotism that attempts to substitute a certain self-legitimizing claim to expertise and a certain auto-declaration of infallibility to replace the intellectual resources by which people grant or withhold legitimation.

This argument may be countered in many ways. One may use the most interesting result in modern social theory: the Condorcet Jury Theorem that the probability of a majority of a group being right increases toward 100 percent as the size of the group increases, providing that the probability of each voter being correct exceeds 50 percent (Sunstein 2006: 25). This means that the citizens need not be omniscient, but only to be more likely than not to give the right answer, for bottom-up participatory processes to succeed. There has also been a substantial body of empirical evidence accumulated that demonstrates that mass collaboration is not only possible but effective (Surowiecki 2004; Tapscott and Williams 2006; Shirky 2008). So it cannot be argued meaningfully that mass collaboration cannot work.

There is no doubt that accessible, timely and credible information is necessary if mass collaboration is to succeed, and that some cognitive infrastructure has to be in place to ensure that collaboration is based on a sound information base (Paquet 2009b). However there is no reason that such cognitive infrastructure cannot be effectively put in place at the local level or that such decentralized infrastructure is of necessity less efficient than the centralized version. Indeed, the reverse is most likely true, as long as it is beyond a certain minimum optimum scale. In any case, there is no reason to presume that capacity and competence can only exist at the top, and that, given the power of appropriate technology, bottom-up governance cannot be effective.

Unworkable, too costly and inequitable

Collaboration, even though it is laudable in theory, is fiendishly difficult in practice. But this does not mean that it is either unworkable or necessarily costly. We now have many experimental studies and documented case studies that have shown that networked social production and other forms of collaboration are both value-adding and sustainable even in social systems where reciprocators are not the majority (Gintis et al. 2005; Benkler 2006; Tapscott and Williams 2006; Parker and Gallagher 2007).

As for the supposedly high costs of variety and collaboration, they represent some sort of myth ascribable to a mindset still dominated by the drive toward uniformity and economies of scale. One of the most important learnings in industrial organization of the last decade is that variety and differentiation need not be costly as long as appropriate modularization of the production process is ensured (Garud et al. 2003). This is the case as much for a whole range of public goods as for the production of automobiles.

Finally, decentralization obviously allows much differentiation to respond to differences in circumstances and preferences. But departure from uniformity generates unease in those for whom simplistic egalitarianism is the golden rule. Deviation from uniformity, being regarded as a violation of the equality credo, entails a refusal of variety even though it would serve the diverse citizens better and more to their liking. In fact, equity does not entail uniformity. Attacks on variety in the name of equity are sheer nonsense.

Consequently, despite the ideological bias against private-public partnerships and other such collaborative arrangements (decreed unworkable) or against differentiation and variety (decreed costly and inequitable), the challenge of serving a pluralistic and heterogeneous citizenry is bound to foster collaborative arrangements generating variety, and this is most likely to result from decentralized arrangements.

Fear of local corruptibility and myopia

One last argument that is broadly used is the fear that a decentralized system is more vulnerable to corruption because it is more likely to allow smaller units to be hijacked by groups planning to make use of the local public assets for private purposes. Undeniably, there is a greater vulnerability to the power being seized by populist local burgomasters à la Danny Williams than the same happening at the national level. But there are obviously ways to prevent such developments or to attenuate the toxic effects of such initiatives considerably. Moreover, it is not clear that immunization from such unfortunate developments is in any way ensured by the sheer presence of centralization.

There has been much evidence of narrow-mindedness and myopia in the strategy adopted by some premiers or local leaders on issues of national import. But there have been equally numerous instances of ideologically inspired destructive interventions and stances by federal leaders. The spiteful behavior of the Rt. Hon. Pierre Elliott Trudeau (both as a prime minister and in retirement) revealed a capacity to deter collaboration and to sabotage collaborative initiatives (Meech Lake and Charlottetown accords) that remains unparalleled at any other level (Burelle 2005).

The capacity for developing a 'super-vision' (i.e., of operating from the high ground and helping others to gain an appreciation of the broad scene that they would not have achieved alone) (Innerarity 2006: 194) has been demonstrated amply by individuals from all sectors and from all levels of government (Blakeney, Castonguay, Lougheed, etc.). For federal officials to pronounce that such super-vision can only be accessed from the federal state level is groundless and self-serving.

Four scenarios

Even though there has been some evolution from 'Big G' to 'small g' in the recent past, and a tendency for more citizen engagement, more mass collaboration, more private-public collaboration, and more inter-governmental cooperation, this drift has been erratic, and it has occurred despite much resistance by the federal government. The brand of federalism of the Chrétien–Martin governments of the 1990s and early 2000s remained state-centric and confrontational, and was built on the dogma that there is a necessity of maintaining a very robust control of the federation from its Ottawa centre.

Nevertheless, for all the reasons mentioned above, Canadian federalism has been forced to adapt somewhat. Figure 2.2 suggests four scenarios that might be regarded as plausible as we look into the future.

Figure 2.2   *Four scenarios of Canadian federalism*

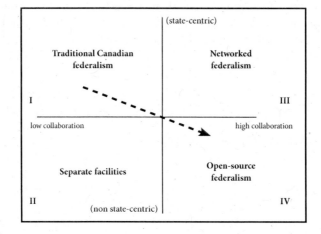

The least likely scenario is the *status quo* traditional Canadian federalism (I): too much has been noted about its ineffectiveness, and the discontent it is generating for this possible future to be regarded as satisfactory and likely to persist.

Two sets of forces are pulling the system in different directions: (i) toward less federal state centricity and more power being devolved to sub-national states; this might entail a drift toward a regime of separate facilities (II); and (ii) toward more collaboration as a result of the realization that only collaborative governance might work, but with the constraint that the central state should/must occupy the dominant position at the centre of the stage, i.e., entailing a drift toward regime (III).

Neither of these two scenarios is very appealing.

The separate facilities scenario is bound to increase the costs of transactions and unlikely to facilitate collaboration.

As for the so-called networked but strongly centric federalism scenario, it has received a good deal of support at the federal level. Still, most discussions of this new form of stewardship (once they are cleansed of their obfuscating rhetoric) would appear to be built on the non-negotiable assumption that the central state must continue to make final decisions even in normal times. This scenario has lost its confederal spirit and is unlikely to provide the degree of flexibility that is considered essential. Central actions since the collapse of the Social Union Framework Agreement have served only to reinforce the non-viability of a deceitful accord built on pseudo-consultation and hegemonic power.

Of course, it has always been assumed that, in abnormal or crisis times, some extraordinary state control might/should be invoked, in the same manner that the *War Measures Act* may be invoked in times of crisis. But scenario III would appear to suggest a permanent state of extraordinary central state control—*un état d'exception permanent* (Agamben 2003)—not well aligned with the need for cooperation today.

The 'Big G' to 'small g' drift has brought forth a scenario of 'softer paternalism' in some more enlightened countries, but in Canada, top-down autocratic and centralized decision making would appear to have remained in force. Canada's approach remains fundamentally Hegelian: the state (always spelled with a capital S) is regarded as the fundamental societal 'organism', with moral purposes that transcend those of its individual citizens, and it is assumed dogmatically that the central state knows best. Warm offers to collaborate (*du bout des lèvres*) is never meant in Canada to challenge the hyper-centralization-driven federal state, because, as we said earlier, without such centralization ensuring that the loot is brought to the centre, there cannot be the massive redistribution which remains a dominant concern and power lever of the federal state. The resilience of this centralized mindset has been amply demonstrated by its persistence even under Conservative (formerly Progressive Conservative) governments, and cannot be ascribed only to the current global economic crisis.

Scenario IV opens the possibility of escaping from both these traps: it emphasizes the possibility of reducing state centricity through allowing individuals, other groups, and/or lower order governments to take on a greater role, while emphasizing the centrality of mass collaboration. It is built on the premise that one does not need to rely exclusively on credentialed stewards (e.g., politicians and bureaucrats) in charge to generate collaboration. Wikipedia, Linux, and VISA have clearly shown that coordination can emerge in other ways.

In this scenario IV, Canadian federalism is 'open-source federalism': the state no longer occupies centre stage:

(i) the people's will and ability to shape their own destiny are the main drivers;

(ii) like in other open-source experiments, prototyping and serious play are of central importance (Schrage 2000); and

(iii) in this regime, geared to promote growth, productivity and innovation, the role of the state would focus on the removal of the major sources of 'unfreedoms' rather than on regimentation.

Open-source federalism would entail a significant amount of experimentation, and the acceptance that experiments will differ from sector/region to sector/region, and will often fail. The guidepost in such experimentation, therefore, cannot be instant success, but minimum regret. Governance and stewardship failures cannot be corrected by simply adding on mechanical contraptions. In the end, some reframing and some cultural change would be required.

We believe that this last scenario, while risky, is the most interesting one.

Key to the evolution in this direction is (1) a drift toward a form of federalism that, to the greatest extent possible, enables each citizen and group of citizens to have access to the 'code' and to tinker freely with the way the stewardship system works within certain well-accepted constraints, and (2) a priority given to 'serious play' (i.e., the development of a premium on innovation and experimentation with the view that, if experimentation is encouraged, necessary retooling, restructuring and reframing are more likely to occur innovatively and productively). The state would remain the backstop in extraordinary circumstances.

Janice Stein has written an important excursus on open-source networks in her 2006 essay on federalism. Open source is for Stein "a story of the governance of shared space" (Stein 2006: 47). Boldly, Stein leaps from her short history of open source to the future of Canadian federalism. One might have expected her to develop her argument in the direction of scenario IV, but unfortunately she did not. She erred on the side of caution. On the one hand, she explicitly states that network federalism and shared policy space are not meant to replace the existing legal and institutional order that govern federalism; on the other hand, she does not restrict their ambit to overlapping jurisdictions and even mentions that "officials from governments and other relevant institutions" should partake in the evaluation of policy "after it was rolled out" (Ibid., 52).

But the cautious, tentative and somewhat nebulous nature of the Stein proposal (that constitutes only a few pages at the end of her essay) leaves it unclear how far she is willing to go in allowing the open source process to come fully into play—that is, to allow all interested parties and not only officials to have access to the code and to tinker with the governing process. One senses that, despite the occasional turns of phrase that would appear to hint at a true open-source process, the shadow of state-centricity-cum-select-elites is omnipresent. Consequently, it is a state apparatus and a select group of leaders that are called to the table, and not, as in true open-source spirit, the whole community of 'hackers'.

Despite the tiptoeing that leads one to surmise that Stein is really veering toward scenario III as the sort of future of federalism she prefers, there are elements in her presentation that entice the reader (and most certainly the authors of this chapter) to carry her suggestions a step further, and to propose a more ambitious program that would boldly develop platforms in different sectors/regions with true open source being allowed to come into play.

Resistance to the emergence of this fourth scenario may be expected from within the world of officials—politicians and bureaucrats. First, it is not clear that 'open-source federalism' will appeal to provincial and territorial officials who have built their discourse on 'acquired rights' rather than on innovation and experimentation. Second, the pundits in the media (who have systematically attacked decentralization and celebrated state–centricity) have echoed the depth of intellectual programming and the resilience of the mindset that have resulted from sixty years of welfare statism. Third, there is already evidence of some concerted efforts by a fifth-column in the uppermost ranks of the federal bureaucracy to suppress and encapsulate all efforts to effect a real reallocation of power toward the provinces and localities, or to open the federal game to experimentation and serious play of the sort open source is built on.

Toward a genuine perestroika

Organizational culture and the whole philosophy embodied in an institutional order are very difficult to transform. They are quite resistant to change. It is much easier to indulge in some tweaking of the structure and technology to tilt the system out of balance, and thereby trigger more fundamental changes. Moreover, there is no recipe for institutional change, and one can easily understand why Albert Hirschman suggests that when dealing with change, citizens should "modestly respect its unpredictability", for "change can only happen as a result of surprise, otherwise it could not occur at all, for it would be suppressed by the forces that are in favour of the status quo" (Hirschman 1995: 136).

So it is with some circumspection that that we suggest a set of prerequisites and the sort of virtuous scheming necessary if a *perestroika* is to materialize in Canada.

Prerequisites

These prerequisites have to do with getting rid of the mental prisons, inherited from the past, that underpin the present over-centralized institutional order. These constraints are not necessarily well understood, but they are deeply anchored in the Canadian soul. So it is perilous to challenge them, and very difficult to uproot them.

Smoothing the Westminster system

The maxims of Westminster-style government are simple: the separation of the bureaucracy in status from elected politicians; the final authority of ministers in office over the actions of officials; and the lines of accountability running directly from officials to ministers to Cabinet to Parliament. The Canadian federation is a non-interlocking set of a dozen such systems—one for each of the two senior orders of government.

While this is an arcane subject, and most citizens would be unable to define the intricacies of the Westminster system, it has remained a robust feature in the mindset of politicians and bureaucrats alike, and a constant reference point. In a world in which boundaries are blurred, roles are becoming fuzzier, and greater collaboration is called for, these maxims cannot be sustained, and yet, as the Gomery reports show, tradition trumps rationality on this front.

New forms of cooperation between politicians and bureaucrats (who have complementary legitimacies), but also between sectors and levels of government, have *de facto* evolved over time, and new ones will have to materialize. Moreover, it is unthinkable to continue to ignore the centrality of the dozen or so major cities in the country that are the true source of the wealth of the nation, and to treat them as mere 'creatures' of the provinces.

Constitutional amendments may not be a workable route to effect such changes. It is more likely that innovative administrative arrangements will be the most useful instruments. But these innovations will require both a new spirit of collaboration (with an end to parties taking refuge in constitutional wrangles to avoid accepting reasonable administrative arrangements) and the acceptance of soft, intelligent accountability in lieu of the rigid accountability framework implied by the Westminster regime.

Already over the last fifteen years, efficiency considerations have led many federations to try to overcome fragmented competencies, and problems of revenue distribution in the face of vertical fiscal imbalance. In Canada, there have been modest and tentative initiatives like the Agreement on Internal Trade in 1994, the Canada Health and Social Transfer in 1996, or the Social Union Framework Agreement in 1999 in Canada. But much more limited progress has been made in the development of collaboration at the strategic level. And when it has materialized, it has been through indirect means and in timid ways. The lack of such strategic capacities is a serious disadvantage in a fast changing world (Braun 2008). It is often through strategic selected inattention and much work under the radar screen that progress has been accomplished.

Softening the egalitarian ideology

The second pillar of the old order is the egalitarian ideology that is so often used to bolster the requirement of hyper-centralization. It is argued that decentralization is unworkable because one could not proceed with the required redistribution without the possibility of bringing a sufficient amount of the fiscal resources to the centre. While there has been a slow and painfully resisted shift from strong to weak egalitarianism over the last few decades, egalitarianism remains a powerful ideology that has prevented efforts to decentralize. There is a need for a decisive attack on this front, and for a change in the language in good currency.

There is something hypocritical about the whole Canadian discourse about egalitarianism. *De facto*, egalitarianism does not guide policy in crucial areas like health and education but only pretends to do so. There seems to be a certain intellectual comfort on the part of both governments and citizens that leads them to collude in wallowing in such rhetorical claims while accepting a significant level of inequality in reality.

One would need to replace the reference to egalitarianism (a most confusing term, that has come to connote a notional and hypothetical entitlement to equality of outcomes) by the more accurate, honest and practical word 'equability'—a term that the on-line *Merriam-Webster Dictionary* defines as "lack of noticeable, unpleasant, or extreme variation or inequality". This word provides a more useful reference point in finding the right balance in the practical search for openness, inclusiveness and high-performance, and the inescapable reality of differences. Equability does not entail uniformity.

Sanitizing the human rights language

Human rights discourse is the new despotism. Do-gooders have been so intent on limiting the damage that the tyranny of a majority may inflict on minorities that they have come to defend the tyranny of minorities lyrically, and have fallen into an idolatry of rights as if they were totems. As Michael Ignatieff rightly underlines, "We need to stop thinking of human rights as trumps and begin thinking of them as a language that creates a basis for deliberation" (Ignatief 2001: 95)

Rights are not a set of trump cards to bring political disputes to closure. Parliament is the place of last resort for deliberation about all governance issues in a democracy. The idea that Parliament is not to be trusted, and that judges, as super-bureaucrats, are like shamen who cannot be contested, is anti-democratic. The Charter of Rights is a creature of Parliament. Rights have been defined by Parliament. As Ignatieff says, they are a "tool kit against oppression" and one should not automatically "define anything desirable as a right", because that would then erode the legitimacy of core rights (Ibid., 57, 90).

Moreover, courts are not infallible in interpreting the Charter. There is nothing sinister in a free and democratic society, in Parliament's use of the notwithstanding clause to suspend for a time the application of a decision by the courts that does not pertain to oppression, and with which the majority of freely elected parliamentarians does not agree. To allow minority groups to obtain everything they would 'prefer' when they dress it in a garb of rights, to make rights into a secular religion, and the courts into its only authorized clergy is the gospel in good currency in certain circles. This has been explicitly stated by the Minister of Justice at the time, Irwin Cotler, in the *Ottawa Citizen,* June 16, 2004 (Cotler 2004).

To reverse this trend will not be easy. Yet the denunciation of the abuse of the rights language and of the indefensible behaviour of human rights commissions and other super-bureaucrats has done much over the last while to question the legitimacy of such claims and the wisdom of the apparatus created to adjudicate them (Leishman 2006; Paquet 2008b; Levant 2009). This might ease the transition to a more balanced regime.

Scheming virtuously

Having challenged the canonical references mentioned above, how can one renew Canadian federalism by filling the gaps where there are weak or non-existent mechanisms or unduly loose ligatures? Are practitioners well equipped to do this work? Can one overcome the degree of disinformation and hypocrisy at play? Can one engineer genuine platforms enabling the citizenry to truly become producer of governance?

For the sort of tinkering that we suggest to be useful, three conditions are necessary: there is a need for practitioners to act locally and 'at the mechanisms level' but also

(i) to develop a super-vision, to maintain a broad holistic perspective, and to keep the theory and its professionals, the experience of the practitioners, and the interests of all the stakeholders in the given area somewhat aligned;

(ii) to ensure the highest and best use of the technologies of collaboration, of self-organization, and of positive deviance by those who have a capacity to confront and to be critical of the ways in good currency; and

(iii) to set various platforms for experimentation in the different issue domains.

Super-vision

The main objectives are to avoid the tyranny of small decisions, to escape from the tyranny of disciplines and ideologies that provide truncated and reductive images of reality, and to take into account the centrality of key complementarities and the power of context (Gladwell 2000; Surowiecki 2004). This is necessary in order to avoid doing more damage than good. But there are very serious barriers to such work that lie in the traditional approaches to social architecture even when the challenges are faced with the best of intentions. There is often misalignment among individual practitioners' skills, issue domains, professional fields, and other stakeholders' interests. Indeed, according to Gardner and others, creativity and good work by professionals are the result of a good alignment of these four realities (Gardner et al. 2001).

Practitioners of public social architecture have a certain specific knowledge and skill set that they have developed through learning by doing—their Delta knowledge (Gilles and Paquet 1989). They maintain somewhat opposed tendencies: a good deal of curiosity and an open mind, but also a quasi-obsessive commitment and perseverance.

Moreover, they operate in a symbolic system: the world of public policy which, like the world of medicine, journalism, carpentry, etc. is built on two sets of codes: a set of procedural ideas (equipment, purposes, identities) and a set of ethical standards (assurance that those ideas will not be used against the common interest) (Spinosa et al. 1997).

But at the same time, these and other professionals are more than skilled persons operating in a domain; they also exercise their profession in a field, that is, a social network of practitioners, a tribe that has its mores, habits, standards, priorities and taboos. As such, they are not only guided by the imperatives of skills and tasks, but also by the values of the tribe.

Finally, the practitioners/professionals, domains and fields all operate in a broader world that involves a wide array of other stakeholders (the corporate world, the general public, etc.) who hold very different views of the world and with whom practitioners and professionals must interact in productive ways.

It should be clear that the super-vision one is striving for must be made to emerge bottom-up through joint work on aligning individual practitioners' skills, issue domains, professional fields and other stakeholders' interests. The state will be only one of the stakeholders involved in this sort of work. Open sourcing entails allowing as many of those with a serious interest to partake in the genesis of the most effective alignment. There may be efforts by the central state apparatus to impose a super-vision in the name of convenience or operational simplicity. Much of the virtuous scheming required may at times be dedicated to ensuring that such efforts to impose unsuitable arrangements are appropriately stunted.

It may be naive to expect that all the components will ever be perfectly in sync (the baskets of skills and interests of practitioners/professionals, the definition of the issue domains, the values of the tribe, and the interests of other stakeholders) since they are all in flux. But one may expect that they will tend to converge toward some evolving configuration that will tend to accommodate somewhat all these constraints simultaneously.

If the alignment is imperfect, practitioners/professionals and stakeholders (of which the state is not an unimportant one) will be led, in the name of efficiency, effectiveness, resilience and innovation to use new or adjusted skills for new or adjusted tasks in the issue domains in which they operate, view the values of their profession in a whole new context, and learn to interact with other stakeholders in new and different ways. The issue domain itself will thereby evolve to match the 'real issues'; the fields will tend to be reconfigured so that the investigation is not unduly restricted by crippling paradigms; and the debating forums and platforms will evolve to accommodate and bring together the various old and new stakeholders, each of whom may harbour quite different values and priorities. Such inter-adjustments may take time but they will evolve as the system thrives to extricate itself from its many conflictive equilibria.

Connexity, self-organization and the failure to confront

A great deal of work is needed to reframe issue domains in a more realistic and wholesome way, to reconfigure the disciplinary fields, to generate more dialogue and deliberation with other stakeholders in order to elicit collaborative governance. Would-be social architects and engineers as "reflective practitioners" will require new skills (Schön 1983) and it is not sure that one can count on the adjustment process unfolding necessarily smoothly and quickly.

Three impediments to smooth adjustment are the dismal neglect of what the new information technologies are making possible for democracy; the obscurantist denial of the forces of self-organization, and the failure to confront that allows so many untruths to remain in good currency.

It is not the place to celebrate information technologies but it is crucial to notice that new bottom-up tools exist that enable mass collaboration, broad-based engagement and deliberation (Mulgan 1997; Lenihan et al. 2007; Tapscott and Williams 2006). These tools are not used half as much as they should. As a result, even though governments and agencies have access to the sort of machinery to make use of the intelligence spread throughout society, share information more readily, and assess the link between policy and outcome more rigorously, the command-and-control military model remains the archetype in good currency.

These new technologies of cooperation are going to play an essential role in demonstrating via pilot projects the possibility of generating new opportunities for complex cooperative strategies that change the way people work together to solve problems, generate wealth and contribute to governance (Saveri et al. 2005, 2008). The new technologies allow organizations to push power to the edge: it is a matter in which both business and military organizations are already familiar, but there has been much resistance in the public governance world to allowing the equivalent of a Green Beret master sergeant on a satellite phone calling up a B-2 bomber to drop ordnances on a specific point (Lawlor 2006). This is a matter calling for a revolution of the mind.

An equally important change in mindset is required in the appreciation of self-organization. One of the most important blockages in the development of effective coordination when power, resources and information are widely distributed is:

(1) the strong reluctance of rational actors to accept the seemingly incomprehensible (and quasi-magical, in their view) emergence of some order from seemingly chaotic environments; and

(2) the strong propensity to make use of episodic monumental failures of this process as persuasive, determining evidence that one cannot ever rely on self-organization and self-steering, and that one must ensure that someone is in charge always and robustly so.

This is not the place to develop a full counter-argument to this skeptical stance, but one cannot ask the reader to accept a paper arguing that this is the most promising way out of the present quandary without at least providing a sketchy plausible counter-argument.

This counter-argument builds first on a better understanding of the way in which collaboration materializes in large groups. Collaboration is first and foremost dependent upon communication generating social negotiation and creative output. Such mass collaboration was first observed and studied in animal societies, where it has been shown that explicit and conscious social negotiation was *not* necessary for mass collaboration to materialize. It is in this context that Pierre-Paul Grasse has coined the term "stigmergy" to connote a method of communication (and implicit negotiation) in which individuals communicate with one another by modifying their local environment. It helps understand "how disparate, distributed, ad hoc contributions could lead to the emergence of the largest collaborative enterprises" (Elliott 2006).

A new literacy about self-organization is needed to understand and make sense of collaboration. Its origin is in the emergence of social dilemmas in which individual rationality would appear to lead to collective irrationality. The best example is the tragedy of the commons, where common property resources are depleted by the overuse of the resource as a result of each myopic individual trying to make the highest and best use of it for himself. A relatively simple and yet powerful avenue out of this sort of dilemma is the development of a broader perspective through generating common knowledge: partaking in rituals producing common knowledge, that is, letting all know exactly what other audience members know. Once, other persons' views are made known, collaboration is made possible. Indeed, increasing common knowledge becomes a way to foster coordination and collaboration (Chwe 2001).

In all such self-organizing worlds, there always are some critical thresholds at which, after gradual change that left the system unmoved, an additional minute change sets the system adrift in search of a new equilibrium. The whole management literature on tipping points is based on the recognition that a better understanding of the cognitive and organizational space reveals where the system might afford the possibility of effective intervention (Shapiro 2003).

The complexity of such adjustments poses wicked problems to potential interveners. On the one hand, unintended consequences, network externalities and cumulative causation at critical points—part of the dynamics of self-organization—often swamp the original intervention and neutralize or distort its impact; on the other hand, these forces may, if one has a fair strategic understanding of the dynamics of self-organization, amplify and enrich the impact of an anonymous intervention in an open-source context.

A third necessary change in the mindset has to do with the failure to confront.

> Conflict is central to the intellectual mode of intellectual life, criticism. Criticism involves the formation of a judgment towards something that the critic believes could—and typically should—have been otherwise (S. Fuller 2005: 149).

Democracy feeds on robust debates; but such debates often entail great personal cost when political correctness becomes *"un nouveau et indolore despotisme"* (Delsol 2005).

Despite strong impressions to the contrary, such tensions and conflicts are the fount of social cohesion. This Gauchet-Dubiel thesis, elegantly defended by Albert Hirschman, suggests that a society with freedom of speech and association that produces "a steady diet of conflicts that need to be addressed and that the society learns to manage" acquires vitality, and a capacity to renew itself. It underlines the important role of the intellectual as conflict-generator, and as the indirect source of social cohesion through the conflicts he/she stimulates (Hirschman 1995: 235ff).

Probably the most important weakness of stewards in all sorts of organizations is the lack of capability or willingness to say "this will not do". Failure to confront is tantamount to deception, to not telling the truth, to misinforming.

The chronic unwillingness to confront may arise from fear of challenges, rejection by others, tribal 'shunning' or disapproval, from being ridiculed, or fear of an interaction one cannot control, or simply as a result of a lack of self-confidence and courage.

Failure to confront entails some reprehensible disengagement, some unacceptable strategic silence in the face of situations calling for correctives. It may also condone and nurture some 'learned helplessness'—a reaction of passivity in the face of unpleasant, harmful or damaging situations where one senses that one has neither bargaining power nor capacity to resolve the problem.

While there has been a good deal of theatrics and antics by politicians (and much disinformation generated in the process), genuine confrontation has been regarded by the citizenry as distasteful. Much has been allowed to survive because of the great deference to authority in Canada, and a quasi-veneration for consensus that has degenerated into some sort of 'collegiality' disease—the obverse of the sort of robust and frank multi-logue that is of foundational importance in collaboration and cooperation.

For open source federalism to have any chance of thriving, critical thinking must be reinstated as a dominant value in lieu of the prevalent conformism. Cleansing the communication systems of 'scorias' (crippling epistemologies, ideological filters, cognitive dissonance, political correctness and the like, that prevent the information and communication system from functioning well, and that therefore generate institutional and organizational pathologies and governance failures) must become the new imperative.

The central importance of critical thinking and confrontation amounts to nothing less than an invitation to subversion (Paquet 2009a, b).

Sectional/regional platforms

A promising way to develop the least inadequate organizational form is not to impose it cold on an assemblage of interested parties, but to allow it to emerge once the nature of relevant prototypes is ascertained on the basis of what the stakeholders will come to regard as non-negotiable constraints.

The key to this evolution on the basis of prototypes is:

- a drift toward open-source governance (i.e., a form of governance that enables each meaningful partner as much as possible to have access to the "code", and to "tinker" freely with the way the system works within certain well-accepted constraints) (Sabel 2001); and
- a priority given to "serious play" (i.e., a premium on experimentation with the imperfect prototypes that might be improved by retooling, restructuring and reframing in productive and innovative ways (Schrage 2000).

What will be required are sectional/regional platforms corresponding to the overall terrain of issue domains and communities of meaning or communities of fate (i.e., assemblages of people united in their common concern for shared problems, or a shared passion for a topic or set of issues). It is tantamount to identifying a vast number of sub-games that each require a specific approach. Each issue domain (health, education, environment, etc.—or maybe some sub-issue domain like mental health) is multifaceted, and dealt with on an *ad hoc* basis with the view of allowing the design of its own stewardship to emerge.

This open-system approach takes into account the people with a substantial stake in the issue domain, the resources available and the culture in place, and allows experiments to shape the required mix of principles and norms, and rules and decision-making procedures likely to promote the preferred mix of efficiency, resilience and learning. A template likely to be of use across the board may not be available yet, but that does not mean that a workable one cannot be elicited *hic et nunc* (Sabel 2004).

However, it is not sufficient to ensure open access, one must also ensure that the appropriate motivations are nurtured so that all those who have a substantial stake are willing and able to engage in 'serious play' (i.e., become truly producers of governance through tinkering with the governance apparatus within certain limits) and that barriers to change and other dynamics of harms and gridlocks are sabotage.

Taking communities of meaning seriously suggests not only that very different arrangements are likely to emerge from place to place, but underlines the importance of regarding any such arrangement as essentially temporary: the ground is in motion, and diversity is likely to acquire new faces, so different patterns of organizational design are likely to emerge.

Consequently, governance would not only rely on a much more flexible toolbox, but would require that any formal or binding arrangement be revisited, played with and adjusted to take into account the evolving diversity of circumstances. It would open the door to the design of more complex and innovative arrangements likely to deal more effectively with deep diversity.

Prototyping would appear to be the main activity underpinning serious play:

- identifying some top requirements as quickly as possible,
- putting in place a provisional medium of codevelopment,
- allowing as many interested parties as possible to get involved as partners in improving the arrangement,
- encouraging iterative prototyping, and
- thereby encouraging all, through playing with prototypes, to get a better understanding of the problems, of their priorities and of themselves (Schrage 2000: 199ff).

The purpose of the exercise is to create a dialogue (creative interaction) between people and prototypes. This may be more important than creating a dialogue between people. It is predicated on a culture of active participation that would need to be nurtured.

The sort of democratization of design that ensues and the sort of playfulness that is required for 'serious play' with prototypes, are essential for the process to succeed, and they apply equally well to narrow or broad organizational concerns.

Conclusion

Innovative 'bricolage' almost necessarily entails some trespassing and some conversations across boundaries. Innovation is a social process and the more successful the innovation, the more social the process. Lester and Piore describe the early stages of innovation as a cocktail party where diverse people gather and chat, casually but seriously, about a variety of topics, in a safe and stimulating environment (Lester and Piore 2004).

If one had to put a finger on the major failure of the Canadian institutional order, it might be the lack of such forums. Our overly rigid governing regime does not allow (or at least robustly constrains) the free-form exchange of ideas, and this rigidity (together with the lack of forums) condemns often organizations to a future of 'unimaginative product extensions' when what is needed is reframing. Emerson's light bulb was not discovered on a journey to improve the candle. Tinkering with information flows, creating new forums, and stimulating new partnerships may appear innocuous, but the sort of trespassing, bricolage and métissage likely to ensue may hold the key to such reframing

It would not be prudent to predict a thawing of the Canadian ethos that will proceed in a revolutionary way or advance quickly. There may be a perestroika in the making, but it will proceed in a hesitant, meandering, two-steps-forward-and-one-step-back and/or oblique kind of fashion. This is the Canadian way.

The broad changes in the texture of the socio-economy brought about by globalization and accelerated technical change have revealed the limits of the nation-state in managing complex problems. Not only has governing become less state-centric, but also the very notion of the public sector itself has been transformed: it has become a multi-level, multi-polar, network-like de-centred reality subject to a new "relational rationality" (Ladeur 2004).

In this sense, the hard core of the 'technocratic state' is becoming eroded not only by the growing intrusion of politics but also by the proliferation of loose regimes that take different forms depending on the issue domain and may not include the public sector as a major player.

Such regimes are the new fabric of the Canadian federation— based on networks that not only go beyond the scope of the state but also do not follow traditional models of organizational design because they are shaped by the expectations and constraints of a variety of actors (mostly non-public sector) often with different perspectives and different contributions to make.

In effect:

> [t]he [S]tate can no longer deliver stable rules of guidance for private actors…but it has to fine-tune limited interventions in the process of private management…In this sense, the possibilities generated from private action create a domain of options which is, at the same time, the pre-structure on which public regulation has to draw (Ibid., 17).

Open-source experimentation at the regimes and issue domains level will create an entirely new dynamic in Canadian federalism. It will allow citizens and emergent publics to become producers of governance, and push the decentralization process one major step forward. While the aim is to re-empower the citizenry, it cannot and will not be done across the board in one sweep: it will have to be built on issue domain experiments and regime building.

Canadians are ready for such experimentation, but, before confederal governance can take hold of them, the citizenry of Canada must build the requisite "negative capacity" (as Keats would call it)—that is, the capacity to keep going when things are going wrong. This entails the construction of the necessary support systems not only to help the citizens to take creative part in this multi-logue but also to withstand the chilling effect generated by the setbacks that will accompany any change venture of this sort. Paradoxically, this will require support from the strategic state and therefore a revolution in the mind first.

Whether the new strategic state is likely to favour such experimentation or whether the right to take part and experiment will have to be wrestled from reluctant state powers remains to be seen. But what is certain is that the contours of the new emerging system are beginning to be perceptible—something that Innerarity calls "social liberalism", a system that has clearly also a Proudhonesque flavour (Innerarity 2006: 235; Proudhon 1850–51).

Federal systems like Canada that have already slaughtered the sacred cow of wholesome and indivisible sovereignty will probably be in the *avant-garde* of this movement even if like Canada they are likely to proceed slowly and cautiously. "Social liberalism" with its emphasis on cooperative freedom is a natural extension of the logic of federalism. Proudhon has been wrongly caricatured as a utopian socialist. In fact, freedom was the fundamental tenet of his social philosophy. His objective was to fight "*la paresse des masses*" (the inertia of the citizenry) which is at the origin of authoritarianism, and "*le préjugé gouvernmental*" (the propensity to rely too much and automatically on the state) instead of having enough confidence that the citizenry can indeed be a producer of governance.

This is the very spirit of our proposals.

PART II

Pathologies of Governance Illustrated

The turbulence of the context, the major transformations in governance, in public governance and in government as such, that are hinted at in the introduction, as well as the extent to which fictions have come to trump reality, have conspired to create strains in the public administration process. Some have even suggested that, in the case of countries like Canada, one might appropriately speak of a latent crisis. There is much denial at the official level of anything untoward, but some perceptive observers have acknowledged a decline of the public domain, as well as anecdotal evidence that would appear to suggest that public administration is in distress.

Our 'windshield' survey of the Canadian experience has revealed that such strains are not new. They are caused by environmental turbulence, by the misalignment not only between politicians and bureaucrats but also among the private, public and social sectors, as well as the different levels of governments, and by misfits between systems of belief and needed practical strategies. These tensions have been resolved differently and more or less successfully over the last century, but with greater difficulty over the most recent decades.

At the core of these heightened tensions is the fact that a new order is emerging that will entail a more modest role for the public sector, and a much different one. We have tried to deconstruct this transition somewhat by identifying some parallel, intermingled processes that would appear to call for a fundamental 'refoundation' of the public administration process.

Part I sets the historical and institutional context, and draws attention to some of the more important aspects of these transition challenges, but before we can begin to reflect on repairs that might help resolve these strains and plug the black hole, it is essential to delve a bit deeper into the pathologies that these strains have generated.

We proceed in two steps.

First, we report on some ethnographic work done over the last three years, with the collaboration of The Association of Professional Executives of the Public Service of Canada (APEX), in order to ascertain the mindset and concerns of senior executives in the Canadian federal public service. These persons are at a level of authority at which they can provide important seismographic data—their daily diet of tensions allows them to experience very acutely and accurately the strains that were discussed earlier in more general terms.

The forty-four forums on twenty-four 'wicked problems' have revealed many key thorny issues. These sessions may be a somewhat unconventional but nevertheless a most effective way to uncover the nexus of problems making the public administration process dysfunctional. We do not claim to have covered the whole territory—indeed, these inquiries are continuing and the exploration remains a work in progress—but we have attempted to review the material collected up to now in a clinical way in order to distill some key dimensions of concern that might help to finesse a more refined diagnosis of what is not working well somewhat.

Chapter 3 reports in some detail on the topics discussed, on the concerns that emerged clearly from these discussions, and on the lessons that we have drawn from these psycho-socio-analyses. We have also attempted to draw attention in the conclusion of this synthetic report to the contours of an overall diagnosis of the etiology of the current malaise that we have derived from our synthesis of the results of three years of probing.

Chapters 4 and 5 analyze two issues raised by our APEX conversations in greater depth: quantophrenia and disloyalty.

Quantophrenia is a crippling epistemology that suggests that, if something cannot be measured, it is of no consequence. This mental reductionism (now a new gospel in public administration) dismisses many important forms of knowledge, and tends to have important negative consequences on public management and public policy resulting from perverse steering effects. Disloyalty entails misalignment between the direction chosen by the principal (the government in power) and the direction chosen by the agents (the senior bureaucrats). It constitutes a breach of trust and a major source of governance failures when public servants usurp the role of responsible government by defining themselves as Platonic guardians who decide the public interest.

Second, chapters 6 and 7 present two case studies. The first one documents the silent revolution triggered by the distrust-paranoia vicious cycle among citizens, elected officials and bureaucrats. It has engendered the neurotic state. The dynamics of the neurotic state are exposed and we use the access to information issue domain to illustrate how the bureaucratic-political interface has come to be corrupted. It should be clear nevertheless, that this is a phenomenon that has contaminated a large number of other issue domains as well. The second case study is in some way a consequence of the neurotic state: it deals with the blatant use of sophistry and disingenuous arguments by politicians and bureaucrats in crucial policy files like the fiscal imbalance debate.

These pathologies should be regarded as the tip of the toxic iceberg revealed by the ethnographic work of chapter 3: nothing more than a sample of what is wrong or some echo effects of a few dysfunctions of the public administration process that have contributed to generating significant pathologies of governance. These illustrations do not in any way exhaust the array of faulty arrangements that have been clinically identified, but they ought to serve as support to our working hypothesis about the poverty of public administration.

CHAPTER 3

Forty-Four Forums on Some Twenty-Four Wicked Problems

> *[T]he earliest collaborative activities are often called 'joint attentional activities'.*
>
> —Michael Tomasello

General presentation

This chapter is a report on forty-four sessions of 'discussions' on twenty-four different topics with approximately one hundred senior executives (EXs) of the Canadian federal government *in toto*. Eight sessions took place in the fall of 2006, four in the winter of 2007, eight in the fall of 2007, eight in the winter of 2008, eight in the winter of 2009, and eight in the fall of 2009—under the auspices of The Association of Professional Executives of the Public Service of Canada (APEX).

APEX's main responsibility has been to provide a safe space where executives could engage in serious conversations about some of the difficult problems that they face. This was an example of what Michael Schrage would call "serious play" with promising prototypes or intriguing hypotheses (Schrage 2000). As animators, we were responsible for the choice of the topics, the conduct of the sessions, the development of the hypotheses and prototypes, and the preparation of the synthesis of these discussions. The participants ran the various 'shows'.

State of affairs

Canada's socio-economic system, like the socio-economy of so many developed countries, is going through a major transition. The institutional order is slowly evolving from a dominance of 'Big G' government towards a dominance of 'small g' governance. This profound change poses significant challenges for senior public servants in the trenches, as the ground on which they operate would appear to be in motion (Hubbard and Paquet 2007a).

This transition entails:
(1) a diminishing capacity of governments to protect their citizens in a globalized world subject to accelerated technical and social change;
(2) a need for governments to continually innovate in order to be able to continue to provide the citizens with the key services on which they depend, in an effective manner;
(3) a major change in the way public policy and regulation are developed, since it is not sufficient any longer to find a policy response that is technically feasible—the response must be socially acceptable, readily implementable, and politically not too destabilizing for the citizenry to put up with; and
(4) a need to reform the public service accordingly.

Such public administration reforms demand a significant change in both the 'what' and the 'how' of public service work. They rattle the very foundations of the shared belief system that the state is best placed to know and to express the common will across a broad range of domains. The result is the raising of questions that are bound to make senior public servants (who have a significant investment in this belief system) quite uncomfortable.

The significant change that is called for must take place in a world plagued with complexity and dilemmas, mixed messages about risk management (manage risks at the same time as no tolerance for error), and tensions between the still highly centralized and top-down governing apparatus and the emerging decentralized and bottom-up governance.

It is against this backdrop that the safe spaces sessions were carried out.

The framework

The idea for such a series of discussions emerged from a number of EXs who expressed a degree of frustration about the fact that new and challenging issues were emerging—that posed ill-structured, wicked problems—and that confronting such problems required serious discussions, and the development of new skills if they were to be handled well. While, at the same time, there seemed to be few safe spaces where such discussions could be carried out, and where the required new skills could be honed and social learning generated.

Ill-structured wicked policy problems have two major characteristics most of the time: the goals are not known or are very ambiguous, and the means-ends relationships are highly uncertain and poorly understood (Rittel and Webber 1973).

To deal with such problems effectively, senior public servants must learn the configuration of both facts and values 'on the job': learning by doing, learning by deliberating. They must learn from the stakeholders as well as from the many peripheral groups who are in possession of important local knowledge, and from colleagues and experts. Without the help and participation of this whole range of 'partners', no meaningful solution can be usefully elicited and implemented (Lave and Wenger 1991; Paquet 1999a: 45).

To deal with such problems, one requires four types of new/enhanced competencies: contextual competencies (acknowledging uncertainty, embracing error, building bridges and strengthening links, reframing problems to explore new solutions); interpersonal and enactment skills (consultation, negotiation, facilitation, conflict resolution, capacity to adopt new roles and attitudes); a capacity to create an effective corporate culture (one of productivity, responsiveness, creativity and learning); and a will to invent new ways (abandoning a focus on rights and autonomy when the actual circumstances of life make the acceptance of obligations and interdependence, as well as experimenting with new tools imperative) (Michael 1980; Paquet 1999a: 37–38).

In each case, the group was faced with a wicked problem: there was no panacea, quick fix or 'solution'. A good deal of discussion was required to clarify the issues at stake. Even though there was no possibility that the issue would be entirely resolved at the end of the two-hour session, and tackling it would very much remain a 'work in progress', it was hoped that the deliberations would produce some learning, hone some skills, and generate 'practical knowledge' (Gilles and Paquet 1989).

The method

On each of the topics, some preliminary reading material was circulated in advance to provide some basic information (see the list of resources at the end of each of the following sections).

One of the authors acted as animator and set the stage for the discussion with a short talk (15–20 minutes). A general discussion followed around one or two provisional hypotheses, but there was no effort to restrict the conversation to them.

For the purpose of synthesizing the outcomes of these sessions, we have put them together in four batches. In each case, we have presented a succinct statement of the topics used and of the discussions that followed, together with some distillation of the lessons learned.

Cat's cradling – the first twelve sessions

No damn cat, and no damn cradle

—Kurt Vonnegut Jr.

'Cat's cradle' is the name of a children's game—producing endless designs using fingers and a loop of string. It has been played around the world for hundreds of years, but, in modern times, the expression has been used to connote intricacy and complexity.

A syncretic view of each topic

For the first series, we selected two topics in each of these following four different areas: contextual issues (diversity and security), interpersonal skills (ethics and disloyalty), organizational culture (corporate culture and the Gomery world), and new governance tools (private-public partnerships and a new partitioning of the public service).

Contextual issues
Diversity (October 4 & 19, 2006)

Great population movements are re-arranging the demographic face of the world. Not only is diversity (linguistic, cultural, ethnic, etc.) growing in most countries, but it is also becoming deep diversity, that is translating into deep cleavages. Are there limits to diversity? What does that mean for the public service both on the policy front and for its own fabric and practices?

The notion of diversity is quite complex. It connotes a range of things from a basic demographic fact, to an ideology about what is desirable, to a plea for 'fraternity lite'. For all sorts of reasons, Canada has been drifting from being a *de facto* poly-ethnic society to choosing to become a multicultural one as a matter of policy. This has generated tensions. In Canada, for the time being, two broad approaches are in good currency: 'interculturalism' in Quebec and 'multiculturalism' in the rest of Canada. *Grosso modo*, the key difference between the two is that, in the former case, many things would appear not to be negotiable while in the latter case, almost everything would appear to be negotiable under the rubric of 'reasonable accommodation'.

Two key questions were discussed: Are there limits to diversity? Can we negotiate moral contracts among groups as part of citizenship building?

There was a clear consensus that some things are not negotiable: acceptance of Canada's legal framework (the Criminal Code and the Charter of Rights and Freedoms) was seen as a minimum. Beyond this, participants generally agreed that there may be additional non-negotiable items that could only be arrived at through conversation and multi-logue.

Paradoxically, while there was a sense that conversations about such issues were necessary, at the same time there was some unease about conducting such discussions. The basic reason was that, while they were clearly seen (from a Cartesian point of view) as essential if the mutual expectations of the different groups were to be clarified and understood, there was concern that these conversations might lead to 'either-or' confrontations rather than compromises of the 'more-or-less' variety. The sense was that, at times, political correctness and intimidating fundamentalism might make it difficult not to be led to unreasonable accommodations that participants would reluctantly accept at a superficial level, but would profoundly resent in their heart of hearts. Tensions would ensue. This makes the emergence and negotiation of 'moral contracts' (i.e., agreement about mutual expectations) very difficult, and explains the tendency for many to prefer a willed *laissez-faire* based on the optimistic faith that peaceful coexistence will somehow emerge.

On the other hand, it was readily agreed that moral contracts are negotiated and renegotiated informally every day through the land. While this was agreed to, the very notion of 'moral contract' generated some concern because of it sounding like 'rules'. So it may be that the best strategy is 'engaging in moral contracting' through extensive conversations but not talking about it as contracting.

Three points on which there was a strong consensus were:

(1) diversity should not be used to obtain special privileges;

(2) more mechanisms are needed to promote dialogue and to clarify mutual expectations; and

(3) priority should be given to eliminating minor irritants, and these minor successes should be used as a way to make for easier discussion about more problematic issues that would require more difficult negotiations and more arduous reasonable accommodation.

Security (December 13 & 14, 2006)

Most of our daily life is orchestrated by rules (e.g., speed limits on the road that have a well-defined probable mortality rate attached to them): they represent a trade-off between willed security and the fact that some costs may prove unbearable. On this front, citizens are attracted by the precautionary principle as a guidepost: in its weak form, it requires taking preventive measure in advance 'just in case'; in its strong version, it claims entitlement to 100 percent protection and rules to ensure that this will be accomplished.

For example, the radically strong version of the precautionary principle asserts that 100 percent security must be provided by the state and by public servants acting on its behalf, and insists that public servants be clairvoyant: 'you should have known' is the response to an unfortunate event (tainted blood, collapsing bridge, etc.) and 'since you did not protect me at the 100 percent level, I will sue and demand compensation'.

The balancing between type I error (rejecting as false what is in fact true) and type II error (accepting as true what is in fact false) is the challenge. Responsible citizens agonize over the terrible ordeal of those suffering from type II error (e.g., Arar's deportation and subsequent imprisonment in Syria) but would certainly never forgive the authorities for not having stopped a home-grown terrorist from perpetrating his/her deed if it were known afterward that there was reasonable suspicion that it might happen (type I error). Citizens want a balance between these possibilities, but are hesitant to confront these issues openly, to talk about the trade-offs that one can and cannot live with.

Two questions were posed: What if the best we can do is to correct both types of errors as quickly as possible, since we are bound to make both types of mistakes? Is Canada too complacent about security as some suggest and therefore more vulnerable to type I error than it should be?

On the second question, there was a general agreement that Canada was too complacent, and too reluctant to discuss the type I/type II error trade-offs explicitly and openly.

Technically, risk depends on the nature of the threat (intent + capacity), and preventive action depends on a mix of the level of risk + the nature of the consequences + the resources available. But from the point of view of the authorities, risk is not only a technical matter: it raises questions about Canadians' confidence in the basic institutions.

As a result debates on these issues often occur behind closed doors, and the discussions may become distorted because they are permeated by both the fear of creating a panic and of contributing to basic institutions losing their credibility.

The result is that security issues are not discussed as much or as openly as they should be, and that the authorities are much more willing to allow terrorists and criminals to remain free (type I error) than to take the chance of having an innocent person incarcerated (type II error). The cost of this structural imbalance may be high.

Interpersonal links
Ethics (November 22 & 24, 2006)

People have a very vague notion of ethics. Usually it connotes nothing more than doing the right thing. But what does this mean? Public servants are constantly faced with ethical dilemmas, and there is a whole industry trying to persuade them that there are codes and rules that may hold the mechanical key to 'ethical behavior'. These devices, like 16th century maps, are usually elegant but not very useful to navigation.

Learning to navigate the 'moral corridor' means taking into account:

(1) the facts of the situation being faced;

(2) an appreciation of the room to maneuver that is regarded as permissible in a given organization (its culture); and

(3) a few fundamental principles that one holds dear—and this can only happen through discussing a great number of cases (real or imaginary).

But it has to be recognized nevertheless from the very beginning that no measuring rod can be devised that can reduce ethical dilemmas to technical problems, and make them mechanically 'solvable' (despite vain attempts by philosophers and others to suggest it can be done).

A useful vocabulary has been proposed by Kolhberg to help the thinking about moral development. He suggests that there are six stages of increasing moral development. The right action is taken:

1. to avoid punishment,
2. to serve one's own needs,
3. so others will view you as a good person,
4. to abide by law and authority,
5. to abide by moral contracts, and
6. as a recognition of principles of justice, fairness and universal rights.

The 'burden of office' of senior public servants requires more in the way of duties and responsibilities than is expected of citizens-at-large or business people (i.e., he or she might be required to operate at Kohlberg's level (5) while for others it may be permissible or tolerable to operate at level (4)) (Kohlberg 1981).

Moreover in today's 'small g' governance world—where power, resources and information are distributed among many partners, and collaboration is an imperative—doing the right thing does not only mean meeting the expectations from higher ups (as was the case in the 'Big G' world) but also meeting the expectations of a vast circle of stakeholders and partners (i.e., a kind of 360° circle of expectations).

Nowadays moral contracts exist between senior public servants and many other groups—citizens, taxpayers, colleagues, partners in service delivery etc.—that may tug them in different directions. And these expectations may neither be compatible nor commensurable one with the other.

This means that senior public servants must find creative ways to 'square this circle' and navigate the moral corridor safely if they are to fulfill their burden of office.

Two questions were discussed: First, is there a decline in the ethics of public servants (i.e., is the senior public service failing more often than was the case in meeting level (5) standards—abiding by the moral contracts they have agreed to)? And are there things that can be done to strengthen the capability of senior public servants to meet this standard, and tools that they can use to enable them to do so?

The ensuing discussion made reference to a variety of pressures on senior public servants that may drive them to stay at level (4)—abiding by law and authority. The multiplication of rules, the lack of safe spaces for dialogue, and the relative lack of support on this front were thought to have caused a chill, and a good deal of risk aversion. There was a sense that the flexibility to do the right thing within the spirit of the law needed to be regained.

It was also strongly felt that the great amount of talk about ethics these days might only mask a reduction of trust. If there is no trust, learning is not easy, working in partnerships becomes more difficult and takes more time, and it is harder to have the discussions necessary to help public servants develop the tools they need to get better at navigating the moral corridor safely and living up to their burden of office.

Nevertheless, several ideas emerged as potential avenues that could be pursued:

(1) taking on more risk personally and for the team ("I will back you in having a bit more room to manoeuvre");

(2) accepting mistakes as necessary for learning (even rewarding well-executed failures);

(3) talking things through with the team and others both beforehand and afterwards;

(4) asking and accepting 'what is reasonable in the circumstances?' that is, 'operating within the spirit as well as the letter of the law';

(5) stopping the cycle of mistrust (e.g., opening the 'books' of an operation to a partner who is mistrustful and not expecting reciprocal action until some trust has been built up);

(6) giving people the opportunity to speak up about their frustrations; and

(7) using one's influence to try to push the envelope a little with bosses or the system.

To enable public servants to navigate the moral corridor safely in today's difficult climate, participants felt that the notion had to be framed as using moral imagination ('scheming virtuously') to live up to the expectations of the different moral contracts of stakeholders; and that learning from individual cases had to be made possible and/or enhanced by senior managers acting as connectors and enablers.

Disloyalty (February 28, 2007)

Disloyalty was a most difficult topic to deal with in these sessions because it involved—of necessity—emotions and a sense of self-incrimination. Every public servant feels 'loyal' and is quite good at rationalizing this conviction. Yet, in reality, the burden of office of public servants is built on many unwritten, even unstated, clauses defining the understandings and expectations of others—bosses, peers, co-workers, clients, possibly subordinates and/or partners—with whom they collaborate. These clauses, of course, may also be incompatible one with another.

Disloyalty is breaking any such moral contract deliberately and knowingly.

A particularly difficult series of problems arises for public servants' burden of office when they are expected to shift their loyalty to the new agenda and policies of a new government. When one party has held power for ten or fifteen years, it would be surprising if the old ways had not come to be regarded as 'normal and preferred'.

Faced with having to forge new direct and indirect relationships that will call for the acceptance of very different perspectives with which they may not be habituated or in accord (for personal or technical reasons), public servants have two choices—leaving ('exiting' physically or hibernating by leaving their souls at home) or trying to propose modifications ('voice' alternative views and propose modifications).

Whichever road is travelled, some have suggested that a measure of loyalty to the organization/institution may be how long one uses 'voice' before 'exiting'. This is a bit simplistic. Openly disagreeing or dissenting is not necessarily a form disloyalty. On the other hand, passive deceit (e.g., silence, reluctance to raise questions, tardiness in questioning when questioning is warranted) might be clearly disloyal.

The questions raised were: what is disloyalty for senior public servants? is disloyalty increasing? what concrete actions are called for, if any?

There was much unease among the participants at the very idea of admitting that there is such thing as disloyalty in the upper ranks of the federal public service. This unease was attenuated somewhat as the conversation progressed, but never disappeared. Indeed, a fundamental denial that any such thing really exists kept popping up.

It was, in part, a manifestation of the classic tension felt by public officials between duty to the public (as they themselves define it) and duty to the higher ups in the particular hierarchy in which they operate. The question squarely put at the centre of the discussion is 'who should define the public interest': the elected government or the unelected public servants who believe that they 'know' more and claim to know what is best?

Examples were cited involving the highest levels of the bureaucracy: the behaviour of one deputy minister who chose to leave because he was unable/unwilling to support the new government's approach, while another chose, instead, to 'put words in the mouth of his unsuspecting minister'. Participants agreed that the first was acting with integrity, while the second was being disloyal.

There was some reluctant agreement that disloyalty had increased recently. It was seen, in part, as a consequence of the increased complexity of the policy issues. Complex issues lend themselves to a multiplicity of interpretations, and feed a greater possibility of differences of opinion. For example, blaming an evaluator for not speaking up 'enough' or scientists for not being 'clairvoyant enough' about future problems may be unreasonable, and may be wrongly associated with disloyalty.

Several participants observed that restoring professionalism and professional pride might play an important part in restoring loyalty. This might entail taking a leaf from the book of professional associations, which instil pride (e.g., taking an oath of office, training, accreditation) and monitor quality (e.g., disciplinary committees). The new requirements to publish information about wrongdoing were also seen as potentially helpful.

Yet, despite individual dedication and effort, it was reluctantly felt that there seems to be a growing culture of disloyalty enveloping the public service today. It would appear however that it is more a 'passive disloyalty' (e.g., responding to the narrowest interpretation of what is expected and required, and, as result, reducing the notion of burden of office to something much less than it should be) rather than 'active disloyalty' (e.g., deliberately undermining the work of superiors and/or betraying the trust of partners and citizens).

Organizational culture
Corporate culture (November 8 & 10, 2006)

The concept of culture connotes the ideas, customs and skills of a people or a group that are passed along from one generation to the next in some fashion, as well as shared beliefs, behaviors and systems of meanings. In general, the culture of any organization is an appreciative system that is both enabling and limiting: it echoes a set of 'readinesses' and capacities, as well as a set of constraints under which the organization labours whenever it faces unforeseen challenges. Corporate culture makes sense of what is, of what actually exists, and of what is important. It helps to create names, interpretations, and commitments—it creates a framework for interpretation and understanding.

In fact, the contrasts among corporate cultures become more visible when organizations face an unforeseen crisis for which there is no routine response, and for which the organizations are technically ill prepared. In these circumstances, the 'soul' and 'instinctive dimensions' of the organization take charge of problem definition, shape the response, and these responses reveal the logic of the underlying culture.

Many schemes have been proposed to X-ray corporate culture. One interesting one (for comparative purposes) has been proposed by Geert Hofstede. It focuses on indices of power inequality, individualism, risk aversion and long-term orientation (among other things). On that scale, Canada and Latin American countries are much more risk averse than the United States, and less likely to accept change readily (Hofstede 2001).

This has had an impact on the corporate culture of Canadian organizations in all sectors. As Andrew Wahl reported, we know that only about 36 percent of Canadian executives regard their companies as having strong adaptive cultures; some 55 percent define their corporate culture as weak (i.e., plagued with top-down managerial arrogance, fear of risk-taking, inward focus and bureaucracy); 64 percent say that corporate culture is important, and 72 percent say that their organization's culture is not what they desire for the future. But nobody appears to know what could be done about it and how (Wahl 2005).

The questions posed were: should we be worried about corporate culture? what can we do to influence it?

Participants felt there were good reasons to worry. Most agreed that the current environment for the public service is one of 'zero tolerance for error + no risk allowed + political expectations must be met', with a drift towards a culture of blaming rather than accepting that making mistakes is a part of learning. Public sector culture is embedded in a societal culture that is risk averse, so the public service has become risk averse.

Many participants thought that any improvement had to start from above: the fish rots from the head. The deputy ministers should be willing to say 'take a risk and we will back you up'. Culture would be affected significantly if the Clerk of Privy Council sent the right signals through his actions: for example, promoting people who are perceived as courageous to the rank of deputy minister. But others believed that this was asking too much and that the focus should be put instead on asking 'what can we do ourselves?'

At the end of the day, it was felt that a more promising strategy would be bottom up: better to help young managers learn how to confront such problems of risk-taking squarely and explicitly—rather than avoiding taking risks at all costs as they are often tempted to do. Over time, these bottom-up efforts were felt to be likely to change the culture.

The Gomery world (February 14, 2007)

The 1995 referendum on Quebec separation from Canada was held as a result of a malaise among a plurality of Quebecers about the existing institutional order and about the ways in which the federation was run. On the occasion of the referendum, a substantial number of Quebecers expressed dissatisfaction with an overly centralized federal system that did not allow Quebec to exercise the full range of public powers needed to ensure its maintenance and progress as a distinct society.

The Gomery inquiry was triggered by a report from the Office of the Auditor-General of Canada about irregularities in the administration of federal sponsorship activities in Quebec between 1996 and 1999. These activities had blossomed in Quebec following the narrow victory of the federalist forces in the 1995 referendum on Quebec secession. Sponsorship activities were intended to increase the visibility and support of the federal government in Quebec, thereby celebrating the benefits of federalism.

Justice John H. Gomery was given a broad mandate: "to investigate and report on questions raised *directly and indirectly* by the audit" (Hubbard and Paquet 2007a: 2). Given the breadth Gomery mandate, one might reasonably have expected that this inquiry would not focus narrowly on possible administrative misappropriation of some federal funds for sponsoring publicity events, but would also examine the 'sources' of the unease that had led the Canadian federal government to use these kinds of social marketing activities. The perceived inadequacies of the existing federal system were obviously questions raised 'indirectly' but sharply by the sponsorship affair.

The inquiry resulted in the publication of two reports—one in the fall of 2005 and the other in the winter of 2006. The reports chose to focus exclusively on the dirty tricks of money laundering, and on how to prevent such incidents in the future by adding many additional sets of administrative controls. They paid no attention to the deeper causes and sources of the problem: the dysfunctions of an existing centralized governing apparatus that is tearing the fabric of the country apart; and the collusion of centralizing groups to defend the *status quo*.

Two questions were tabled: is the system of Canadian federalism unduly centralized? does the existing model of Canadian public administration in place today perform as well as is claimed?

Participants generally felt that the current systems of federalism and of public administration were far from perfect, especially in light of the drift underway from 'Big G' government toward a 'small g' world in which no one is 'in charge' anymore.

On the issue of federalism and the federal role, participants noted that the federal government was downloading responsibilities and cutting (or increasing) transfers to the provinces in a whimsical way. It was felt that there was a need for some overhauling of fiscal federalism to deal with the current vertical fiscal imbalance (federal/provincial/municipal).

On the issue of public administration: some suggested that the problems were mainly ascribable to 'political' interference, while others felt that "some public servants may be too anxious to please and thus end up becoming too attached to the government of the day". There was some mention of the fact that deputy heads are moved around so quickly that departments/agencies are often left rudderless for quite some time.

This provoked a conversation about the vulnerability of a system that is built around specific 'leaders' when what Canadians assume is needed (and what is required) is 'system trust': trust that, despite individual failings, the entire system catches mistakes or missteps very quickly and corrects them fast. This is regarded as the basis of effective governance.

Most participants concluded that experimentalism and 'open–source federalism' might well provide an avenue for greater effectiveness, with the federal government acting more as 'coach' than a player itself.

With respect to the second question—is the Canadian public administration model as good as claimed?—a good deal of defensiveness was evident. Whether this arose as a result of sheer corporatism or as a lack of interest in and/or appreciation of the broader contours of the 'public administration machine' was not clear. Participants seemed keenly aware of the complex arrangements in their own issue domains, but the contours of the broader administrative apparatus appeared to remain not fully understood by many of them. This was somewhat surprising for executive level public servants.

It is not unfair to add that the conversations revealed a profound attachment to state-centricity, and an equally strong commitment to the 'need' for a strong federal government (and consequently a powerful and influential senior federal public service). References were made to the need for strengthening the role of the federal government, to government being essential to articulate the public interest, and to the state, in our complex world, being the 'sole actor' having the cognitive power and muscle necessary to identify the public good and effectively pursue it. As a result, participants were quite reluctant to chastise the federal government for its centralized mindset or its state centricity. Indeed, it was felt that its final role as arbiter in most files was essential. This should not be surprising from executive-level career federal public servants.

So while experimentalism and open-source federalism 'as general ideas' were received favourably, when it came to making these ideas operational through a robust departure *de facto* from state centricity and from hegemonic overall federal controls, the support for these bold ideas almost disappeared. Consequently, one had a sense that, despite conceding that the Canadian model of public administration was far from perfect, the participants were at best willing to entertain some redecoration of the public household but not any major architectural repairs.

This state of mind would appear to echo the substance of a recent lecture of Jocelyne Bourgon (2007):

(1) a recognition, as a result of some factual evidence, but at the most general discursive level, that public administration is a work in progress and requires serious overhauling in Canada and elsewhere; but

(2) an equally strong feeling that there is no need to question the fundamental underlying assumptions on which the traditional model is based.

This allows not only an escape from the old Hegelian mental prison that makes the state the sole source of the 'common will' (an assumption that is now openly challenged), but also a continued belief in a state (in this case with the federal government in the lead) in the form of a re-invented, quasi-Hegelian intermediary institution that can do almost the same thing in the name of effective provision of public services to the citizenry because it has the unique capacity to read the collective mind appropriately and to serve the citizens well.

New management and governance tools
Public–private partnerships (March 19, 2007)

Everyone agrees that there may be things that one particular sector (private, voluntary or public) does better than the others. Equally, there may be some things done best by combining forces across sectors. In recent decades, public–private partnerships (PPPs or P3s) have become popular with reform-minded (and cash-strapped) governments—reducing administrative and operating costs by some 20–50 percent in some areas. Yet there have been also some spectacular P3 failures because the 'winning conditions' were not in place. Moreover, a strong ideological opposition to P3s still prevails in certain circles and is epitomized by Jane Jacobs (1992) who argued that such things can only produce 'monstrous hybrids'.

There is a poor understanding of the whole panoply of 'winning conditions' necessary for P3s to succeed: engaging the mega-community effectively and continually, ensuring that there is value adding and a fair sharing of the benefits and risks among partners, well designed contractual arrangements and procedures, and social learning that ensures that the arrangements can be adapted continually to new circumstances.

The questions posed were: has the case for P3s been made persuasively? what are the winning conditions for successful P3s?

Participants quickly agreed that the case for P3s had been easily made in the case of physical assets (e.g., bridge, road or building construction)—that is, where a clear contract could be written and where there is a strong element of predictability about the outcome. They pointed out nevertheless, that the case has not yet been made persuasively about the use of P3s in the delivery of social services.

Participants felt that using small steps and proceeding gradually would be the best approach to successful implementation of P3s. A number of successful experiments seem to have been conducted piecemeal, slowly, experimentally, and 'under the radar screen'. Experiments have the advantage that, when they are shown to be successful, they can be generalized more readily and will gain popular support. It was also suggested that the focus at the beginning might usefully be on experiments outside 'core areas'—for example, in health care, P3s might be used in sub-areas where people are in significant pain or discomfort but where the problem is not life threatening (e.g., joint replacements and cataracts).

Much was made of the need for the public sector to develop the required competencies to negotiate and govern P3s effectively. Such competencies are scattered around many departments and may not be easily mobilized by a single agency. This may be the Achilles' heel of the P3 process.

Possibly more important, and often unnoticed, is a major ideological blockage about P3s: P3s might not ensure equal access for the very poor or disadvantaged to the extent that a pure public agency would. A discussion followed about the dark side of egalitarianism ('if I can't have it, then neither should you' is making envy into a national virtue), and the emergence of the new norm of 'equability' (i.e., a willingness to eliminate unacceptable inequities only) to replace the old norm of radical egalitarianism (Kekes 2003).

The three main challenges would appear to be:

(1) a great distrust of the private sector;
(2) a difficulty for the public sector to mobilize the high-level competencies needed to govern the P3 process effectively; and
(3) some deep-rooted commitment to egalitarianism in the Canadian psyche and a sense that P3s must be anti-egalitarian.

These stand in the way of a greater use of P3s. Nevertheless, P3s are here to stay and their use and scope will continue to expand, although low-key approaches are probably more likely to succeed than 'frontal attacks'.

A new partitioning of the federal public service (March 28, 2007)

An important myth in good currency suggests that one of the reasons why state employment cannot be reduced without generating an impoverishment of governance is that *all* work done in the public sector is, by definition, both homogeneous and of a different kind—of a 'higher order' than other work—(i.e., there can be no substitution of 'lower order work' (private or social sector types) for 'higher order' (public sector employment).

In a world that puts a premium on flexibility and innovation, such rigidity cannot easily be defended. A case can be made that public sector employment is neither as different in kind nor as homogeneous as has been presumed. Recognizing these facts leads to the suggestion that partitioning public service employment in line with their differential burden of office—with quite different human resource (HR) regimes for each grouping—would tend to increase flexibility, effectiveness and efficiency.

Federal public servants could be partitioned in the following way:

I. Super-bureaucrats (e.g., Auditor-General, deputy ministers and the like: approximately 500 individuals) whose burden of office is co-governing with the elected officials and safeguarding the fabric of society;.

II. Guardians (e.g., EXs and persons of that sort: approximately 10,000) whose main job is senior management of the public household to ensure optimal productivity;

III. Professionals (e.g., scientists, lawyers and the like: approximately 40,000) whose main job is to ensure reliable regulation, innovation and horizontal coordination; and

IV. Employees (e.g., most 'PM' and 'AS' levels: approximately 185,000) whose main functions are to ensure service delivery with a modicum of reliability and fairness.

The questions raised with the participants were: is the 'one lump of labour' myth referring to the federal public service still alive? what sort of partitioning of public employment might be workable?

Participants generally felt that, despite the existence of different unions (e.g., PSAC (Public Service Alliance of Canada) and PIPSC (Professional Institute of the Public Service of Canada)) with different approaches, the notion of 'one lump of labour' is still in place and it is an important impediment to getting work done in an environment in which there is a need for a great variety of organizational arrangements.

Tackling the professional grouping first (i.e., III) seemed an attractive idea for there is a sense of communities there. But starting with grouping II (primarily EXs) might be easier. Another way to approach the problem might be to introduce the partitioning in one small organization as an experiment. The concept, if successful, might then be generalized. Unions might be prepared to tradeoff some things (e.g., higher barriers to entry and exit in group IV) in return for being able to bargain new elements (e.g., classification and promotion). Regional rates of pay were also felt to be important. For any such re-partitioning to be successful, it would be crucial to demonstrate that different HR regimes provide better results both for the organization of work and for the welfare of the workers.

One would also need to initiate discussion with a view to modifying not only the HR regimes but also the underlying frames of reference—from the current one that emphasizes accountability almost exclusively (doing only what one has been mandated to do), to one that put the focus back on the organizational goals of efficiency and effectiveness, and explicitly link the HR regimes to these broad organizational goals (i.e., doing anything one is not prevented from doing in order to pursue the organizational goals).

A personal distillation of what we learned

The intent of this section is neither to second guess the perspectives of the public sector executives we conversed with nor to psychoanalyze them on the basis of these few conversations. Rather our intent is to draw some more general conclusions about the challenges facing the Canadian public sector on the basis of what these conversations have revealed to us.

The decline of open critical thinking

First, it has become clear over those months of conversations that there is a lack of safe spaces where executives are allowed and enabled to explore these thorny issues—where there is no precise or definitive solution, but only responses with varying degrees of usefulness. Safe space discussions automatically generate: a degree of critical thinking, some recognition that organizations have failed, and an appreciation of what might have been done better. A sense developed during our conversations however, that this kind of forum might not be universally welcomed precisely because it generates critical thinking. The shadow of yesteryear is still present when criticism was considered as a light form of treason.

While the taste and the need for such safe spaces was felt very strongly by the executives we met, and the usefulness of such exercises in critical thinking was much appreciated, it was clear that a great majority of executives have chosen to avoid them completely. A certain demoralization of a large segment of the executive group has led many to withdraw into the 'technical' aspects of their work, to 'hibernate' as some called it—seeing no merit in engaging in discussions that can only get them into trouble.

The general quality of intra-public-service conversations seems to have declined, in part also as a result of a very high degree of political correctness that has come to prevail over the years. The 'real' conversations are more likely to be carried out in the washroom than in the boardroom. Indeed, many participants remarked on the higher degree of self-censorship that has led to a much less effective degree of social learning than is desirable.

Some paradoxes and some differences in our difficult conversations
There were some paradoxical reactions to the discussions about certain topics—corporate culture, the Gomery world, disloyalty.

While most participants agreed that these 'realities' were an important source of *malaise*, there was also, at the same time, even in our 'safe space', a reluctance to engage fully in discussion about their toxic effects. For instance, there was quite a hostile reaction to the results of an exercise (suggested by Kets de Vries 2001) designed to identify the dominant type of neuroses present in different federal public sector organizations. The very word 'neurosis' was clearly a term that was seen as loaded (implying some kind of disease or unhealthiness) and as a result provoked strong cognitive dissonance and sharp denial.

A similar denial syndrome plagued the discussion about the Gomery world: acceptance of a need to change in general (given the difficulties encountered by the federal state) but an unwillingness to accept that there cannot be change without changing some of the basic assumptions on which 'Big G' government is built. There would appear to be a profound unease about questioning the fundamental assumptions of state centricity and centralization.

The same sort of difficulties arose in the session on disloyalty. Participants volunteered numerous examples of blatant disloyalty but were in denial generally about the existence of a culture of disloyalty. There were a number of instances when reference to behavior that might be construed as 'disloyal' was explained as loyalty to the higher purpose of the public interest.

In each of these cases, there seemed to be a visceral need to defend questionable practices on the basis of superior motives— which is not unusual (Brewer et al. 2000)—and a particular and better appreciation than others of 'Canadian values' on the part of federal public servants. In this latter case, it would appear that the "myth of Canadian values" as the basis for federal paramouncy is still alive and well in the higher echelons of the Canadian federal public service despite it being quite problematic (Heath 2003).

The concern with ethics and moral contracts generated an extremely high level of interest. These issues are of a very personal (as opposed to organizational or institutional) interest and participants felt freer to express their sense of frustration as individuals. The use of the notion of moral corridor to provide a framework for talking about ethical issues and the use of moral contracts as instruments to frame moral choices were embraced. It is as if one could openly talk about 'personal dilemmas' but one could not entertain it as permissible to indict the organization (culture, disloyalty).

The discussions about diversity and security, although difficult and permeated with a lot of guarded language, revealed that it was much easier to deal with tough contextual features than with matters of internal organizational culture.

It was also clear that those issues could be discussed a lot more freely in our safe space than in public meetings. Indeed many participants noted that the need to be politically correct had kept them from expressing themselves as fully as they would have liked on the issue of diversity at a recent APEX symposium.

On issues of a more instrumental nature (PPP and public service partitioning) the safe space may not have been necessary. Those topics were discussed openly and clinically. They were regarded as managerial issues that lent themselves to critical analysis. Interestingly, the undertones of ideology (*à la* Jane Jacobs) that were felt constantly during the discussion did not seem to be sufficient to prevent hard-nosed debate and useful conclusions on which most participants agreed.

Conclusion

It is far from certain that observations derived from conversations with a relatively small number of federal public sector executives can be generalized beyond our sample group. As a result, our intent is not to pretend to do so.

Today's world puts a premium on innovation in a climate of significant, on-going, permanent change. It demands a great deal of exploratory work with new tools and perspectives, rapid prototyping and serious play as a vehicle for innovation in all sorts of domains, and social learning as a new imperative.

This experience with conversations on 'wicked problems' (and the follow-up conversations we have had with some participants) has reinforced some of our presumptions: safe space discussions foster more rapid and better prototyping and enhance learning about the 'what' and the 'how' of changing public service work. They break old moulds and open new vistas. But most importantly, such conversations perform many cleansing functions:

(1) they reveal assumptions people are not aware they are making and challenge them;

(2) they kill or at least expose and wound bad ideas; and

(3) they create a taste for more experimentation and adaptation, for exploration, for more prototyping and more serious play.

At the same time, critical thinking generated by intelligent conversation also feeds speculation and exploration about the sorts of institutional repairs that are needed for the governance process to meet the new challenges. Critical thinking reveals the weaknesses of the existing institutional order: what information, what forums and what permissions are missing so that the requisite amount of consultation, negotiation, collaboration and experimentation are allowed to emerge? A supply of new ideas ensues.

While supply does not create its own demand, it has quite a subversive impact on subsequent conversations. It allows participants in such further discussions to hold a trump card: a subversive question—why do you say that such an additional fixture is not necessary? Why do you say it cannot be done?

It cannot be denied nevertheless, that there is much reluctance for a large number of EXs to enter this danger zone of critical thinking: it would appear to be a terrain that they are not anxious to explore. This is not surprising. Groups are prone to suppress evidence that runs counter to their basic premises, and holding the same set of pre-suppositions allows individuals to confirm each other's interpretation of evidence (O'Toole 1995–96: 168). Critical deliberation may bring down these defence mechanisms.

It is possible that the fundamental calling into question of such a fundamental belief system caused by the drift from 'Big G' government to 'small g' governance demands too much of a reframing to be accepted lightly. This might explain the differences in the nature of the conversations when it dealt with 'technical and somewhat peripheral' management issues as opposed to when it dealt with issues that raised 'fundamental' questions about governance—where paradoxes and denials served to immunize the hard core of assumptions one is not allowed to challenge.

Basic documentation for each session

Diversity

G. Paquet and P. Reed 2003. "Are There Limits to Diversity?" www.optimumonline.ca, 33: 1: 13–19.

R. Higham 2005. "Governance of Diversity: What mechanisms?" www.optimumonline.ca, 35: 4: 60–67.

G. Paquet 2006. APEX 2006 "Two-Tracked Symposium: A curmudgeon's commentary." www.optimumonline.ca, 36: 2: 54–62.

R. Higham 2006. "The passport of convenience phenomenon." www.optimumonline.ca, 36: 3: 8–11.

G. Paquet 2006. "Moral contract as enabling mechanism." www.optimumonline.ca, 36: 3: 12–21.

Security

Wikipedia: Security , Precautionary principle , Type I and Type II Errors.

M. Ignatieff 2004. *The Lesser Evil – Political Ethics in an Age of*

Terror. New York: Penguin.

P. Bruckner 2006. *La tyrannie de la pénitence*. Paris: Grasset.

C. R. Sunstein 2005. *Laws of Fear – Beyond the Precautionary Principle*. Cambridge, UK: Cambridge University Press.

Ethics

P. Lecours and G. Paquet 2006. "Communication and Ethics: How to Scheme Virtuously." www.optimumonline.ca, 36: 2: 12–26.

Disloyalty

A. O. Hirschman 1970. *Exit, Voice and Loyalty*. Cambridge, MA: Harvard University Press.

Google: exit + voice + loyalty for examples of the use of this framework

Corporate culture

A. Wahl 2005. "Culture Shock: A Survey of Canadian Executives reveals that corporate culture is in need of improvement." *Canadian Business* 10: 23.

G. Paquet 2006. "Corporate Culture and Governance: Canada in the Americas." In P. Imbert (ed.) *Converging Disensus, Cultural Transformations, and Corporate Cultures*. Ottawa: Research Chair in Social and Cultural Challenges in a Knowledge-Based Society, 79-115 (Available also on www.optimumonline.ca under Publications).

The Gomery world

R. Hubbard and G. Paquet 2007, *Gomery's Blinders and Canadian Federalism*. Ottawa: The University of Ottawa Press.

J. G. Stein, M. Gibbins and A. Maioni 2006. *Canada by Picasso: The Faces of Federalism*. Ottawa: Conference Board of Canada.

Public-private partnerships

R. Hubbard and G. Paquet 2007. "Public-Private Partnerships and the 'porcupine' problem." In G.B. Doern (ed.) *How Ottawa Spends.* Montreal, QC and Kingston, ON: McGill-Queen's University Press.

B. Aubert and M. Patry 2005. "Les partenariats public-privé : le long et tortueux chemin du Québec. " www.optimumonline. ca, 35: 4: 68–74.

Partitioning a new the federal public service

R. Hubbard and G. Paquet 2007. "The myth of public service as a lump of 'guardians." www.optimumonline.ca, 36: 1: 9–26.

Cat's eyes—the next sixteen sessions

Cat's eyes are particularly valuable in fog.

—Wikipedia

Cat's eyes connote raised lane markers on paved roads—two pairs of reflective glass spheres set into a rubber dome and mounted in a cast iron housing used for lane marking, with one pair of cat's eyes pointing in each direction. Patented in 1934 by Percy Shaw, this invention has done more to save lives on the road than anything since.

For this second series, we focused our attention on two families of topics. First, we dealt with four challenges facing public servants in meeting the legitimate expectations of the citizenry: how to succeed in ensuring intelligent accountability, intelligent regulation, intelligent organizational design, and intelligent public service. Second, we dealt with what we felt were some of the most important sources of 'unintelligence' buried (not exclusively but most importantly) in questionable if not perverse incentive reward systems: rewarding failure and deception, punishing success, positive discrimination, and failure to confront

A syncretic view of each topic

This section provides a brief sketch of the introductory statement on each topic, and a summary view of the general substance of the conversations that followed.

Intelligent work

The first four topics dealt with intelligent work in four dimensions: accountability, regulation, organizational design and public service. Each of these labels connotes both a familiar terrain and a nexus of somewhat poorly-understood and contested issues. It is not always clear what is meant when such issues are raised because the complex mechanisms behind the labels are varied, and are often defined in significantly different ways by the key players involved. At the same time, whatever arrangements have been put in place to deal with the original concern have often been used in ways that can only be called 'unintelligent' (frequently with disastrous results). Yet, most of the time, the frustrated observers have been unable to determine what would be necessary to make these arrangements more 'intelligent'.

Intelligent accountability (October 17 & 19, 2007)

Accountability is the new mantra. It has emerged from the autopsy of recent mishaps as a panacea supposedly capable of resolving all conundrums by connecting each action and/or inaction to a source or cause to which it can be attributed, and therefore to a person or group that could be asked to render an account. Unfortunately, the world is much more complex than this simple mechanical depiction might suggest. There is not always a simple and direct connection between an outcome and a person who can be held responsible for it. As a result, accountability has become a weasel word: it has come to mean a variety of things ranging from true responsibility to the simple obligation of formally offering an official account of what has happened.

A key foundational concept at the core of the notion of accountability is the notion of the 'burden of office' on which accountability rests: what can be legitimately expected from an official. While the burden of office is relatively simpler to define in a strictly hierarchical organization (to do with what the superior may legitimately expect from her subordinate), it becomes much more complex in organizations where officials have to deal with a variety of stakeholders (bosses, partners, citizens, etc.) who all have legitimate expectations that may or may not be compatible. This complex context underpins the need for 360° accountability, makes the burden of office immensely more complicated, and the notion of accountability much fuzzier—less narrowly defined and focused, less hard, less strictly financial, and less manageable. The resulting challenge has not always been acknowledged. Indeed, many officials have been in denial *vis-à-vis* this new reality, and have continued to pretend that all issues can be defined as capable of being deconstructed into cause-effect relations where officials have a unique and narrowly defined burden of office for which they have to render an account to a unique overseer.

This is the dreamland in which too many adjudicators in all sectors have chosen to live. Unintelligent accountability obviously ensues, and unfortunately, as a result, too many auditors, evaluators and adjudicators have felt empowered to declare or imply guilt and innocence willy nilly and to impose praise or blame somewhat speciously.

Intelligent accountability entails a more realistic appreciation of the complexity of the context, and of the complexity of the notion of burden of office that ensues. This in turn calls for a more diffuse and a softer notion of accountability, and one that is truly dynamic in the sense that it evolves through time. Moreover, it is not (as it has come to be used in the language of auditors) the lynchpin of an *ex post* process of allocation of blame, but the basis of an *ex ante* process of social learning. Intelligent accountability is therefore learning accountability, soft accountability, and experimentalist accountability: it is the process through which an organization, in the short run, must deal with deception and disinformation, and in the longer run, must organize social learning in a forward-looking perspective (Paquet 2008c).

In the discussions, there was general agreement that accountability is too narrowly defined, and that in the public service one lives in a world of excessive rules and omnipresent watchdogs. It was also felt that common sense and trust might be brought back but that it would require action on many fronts: small steps in one's own shop, better use of training to instill the new culture of responsibility, some initiatives by communities of practices (e.g., human resource managers, regulators, procurement experts) that could be instrumental in promoting a broader perspective and in finding ways to operationalize such a renewed perspective with the development and use of instruments that were likely to keep the watchdogs at bay. Small steps and caution were seen as mandatory in this minefield.

Intelligent regulation (October 30 & November 2, 2007)

Regulation is a central feature of our lives. It affects all of us daily. Yet it is poorly understood, badly managed, and often has unintended consequences that make it ineffective and sometimes even toxic. These unintended consequences and the costs of regulation have led most governments to launch processes of 'regulatory reform': trying to get most of the benefits of intelligent regulation while avoiding the costs of dysfunctional regulation. These efforts have gone by many names: deregulation, smart regulation, responsive regulation, etc. Progress on these fronts has been slow.

The basic aim of all these reform movements has been a broadening and smoothing of the regulatory process:

(a) an attempt to take into account the broader mega-community in order to help it avoid ensnarement in the regulator's web;

(b) a shift from hard to soft regulation, from enforcement to assistance, from reactive to preventive, and from adversarial to collaborative action, from incident-driven to problem-solving approaches;

(c) a new focus (1) on risk management that entails a new attention to impact and not only to outcome measures, and (2) on materiality of risk in defining priorities;

(d) a recognition that this different approach is more demanding intellectually, analytically and organizationally, and more difficult as a result of the effort it demands unrelentingly.

The slow evolution from traditional to smart and responsive regulation has meant a shift toward a focus on more flexibility, more efficiency, more timeliness, more transparency and the use of a broader range of instruments, toward a sort of significant climbing-down of the enforcement pyramid toward less policing and more self-regulation, and a focus on preventing bad things through behavioural change.

In this transformation of the regulatory process to make it more intelligent, what is involved is nothing less than a change in the nature of the task, and a redefinition of the categories of harm. Such a transformation entails a much greater role for the mega-community and for the community of practice of the regulators (Gerencser et al. 2006; Wenger 1998). Even more importantly however, it is a redefinition of the very nature of the regulation work: away from policing to harm reduction.

This is not simply a semantic nicety. While on the surface promoting good things and working at reducing bad things may look the same, at the operational level it makes a considerable difference:

> ...scrutinizing the harms themselves, and discovering their
> dynamics and dependencies, leads to the possibility of sabotage.
> Cleverly conceived acts of sabotage, exploiting identified
> vulnerabilities of the object under attack, can be not only
> effective, but extremely resource-efficient too (Sparrow 2008: 27).

Climbing down the regulatory enforcement pyramid however, runs afoul of the trend toward more regulatory intervention in our age of distrust. In the face of complex circumstances nevertheless, such a propensity to over-regulate has generally failed. The first reaction to such failures has been to deregulate. Unfortunately, this has not proved necessarily very satisfactory either. A second wave of reaction has been a mix of smart regulation and responsive regulation, with an emphasis on the latter.

The discussion led to the realization that the risk tolerance of Canadians may be lower than that observed in other countries. So experimenting with radical elimination of regulation (like eliminating all traffic lights as has been done elsewhere) is unthinkable.

There was also much concern expressed about the focus on the 'how' of regulation instead of the 'why', and about the fixation on metrics (quantophrenia).

Much hope was put in the development of communities of practice: cultivating the community of regulators would enable interested public servants to share best practices.

Several actions could enable them to do a better job:

(1) allowing them to engage in discussions with their political leaders about the 'what' and the 'how' as well as about the true nature of the challenges they face;

(2) increasing the scope and discretion the regulators have (pushing them to understand and accept tradeoffs);

(3) finding ways to provide more time and resources to engage the relevant mega community; and

(4) perhaps most importantly, eliminating the trust-destroying philosophy of "trust but verify" that is in good currency.

Intelligent organizational design (November 14 & 16, 2007)

Organizational design is to governance what engineering is to science: the essential process of operationalization without which much of the good reflective work on governance is bound to remain fruitless. Yet this design work is quite difficult, is not well done, and is likely to be a cause of governance failure and poor performance.

An organization may be X-rayed as a mix of *people* (stakeholders of all sorts with their skills, talents, and responsibilities), *architecture* (relationships of all sorts defined by the organization charts and the like), *routines* (process, policies and procedures), and *culture* (shared values, beliefs, language, norms and mindsets) (J. Roberts 2004). At any time, these components (**PARC**) are assembled within organizations in various ways—bound together by ligatures making them into a more or less coherent whole. Any shocks disturbing any of these components (whether they originate within or without the organization, whether they modify a physical or a symbolic dimension) obviously trigger some re-alignment in all the other dimensions. So the organization continually evolves.

The main reason for effective organizational design failing to materialize is probably because it is wrongly assumed that organizational design amounts to little more than tinkering with organization charts. In fact, the sort of architectural work required is immensely more demanding and commands a wholly different way of thinking. It is not (and cannot be) guided by the sole sort of logic that dominates science (the search for general knowledge and the subsequent test of its validity) but by an inquiry into systems that do not yet exist: the logic is that of disclosing and crafting a new 'world', with the sole purpose of ascertaining if it works, and to ensure that it does (Romme 2003: 558).

The organization is a living entity. Buildings evolve despite their constraining structures as their occupants take hold of them, and transform their functions and missions in ways that were never planned. The same evolution occurs in organizations but much faster and more dramatically, as a result of unintended consequences of unplanned interactions.

The role of the organizational designer is to intervene in real time in an existing assemblage to improve the four-dimensional PARC configuration of the organization in a manner that generates better dynamic performance and resilience, given the nature of the environment in which the organization operates, but as well taking into account its turbulence and its evolution, and fully recognizing the limits of such exercises.

These four dimensions may be tweaked in a creative way to provide effective dynamic coordination, but unintended consequences may thwart the whole experience. This sort of work:

(1) requires a new vocabulary because critical description is crucial at the diagnostic phase;

(2) demands a new form of knowledge, a new type of exploratory activity and a new process of experimentalism-based creative thinking; and

(3) presumes a new type of competencies;

(4) however, this process will lead to nothing substantial unless one has been able to develop a mental tool box of levers usable in such design work and capable of guiding the tentative work of crafting new organizations;

(5) because organization design is akin to creating a new world, none of the above will suffice unless the design process truly discloses a coherent world (a body) and

contributes to impart it with a style (a soul) that provides it with a sextant, focal points that underpin its being able to sustain effective coordination and change (Simons 2005; Paquet 2007a).

This topic proved difficult to discuss. In large part, this likely stemmed from participants' lack of direct involvement with the process of deliberately attempting to change organizations, along with the false impression that 'organizational design' refers simply to the definitions of roles and reporting relationships. Moreover, the very notion of re-organization came with some baggage: it is often perceived as a decoy for scaling down the operations. Consequently it often generates a culture of 'resistance to change' that tends to discourage prototyping or redesign initiatives.

Demographics were referred to as a determining factor as young people are often more willing than their older colleagues to experiment. However, it was also felt that oblique strategies may be more effective because existing structures may correspond to important vested interests. The human resource (HR) function was the common ground that proved most congenial for the discussion both as a result of familiarity with the field, and as there was some agreement that this might be the locus where redesign might be regarded as a top priority.

Intelligent organizational design is not a matter of recipes, but a way of thinking that is non-linear, uses a holistic approach, and entails the practical use of prototyping. In the case of HR, without better information about people, a more accommodating classification system, a reduction in institutional rigidities and the avoidance of the current mixed messages seeking both permanence and fluidity—significant improvement is going to be hard to achieve.

Intelligent public service (November 28 & 30, 2007)

In a Westminster model, the public service serves elected officials by ensuring that the programs of action and inaction of the government in place are carried out as effectively, efficiently, economically and creatively as possible within the constraints imposed by the rule of law.

In Canada, at the federal level, the governing of the public service is carried out by a multiplicity of intermediary institutional players: Treasury Board Secretariat, Privy Council Office, Public Service Commission and Canada School of Public Service, etc.— over and above a myriad of actors at the departmental and agency level. It has been guessed that, at the central agencies' level, no less than the equivalent of 2,000 full time employees are involved, and close to another 1,000 at the department and agency levels. This entails expenditures of between CA$ 300 and $400 million per year.

It has been argued that the present arrangements are far from satisfactory. The public service is often regarded as not serving elected officials well, as doing so in a rigid and not very innovative way and, therefore, as performing at a level that is below expectations.

This should not be interpreted as denying in any way the general quality of the Canadian public service by comparison to the public service apparatus in other industrialized countries. It is simply that much room for improvement has been perceived by observers in a number of recent reports.

Two of those reports have been receiving much attention of late: the work of the Prime Minister's Advisory Committee on the Public Service (Mazankowski, Tellier et al. 2009) and the 2008 report of the Public Policy Forum, "Canada's Public Service in the 21st Century – Destination: Excellence".

While these reports made a number of helpful suggestions, it is fair to say that they were both very cautious and circumspect about the way to deal with the tensions between the elected officials and the bureaucrats. They focused narrowly on human resources management issues (including performance management) that, if dealt with satisfactorily, might help the Canadian public service to perform better. Issues like the burden of office of the public service, the moral contracts binding them to the different stakeholders they serve, and the professionalism that is fundamental to their activities in our Westminster system of an independent and non-partisan public service were largely ignored.

Yet those latter issues were clearly on the mind of many observers who have been wondering whether the public service in its present form can survive; they have pondered the question of what intelligent public service really means.

The discussion on this topic was painful as it is quite difficult to assume (even temporarily and for the sole purpose of discussion) that the public service (to which one belongs) might be 'unintelligent'. However it became clear as the discussion proceeded that the cumulative impact of poor accountability, regulation and organizational design could only add up to a less than perfectly intelligent public service. Again, the HR dimension dominated the discussion because it provided more palpable evidence of the sort of dysfunction referred to in the general discussion. It provided much evidence of the difficulty of striking the right balance between reliability and innovation. It also led to the recognition that there is much more need for innovation, measurement of the right things the right way, and for sensible reporting.

The need for being given an 'objective not a template' and 'a goal without being told how to achieve it' were regarded as necessary prerequisites to producing good results. Mentoring and coaching were noted as important for improving capability. The participants deplored meaningless reporting, observing that the centre did not have the capacity to analyze all the information being sought. In a general way, intelligent public service was seen as building on three conceptual pillars: the 'burden of office' of public servants, the many 'moral contracts' created with different stakeholders, and the 'professionalism' that public servants bring to their work. Nevertheless, without a real capacity for pushing back when rigid and ineffective action is ordained, for cultivating communities of practice, for empowering managers and for measuring the right things the right way—moving towards an intelligent public service will be hard.

Perverse incentives

The second set of topics tried to probe some of the sources of the lack of intelligence noted in the discussions of the last four topics. Those sources and causes are many: some are structural, others organizational, still others behavioral. We focused on some of the behavioral dimensions and particularly on toxic and perverse incentives, which may help explain some of the most destructive tendencies and proclivities that would appear to undermine the governing of our social system in the private, public and social sectors: rewarding failure and deception, punishing success, positive discrimination, and failure to confront.

The issues discussed in the last four topics were not, in general, disturbing emotionally (at the end of the day, who could be in favour of unintelligent anything) and led to engaged but relatively serene discussions in all but the last session. The issues discussed in the following sessions were emotionally-loaded. A very sensitive approach was needed to deal with each of the four issues by working carefully through four stages: is there evidence of such behavior? is there evidence that it has become more important of late, and that it creates problems? can one speculate on the root causes of such behavior? can one design correctives in the short and longer terms?

It is fair to say that consensus was neither sought nor reached on these difficult issues. Moreover it is also true that, in general, conversations about these issues were rather difficult. Disagreement, often sharp disagreement, was recorded on all four questions about all four issues. It ranged from vibrant denial that any of these issues were relevant or had any materiality by half of the groups, to the sad recognition by the other half that they were rampant viral afflictions that were slowly destroying the culture of the public service as well as our social system. Our summary of these discussions is clinically sanitized but in ways that try to echo the temper of the debates as fairly as possible.

Rewarding failure and deception (February 13 & 15, 2008)

Incentive reward systems are foundational in organizations. When an organization sends wrong signals (as when it rewards failure and deception), it conveys to all members of the organization that performance and dedication are not required. This can only corrupt the whole incentive reward system. While one wants to be tolerant of mistakes as an essential component of the learning process, when confirmed and systematic failure and deception are rewarded by lateral moves or promotion, this can only be destructive.

The challenge is to strike the right balance: encouraging experiments, innovations (and therefore potential failures) without being seen as rewarding gross incompetence, misleading messages and deception. Punishing deception is indeed the first step in establishing intelligent accountability as was explained in that earlier session.

After a moment of discussion about what could be meant by 'failure' (and the need to understand that there may be some confusion and legitimate differences of opinion depending on where one stands), it was agreed that *grosso modo* rewarding failure was 'endemic'. Why? Much was made of the extreme difficulty in dealing with poor performers, and the consequent minimal incentive for executives to keep the public interest in mind on these matters, and to take punitive action. Too often, there is a tendency to off-load problem cases by getting non-performers shunted off or promoted elsewhere.

Perversely, this is often encouraged by the 'higher ups' who want to avoid the short term havoc of quarrelsome and disruptive dismissal procedures for 'their' organization. Fear of harassment charges or of damaging personal relations encourages this culture of 'playing nice' and hyper-tolerance, and it discourages criticism. Even though one may be said to live in an age when audit and oversight have become pervasive, bad results are often camouflaged and bad performers not punished. While all agreed that the private benefits of such practices are not negligible, it was also agreed that the social costs are huge.

It was felt that it is naive to expect that there will be any change until each executive accepts that addressing this problem should be regarded as his or her own responsibility. This requires educating persons upward that responsible action calls for:

(1) refusing to indulge in camouflage or beggar-thy-neighbour practices;

(2) acting responsibly as a cadre of executives to reinforce this commitment; and

(3) providing unfailing support to managers trying to deal with these kinds of problems.

Mechanisms or practices that help prevent such pathology from being eradicated should be questioned explicitly, and raised at executive retreats. For example, it should be common knowledge and widely publicized within the organizations that harassment allegations will not be entertained if there is a performance problem. The burden of office of an executive is not first and foremost meant to be focused on being nice, but on ensuring that important public functions are performed as effectively, efficiently and creatively as possible. Those unwilling to subscribe to these principles should be relieved of their executive functions. The public expects nothing less from professional executives as professionals.

Not surprisingly, the official public service document listing key leadership competencies (a document widely used in executive training) includes two pages of 'generic' ineffective behaviors that need to be avoided by all personnel, from supervisors through deputy ministers (Canada 2006a).

Yet, in this official document, a list of the ways of 'dealing with ineffective performers' is explicitly provided 'only up to' the director level: it then vanishes, as if it could not happen or even be entertained at the higher level. This is perplexing especially in view of the second (2008) and third Mazankowski-Tellier reports in which the need to "deal with poor performers" (wherever they are in the hierarchy) is singled out as particularly in need of more attention to improve performance (Mazankowski, Tellier et al. 2009).

Punishing success (February 27 & 29, 2008)

Punishing success is even more toxic than rewarding failure. It is a form of organizational violence and indicates that personal likes and dislikes are much more important than performance. If tolerated, not only does it destroy people but it also weakens and brings organizations down by discouraging initiative, creativity and innovation. Allowing executives to endanger the health of their organization through the pursuit of personal vendettas or sheer spite puts in question the very notion of fairness; it is no more defendable if such action is taken in order to preserve one's empire or to prevent its erosion.

Again the discussion focused at first on the notion of 'success'. In a world of greater complexity, faster change, and much pluralism, there may be some legitimate differences of opinion about what is 'success'. The general view of half the groups was that 'punishing success' was not as endemic as 'rewarding failure and deception'. Nevertheless numerous examples were cited.

There was sharp disagreement also about whether or not organizational violence (in this form or in other forms) is or is not on the rise. Some argued forcefully that it was on the rise. On the other hand, there was much denial of the problem: its reality, its increasing importance, its toxicity. The sense of denial permeated the discussion, despite the strongly held view by a plurality of participants that such denial was unconscionable.

Despite the resistance to the idea that such psychopathic behaviour may be rampant, some support was lent to the view that some '*bricolage*' was in order—a number of small things that make this perverse behaviour more well-known and better exposed might make it less likely. For executives, a focus on symbolic and oblique measures (e.g., referring systematically to values and ethical code) as well as 'in-your-face' demands of account in such cases may represent avenues to explore.

Even though many examples were given of individuals (Allan Cutler) having been punished for doing their job well and in a very professional way, and of organizations (Service Canada) having been savaged despite award-winning experience, there was a deep reluctance to recognize that punishing success may be a viral affliction in public sector organizations. The assumption that officials are knights and not knaves was put forward so strongly that the very idea of entertaining the thought that success was punished seemed to be impossible for many participants to entertain.

At no time since the discussion on disloyalty (in the first series) can one say that the denial was stronger. The vocal minority was exercised by this cognitive dissonance and expressed its views sharply, but to no avail. The discussion was derailed into a philosophical disquisition on what is 'real success', and denunciations of 'pseudo-success' reached at great human costs. It is not unfair to say that some aspects of the conversation brought to mind the famous line of Lewis Carroll's *Humpty Dumpty*: "when I use a word, it means just what I choose it to mean". It is therefore unlikely that this conversation will have much follow-on impact.

Positive discrimination (March 12 & 14, 2008)

The topic was squarely defined as *not* dealing with persons with equal capabilities on all counts but different only on the basis of markers like race, gender or color, etc., but dealing explicitly with the choice of a lesser quality candidate when candidates of higher quality are available and by-passed only because they are not from the minority group being targeted. There is little discussion of these issues: is it because the problem does not exist or because of political correctness?

Positive discrimination (in this very particular and narrow sense) is the deliberate setting aside of key performance objectives discussed in the last two sessions (success, failure) in the name of higher goals and objectives. Wittingly or not, it amounts to rewarding lesser performance and punishing higher performance in the name of some 'greater good' like making reparation for past wrongs, improving the representativeness of the bureaucracy, and the like. Moreover, it is done with a great amount of self-righteousness.

There was no denial that the problem exists and is important, but it was argued that, in the public sector, one cannot be restricted to matters of efficiency or fairness: it is also a matter of legitimacy. Therefore the 'need to have a representative public service' may be legitimately used as a basis for 'corrective measures'. In other words, there was an acknowledgement that positive discrimination may be regarded as necessary in some situations in order for some barriers to be eliminated, so that one may generate a 'representative' bureaucracy.

A contrario, there was also a substantial agreement on the part of a plurality of participants that too much is made of the problem of an un-representative public service. While the structure of the public service may not match perfectly the fabric of Canadian society as it stands today (as a result of rapid transformation over the last 50 years), it is unreasonable to expect instantaneous adjustments. The expertise and experience necessary for promotion to higher levels in the public service take time to develop. It was pointed out that market forces, demographics, and time will take care of the problem (and faster than anticipated as a result of the massive retirement cohort that is forthcoming). This suggested that positive discrimination might be overused: some argued that it might be needed to achieve a critical mass of targeted groups to break down a systemic barrier, but, beyond that level, what is needed is simply good management of the interface at group boundaries.

Nevertheless, the culture of political correctness is very strong, so that the trade-off between representativeness and efficiency-effectiveness of the public service is unlikely to be a topic that can be easily and openly discussed.

There was broad agreement that implicit discrimination (unintentional and outside the discriminator's awareness) will also require more attention.

Failure to confront (March 26 & 28, 2008)

It is always unpleasant (except for sadists) to confront a person whose performance is unsatisfactory, and to demand that some corrective measures be taken. Yet, it is probably the most important weakness of stewards in all sorts of organizations: the lack of capability or willingness to look a person directly reporting to one in the eye, and to say that "this will not do". Yet this is a fundamental requirement for any steward; it is part of her/his burden of office. Failure to confront is tantamount to deception, to not telling the truth, to misinforming.

The chronic unwillingness to confront may arise for many reasons. It entails, nevertheless, some reprehensible disengagement, some unacceptable strategic silence in the face of situations calling for correctives. It may also condone and nurture some 'learned helplessness'—a reaction of passivity in the face of unpleasant, harmful or damaging situations where one senses that one has neither the bargaining power nor the capacity to resolve the problem.

While there was a general agreement that this was a crucial problem, and that this was on the rise, there seemed to be a strong reluctance to focus any energy on designing mechanisms aimed at resolving this difficulty. The need to find ways to foster more courage was underlined, but it went no further.

Even though it was recognized that, at this time, 'strategic silence' may have become too much of a survival strategy for executives, and that it may prove very costly for organizations, relatively little in the way of positive action was argued. Yet, it was recognized that taxpayers may soon ask why they should surrender money to a state so badly equipped to exercise due diligence, and to demand that public servants perform their duties efficiently, effectively and creatively, or leave.

Participants concluded that 'failure to confront' was not only a problem on the rise in the public service in connection with ineffective performance, but also a cause of the weakening of the challenge function with respect to policy.

Training could play a role in increasing awareness, and in teaching techniques for handling difficult conversations. Nevertheless, participants emphasized that, in many cases, people knew how to confront but that the blockages arose elsewhere—in particular, the lack of support by superiors. It was also telling that many participants found 'failure to confront' to be offensive language in Canadian culture: promoting dialogue was seen as preferable to bemoaning 'failure to confront'!

A personal distillation of what we learned

Any effort to distil lessons from such disparate discussions on difficult topics with different groups over the period of more than six months is bound to fail in being as comprehensive as it should be ideally. Most certainly, every participant might well come up with a slightly different list of key issues if the task were delegated to him or her. So this particular distillation does not claim to be more than one set of observations by two of the participants. We have presented our observations under four rubrics, but these sections are preceded by a cautionary statement.

A cautionary statement

No conversation can make any sense without some contextual information being supplied. The conversations referred to above were held in difficult times for the Canadian public service both as a result of a troubled conjuncture (minority Conservative government after more than a dozen years of Liberal rule, decline in the trust in government and bureaucrats in general, etc.) and of a period of fundamental questioning about Canadian political institutions (*remise en question* of the role of an independent public service in dealing with elected officials in a world drifting from 'Big G' government to 'small g' governance, new complexity of the issues as one enters an era of distrust where collaboration among a much larger number of partners is necessary but rather difficult as it remains uncharted territory, etc.) (Hubbard and Paquet 2007b).

This context could not but influence the nature of the conversations. And this turbulent environment has of necessity made it difficult to disentangle the roles of external (i.e., contextual) and internal (i.e., emerging from the fabric of the public service) factors in making sense of what was said and in explaining why such reactions were elicited by the conversations.

The temptation to ascribe much of the pathologies we observed to external factors had to be contained. Such an approach would appear to characterize senior executives of the Canadian public service as passively suffering these pressures and without a capacity to act as *définisseurs de situation* in a learning organization. A more reasonable perspective is to ascribe a portion of the difficulties to the context, but a very significant portion of it to failures of the executives in fully mastering the technologies of survival, adaptive and generative learning (Senge 1990).

The purpose of our conversations is obviously to foster a better understanding of the complexity of the environment and of the wickedness of the problems faced by public sector executives, and as well to help develop what Peter Senge calls 'personal mastery'—the capacity and discipline of continually clarifying and deepening their learning process and of becoming "acutely aware of their ignorance, their incompetence, their growth areas" (Ibid., 142). This cannot be done without sharply identifying what one can detect as internal (behavioral and organizational) features that need to be transformed by executives themselves.

So our clinical and provocative diagnoses have to be interpreted not as putting the onus of adjustment entirely on the executives (for there are things that will require nothing less that a modification of Canadian institutions and of the Canadian mindset), but as putting much responsibility on their shoulders to deal with those portions of the undeniable pathologies that are under their control.

Two major contextual factors should however be kept in mind in interpreting what might be regarded as a stark diagnosis.

First, debates are going on about the unresolved questions about the legitimate role of the senior public servants. As Paul Thomas put it:

> …we want an independent public service. Is this independence
> mainly important for the implementation of public policy to
> ensure fairness and impartiality in the delivery of programs and
> services? Is the same amount of independence required with
> respect to the provision of policy advice? Does independence
> for the public service guarantee objective advice to government?
> Are objectivity and independence the same quality in an
> institution?…Acceptance of the notion of a separate place in the
> constitutional order for an independent public service [i.e., the
> presumption behind Gomery and perhaps the Public Accounts
> Committee of the accounting officer concept] has far reaching
> implications. It implies, for example, that the public service has
> a legitimate role in helping to define the public interest (Thomas
> 2008).

In the face of such indeterminacy, it is difficult for senior executives not to be confused, and there is little any one can do about it until some clarification materializes.

Second, the nature of the problems faced by elected officials and senior executives is immensely more complex in the world of 'small g' governance than it used to be in the old 'Big G' government institutional order. Yet there is a great reluctance in accepting the fact that these 'more wicked' problems may not be capable of being handled adequately by the old artillery. This would entail a transition in the nature of the burden of office of senior executives and the development of a full acceptance that the old ways must change accordingly.

Again, the fact that this transition is far from over, and that many senior executives in the public service at all levels, and many crucial partners, are still in denial about the need to change significantly, cannot but paralyze action by senior executives, and generate much frustration that cannot be overcome by wishful thinking.

This being said, we could not fail to observe the following perplexing phenomena as a result of our discussions.

Somebody is in charge and it is not me

A rather perplexing set of assumptions about the 'real' place of the executives in the overall governance apparatus and in the public sector cast a shadow on our conversations. One could feel a tension between the willingness of executives to take charge and to accept responsibilities for success or failures, with some sense that they are not in charge. When faced with the hypothesis that they have to take charge, because nobody is truly and completely in charge, there was a forceful reaction of disbelief.

The executives seem paralyzed by the triple presumption:

(1) that it cannot be that truly nobody is in charge;
(2) that, since they (the executives) are not in charge themselves;
(3) these 'somebodies' in charge should provide guidance.

Faced with the hypothesis that we are drifting from the world of 'Big G' government to 'small g' governance, the senior executives seemed *unready* to accept (at least initially and easily) that they are key producers of governance, that they are the ones holding the key to most of the challenges discussed. They are torn between two uncomfortable positions: the old Westminster model that tells them that they are the 'servants' of Parliament, and the new credo that claims that the super-bureaucrats and senior executives are more legitimate than the elected officials, and therefore should be in charge (Paquet 2008b, c). Neither position would seem to fit their circumstances: they simply perceive themselves as 'subordinates', and therefore as not really being in charge.

This (added to the great confusion in the context) seems to have created a climate of 'learned helplessness' that even constrained the ambit of permissible discussion to a considerable degree. Much of the casuistry displayed during the discussions (about what is success, failure, etc.) is ascribable to the fact the executives cannot bring themselves to believe that we can live in a world where nobody is in charge: they cannot but search for some 'person in charge' either in the political sphere or in the upper sphere of the bureaucracy. This acts as a self-restraining mental prison that prevents them from claiming their just place in the governance structure—however constrained that just place might be. How much is ascribable to the complexity of the context and how much to this mental prison is a moot point: both factors would appear to prevent the senior executives from exercising their full role of 'governors'.

One must add that this malaise was somewhat shaken off along the way as the different conversations proceeded. Indeed, the slow disappearance of the 'us-them' cleavage is probably one of the most positive results of the conversations conducted over the last year, especially for the younger participants: the slow evolution of a perception where the problems were being ascribed to 'them' (whomever they are), and the responses expected from 'them', toward a position reached, later in the 2007-08 season, where the participants came to reject that *servitude volontaire*, began to recognize their share of the causal factors and their responsibility in generating meaningful and effective responses, and did it in a more and more forceful way. There was no mind quake, but a significant change in mindset.

Déformation professionnelle

H. L. Mencken wrote somewhere that for every complex problem, there is a solution that is simple, clear and wrong. This is an aphorism that echoes both:

(1) the presumption that the degree of complexity of the discussion of or of the response to an issue has to be as great as the nature of the issue being debated; and

(2) the dangers of particularly reductive *manières de voir* that often lead specialists to be no better than one of the blind men, in the Indian tale, trying to describe an elephant.

The prevalent mindset of executives (ascribing so much authority to external powers at least at first, and claiming so little real governance as being in their hands) explains why the executives were so reluctant to be dragged out of the concerns about the 'how' toward a better appreciation of the context, of the need to understand the 'why', and of the obligation to engage in critical and reflective thinking on these broad issues. A grander way of dealing with issues was simply seen as out-of-bounds.

This *déformation professionnelle* explains the impatience with contextual issues and the pleasurable satisfaction with dealing in operational details. While such a bias was not universal, it was omnipresent: enough in any case to drown efforts by many to cast a wider net, to frame issues in a broader way, and to deal with non-operational issues. This led the discussion to founder on the search for recipes and ways out, or to focus on some tractable aspect of the question (like HR) instead of spawning reflections on the broader sources and causes of the problems raised. If you think that you only have a hammer, everything starts looking like a nail.

This was in no way the result of a lack of intellectual capability for appreciation of such complexities, but rather the result of a sort of professional bias that would appear to have struck the federal executive class and drawn it away from the shoals of critical thinking into the quiet waters of operations. In a world where critical thinking is not valued as much as it used to be, and is even seen unfavourably, it is hardly surprising that in dealing with taboo topics one would be naturally led to search for a technical fix rather than for an appreciative system.

This professional bias may be ascribable to the decline in the valuation of critical thinking since the 1990s when, in certain federal quarters of the public service, criticism became a synonym for treason. This was the time when the programs of the Canada School of Public Service were stripped of their critical edge, and when training became clearly much more focused on logistics than on appreciation. This bias has come to define the norms in good currency. So much so, that even groups as venturesome as the ones we met in these series of discussions tended often to shy away from tackling problems in a reflective manner to focus on instrumental and highly focalized avenues.

Cognitive dissonance and political correctness

The two mental prisons mentioned above (*servitude volontaire* and *déformation professionnelle*) seem to go a fair distance in explaining the mix of cognitive dissonance and political correctness that marred our conversations. The great amount of tiptoeing around the difficult topics would appear to flow from two imperatives: avoiding any self-indictment of the public service *per se* as much as possible, and any statement that might sound politically incorrect. On the first front, this entailed much cognitive dissonance: the denial of unintelligence and of misbehavior by authorities was in most cases the *position de départ*, and there was much defensiveness whenever it was suggested that some particular event or some particular action might prove the point that something untoward was averred.

When an official key leadership competencies document was tabled (Canada 2006c) showing that it was presumed that nothing untoward could be expected from the very senior ranks, the reaction was straight-faced denial until the particular pages could be shown. The examples of misbehavior tolerated by deputy ministers and then rewarded were greeted with much *malaise* but readily dismissed as exceptions to a general diagnosis that 'things were not that bad' and that it was unreasonable to generalize on the basis of a few examples.

One could notice, even in a group that can only be characterized, by all accounts, as enormously more open-minded and venturesome that the average public sector executive, a disposition and even a propensity to defend the system not only by blanking out the implications one might reasonably derive from the observed phenomena, but also by systematically down playing the weight of the evidence brought forth. Not only was there denial that there has been much misbehaving, but there was even some disingenuity at times in the rationalizations proposed to make sense of them.

On the political correctness front, the lines were less sharply drawn. Decades of guarded language and human rights commissions' denunciations have taken their toll. Robust language was not well received, but there was a willingness to insist on a softer language as a strategy to ensure that the issue would be dealt with. Avoiding provocative formulations was a tactic used by some not to frighten others who were particularly sensitive about such things.

Taboo topics were defanged by flats and sharps, and the issues were de-generalized in a manner that helped to exorcise their damnable aspects. The group tended to focus on particular instances and circumstances to illustrate ways in which difficult issues like positive discrimination had been handled aptly. This approach allowed the group to be much bolder on this external front than it allowed itself to be on the internal front (i.e., when dealing with the public service proper). Still, there was some defensiveness and a sharp contrast between the evenly balanced sub-groups—those yearning for sharp and forceful exchanges, and those hesitant about allowing it to proceed too far.

The presence of latent fear

The most elusive sense that permeated the discussions was one of latent fear.

This had nothing to do with any sort of edicts but rather some form of self-censorship that has become habitual, it would seem, as a survival instinct in a world where critical thinking and sharp exchanges are no longer valued as they used to be. This is where the rampant sense of organizational violence would appear to take its toll. To a person, participants testified that *prudentia* was *de rigueur*, that it was by far the most important of the cardinal virtues in the public service these days: much more than the other cardinal virtues, *temperentia* (the sense of limits), fortitude or courage, and justice (van Hooft 2006). This would appear to flow from a profound culture of distrust that has come to imbibe the Canadian federal public service.

This culture of distrust has much to do with the evolution of the nexus of moral contracts among the politicians, the bureaucrats, the diverse interest groups, and the citizenry as the regime drifted from 'Big G' government to 'small g' governance

(Paquet and Pigeon 2000). In the stylized world of persons like Donald Savoie, there used to be a simple loop—linking voters to their MPs and through them to the PM and Cabinet, and then from Cabinet to ministers, departments and the cascades of public servants back to the citizen—that has now (as he would have it) been broken (Savoie 2008). If such a loop of accountability ever existed is a moot point; it is clear that it has not existed for a long time, and that we have lived much more in a power matrix whose organizational chart would look instead like a knotted fishnet.

What has changed is the structure of moral contracts binding this set of public actors: from contracts based on trust to contracts based on distrust. Disloyalty need not be generalized for distrust to prevail: if only a small fraction of a group is disloyal but there is no way to know who they are, distrust will become endemic (Paquet 2008b). Indeed, this has been the sort of drift one has observed, not only in Canada but in many advanced democracies, with the result that executives are now living in an age of distrust (R. Hardin 2004; Rosanvallon 2006)

This sort of distrust, together with the growth of organizational violence, is at the source of the latent fear that permeated our conversations. It is ascribable to a much greater extent than is usually attributable to poor organization design, leading to a growing gap between what is expected and what can be delivered, and consequently a source of both stress and harassment. Again, how much of it stems from context (and therefore beyond reach for the executives interested in engineering needed repair) and how much from cultural factors within their reach (even though it might be a daunting task to deal with them) is quite difficult to ascertain.

In this case therefore, it is hardly sufficient to suggest that order can be restored only by super-bureaucrats and senior executives being given more power (as Savoie suggests). Rather if fear is to be attenuated, what is required is recognition that in a world of governance, new structures have to be designed and new rules of the game have to be put in place that build much more on trust than distrust.

What this refurbished system might look like has not crystallized yet but some of its contours have been sketched by Sunstein and Thaler under the generic name of "libertarian paternalism" (Sunstein 2005: ch.8; Thaler and Sunstein 2008). It argues for a soft, non-intrusive type of public sector intervention to nudge citizens in certain directions without forbidding, very much along the lines suggested in the governance literature.

Clearly, until such time as the very notion that 'nobody is in charge' takes hold of the mindset of public sector executives at all levels (including deputy ministers), there is little hope that the necessary redesign will be put in place, that intelligent work will unfold, that perverse incentives, organizational violence and fear will be subdued, and that moral contracts among the different actors can be renegotiated. Unless this can be done, there is little sense in hoping the complete dominance of *prudentia* over fortitude, courage and justice will be shaken off by executives in the public service.

Conclusion

It may be useful to remind the reader that one cannot and should not forget that these conversations with a few dozens self-selected executives in the Canadian federal public service constitute a small basis from which one can only generalize very prudently. We have chosen to do so somewhat carefully but also boldly in the hope that conversations around these topics, and around our conclusions, will generate useful discussions.

It is our view that discussions in safe spaces constitute an extraordinarily powerful instrument to accelerate the transition that is required. Not only do such discussions provide an opportunity to deal with difficult issues with a view to generating both better understanding and closer collaboration (i.e., trust), but they are also a good cauldron where professionalism is reinforced and solidified. For, in the absence of real-life experiments, such discussions are a substitute for experimentation. Indeed, as Albert Hisrchman has so aptly said, a diet of conflicts that a group is capable of resolving does marvels to generate a sense of community (Hirschman 1995).

Whether our observations are confirmed or challenged, the topics raised remain crucially important, and deserve the attention of those who have chosen a career in the public service, and find themselves less able to serve as well—to do intelligent work or to fend off perverse incentives—as they would like. Without such conversations, there may be a danger that unwittingly some of the foundational institutions that we Canadians have invented to govern ourselves will be eroded. Moral contracts need to evolve constantly with circumstances, and they need to be kept in mind, to be in the forefront of our consciousness, if they are to be re-negotiated as and when appropriate.

Otherwise, one may fall prey to simplistic fixes like the argument in good currency among columnists these days, *ces magistrats de l'immédiat,* that elected officials have lost legitimacy and that the 'solution' is that super-bureaucrats and senior executives need to be given more power. This sort of pretension to superior legitimacy by the managerial class is in the air in Canada and elsewhere, and it has not been critically chastised in Canada in the manner it has been in Australia (Rhodes and Wanna 2007).

For those tempted by such stratagems of hijacking by the managerial class (and they are many in the ranks of the public sector executives) a re-reading of the parable of the wicked tenants may be in order. This is the parable of the vineyard planter who leases his vineyard to tenants who turn out to be wicked, and subsequently murder the planter's son to try to inherit the vineyard. The fate of the wicked tenants was predictably tragic.

Basic documentation for each session

Intelligent accountability

J. Tussman 1989. *The Burden of Office*. Vancouver: Talonbooks.

G. Paquet 2008. "A Plea for Intelligent Accountability." *Financial Management Institute Journal*, 19: 2: 9–14.

Intelligent regulation

M.K. Sparrow 2000. *The Regulatory Craft*. Washington, DC: The Brookings Institution Press.

W. Leiss 2003. *Smart Regulation and Risk Management*. Paper prepared for the External Advisory Committee on Smart Regulation, November.

J. Graham 2005. "Smart Regulation: Will the Government's Strategy Work?" *Canadian Medical Association Journal*, 173: 12: December: 1469–1470.

I. Ayres and J. Braithwaite 1995. *Responsive Regulation: Transcending the Deregulation Debate*. Oxford: Oxford University Press.

Intelligent organizational design

G. Paquet 2007. "Organization Design as Governance's Achilles' Heel." www.governancia.com, 1: 3: 1–11.

J. Roberts 2004. *The Modern Firm*. Oxford: Oxford University Press.

A. G. L. Romme 2003. "Making a Difference: Organization as Design." *Organization Science*, 14: 5: 558–573.

Intelligent public service

G. Paquet 1997. "The Burden of Office, Ethics and Connoisseurship." *Canadian Public Administration*, 40: 1: 55–71.

Prime Minister's Advisory Committee on the Public Service, Second Report to the Prime Minister. *Pursuing a High*

Performance Public Service, February 2008.
Public Policy Forum 2008. *Canada's Public Service in the 21st Century Destination: Excellence.* Ottawa.

Rewarding failure and deception

O. O'Neill 2002. *A Question of Trust.* Cambridge, UK: Cambridge University Press.

Punishing success

G. Paquet and L. Pigeon 2000. "In Search of a New Covenant." In E. Lindquist (ed.), *Government Restructuring and the Future of Career Public Service in Canada,* Toronto: Institute of Public Administration of Canada, 475–498.

Positive discrimination

G. Paquet 2006. "APEX 2006 Two-Tracked Symposium: A Curmudgeon's Commentary." www.optimumonline.ca, 36: 2: 54–62.
M. Bertrand et al. 2005. "Implicit Discrimination." *American Economics Association Papers and Proceedings,* May, 94–98.

Failure to confront

C. Peterson et al. 1993. *Learned Helplessness.* New York: Oxford University Press.
K. L. Stewart 2002. "Confrontation – Some Practical Guidelines for Confronting Others Effectively." April 25. http://www.somc.org/NRSOMCPress/Confrontation.ppt [accessed May 5, 2010].
T. Lenski, "7 Fears of Confronting Conflict," http://lenski.com/7-fears-of-confronting-conflict/ [accessed May 5, 2010].

Not in the catbird seat – the next eight sessions

The catbird seat is an idiomatic phrase used to describe an enviable position.

—Wikipedia

For this series, we focused our attention on some flaws in the public governance process in Canada: the propensity to develop a cult of quantification that we have called quantophrenia; the ineffectiveness of personnel performance review as a process, the puzzling notion of speaking truth to power as an ill-understood imperative, and the occlusion of cities in the national governance process.

A syncretic view of each topic

This section provides a brief statement of the introductory context for each topic, and a very sketchy summary view of the general substance of the conversations that followed.

Quantophrenia (January 21 & 23, 2009)

Quantification *per se* is not reprehensible. Quantitative methods have been used from time immemorial as a powerful instrument of reasoning. The problem arises when the use of such tools becomes the basis of a *cult* roughly captured by the motto that if it cannot be measured, it does not matter. Such a cult distorts the appreciation we have of socio-economic phenomena, and this mental prison acts as a pair of blinders that have toxic unintended consequences for public policies when they become shaped by an apparatus thus constrained.

If this happens, an unduly sanitized view of policy ensues that generates perverse incentives and increasing disrepute for program evaluation. The idea that any socio-economic measure that becomes a target becomes a bad measure is known as

169

Goodhart's Law. Measuring a system usually disturbs it: the more precise the measurement, and the shorter its timescale, the greater the energy of the disturbance, and the greater the unpredictability of the outcome (Hoskin 1996).

Many examples were offered of the toxicity of Goodhart's Law: fixation on quantified benchmarks that had perverse effects (e.g., steering decisions on the basis of measurements rather than whether it serves a purpose), and turning attention away from either maintaining professional quality or doing real work in order to focus on 'feeding the beast', that is, the administrative machine.

Pointed pressures for ever more rigid accountability (e.g., to provide elaborate defences of choices and effectiveness to political masters or the Office of the Auditor-General) generate a futile attempt to impose a command-and-control system on an increasingly complex and unpredictable world that requires ever more flexibility and capacity to adapt to rapidly changing circumstances if the necessary social learning is to be enabled. This had led to much energy and time being expended to 'find' particular concrete (numerical) evidence to support a choice once made, rather than on implementing the best possible response as effectively and efficiently as possible.

A good deal of quantophrenia is self-imposed by the bureaucracy: not by either politicians or the public. Why? Perhaps it is nothing more than a futile attempt to look scientific in order to minimize the likelihood of blame. A current example (summer 2009) is the Treasury Board Secretariat's 2005 management accountability framework (MAF)(Canada 2005b). It originated in the development of two simple gauges for service delivery:

    (1) are the service deliverers relatively happy with the service process and their part in it? and

    (2) are those receiving the service relatively satisfied with it?

This innocuous pair of questions has, however, grown into a monstrously complex exercise in quantophrenia.

The real challenge is to engage in an evidence-based exploration of the issue (wherever the evidence is and whatever form it takes) without relying exclusively on a numerical representation of reality diverting public servants' attention towards artificial targets and away from doing their job as effectively as possible.

Opinion was divided over the likelihood of things changing relatively soon. Many seemed to feel that this mania would eventually fade away as earlier versions of this obsession have in the past (e.g., the failed financial management attempt that lasted most of a decade, Planning Programming and Budgeting Systems (PPBS) introduced in 1969), but that it might take years. Some felt that—unlike the boomers who are retiring—generation Y public servants would simply leave rather than get bogged down in such nonsense, and thus change would become inevitable relatively soon.

Notwithstanding the difficulties, legitimate pressure of citizens wanting value for money, and politicians demanding to know if the right thing is being done the right way, mean that ways need to be found to improve performance in a world in which 'no one is in charge'. This means putting in place instruments to gain a sense of the overall direction (e.g., east or west) and then allowing much more self-steering of the vehicle (depending on context), but with consequences for those responsible if the vehicle gets and stays 'off the road'.

There is already some 'push back' with respect to the MAF: for example, agents of Parliament creating a 'common front' and refusing to report some things to the centre; managers who have acquired more authority under recent human resources modernization arrangements, presenting clear and timely explanations to defend their judgments rather than subjecting themselves to the quantophrenic exercises that some try to inflict on them.

An alternative to quantophrenia (for an alternative is necessary) might be an 'ergonomic' approach—focus on continuous improvement by providing easily learned and implemented tools that focus attention on possibilities for action aimed at the real problem to be solved (like checklists in operating rooms that have been shown to reduce both avoidable deaths and follow-on complications by 35–40 percent).

Personnel performance review (February 4 & 6, 2009)

A critical review of the performance measurement agreement (PMA) in use has shown that its effectiveness depends on how it is used. A knowledgeable expert in good human resources management could increase the likelihood that ongoing key commitments are realistic and well spelled out, and that bosses and subordinate executives are enabled to have constructive discussions about achievements as well as about 'goodness of fit' between person and context (not simply concluding that someone was a 'poor performer' in general). But this is in no way the general experience with the personnel performance review.

Participants pointed both to the futility of trying to stimulate regular boss-subordinate discussions using the PMA, and to the distortion effects flowing from the way it was used for determining performance pay. Mostly the instrument in use tends to focus on ensuring boxes are checked, mentioning that the discussion has occurred and the required percentage of discussions were held before a specified date—rather than focusing on the substance of the communication to ensure that good results were achieved. The efforts to justify a boss's decision (to peers, higher ups, etc.) is often more important than the PMA scores. The PMA becomes a lengthy distraction from both the organization's real results and the necessary boss-subordinate discussions. Moreover, insistence on hard percentages of over and under performers at the top and bottom of the scale, and consequential pay at risk, regardless of the size of the organization or the nature of demands put upon it, can (and do) lead to 'game playing' and perverse incentives.

S. Culbert (2008) proposes a two-sided, reciprocally accountable, performance *preview* as an alternative—the traditional performance *review*—that he scathingly calls a "mainstream practice that…is negative to corporate performance, an obstacle to straight-talk relationships, and a prime cause of low morale at work" (Culbert 2008: R4).

Generally participants felt that Culbert's assessment of the downsides of performance review echoed (albeit in radical language) some of their concerns, and that the idea of a performance *preview* with its two-way accountability had some merit. In fact, some (but not enough) good and regular boss-subordinate conversations are taking place. What appears to be needed is a combination of hard and soft measures, of prospective and retrospective views, possibly using a rolling timeframe that extends beyond one fiscal year.

It was observed that what underpins effective performance is often the organizational culture with the tone being set 'at the top' being an important influence. The nature of the work and the organization's history are also important. An enriched evidence-based exploration of performance issues before, during and after the fact—wherever the evidence comes from, whatever form it takes, and whenever it is observed—needs to be the focus of effective performance management if it is to enable and support necessary organizational innovativeness, nimbleness and resilience.

Speaking truth to power (February 25 & 27, 2009)

'Speaking truth to power' is a sanctimonious-sounding phrase that is often used today to remind senior public servants of their burden of office—to serve the government of the day (subject to the laws of the land) first and foremost by speaking truth to elected officials. Some see it as an arrogant, value-laden and self-serving stance: public servants assuming that they are in possession of the truth, the only truth, and as such charged with the duty of enlightening the unenlightened. Others avoid reflecting on the nature of the stance, and focus only on the challenges of telling people what they may not wish to hear.

While there is no doubt that politicians and bureaucrats have possibly different legitimate views of the public interest (the former's legitimacy being based on their electoral support, the latter's being based on expertise) and there is a need for these different views to be merged in some way; it is pretentious to assume that the bureaucrat's views represent a superior untainted truth, and should trump the politicians' views which must, by definition, be tainted.

Some view the duty of the bureaucrat as purely informational (making the politician aware of what the bureaucrat feels to be the public interest); others perceive this duty as a duty to influence the politician's view so as to have the bureaucrat's view prevail; still others see the challenge as a duty to ensure the best blurring and blending of these two perceptions of the public interest (when they are in conflict) through an imaginative reframing that enables the crucial aspects of both views to be preserved—in the search for superior solutions likely to serve the citizenry best. In today's world, fraught with mistrust, carrying out that burden of office in the third sense may be particularly difficult. Crippling results may ensue as a consequence.

Trust is a central feature in this process of reconciliation of different views of the public interest. Forceful confrontation may be useful at times, but using imagination may be a much better way to deal with the search for superior solutions through alignment of interests, benevolent concern, competence and integrity. This raises questions about the common perception that what senior bureaucrats require to fulfill their burden of office (i.e., 'speaking truth to power') is primarily courage.

The bureaucrat's burden of office does not entail staring down the elected officials but rather (in virtually all cases) reframing issues so as to make the views of politicians and bureaucrats compatible. It requires a new mindset, some new principles and some new mechanisms. The political-bureaucratic relationship has been aptly compared to the relationship between a wife and her mother-in-law—both loving the husband/son but each defining 'love' in a different way, and having to find some way to rub along together as a result. For the political-bureaucratic relationship, the common interest is the public interest, and constructive ways must be found to manage the natural tension between different views of the public interest for the sake of the citizen.

The transformation of our governance system towards one that is collaborative rather than hierarchical has begun in earnest, so that dealing upwards (with political or bureaucratic bosses) has become an exercise in finding effective ways to create a new frame setting out the public interest: one that is a blending of the separate views (e.g., political and technical), into a 'super'-vision (a more comprehensive vision than the ones held by the different parties) in order to get both parties to see what they cannot see separately on their own.

What role for cities in public governance? (March 11 & 13, 2009)

Canada is a nation of cities. And yet, in the Canadian governance scheme, cities are occluded. Even though most citizens live in cities (50 percent in the four largest cities in Canada; close to 75 percent in the largest 25 cities) and receive most of their daily public sector benefits at this level, this level of governance is starved for resources and prevented from playing its role by very rigid restrictions on the range of powers that it can exercise.

There are feeble signs that this is slowly changing as some Canadian cities acquire city charters. But, *de facto*, the invisibility of cities in the public governance system of the country is a measure of the system's incapacity to take the new realities into account. How much of what is done at the federal and provincial level could be effectively delegated to cities? What would be necessary to bring it forth in key areas? Where should we start? What would it mean for federalism?

A large number of national concerns and issues are defined and lived in an urban context. Cities are not only the engines of economic prosperity, but also where Canadian society and polity thrive. Yet, a silly mental prison would appear to suggest that, because provinces utilized their powers to establish cities, way back then, this entails the servitude of cities as creatures of the provinces in perpetuity.

Reframing our notion of fiscal federalism to include and fully engage the city level is an obvious solution, and some proposals have already been put forward that would allot to cities a portion of the sales tax and of the personal and corporate income taxes (the Winnipeg proposals). But there is also a need to modernize the governance framework of cities in order to give them a broader range of powers defined not by general municipal acts but by stand-alone charters known as city charters. A new set of arrangements inspired by subsidiarity would appear to respond well to the present needs.

Provinces have resisted such moves. The federal government has of late begun to transfer more and more resources not to cities as such but to urban corporations (universities), other entities, and individuals at the local level—doing an end-run around the provinces. It is bound to increase with the infrastructure programs. A sort of hourglass federalism is in the making: the federal government trying to retain as much power as possible, but also to enter into non-formalized arrangements to bolster the authority and resource base of the cities. This is generating staunch opposition from the provinces.

A personal distillation of what we learned

The set of issues discussed in the winter of 2009 pertained to pathologies of governance.

The first two topics (quantophrenia and personnel performance review) pertained to 'flawed instruments' that have had a negative impact and an unfortunate steering effect on public sector governance: the propensity to quantulate, generating in both cases a fixation on very imperfect measurements instead of promoting a better use of judgment.

The latter two topics (speaking truth to power and the occlusion of cities) revealed different forms of schizophrenia resulting in governance failures:

(1) an inability to effectively merge the contributions of the different types of officials (elected officials, bureaucrats, but also citizens as producers of governance) and, as a result, poor collaboration and governance failures; and

(2) an inability to give an adequate role for cities (occlusion and exclusion) in public governance as a result of a reluctance to decentralize the governance of the country—this reluctance is well documented at both the federal and provincial levels, but the denial of a larger role for cities is largely ascribable to the centralized mindset of the provinces.

These two families of pathologies of governance (ascribable to flawed instruments and schizophrenias) are deeply rooted in crippling epistemologies, and in a deep risk aversion and fear of experimentation.

Crippling epistemologies

Gerd Gigerenzer has underlined the important differences between topic-oriented and discipline-oriented research (Gigerenzer 2008: v-vi). The latter sort is rooted in an angle of vision that is quite crippling because it systematically limits what is considered as relevant knowledge, and produces quite a reductive representation of reality. One would have expected practitioners of public management to have a natural tendency to work à la Dewey in a topic-oriented way, and to insist on the guidepost—'In the beginning is the issue'. This unfortunately may not be the case.

Scientism (after having perverted many of the social sciences over the last decades, and having imposed a reductive framework on their activities) would appear, of late, to have succeeded in pervading the field of public administration. As a result, it has imposed an artificial notion of rationality on the operations of the public household: a norm of idealized technical rationality or optimization under constraint whereas a notion of 'ecological rationality' (the co-evolution between heuristics and environments) has long been perceived as much more adequate, and therefore warranted (Ibid., 8; Vickers 1965).

The seduction of quantophrenia and the desire to construct an idealized numerical model of the public household have been the result of the ambition to apply management science and operations research approaches (that have proved useful in handling logistics and well-structured problems of service delivery) to the ill-structured and much fuzzier edifice of public policy. Such an elaborate ethereal (idealized and sanitized) model is put forward as substitute for the messy reality out there (McCormack 2008).

The dual process of sanitized models and of exclusive reliance on quantitative indicators has cartoonized the public administration process. There is nothing inherently wrong about simplifying a complex process in a meaningful way for analysis, or quantifying anything that can meaningfully be quantified. The downside of the quantophrenic modelling cosmology becomes toxic when quantification becomes a camouflage, or verges on becoming a mystification, sweeping unpleasant intractable issues under the carpet while focusing attention on a reductive vision of the policy process. This is not unlike the pretensions of those naive psephologists, claiming to give an adequate account of power politics and political behavior through counting votes. It is not unlike pretending to build meteorology "on elaborate computations of the flutterings of flags" (Andreski 1974: 132).

It would be natural for academics to fall prey to this mode of thinking—they have always been *terribles simplificateurs*! It is less obvious how strata of practitioners have come to be mesmerized by this reductive way of thinking. While the massaging of numbers probably provides much intellectual satisfaction to massagers, and may provide some comfort for operatives who can use them to immunize themselves from blame, the process can easily degenerate into an exercise in the management of a fictional numerical representation of reality, rather than remaining an effort to painfully nudge reality into a preferred direction.

The discussion of the first two topics revealed that crippling epistemologies have taken hold of a significantly powerful portion of the upper echelon of the Canadian public service. In the post-Gomery world, quantophrenia has become a security blanket for public servants under surveillance. Consequently, even if such exercises are regarded as mostly futile and rather costly in terms of resources required, junior executives simply have bowed to the edicts from above, and developed the habit of filling the required forms 'creatively' so as to keep the 'beast' satisfied.

Creatively is the operative word in the last paragraph: we were informed that MAF numbers are not only massaged but manufactured and/or invented.

To the extent that it has remained possible to keep these fictions from interfering too much with the real work, it may be said to represent nothing but an additional element of waste. To the extent that these fictions are becoming a conceptual framework that is inculcated in junior staff and that this mindset triggers meaningful perverse steering effects, the costs of these crippling epistemologies in derailing policies or in generating governance failures can be enormous (Paquet 2009a, b).

Middle-ranked senior managers (EXs) are trying to immunize themselves against the new quantulators. This requires much *fortitudo* (a capacity to take into account context and long term) and some scheming virtuously. In particular, foot dragging is quite popular. As Georges Brassens would put it, "*mourir pour des idées bien sûr, mais de mort lente*"—for often new ideas turn out not to be in good currency for long, and often the same language is used to propose and dispose of the same apparatus.[1]

Risk aversion and fear of experimentation

One of the immense costs of those fictional representations of the social system is that, for survival sake, much of the public service at the mid-ranked EX level may have been driven into a state of suspended animation. Having succeeded in keeping the quantulation machine at bay through sheer creativity, and knowing that good scores may do no more than ensure peace but that bad scores entail retribution, there is a likelihood of an increase in risk aversion and in fear of experimentation—matters that the new metrics are unlikely to pick up and most unlikely to value positively.

Indeed, experimentation seems to be explicitly discouraged if it creates disturbances in any way. It is especially meaningful as a deterrent to innovation when it comes to efforts to accommodate a diversity of preferences or to foster new forms of collaboration. For in such cases, the heavy costs of revamping the system (while ensuring satisfactory MAF results) may be sufficient to kill innovation altogether.

The whole importance of a redefinition of the notion of speaking truth to power as calling for more imagination than courage, and for the need to invent new ways of making the federal apparatus more inclusive and more innovative allows one to fear the full extent of the chilling effect that the quantophreniacs inflict on the system.

On neither of these last two fronts (the politician-bureaucracy and federal-provincial-local interfaces)—despite the central importance of overcoming crippling schizophrenias—was there any appetite for executives to indulge in experimentation. Indeed, it became quite clear that EXs did not feel that these issues were in any way on their radar screen. It is as if the machinery of government was regarded as arrested in time, and their burden of office had nothing to do with the organizational redesign of arrangements that are regarded as dysfunctional. When probed about whose responsibility might it be since it would not appear to be theirs, the unease was palpable, but it remained clear that it was not a responsibility that they felt they could or would shoulder.

In fact the whole notion of collaborative governance—and its core concern about designing new technologies of cooperation (Saveri et al. 2005)—would appear to have ceased to be of concern to EXs. They define the structures as givens, and only envisage their responsibility as operating smoothly within these structures. Organizational design does not appear to fall within their jurisdiction.

In the mid-ranked federal EXs cadre, it would appear that the challenges of design have come to be regarded as the sole prerogative of some higher-ups and as not part of the on-going responsibility of all EXs. Most certainly, the post-Gomery accountability craze and the chilling effect it has generated have done much to reinforce this sort of disengagement.

Conclusion

We are not sure what to conclude about the implications of what would appear to be some evidence of an uncritical accommodation to flawed instruments and quantophrenia, and a lack of engagement on macro-issues calling for organizational redesign by the EXs with whom we conversed. It most certainly revealed a tamed critical sense and an unwillingness to engage in bold speculation about modifications to the social architecture of the federal arrangements.

Whether this sort of diffidence about engaging in anything but the functioning of the machinery of government reveals a long-term steady state, or whether it is the result of the closing of the public service mind by the extraordinary circumstances generated by the Gomery inquiry and the numbing impact of the financial crisis in the winter of 2009, cannot be ascertained at this time.

The degree of *anomie* in the federal public service system has undoubtedly grown in the last while, and it is hardly surprising that, in times of crisis, quantification as a rampart against attacks, and hyper-prudence when dealing with institutional change appear. Battle fatigue may also be playing a part: the dual shocks of the recession and of the political instability of the minority government may have forced EXs to keep their noses close to the grindstone.

The need to perform the governing task, in as flawless a way as one can, may mean that broader philosophical issues may well have been deleted from the priority list. At the same time, the battle fatigue may also result from the impending changing of the guard. So many EXs are going to retire in the next while, that it may be that they are unwilling to question in public many of the assumptions that they have come to question in private. If this is the case, one may regard the observed despondency as a temporary phenomenon.

There are some grounds to believe so. The spirit of the new cohort is already making itself known, and it would appear to be more subversive if one is to believe some of the mottos they brandish—like "scheming virtuously" (Charney and Mangulabnan 2008).

Basic documentation for each session

Quantophrenia

G. Paquet 2009. "Quantophrenia." www.optimumonline.ca, 39: 1: 14–27.

Performance Review

S. A. Culbert 2008. "Get Rid of the Performance Review!" *The Wall Street Journal*, R4, October 20.

Speaking Truth to Power

R. Hubbard 2009. "Speaking Truth to Power." *Canadian Government Executive*, 15: 1: 10–11.
C. Wilson 2007. "Facilitating Contingent Collaboration." www.optimumonline.ca, 37: 1: 1–8.

What role for cities in public governance?

M. Harcourt 2006. *From Restless Communities to Resilient Places*. Final Report of the External Advisory Committee on Cities and Communities, Ottawa.

The unwisdom of cats—the last eight sessions

In a cat's eye, all belong to cats.

—English proverb

For this last series, we focused on four difficult topics that go to the core of public administration in Canada: the multi-dimensional principal-agent problem in public management, and the need to develop truly collaborative governance.

A syncretic view of each topic

This section provides a brief introductory statement on each topic, and a very sketchy summary view of the general substance of the conversations that followed.

The politico-bureaucratic interface (October 7 & 9, 2009)

Both politicians and bureaucrats are legitimate officials: the former draw their legitimacy from elections as representative of the citizens, and the latter from competitions that have confirmed their expertise and professionalism for particular sets of responsibilities. Both groups may have views about the public good and the public interest that may be at variance. However, what is not always as clear as it should be is whether the view of politicians, of bureaucrats, or a blend of both ought to prevail, and how one ought to arrive at the answer to this question.

Some brandish the Westminster philosophy to remind everyone that, in the final analysis, the politicians should have the ultimate say, and that bureaucrats should serve them loyally. Others view the public service as the 'Platonic guardians' of the public interest and of the Constitution against the claims of responsible government, and as echoing a truer version of the public interest than the politicians. Indeed it is said by some that the loyalty of the public servant to government and minister is secondary to the loyalty to the institution of the public service. A third group argues that these polar-opposite positions are too absolute, and that mechanisms have to be found to ensure that workable and effective collaboration materializes between both groups.

In a world where the level of mutual understanding and trust on both sides appears to have declined significantly in the recent past (Paquet and Pigeon 2000; Savoie 2003; Paquet 2010), it has been said that the 'traditional' bargain between politicians and bureaucrats (non-partisanship, loyalty, impartiality, discretion and professionalism provided by bureaucrats in exchange for anonymity and security of tenure) has been broken. The consequence is that the interface must be redefined: whether it should be as a result of revisited conventions or of rewritten legislation is not clear. What is not always clear either is how bureaucrats are to ensure a right balance between responsiveness and loyalty on the one hand, and independence and impartiality on the other.

Participants pointed to many important factors that have contributed to the erosion of the traditional bargain. Some of these factors are externally generated—such as the greater complexity of the issues and the greater possibility of honest differences of opinions arrived at on the basis of mountains of information of varying credibility, and citizens demanding more say in policy making. Others are the result of internal factors—such as the more limited face-to-face interaction between politicians and bureaucrats as well as a decline in basic civility in their encounters. Still others seem to be constraints self-imposed to varying degrees—such as the fast-paced 'churn' in senior ranks that has reduced the reservoirs of deep technical expertise available in strategic positions (making creativity more difficult), the loss of some capacity to think critically, and constrained budgets (e.g., limiting travel, consultation and resources for educating publics) that impede the enriched relational connections necessary for effective exchanges between politicians, bureaucrats and the citizenry.

These factors are over and above the understandable deep mistrust of the public servants in place by a party that takes power after many years in opposition, and the pressure of permanent campaigning by minority governments: this is pushing ministers to 'do something quickly', so that if the public service has nothing to offer immediately, the minister has to improvise and find advice wherever he can.

In the United Kingdom, two robustly enforced initiatives were announced recently—one reminding ministers to listen carefully to the advice of their public servants, and another underscoring the importance of public servants providing complete, accurate and timely information to ministers, Parliament and the public. While such a system-wide and public restatement of basic principles has not happened in Canada, it was felt that there might be a need for it.

In terms of repairs, some pointed to the need for better use of 'competitive intelligence' (as the private sector organizations do), better sifting of information in terms of reliability and credibility, distilling the main points of view emerging from a confusing plethora of voices more effectively, and developing improved ways to engage groups across the country and to network with them. There was also some mention of the importance of building new loci for dialogue if the necessary trust is to be rebuilt.

The federal public service as a nexus of moral contracts (October 21 & 23, 2009)

The first sessions dealt with the major interface between politicians and bureaucrats. The second ones dealt with a more complex territory: the broader texture of the Canadian federal public service as a nexus of a variety of moral contracts of which the political-bureaucratic bargain is only one.

The world of governance has become more complex, the environment more turbulent and—given the wide distribution of information, power and resources among many persons and groups—no one can be said to be fully and solely 'in charge'. This means that all (including the citizens) must maintain rapport and interactions with many parties in the process of governing.

This entails the involvement of most officials in multiple moral contracts, and therefore the need to honour multiple loyalties. The collaborative governance process that has emerged (including more actors, more consultation and negotiation, more horizontal and transversal partnerships, etc.) has transmogrified public administration. Yet, many officials are in denial *vis-à-vis* the fact that top-down 'Big G' government is being replaced by 'small g' bottom-up governance. This is a hard sell even though the verdict of one of the leading thinkers about public administration, H. G. Frederickson, would appear eminently clear: "What happened to public administration? Governance, governance everywhere" (Frederickson 2005).

Four moral contracts were presented as underpinning the corporate culture of the Canadian federal public service: moral contract I: (citizens)–(bureaucracy); moral contract II: (upper bureaucrats)–(other public servants); moral contract III: (citizens and bureaucrats at all levels)–(politicians); and IV: the moral contract about the style of communication (based on tact and civility) that ought to prevail among all parties. The nature of these contracts as they stand now (burdened by confrontation, distrust, *anomie*, and incivility) seems to fit poorly with the governance requirements of the day.

What seems to be needed in the public service is **a new philosophy of governance**: that fuels a continuous use of a sort of program review lens—recognizing the existence and importance of multiple loyalties, of wicked problems, and of the new centrality of social learning, and **a new philosophy of stewardship**: recognizing the importance of new competencies and the need for a refurbished human resource management system (to select, evaluate and promote people differently), for more mentoring and coaching and for refurbished incentive reward systems.

Participants chose to focus their attention on two moral contracts as most urgently needing to be revisited:

- moral contract I (between citizens and the bureaucracy); and
- moral contract II (between the top of the bureaucracy and other public servants).

The central concern was best illustrated by participants underlining a sort of schizophrenia in the federal public service in these sessions, saying for example, the people in the regions think they work for Canadians, and the people in Ottawa think they work for the minister.

With respect to the first moral contract, the vertical structure and top-down mentality of the state apparatus make the kind of horizontal collaboration amongst stakeholders needed today significantly harder than it ought to be. As an example, the current strategic reviews were described as focussing not on serving Canadians better but rather on matters of financial stringency.

With respect to the second moral contract, the self-censorship of risk-averse upper bureaucrats and the pressure from above to massage results in order to reduce controversy (making reported results odourless and colourless and therefore stunting social learning) were seen as crucial sources of the problem.

Two mechanisms (currently under revision) were noted as potentially helpful despite their acknowledged limitations. An improved code of values and ethics could in principle improve the citizen-bureaucracy moral contract, while an improved management accountability framework (MAF) could help link the top of the bureaucracy to the rest of the public service.

Taking the long run seriously and taking time to communicate better were seen as crucial, but also as under-appreciated challenges. Little time is made available for enabling upper bureaucrats to talk to their senior staff (e.g., DMs and assistant deputy ministers (ADMs)). It is often only at glitzy public events that some ADMs learned of the expectations of their own DMs. Participants put a lot of emphasis on communication (broadly defined) to overcome the failures within the public service: this was seen as offering the most promising tool for improved collaborative governance.

The suggestion was made that more attention should be focused on getting people to feel so engaged that they would naturally go beyond the call of duty—and ensuring that this engagement is evaluated (*quantophrénie oblige!*) for only if it gets measured (however badly) will attention be paid to it. Recent public service surveys suggest that employee engagement might be slipping, and that engagement intensity in federal crown corporations would appear to exceed that of the core public service at aggregate levels. This might suggest a general direction to generate more engagement: de-concentration—an effective effort to counter the organizational diseconomies of scale and to acknowledge that issue domains are probably the best loci of engagement.

From leadership to stewardship (November 18 & 20, 2009)

This third topic was considered by all participants to be the most difficult one to tackle for it suggests that nothing less than a change of paradigm is required to ensure effective collaborative governance: the shift from 'command and control' to an 'organic/ on-going direction-finding process', the shift from leadership to stewardship.

We see the usual meaning of 'leadership' as problematic in a world where nobody is in charge, and where shared values are a myth. It reeks of hierarchy, and has a mystical garb. Exceptional individuals exist, of course, who inspire colleagues and are truly charismatic leaders, but they are the exception rather than the rule. In most cases, the governance regime ensures 'stewardship'. The least inadequate metaphor is that of an 'organic automatic pilot': an ensemble of mechanisms, always in evolution and emergence, capable of keeping the organization on the track, that is, continually adapting to the context in its social learning and direction-finding process.

One may reasonably reflect:

(1)   on the emergence of such regimes,
(2)   on how they gain support and legitimacy, and
(3)   on how stewardship ensures effective coordination.

The rise and fall of Stéphane Dion is a case that can be fruitfully analyzed through that lens (Paquet 2008f).

If one had to stylize the stewardship process through social learning in a simple sequential way, one might make use of the template used by practitioners (Parr et al. 2002).

Stage A begins with some perceived gap between current reality and some desirable outcome as a trigger to direct attention toward initiating action. There is recognition that action is required (either individually or collectively) and then an exploration of action possibilities.

Stage B is the concurrent search for the mobilization of required partners, and the nurturing of the necessary collaboration. These dual and interactive sub-processes unfold in two steps:

(1) the correct framing of critical issues and opportunities, the focusing of attention on what needs to be done, and the creation of platforms for people to work together, and

(2) the communication of key information likely to inspire, rally and motivate a broader set of people to take part in the diverse networks, and the development of new relationships capable of generating tangible results and thereby of changing mindsets, and encouraging creative thinking.

Stage C has to do with efforts to sustain change through creating and renewing institutions, and re-igniting the process by focusing again on new challenges and opportunities. This entails much conceptual refurbishment, and efforts to agitate and rekindle the social learning process through reframing the very notion of what is possible.

What is required is a capacity for an organization to learn, that is, to reflect on its own experience, to make sense of it, and to retool, restructure, and even to reframe the basic questions facing the organization in order to generate effective ways to grapple with the issues of concern.

These requirements have been spelled out by practitioners of reflexive governance: knowledge integration and learning by doing; capacity for long-run anticipation of systemic effects; adaptivity of strategies and institutions; iterative experimental and participatory definition of broad directions; and interactive strategy development (Voß et al. 2006). In order for dynamic adaptation to unfold, stewardship requires competencies that need to be nudged into existence, not only by leveraging the existing forces of self-organization, but also by harnessing them to a degree.

The required competencies can be divided into five categories (Michael 1993; Hughes and Weiss 2007; Paquet 2009a: chapter 5):

    (1) contextual (that is, embracing uncertainty and error, building bridges, reframing, improvising, adapting, overcoming (in the manner of Clint Eastwood's Heartbreak Ridge));

    (2) interpersonal (that is, consulting, negotiating, deliberating, resolving conflicts, facilitating, brokering, preceptoring, educating, animating, changing roles);

    (3) enacting (that is, enabling, empowering, responding, being creative);

    (4) paying attention to systems values (that is, the ethics of inter-connectiveness and interdependence, removing obstacles, freeing others to act better);

    (5) staying the course while rocking the boat (that is, imagining, experimenting, feeling the responsibility to explore, putting the emphasis on sins of omission, learning by prototyping).

It is hardly surprising that such a complex transformational process proved so difficult to discuss. The propensity to presume that there must be someone in charge is culturally prevalent, and coming to terms with the fact that the context is powerful, that self-organization is very potent, and that, at best, one can nudge things a little through '*bricolage*' and tinkering is not in good currency in a world where capturing and wielding power is the name of the game.

The participants granted that power, resources and information were widely distributed, and that the new game might resemble a game of "GO" much more than the old chess game. Nevertheless, there was a good deal of effort to avoid confronting the stewardship challenge by suggesting some elasticity for the notion of 'leadership' (relational leadership, shared leadership) rather than replacing the term with a different one that signaled the discontinuity clearly. The term 'leadership' would appear to serve as a security blanket.

Notwithstanding this, the group realized that what was involved was a dramatic cultural change. They pointed out that it would be hard to bring about this kind of change in a top down system in which everything is entrenched. The current ethos of control and accountability promotes a climate of fear rather than an incentive to achieve results (Thomas 2009a). This kind of change to the incentive reward systems would require some probing of the reasons why people cooperate and of the forces at work to maintain cooperation (D. W. Brown 1995).

Many examples were given of officials suffering from acute cognitive dissonance with respect to the profound nature of the cultural change involved, and indulging in a good deal of dynamic conservatism, that is, preserving their view of the world they know at all costs despite evidence that the world is changing. The most promising road to promote the development of this new view of the world appeared to participants to be likely to come through executive development, enabling public servants to better appreciate what is required to be effective in today's world. The role of the Canada School of Public Service (that used to be focused on this kind of reframing in the 1990s and has changed since that time) may need to be revisited.

Deputy minister: then, now and future
(November 3 & 5, 2009)

From earlier sessions, a number of considerations emerged:

(1) the political-bureaucratic interface operates less smoothly than before;

(2) there is a new complexity of the moral contracts between citizen and bureaucrats, and between uppermost bureaucrats and the others;

(3) the different notions of 'public interest' often held by elected officials and experts have flared up of late;

(4) the lack of awareness of the foundational importance of democratic values by most public servants, and their growing loyalty to profession (e.g., scientist, regulator, etc.) have become important forces that have fractured the public service further; and

(5) there has been a silent very slow drift from leadership to stewardship, even though much denial about it subsists.

The gradual drift in loyalty towards 'profession' (or the tribe) in the case of deputy ministers is documented in the book *Profession: Public Servant* (Hubbard 2009) that describes the experiences of one DM through three periods: before PS2000, during a transition period (late 80s to the turn of the 21st century), and in the current period.

In the heyday of the mandarins (in the decades around the middle of the 20th century), a few senior federal officials (elected and unelected—sometimes interchangeably) were able to collaborate to transform the country (Granatstein 1998). These intelligent generalists were able to achieve the results they desired, informally and organically.

The extraordinary expansion of the federal public service rendered 'informal coordination' unworkable. Scientific management became the rage and was imposed in a top down, centralized way to try to 'control' the actions of the burgeoning public service. This era led to some experience of the limits of central control, and saw the beginning of the worldwide drift from 'Big G' government to 'small g' governance: 'what was needed' was no longer imposed by a few people with hierarchical power.

Starting in the late 1980s, waves of reform led by the senior bureaucracy tried to bring about the necessary 'cultural change' in the federal public service, but with mixed success. The drivers of change in public management came from external developments (e.g., political, economic, social and technological) pressuring governments everywhere to adapt and adjust (OECD 2005), but the resulting changes in the role of the state represented an attack on "the psychological comfort of the powerful" (O'Toole 1995–96: 238). Faced with this kind of profound change, senior officials have been led to gradually redefine the balance between responsiveness and loyalty on the one hand, and independence and impartiality on the other. The balancing of the burden of the DM role (in which democratic values are squarely front and centre) with personal, institutional and group interests and inclinations seems to have become more problematic.

Participants acknowledged that, because of a general worldwide increase in moral relativism, groups of public servants do not accept any longer that they have to loyally implement legal government decisions if *they* feel the decisions are 'not in the public interest' as defined by them. Professionalization and a guild-like mentality are becoming important for all sorts of groups, be they DMs or regulators: an emphasis on the survival and welfare of the group (i.e., the 'tribe') trumping even democratic values at times. This is an echo of the same general phenomenon in Canadian society at large.

Many participants pointed to a lack of clarity in the definition of the role of DM (e.g., the relative emphasis that ought to be placed on helping the minister, engaging the 'departmental team', and dealing with clients and stakeholders).

A need was felt to re-emphasize the importance of selecting the right people with the right skills (e.g., change management) with their performance assessed to a greater degree on the basis of what their subordinates think (e.g., an obligatory 360° performance review). Better talent management is crucial (e.g., succession planning and differentiating DM jobs demanding policy skills versus those where managing is essential).

The importance of DMs being able to work horizontally (e.g., in portfolios) in ways that required collaboration rather than control was underscored. They also need to have the tools and skills to be able to do so effectively. There might be real advantages in bringing in people from other jurisdictions or other sectors—persons who, by definition, would have a different perspective and fresh ideas.

Conclusion

Whether or not a new culture can be cobbled together that will re-invent the fabric of public governance as a complex adaptive system is unclear. In a world of hyper-turbulence, social triage occurs—an effort to allocate and protect scarce resources. This triage triggers a partitioning into social enclaves (where members attempt to create a shared identity to protect adaptive capacities) and social vortices (low capacity segments lacking the necessary resources to survive and incapable of avoiding implosion and encapsulation) (McCann and Selsky 1984).

There are signs of an enclave movement and of strategies designed to protect professional capacities. It is not clear that these enclaves will serve the public good rather than guild interests. At the same time, those from within who might be most able to sabotage this dynamic which, if left unfettered, is likely to generate harm find themselves hesitant and indecisive, because entering the fray entails a change of paradigm.

Despite numerous attempts at reform of the Canadian federal public service, there would appear to be no workable solutions being proposed. It may be because of the limits to integrative strategies and collaborative governance—regarded as too expansive, too threatening, and blocked by the inability of members to cooperate. But it may also be because of deeper cultural and psychological reasons or ideological mental prisons that are preventing analysts from seeing the meaningful patterns that lie within the mess of evolving dots on the screen.

Since we are persuaded that collaborative governance is not unworkable, the only way out of this quandary is to launch an attack on these cultural, psychological and ideological blinders—the slaughtering of some sacred cows (Paquet 2009b).

Basic documentation for each session

The politico-bureaucratic interface

Paul G. Thomas 2008. "Political-administrative interface in Canada's Public Sector." www.optimumonline.ca, 38: 2: May: 21–29.

Federal public service: a new covenant

Gilles Paquet 2009. "Gouvernance publique: (G → g) ∩ (G₁ → G₂)." www.optimumonline.ca, 39: 4: 17–34.
Gilles Paquet 2009. "An Agenda for Change in the Federal Public Service." In G. Paquet. *Scheming Virtuously: The Road to Collaborative Governance*. Ottawa: Invenire Books, chapter 8.

Stewardship versus Leadership

Gilles Paquet 2008. "Stéphane Dion: Source ou symptôme du malaise?" *Policy Options*, May: 35–40.
Gilles Paquet 2009. "Stewardship versus leadership." In G. Paquet, *Scheming Virtuously: The Road to Collaborative Governance*. Ottawa: Invenire Books, chapter 5.

Deputy minister: then, now and future

Ruth Hubbard 2009. *Profession: Public Servant*. Ottawa: Invenire Books.

General conclusion

There would be little sense in conducting conversations with some one hundred executives, and having reported carefully and clinically about them, not to attempt to provide some provisional conclusions of a more general nature about the situation they appear to reveal. This must be done with great care so as not to generalize unduly from a small sample. At the same time, it would be unconscionable not to draw attention to features that would appear to characterize the present state of mind of the federal public service.

Our general diagnosis may generate ire and contestation: a predictably irrational defence of a dysfunctional system by many who are in denial when it comes to the pathologies of their life world. Panglossian defenders of the federal public administration as flawless are not friends of federal public service but its worst enemies. Their denials of flagrant problems can only lead to further deterioration, and maybe ultimately, to the disappearance of an institution that has served Canadians well but is at present in distress.

Our diagnosis is presented in five steps.

First, it is clear that the context faced by the Canadian federal public service has become immensely more complex over the last decades. This globalized and pluralistic world has experienced accelerated change and posed wicked problems to decision makers as it became ever clearer that nobody was fully in charge, that the public domain was shrinking, and that the false impression of a secure Gaussian view of the world (with tamed variance) had to be replaced by one that is immensely more chaotic. Clearly a significant portion of the difficulties experienced by Canadian public governance is ascribable to this transformation of the environment—a matter beyond its control but one that it has had to confront and that was not handled as well as could have been expected (Taleb 2007).

Second, it is also clear that one of the main reasons why good governance has not been achieved—effective coordination when resources, power and resources are widely distributed and nobody from the private, public or social sectors is fully in charge—is the hysteresis of the Canadian system: its memory, its path-dependence, its baggage of mental prisons carried over from another era.

This antiquated system of beliefs (the dogma that someone must be in charge, the necessity of centralization, state centricity as a must, the belief in mythical Canadian values, the fixation on ethereal egalitarianism, etc.) has remained vibrant in the Canadian public service, and the executives have come to see their role as guardians of those mythical values. The pursuit and defence of these non-negotiable beliefs has blinded the Canadian public service to the challenges of the new realities and to the imperatives these challenges impose.

Third, this has had a dramatic impact upon the state of mind of the Canadian public service. The executives have been torn between the old fundamentalism and the new relativism, the mental prisons of the past and the new imperatives, the former dominance of the public domain and its recent decline. These tensions have traumatized the state and its officers. Old techniques have failed, public confidence has declined, deference has disappeared, and learned helplessness has invaded the world of public administration. This has led to latent fear, denials, risk aversion and fear of experimentation. Neuroses have surfaced, and fictions have been invented to tame the chaotic world.

Fourth, this state of mind has translated into a multitude of bad habits. The seeming unimportance of cognitive dissonance and political correctness has led to an erosion of critical thinking and to the celebration of crippling epistemologies. More perverse bad habits have followed: rewarding failure, punishing success, failing to confront, and disloyalty. Various forms of organizational violence have ensued.

Fifth, this could only entail growing systemic failures and pathologies of governance: a growing dynamic conservatism, a decline in the capacity to transform and to learn, deepening symptoms of neuroses, and consequent efforts to rationalize one's own incapacities and inertia, etc.

Summarizing these points starkly in closing may generate a sense of inexorability and hopelessness. This is not our goal. The key objective is to make these forces visible, to question the mindset of denial, and to suggest that one must face the fact that the Canadian federal public service is facing critical times.

The various toxic forces mentioned above have strained all the crucial interfaces in the public administration process (among the citizens, the politicians, the bureaucrats, the different sectors, and the different levels of government). Collaborative governance may be the new categorical imperative but the Canadian federal public administration would appear to be ill-prepared for its role as *animateur*—even though it is a very crucial role.

It is not unfair to say that our broad brush conversations with executives did not provide an opportunity to analyze all the pathologies hinted at in depth. For this reason we have felt that it might be useful to look a bit more carefully into the dynamics of harm generated by some of these pathologies. The sample of issues that follow, analyzed with a bit more care (quantophrenia, disloyalty, the neurotic state, and the fiscal imbalance debate to name a few), clearly reveal that the concerns raised by our conversations with federal government executives are warranted. The more careful analyses of these phenomena ought to provide some preliminary insight into possible ways in which some of these pathologies may be countered.

Endnote

[1] It would appear that the spirit of 'streamlining' can be used to explain both the creation and the dismantling of the Canada Public Service Agency. December 12, 2003: "As part of the streamlining of the Treasury Board Secretariat, a new Public Service Human Resource Management Agency of Canada will be established." (http://epe.lac-bac.gc.ca/100/205/301/

prime_minister-ef/paul_martin/05-10-06/www.pm.gc.ca/eng/news. asp@id=2). February 6, 2009: "Prime Minister Stephen Harper today announced changes to streamline and improve the management of human resources in the Public Service of Canada." (http://pm.gc.ca/eng/ media.asp?category=1&id=2413).

CHAPTER 4

Quantophrenia

> *Not everything that counts, can be counted, and not everything*
> *that can be counted, counts.*
>
> —Albert Einstein

Introduction

This chapter addresses some concerns raised by Pitirim Sorokin some 50 years ago (Sorokin 1956). At the time, Sorokin was somewhat distraught by social sciences falling prey to all sorts of manias and foibles—mindless application of methods in use in experimental sciences to issues in social sciences, sterile formalization, useless number-crunching, and the like—that were in danger of shifting socio-economic inquiries away from the purposes that had given rise to social sciences to begin with (to respond to *une fringale de sens*).

Sorokin's book attacked a variety of pathologies, but spent two chapters on what he called *quantophrenia*.

It should be clear that Sorokin's attacks were not directed at quantification *per se*. Quantitative methods have been used from time immemorial as a powerful instrument of reasoning. The problem arises when the use of such tools becomes the basis of a *cult* roughly captured by the motto that 'if it cannot be measured, it does not exist'. Such a cult distorts the appreciation we have of socio-economic phenomena, and this mental prison acts as blinders that have toxic and unintended consequences for public policies when they are shaped by an apparatus constrained in this way.

Sorokin's *mise en garde* has generated some prudence in the use of quantitative methods in most social sciences, as experience revealed the deleterious nature of this cult, and as it has become clear, over time, that crippling epistemologies generate governance failures (Paquet 2009b).

Public management (and management in general) has resisted this sort of contamination for a long time, but it has been infected by numerology in recent decades. Reading Chester Barnard (1938), Herbert Simon (1947) or Geoffrey Vickers (1965), one might not have anticipated that management studies would become obsessed by quantification as a result of the viral influence of operations research. But it has happened.

In this chapter, we only wish to reiterate the Sorokin message that some prudence is *de rigueur* when it comes to quantification in public governance.

Crippling epistemologies and policy pseudo-sciences

Quite sensibly, Sorokin ascribes the propensity to "quantulate" to some fundamental deficiencies at the philosophical and epistemological levels.

It all began with the quasi-theological fundamentalism echoed by words like 'objectivity' or 'truth' when they began to serve as references in the mushy world of public administration. Under the influence of Emile Durkheim and others, it was argued that "*les faits sociaux sont des choses*" and that one should generalize the application to them of the sort of 'scientistic' methods in use in the physical sciences.

This has percolated, after quite a lag, into the promises of the so-called 'policy sciences', erected on the model of management science. Those policy sciences are based on the presumption that public, private and social organizations are directed by omniscient leaders who have a good understanding of their environment, of the future trends in that environment if nothing were done to modify it, of the inexorable rules of the game they have to put up with, and a clear view of the goals pursued by their own organization.

Policy sciences were and are starkly 'Newtonian'. They postulate a deterministic, well-behaved world, where causality is simple because the whole is the sum of the parts. Given the well-defined goals of the organization, and the more or less placid environment, the challenge is purported to be the design of control mechanisms likely to get the organization to where it wants to be. Many issues were and still are tractable with this approach, but most are not.

In the last few decades, the pace of change has accelerated, and the issues have grown more complex. Private, public and social organizations have been confronted more and more with 'wicked' problems (Paquet 1999a: chapter 2). In this *quantum* sort of world, there is no objective reality, the uncertainty principle looms large, events are at best probable, and the whole is a network of synergies and interactions among the different parts of the system that is quite different from the sum of the parts (Becker 1991). To deal with these wicked problems, a new way of thinking about governing is required.

In this quantum world, "nobody is fully in charge" (Cleveland 2002). This has forced the governing system to evolve. It has been transformed (through a number of rounds of adaptation over the years) so as to accommodate the presence of multiple stakeholders, to respond to a plurality of groups in possession of part of the resources, the power and the information, and to provide the requisite flexibility and suppleness of action. The ultimate result of these changes is a multi-stakeholder governance system, built on unreliable control mechanisms, in pursuit of ill-defined goals, in a universe that is chronically in a state of flux.

When dealing with such a universe in a reasonable and practical way, the 'scientistic' apparatus proves pretentious and inadequate, and Fukuyama could recently refer to "the black hole of public administration" without generating much outrage (Fukuyama 2004).

In this world of 'small g'-network-governance (that has replaced the world of top-down 'Big G'-government), labels that apply equally well to organizations in the private, public and civic sectors, organizations govern themselves by becoming capable of learning both new goals and new means as they proceed. This can only be done through tapping the knowledge and information of all the citizens, and by ensuring the collaboration of members of the organization that have a relevant portion of the resources, power or information, and by allowing them to invent ways out of the predicaments that they are in (Sullivan and Skelcher 2002; McCarthy et al. 2004; Parker and Gallagher 2007; Bradwell and Reeves 2008).

Such a governance system deprives so-called leaders of any illusion that they have a monopoly on the governing of the organization. For the organization to learn fast, everyone must take part in the conversation, and bring forward each bit of knowledge and wisdom that he or she has that may have a bearing on the issue (Paquet 1999a, 2005b). We are in a world of governing by experimenting and prototyping, of "governing by learning" (Michael 1993).

This process of social learning requires new governance structures (more modular, network-like, making use of integrated, informal moral contracts). Yet this is only one half of the learning process. The other half is the work of stewardship. Instead of building on the assumption that the leader is omniscient and guides autocratically top-down, the new distributed governance process builds on critical dialogue with the stakeholders, ensuring that everyone learns about the nature of the problem, and about the consequences of various possible alternative initiatives (Paquet 2008d, 2009a: chapter 5).

The citizenry learns in this manner to limit unreasonable demands; managers and administrators learn to listen and consult; other stakeholders learn enough about one another's views and interests to gauge the range of compromise solutions that are likely to prove acceptable and workable. The distributed governance process, predicated on social learning, builds on the answers to four questions posed to all stakeholders: is it technically feasible? is it socially acceptable? is it too destabilizing politically? Can it be implemented? (Friedmann and Abonyi 1976; C. A. Taylor 1997).

This is the world of public policy in which the essential fuzziness of goals and targets and the essential uncertainty of means-ends relationships force the adoption of the social learning mode, a strategy of learning by doing, of learning by monitoring.

Whatever may be done to improve this process of learning must therefore be applauded—

(1) a more outcome-oriented focus of the conversation;
(2) a more timely and performance-related reporting/ monitoring processes; and
(3) shorter learning loops

—all for a more effective social learning process.

It is not a matter of objectivity, truth, or testing of hypotheses, but a matter of experimenting, designing mechanisms, and disclosing and designing new worlds (Spinosa et al. 1997; Paquet 2009a, b; Hubbard and Paquet 2009).

Words of caution about the quantophrenic cosmology

The capacity to transform is a measure of the organizational learning: the speed with which the public policy process is able to ensure the requisite restructuring (changing the set of roles and responsibilities of the actors in the process), retooling (changing the technology and tools used), and reframing (changing the view held by members about the process, its purposes, environment and future) in order to enhance its triple-E performance: effectiveness (doing the right thing), efficiency (doing it right), and economy (doing it spartanly), while carefully maintaining due process and fairness, not only in the outcomes, but also in the very process through which these outcomes are generated (Schön 1971).

One may usefully stylize the public policy process as a funnel—from a broad taking into account of the socio-technical environment to be regulated, through the mediating lenses of ideology, culture, institutions and the structure of power, towards program definition, and service delivery.

The new 'quantophrenic cosmology' has tended to simplify this very complex public policy process somewhat and to approach it in a rather parsimonious way: by truncating the policy process and zeroing in on the sub-process of delivery of services, and by focusing, within the service delivery segment, mainly on the way to clarify goals and to sharpen reporting/monitoring indicators to increase, through clarity and transparency, the efficiency of the delivery process.

This approach has undoubtedly proved useful in some cases at the service delivery end of the public policy funnel; for example, measuring how much time it takes to have cheques mailed and delivered, and improving this sub-process as a result. It is less clear what this clarification/reporting improvement may or does contribute at the other end of the funnel, that is, for environment scanning/policy formation.

However, the prophets of the new cosmology suggest that the clarification/reporting improvements hold the key to much more than the simple efficiency of service delivery. We are told that this quantification will soon guide the conduct of the different programs, and determine the appropriateness of the allocation of roles and relationships in programs. We are even promised that through an aggregation of these local and partial measures (as building blocks) soon will emerge macro-machines, generating indicators of performance for whole departments, and even for whole provincial or federal governments. Indeed, there are already prototypes of such mega-models and mega-measures being developed in the bowels of the Treasury Board Secretariat. The tail we are told will soon wag the dog.

This ambitious new cosmology runs into difficulties: one danger, one seduction, and one quagmire.

The danger of an overly sanitized stylization of the public policy process

The new cosmology has boldly sanitized the public policy process. The goals are presumed to be known and precisely measurable, the means-ends relationships clear, and the business plans transparent. This stylization brushes aside many of the complexities of the multi-stakeholder power game that underpins much of public policy formation. It flies in the face not only of the day-to-day experience of any Ottawa watcher, but even of the stylization of the public policy process that is presented to would-be policy-makers by the official Canada School of Public Service (Smith and Taylor 1996).

The new cosmology excises political haggling and the socio-technical milieu from the world of public management. This view of the public policy process tends to suggest:

- the separability of the different phases of the policy process: policy formation, program design, and delivery mechanism;
- the sacred nature of the Westminster model of government, and the consequent assumption that accountability to the minister must remain untouched as the process is amended; and
- the presumption that explicit detailed contracts are sufficient to ensure that the policy intended by the senior executives (political and bureaucratic) will be carried out.

All this represents an idealized world.

When it is suggested that what may be gathered from examining the service delivery portion of the policy funnel carries results that may be regarded as capable of being generalized to the whole policy funnel, one may reasonably claim that it is a *non sequitur*. The production of useful but limited observations merrily blended into broader aggregates may not constitute meaningful syncretic measures of the performance of the whole cluster of policy arrangements.

The seduction of quantophrenia

The greatest appeal of the new 'quantophrenic cosmology' is that it is a 'numerical' model. Goals, targets, outcomes and results are quantifiable, and performance indicators are to be computed to ensure that what has been promised can be compared to what has been realized. This is meant to bolster the legitimacy and credibility of the stylized policy process.

This magic transmogrifies reality into a numerical representation, and performance into a set of *clignotants*. This fixation gives a false impression of certainty, and unduly simplifies a notion of performance that is essentially fuzzy. In fact, performance in public policy making is an essentially contested concept.

W. B. Gallie has characterized a whole range of concepts as "essentially contested concepts...the proper use of which inevitably involves endless disputes about their proper uses on the part of the users" (Gallie 1964: 158) and he has identified five conditions for a concept to be essentially contested. He describes it this way:

(1) appraisive, in the sense that it accredits some kind of valued achievement;

(2) this achievement must be complex in character, and its worth attributed to it as a whole; but

(3) variously describable in its parts, with the possibility of various components being assigned more or less importance; and

(4) open in character to the extent that it admits to considerable modification in the light of changing circumstances;

(5) moreover, to qualify as an essentially contested concept, each party must recognize that its own use of the concept

is contested by other parties, and that the concept can be used both aggressively and defensively (Ibid., 161).

A good example of such a concept might be "championship" in a sport like figure skating, which can be judged in a number of different ways, with attention being paid differentially to method, strategy, style, etc.

While the massaging of numbers probably provides much intellectual satisfaction to massagers, the process easily degenerates into an exercise in the management of a numerical representation of reality, rather than the governance of reality.

Again, it must be restated that there is nothing inherently wrong about quantifying anything that can meaningfully be quantified. The downside of the 'quantophrenic cosmology' is underlined when quantification becomes a camouflage, or verges on being a mystification, because it is used for sweeping unpleasant issues under the carpet, while focusing attention on a reductive vision of the policy process. This is not unlike the pretenses of those naive psephologists claiming to give an adequate account of politics and political behavior through counting votes, or pretending to build meteorology "on elaborate computations of the flutterings of flags" (Andreski 1974: 132).

The quagmire of performance evaluation

This sacralization of numerology generates a real danger that such an 'essentially contested world' might generate whimsical measurements and perverse adjustments to them. Scoreboards and social indicators of performance become the dimensions steering the game; agents adjust their behavior accordingly. And since whatever sets of indicators are chosen are bound to be partial and imperfect, social learning may be misguided, slowed down, or even derailed.

These numerical indicators are bound to attract the attention of auditors, and can steer organizations in unproductive ways, whatever their fragility. This has been observed most dramatically in the world of 'phynance' (so spelled by Alfred Jarry so as to remind all of its shamanic quality), where failing to meet quarterly sales or profit forecasts can generate disastrous results whatever the soundness of the organization from an economic point of view.

It is therefore crucially important not to fall prey to 'indicators-for-the-sake-of-indicators', nor to be tempted to use them in complete isolation from the array of other evaluative instruments available, which, although more evasive, have had a reasonable track record at guiding the learning of organizations.

The graft onto the public policy process of a battery of performance indicators, and of a gross and imperfect monitoring protocol, without the complementary change in organizational culture to ensure that the requisite degree of skepticism is attached to such indicators, will not produce a dramatic improvement in the process of social learning. Certainly, improvement does not automatically follow.

The crippling potentialities of quantophrenia

Undoubtedly, there have been benefits derived from some of that work. Yet we have no clear appreciation as to whether the quantophrenic experiments carried out over the last decades have generated reasonable cost–benefit ratios.

The cynicism that has surrounded such discussion can best be captured by a crude comment made in yesteryears about PPBS (planning, programming, and budgeting systems) the mother of all those quantophrenic experiments—launched in the 1960s in Canada (Balls 1970). The perplexing question in Ottawa in the early 1970s was: is it more PP or more BS? A less crude way to put this matter is that the general agreement in Ottawa (except among the operatives) was that the costs of this experiment had been greater than the benefits.

It would be nice if one could establish the necessary and sufficient conditions to ensure that the quantophrenic perspective would yield all the benefits attached to better marksmanship (for there are many), while avoiding the important distortion-generating impacts mentioned earlier. Unfortunately, one cannot define such necessary and sufficient conditions. One may, however, at the very least, identify a few major sources of concern.

Uniformization in the face of pluralism and change

In a world that is pluralistic and continually evolving, one of the great dangers of formalization and quantification is the tendency for measures of central tendency to evolve into standards and norms that are applied across the board in the name of uniformity. These uniform standards have quite differential impacts on differentiated publics, and tend to acquire a certain degree of non-negotiability over time. Indeed, it has been shown that such measures tend to foster centralization, and that such a propensity to impose uniformity does result in effectively balkanizing the country (Migué 1994).

The uniformity frenzy coupled with the egalitarian ideology (Kekes 2003), the folly of accountabilism (Weinberger 2007) and the passion for transparency (Bennis 1976a) amount to a very toxic potion. Vibrant dynamic conservatism ensues, and extraordinary disinformation in arithmetical garb often mauls citizens into catatonic states where common sense and the fundamental purpose of policy interventions easily get lost.

Steering effects

We have mentioned earlier the steering effects of perverse incentives. The fixation on certain metrics to measure the performance of manpower agencies (number of job placements) or police forces (number of crimes resolved) and the like has led such agencies to redirect their action away from difficult tasks (the placement of long-term unemployed or the effective resolution of complex crimes) into activities that would simply make the organization look good according to the metrics in use: getting involved in routine hiring or the practice of plea bargaining with criminals to get them to admit to other crimes in exchange for reduced penalties. Metrics have often become powerful slogans (Schrage 2008).

MAF as an innocuous illustration

The incentive for the regulatees, faced with such numerical targets that must be met if one is to escape blame from the regulators, is to indulge in deception and lies when they realize that such numbers are often in the realm of the unverifiable.

As mentioned earlier, we were not as astounded as some colleagues to hear about bizarreries of the world of MAF (the management accountability framework) of the Treasury Board Secretariat. Originally, the intention at the Treasury Board Secretariat was to gauge in a very rough way whether the public service providers were satisfied with their job, and whether the citizen was satisfied with the service provision. It was felt that if both parties felt satisfied, it might provide a rough gauge of quality.

However, when the quantophrenic enterprise was finished with this simple effort at providing a guesstimate, what had been put in place comprised: a framework based on ten inter-dependent expectations, ten series of indicators meant to convey the breath and meaning of the expectations, and ten series of measures meant to assess the progress toward the objectives described by the indicators. Responding to such requests has become a fairly demanding task, and the MAF scores have been used not only as record of 'what is' but as a basis for evaluation and blaming, and to define what 'ought to be'.

In a moment of candor, one participant confided that upon his department having been chastised for having poorly 'MAFfed', and being compared poorly with another department that had 'MAFfed' quite well, he became quite astonished since he had worked for years in the other place, and did not feel that they were performing that well. Upon discreet inquiry, it turned out that the other department had simply cooked up the numbers. And since the central bureau is flooded with masses of such numbers, it has no way to check and the whole system becomes an invitation to deception.

The unintended costs of quantophrenia

It is difficult to measure the unintended costs of quantophrenia, in the same manner that it is difficult to measure the unintended costs of the demoralization of the federal public service as a result of 'Gomery'. The fact that it is difficult to measure them precisely however, does not mean that such costs do not exist. The most important costs are obviously the result of a redirection of the efforts of the public service toward meeting artificial targets rather than doing their job with the maximum effectiveness, efficiency and economy through making the highest and best use of their judgment and imagination. This leads to a form of reification of the burden of office, and to the development of ever more clever methods to generate metrics-satisfaction rather than doing a good job.

One may easily gain a sense of the momentous sums of waste generated by enforcing the rituals like personnel performance reviews (that have been in good currency for years) that focus on formalizing and quantifying. Samuel Culbert has suggested that one might usefully get rid of such perfunctory performance reviews, and develop rather more iffy and less easily quantifiable performance *pre*views based on conversations designed to determine what an employee needs in order to be able to deliver what is expected of him or her (Culbert 2008).

Another important cost of the 'quantophrenic cosmology' is the so-called Goodhart effect—a phenomenon akin to the Heisenberg principle that suggests that quantifying transforms the world it tries to measure. Hoskin has suggested a formulation of the Goodhart effect along the following lines: "every measure which becomes a target becomes a bad measure" (Hoskin 1996: 265). This is so because the calculative fantasies of managerialism transform the environment into which they are introduced. Individuals and organizations come to think of themselves as auditees, and quantification distorts the character of the universe to which it is applied (Shore 2008): its effects are irreversible and generate a fixation on the metric rather than on the creativity and initiative that any practice requires. Getting results may be the explicitly stated goal mentioned, but numerology transforms the very notion of what the goal is, of what the organization is about.

The ergonomics of the public policy process: focus on affordances

In order to engage stakeholders in action to eliminate or attenuate the 'malefits' engendered by quantophrenia, it is not sufficient to denounce the quantophrenic perversion. One must provide an alternative cosmology, one less mesmerized and polluted by numbers. Otherwise, many stakeholders may not be willing to reconsider existing practices because they feel that some form of monitoring and performance-enhancement mechanism is necessary, and that the present one is better than none.

One alternative might build on the basic idea of ergonomics that "physical and cognitive affordances can help people to think about, know and use something more easily and to make fewer errors" (Rao and Sutton 2008). These are concrete ways in which one draws attention to the problem to be solved and provides easily learned and implemented tools that tend to generate a context that "affords 'action possibilities' and not others".

The context includes affordances that individuals and collectivities perceive or learn to perceive. Learning to perceive affordances is a key kind of perceptual learning (Gibson 1982; Norman 1999). But "affordances are not fixed properties: they are relationships that hold between objects and agents…to discover and make use of affordances is one of the important ways" to deal with novel situations (Norman 2007: 68–69). Learning to perceive affordances better or developing ways to improve such perception is the substance of social learning, and is at the core of innovation and innovative design.

Consequently, one can and should see the development of affordances as simple ways to lower the costs of thinking, to focus the mind and attention on key issues, to make sure that best practices and key ideas are communicated to neophytes in ways they can understand and apply.

A good example of affordance is the checklist of things to verify used by pilots before taking off: an idea that would appear appallingly simplistic to policy makers or university professors. Yet, as Steven Tremain would say: would you board an airplane if the pilot were to be overheard saying "I don't use checklists. I have been doing this for 20 years" (Rao and Sutton 2008). How many lives could be saved or policy failures avoided if the health care system and the public policy community were to emulate the aviation industry on this front. We already know the answer to this question from recent studies that have shown the extent to which such simple affordances as checklists in operating rooms have generated momentous improvements: "death rates fell overall by more than 40 percent and major complications by more than a third" (Priest 2009: A-4)

The intent is not to provide a general ergonomic template for the public policy process *in toto*. This would be a futile utopian effort. As Weick and Daft have shown in a classic article, such big daunting problems are discouraging because they seem to pose insurmountable challenges (Weick and Daft 1984). Consequently it leads many to do nothing. Such big problems must be reframed as a series of smaller problems that can be tackled through concrete and manageable steps—issue domains and the like.

Yet, one may suggest a list of ways in which affordances can be developed in the different issue domains in public policy.

First, there is a need to name the issue of interest. 'Naming' (as many activists know) has the great merit of making the issue more tangible, and focusing attention and energy on what the issue name has identified as being of prime importance.

Second, 'an enriched evidence-based exploration of the issues' grapples with 'evidence' wherever it is, and whatever form it might take, and is not restricting itself to hard material or quantophrenic evidence. It also takes into account intentionality, frames of reference, belief systems, and culture to the full extent that these realities impact on the issue at hand.

Third, a refurbished mindset would put a premium on 'the highest and best use of imagination, experimentalism and serious play' in the exploration of promising avenues for the design of viable responses to difficult situations. In that sense, it puts at the core of its inquiries an explicit social learning machine. The issue must not only be properly contextualized, but also subjected to a probing that attempts to make explicit the partiality of the frames used by the different stakeholders in order to generate the requisite blending and blurring of frames that allows fruitful multi-logues (Sabel 2001). This calls for a certain process of reconstruction: not only searching for responses to the original questions, but wondering whether the original questions are the most useful ones, and exploring ways in which such questions might be modified, transformed and reframed.

At the core of experimentalism is prototyping. Prototyping means:

(1) identifying some top requirements as quickly as possible;
(2) putting in place a quick-and-dirty provisional medium of co-development;
(3) allowing as many interested parties as possible to get involved as partners in designing a better arrangement;
(4) encouraging iterative prototyping; and
(5) as a result, encouraging all the stakeholders, through playing with prototypes, to get a better understanding of the problems, of their priorities and of themselves (Schrage 2000: 199ff).

The purpose is to generate creative interaction between people and prototypes. This may be more even more important than creating a dialogue between people. It is predicated on a culture of active participation: a democratization of design and the sort of playfulness and adventure that is required for serious play with prototypes. This is a lesson worth re-iterating.

Fourth, this new mindset is meant to be 'transformative'. It does not propose an exercise in hypothesis testing but a commitment to entering a process of inquiry with a view to transforming the context that has led to the emergence of the thorny issue (Chait et al. 2005).

The traditional approaches, aimed at attempts to falsify hypotheses about some objective reality, have generated too narrow a focus. For the social practitioner, what is central is an effort "to create a wholly, new, unprecedented situation that, in its possibility for generating new knowledge, goes substantially beyond the initial hypothesis" (Friedman and Abonyi 1976: 938). This in turn calls for a different notion of 'success' or 'failure' that goes far beyond those in use in the usual physical science-type-based process.

Conclusion

This chapter has underlined the foot-binding effects of quantophrenia. It has tried to exorcise the futility of the quest for certainty through quantification, but it has also has bemoaned a major loss ascribable to the quantophrenic frenzy: the loss of the centrality of experimentalism and social learning in most non-trivial aspects of public policy.

Far from being a panacea, quantification may be a bane especially in the world of Kahneman and Tversky in which it has been shown that 'objective' results are elusive: when a slight change in the framing of a question, based on the same quantitative data, can generate very different responses even from experts in the field, it is clear that the pretence of absolute illumination by quantification is untenable (Kahneman and Tversky 1979).

Consequently, unless auxiliary conditions are in place to ensure that the requisite social learning remains the main driving force, reification, distortion and mystification will ensue from quantophrenia (Paquet 2009c).

The main message is simple: prudence is *de rigueur*.

A better way to summarize this message might be to borrow a phrase from Joseph Tussman, and suggest that it be inscribed at the top of the screen on the computer of all the would-be quantulators…something that would remind them of the state of mind they have to maintain:

> …the state of mind of the magician who tremblingly invokes the powers he would use, knowing that if he gets the ceremony wrong what he invokes will destroy him. Neither romantic nor puritan, merely sensible (Tussman 1989: 25).

CHAPTER 5

Disloyalty

Some circumstantial evidence is very strong, as when you find a trout in the milk.

—Henry David Thoreau

Introduction

This chapter examines the notion of disloyalty, and obliquely the notion of dissent. First it deconstructs the notion of disloyalty and the reasons why disloyalty is usually regarded as reprehensible. Then it looks briefly at the mechanisms through which disloyalty might emerge. In each case, it deals with these issues at a general level before focusing on the Canadian federal public service as a world in which this kind of issue is a matter of great consequence.

In passing, it also probes the virtue of dissent—not be confused with disloyalty—and examines the problems of whistle blowing and *affectio societatis* (a term in French law for the spirit of collaboration), and the myth of the state clergy—as interesting phenomena illustrating the richness of the notion of disloyalty.

Loyalty and disloyalty as different nebulas

Some basic points

The notion of loyalty is usually associated with the honoring of a moral contract, with living up to the legitimate expectations of those with whom one is interacting and who have invested trust in that person. This means that disloyalty is a breach of trust.

Along the loyalty-disloyalty spectrum, those whose loyalty is 'blind' give an absolute and transcendent value to this moral commitment. This kind of loyalty is echoed in the motto 'loyalty to country right or wrong'. It allows a particular commitment to take precedence over all others, and disallows any interference from critical thinking. In a world of absolute loyalty, there is no possible questioning of loyalty to a person or to a cause, and no possibility of a review in the light of circumstances. Moreover, there is neither the possibility of certain loyalties acquiring different valences in certain circumstances over time, nor of the many loyalties requiring difficult trade-offs. This amounts to 'degree zero' of critical thinking.

At the other end of the spectrum is 'degree zero' of loyalty: this is the situation where any moral contract is totally contingent and revisable in view of evolving circumstances as a result of benefit-cost analyses or of sheer whimsicality.

In between these two positions lies a wide range of shades of loyalty or disloyalty: from the quasi-blind loyalty of public servants to their political masters (except in matters violating basic moral principles or the law) on the one hand, to disloyalty as opportunistic self-serving choice because the opportunity cost of loyalty is judged as too high, on the other.

This one-dimensional characterization is a bit simplistic: the range from total other-directedness to total self-directedness is defined in connection with only one moral contract. It ignores the complexities of the multi-dimensional real world:

(a) where loyalties to person or cause are many,
(b) where their intensity varies and evolves,

(c) where trade-offs are constantly renegotiated depending on circumstances and values that are themselves evolving, and

(d) where pluralism thrives (Kekes 1993).

A more realistic view of the world sees multiple moral contracts nested in a network of heterarchical relationships and encompassing a variety of dimensions. According to circumstances that are ever changing, and to levels of knowledge and competencies that are varied and imperfect, the legitimacies of the claims of the different parties to moral contracts differ and evolve. In this kind of world, the multiple loyalties may be starkly incompatible. In such a context, blind loyalty and chronic disloyalty *vis-à-vis* any other party on one particular issue (without some appreciation of the complexities of the situation and some critical thinking about the ordering or priorities of the different loyalties at play) are equally problematic. In reality then, moral pluralism prevails: a balance of claims must be reached that allows no absolute over-riding by any claim or value (Ibid.)

The balancing of claims that this demands is quite daunting. Critical thinking can only lead to what amounts to negotiations about the relevant burden of office, and then to a decision about *which* loyalties will take precedence here and now, and with *what* intensity.

The notion of burden of office—a nexus of moral contracts— refers to the duties that all officials are expected to accept as producers of governance. Such officials are not necessarily rulers. Citizens who claim civil rights like freedom of conscience, expression and association are officials of a sort, and are assumed and expected to accept duties as the *quid pro quo* in the moral contract that makes them producers of governance.

In a complex modern society, the citizen and all other officials have a multitude of relationships with the rest of the society and each is defined more or less well by a moral contract that spells out the legitimate expectations of those with whom they interact. As a result, all citizens or officials are embedded in an n-dimensional network of relationships. Corresponding to duties accepted (perhaps unconsciously, carelessly, or unwittingly) are rights that are more or less clearly agreed to, and that are provided to secure the required powers to perform these duties. Of course, exceptional duties are usually accompanied by exceptional rights and/or privileges.

Since most moral contracts are largely tacit, ill defined or incomplete, and since their terms can be regarded as inherently contestable by reasonable persons, there is much scope for disagreement and misunderstanding. This means that the benchmark by which loyalty or disloyalty may be gauged can be less clear than one might like, and very often contestable.

The notions of accountability (the nature of accounts to be rendered), of ethics (the nature of what is an acceptable and fair way to carry one's burden of office in the view of other parties) and of loyalty/disloyalty (what can be reasonably and legitimately expected by and from other parties to the moral contract) furthermore, are necessarily similarly contestable and contested.

It is quite difficult to pin down the notions of loyalty and disloyalty in the abstract. The benchmark by which one can measure them will vary; the various players may have different perspectives on them; and a different lens is used for the notion of loyalty as opposed to disloyalty.

In addition, the idea of a continuum from loyalty to disloyalty (like the idea of the continuum from trust to distrust) has proved less robust and helpful than anticipated. It has proved not unlike the evolution of H_2O as one proceeds up or down the Celsius scale: there are not only changes of degree along the way, but also changes of state—from solid ice to liquid to gas as temperature increases. Loyalty and disloyalty are in fact not the simple opposite or negative of one another, but realities that have been perceived as quite different in nature. As in the case of trust and distrust, it may be difficult to determine exactly at what point there is a change of state, but it definitely occurs nevertheless (R. Hardin 2004).

Loyalty is a very 'thin concept': one can be loyal to anything and anyone, and indeed may be loyal without knowing it, and even without any idea of what loyalty is. It connotes perseverance in meeting the expectations built into a relationship. Most often, loyalty connotes an unquestioning, non-discriminating and undiscerning force: "loyalty is a dog without moral judgment" (Tussman 1989: 66)—that is with no critical thinking.

Disloyalty on the other hand is a very 'much thicker concept'. It "is more of a moral, social, public or institutional phenomenon, requiring more in the way of context. Before we can have disloyalty, we need a setting sufficiently rich to give rise to normative expectations" (Keller 2007: 213). Moreover, most of the time there is a much higher degree of deliberateness in disloyalty than in loyalty.

Neither loyalty nor disloyalty is of necessity enlightened: it may be self-serving and may threaten the social order. But loyalty has acquired the garment of a virtue in many circles, while disloyalty is most often regarded as a vice.

Shades of disloyalty

The thick nature of the notion of disloyalty makes context and burden of office immensely important: since disloyalty needs a sufficiently rich setting to give rise to strong normative expectations, it is difficult to ascertain disloyalty without a fair understanding of the nature of the issues involved. As a result, this cannot be a discussion conducted in general, but rather must take place at the level of particular issue domains.

Two important dimensions of the context are worth exploring in a preliminary way: the difference between convergent and divergent issues, and a concrete sense of what the notion of issue domains might mean.

One of the important sources of the growing degree of 'dissensus' among officials (citizens and all other officials) is obviously the greater complexity of current policy issues, the hyper-turbulence and uncertainty of the external environment, and the greater degree of pluralism of the texture of society. But the growing acuteness of these differences of opinion may also be due to the fact that issues under discussion are now, more often than before, raising not 'convergent problems' (for which the multiplicity of diverse responses offered tend cumulatively and gradually through time to converge toward an agreed-upon response or consensus) but rather 'divergent problems' (for which *a contrario* the more the problem is clarified, the more divergent and irreconcilable the points of view become).

Fritz Schumacher, who proposed this distinction, used education as a fair example of an issue that raises a family of divergent problems—the more one delves into what would be necessary to better raise and educate a child, the more complex and intractable the problem becomes (Schumacher 1977: chapter 10). This is the reason why Freud used to say that to govern, to cure and to educate are "impossible professions" (Innerarity 2006: 193).

In the face of divergent problems, there is an ever-greater possibility of different stakeholders reasonably defending incompatible approaches, and therefore more scope for dissent and for the possibility of disloyalty of one sort or another. In the many-dimensional world of governance, where 360° loyalties are likely to be difficult if not impossible to reconcile, divergent problems are the rule.

Disloyalty as a breach of trust depends on the intensity of the normative expectations: the greater the intensity of the legitimate normative expectations, the more egregious the breach of trust, and the more reprehensible the disloyalty.

In any governance context (where governance is defined as effective coordination when power, resources and information are widely distributed), the different sorts of accountabilities involved are a useful gauge of the normative expectations attached to the burden of office: ethical relations are the flip side of these accountabilities. One may therefore categorize disloyalties according to the valence and intensity of the accountability/ ethical relations and to the depth of the trust violated when there is a breach of trust.

De-squishing the concept of trust is therefore crucial to an understanding of disloyalty. Trust is domain-specific—you would not trust your dentist to repair your car! (Keen 1999). Therefore disloyalty has to be dealt with at the issue domain level: one is not disloyal in general, but disloyal with reference to normative expectations in a given issue domain as defined by the burden of office and as gauged by the community of practice. Without specificity, the sort of trust that is betrayed is rather difficult to define.

The more convergent the problem, and the more fully integrated and mature the community of practice, the sharper is the definition of the burden of office, and the easier it is to identify disloyalty. The more divergent the problem and the more diffuse and anomic the community of practice on the other hand, the fuzzier is the burden of office, and the more difficult it will be to identify disloyalty. Both hard and soft disloyalties can ensue.

Setting and source of an hypothesis

The burden of office of public servants is built on many unwritten (even un-stated and ill-understood) clauses defining the understandings and expectations of others—bosses, peers, co-workers, clients, possibly subordinates and/or partners—with whom they collaborate. In the simplest of terms, disloyalty means breaking any such moral contract deliberately and knowingly.

The emergence of our hypothesis about the existence and increase of disloyalty in the Canadian federal public service took shape in discussions with senior public servants at an Association of Professional Executives of the Public Service of Canada (APEX) seminar on February 28, 2007 (see chapter 3 of this book). From the very start, and unsurprisingly given the nature and scope of the expectations mentioned above, they declared emphatically that they felt 'loyal'. This was both a matter of personal comfort and pride, but without being very specific about either their burden of office or about the norms they felt had to be honoured.

Yet as the discussions progressed, almost all participants recalled and described instances of disloyalty that they had observed, and reluctantly came to the conclusion that it would appear to have increased. The reasons mentioned to explain such phenomena were that their group had been experiencing a dual series of shocks over recent decades.

The first series of shocks occurred in the late 1980s and mid–1990s. These shocks have been well documented (Paquet and Pigeon 2000; Paquet 2009a: 179ff) and came to challenge the public service culture as it stood *circa* the 1980s: permanent employees, appointed on the basis of merit, a job-description, generous fringe benefits, job security and a career-path, expectations of anonymity, impartiality and clear accountability to ministers.

This traditional culture was challenged 'from within' in a timid way in the late 1980s by Public Service 2000. That initiative pointed to the need for public employees to attend to the needs of the citizens better, and to make the highest and best use of their creativity in their work; as well, it outlined the need for the employer to improve training, development and career planning, and to develop a new focus on accountability as responsibilities were devolved to managers so that they could manage. This challenge did not however, shake the traditional culture in a fundamental way.

It was only in the mid-1990s, as a result of the fiscal crisis, that the culture was hit by strong pressure 'from without'. While it is difficult to establish clearly the exact moment of the hit, the message of the "purple book" and of the "grey book" tabled by the Rt. Hon. Paul Martin (Minister of Finance at the time) had implications for the federal career public service. The message was first presented starkly in the "Directors of Personnel" discussion paper in the fall of 1994. This document, inspired explicitly by David Noer's *Healing the Wounds* (1993), sets out to "define the steps required to achieve a new public service model for Canada" (Canada 1994a: 2). Noer's message is simple:

(1) to acquire the new required flexibility, the old employment contract guaranteeing much security to the employee must be abrogated;

(2) traditional notions of employment contracts might not have been very healthy in any case for it fostered an

undesirable sort of co-dependency between employees and their organization.

The "Directors of Personnel" discussion paper was even more stark: it diagnosed the traditional employment contract as "unrealistic", "not necessary or affordable", and "an unhealthy expectation" (Ibid., 5). The document suggests the termination of the then current policy of conversion from term to indeterminate employment after five years; it put forward a framework where "employees not the employer, are responsible for their own employment options, but the employer would provide support to enable the continued employability of staff" (Ibid., 17). The document stated that the "moral framework" has to be renegotiated (Ibid., 9).

In May 1995, the President of the Public Service Commission, Ruth Hubbard, sketched a three-tiered system model of the public service as it might emerge with a small "core of permanent and highly skilled knowledge workers, supported by a pool of short term employees who work in government for stints of several months or years and move on"...(plus) a "para-public service that could emerge as various levels of government cooperate on delivering services and as private–public partnerships take over services that were once provided by government" (Hubbard 1995). While the contours of the new employment contract(s) Hubbard had in mind remained vague, the strategic direction hinted at was congruent with the contents of the "Directors of Personnel" document.

The changes necessary to breathe new life into the traditional culture were never introduced, were short-lived, or were prevented from evolving as hoped for. Donald Savoie could indeed say that the deal that ensured that bureaucratic officials would provide the government of the day with "non-partisanship, loyalty, impartiality, discretion and professionalism, in return for anonymity and security of tenure" had all but disappeared (Savoie 2003: 17).

The second series of shocks came as a result of the recent switch in government regimes—from majority to minority and

226

from Liberal to Conservative—that has exacerbated the strains as bureaucrats came to be expected to shift their loyalty to the agenda and policies of the new (and yet perhaps temporary) government, and to serve it creatively and loyally. When one political party has held power for ten or fifteen years, many of the old ways come to be regarded as 'normal and preferred' by public servants who have been hired, promoted and engaged during the tenure of the former government. Moreover, when the new government is a minority government that could be toppled soon, the urge to shift one's involvement and engagement may be considerably slowed down and attenuated.

Faced with having to forge new direct and indirect relationships that call for the acceptance of perspectives very different from those to which they have become accustomed, public servants have two choices: leaving ('exiting' physically or hibernating by leaving their souls at home and focusing only on fulfilling a modicum of technical duties) or trying to propose modifications ('voice' alternative views and propose alternative ways to define and implement what the new government has in mind). Some have suggested that a measure of loyalty to the organization/institution may be how long one uses 'voice' before 'exiting' or before beginning to indulge in passively or actively disloyal behavior.

There is a clear distinction between open dissent and disloyalty. Passive assent (e.g., reluctance to raise meaningful questions in a positive way, tardiness in questioning when questioning is warranted, silence when innovative ways of handling contentious issues are thinkable and available) is often an instance of disloyalty.

It is hardly surprising that the broken bargain of the 1990s (that had already generated a great cooling-off in the relationships between politicians and bureaucrats, followed by a degree of circling of the wagons by the tribe of senior bureaucrats intent on protecting its privileges and on using all the means at its disposal to immunize itself from the fate promised by the new planned bargain) (Hubbard 2009: 97–113), combined with the new strains added to politico-bureaucratic relations by the shift to a minority Conservative government, has generated tensions. Tensions that would lead inevitably to increased disaffection, and consequently to lesser engagement, and a tendency to re-affirm the legitimacy of *their* expertise ever more strongly as opposed to one which is churned out by the democratic election process. Tensions that, as might be expected, translate into forms of passive and active disloyalty.

Such at least has been the hypothesis that has emerged from preliminary interviews and discussions with senior federal public servants.

Is disloyalty increasing?

Disloyalty entails some disagreement leading to misalignment between the direction chosen by the principal (the government in power) and the direction followed by agents (the senior bureaucrats). This disagreement and misalignment can have many sources and take many forms. For instance it may simply be ascribable to miscommunication or to poor motivation or to a lack of effort (e.g., free riding and laziness), but it may also be due to deliberate sabotage. Consequently, while a portion of what has been called X-inefficiency (Leibenstein 1976, 1987) is clearly ascribable to casual organizational slack, some of it may well be ascribed to a lack of motivation and effort due to resentment and disloyalty to the organization.

One important source of friction has to do with differences of opinion as to who is authorized to define the public interest: the elected officials or the unelected public servants who may believe that they 'know' more (because they are experts) and may claim to have a better appreciation of what is best for the country. Democratic values dictate what must happen when there is dissent between politicians and bureaucrats on the matter of what is in the public interest. The bureaucrats must first use their 'voice' to bring the full force of persuasion based on their expertise to get the political authorities to modify their view. In the discussion however, the bureaucrats may discover that there is no possible meeting of minds and, depending on the criticality of the issue, if there is no possible reconciliation of the different points of view, the bureaucrat may either choose to resign or to use creativity to help the politician carry out the policy of choice in as effective a way as possible despite his/her reservations.

The rise in disloyalty however, may not depend only on the circumstances as defined by the narrow context. Federal public servants do not live in isolation from the broader society, and the broad context may have an impact on the coefficient of loyalty in good currency in a society. William Safire has denounced what he has called the rise of a "new disloyalty"—a pernicious worldwide devaluation of loyalty that has permeated the workplace everywhere (Safire 1994). The forces at work here, one would expect, have affected the work place at the federal public service level, and have generated some disloyalty as a result. In that sense, the public sector is no different from the private sector in Canada, where polling data appears to support strongly the hypothesis of rising workplace disloyalty (Rynor 2009).

Finally, the very wide range of definitions of the phenomena covered by the notion of 'disloyalty' has made it easier to arrive at a consensus on the general fact that disloyalty is growing. Definitions that include not only passive and active disloyalty, but the whole, more-difficult, terrain of lessening engagement and commitment, of 'hibernation', of a systematic dwarfing of the notion of burden of office, and of an erosion of the sense that democratic values must prevail on so-called expertise. There has however, been disagreement about the form it has taken. Insiders who were interviewed felt that active sabotage has always been limited in the federal public service, and has probably not increased significantly over the last decade. Most felt nevertheless, that the rest of the disloyalty nebula had increased.

In fact the cautious conclusion of our 2007 discussions was that one could observe a growing 'culture of disloyalty' enveloping the public service today as a result of the whole array of forces mentioned above. This may be perceived as rather weak anecdotal evidence from a few dozen senior executives. Yet the result of these discussions and interviews is no weaker than most of what is found in the traditional public administration literature—passing references to anonymous interviews.

Disloyalty as akin to the underground economy phenomenon

Understandably, there has been a good deal of vibrant denial by the Canadian federal public service' uppermost officials when confronted with the airing of these conjectures.

We could not but be reminded of the impact of a paper one of us wrote some twenty years ago on the size of the underground economy in Canada, and on the consequent loss of tax revenue to governments (Paquet 1989). In it (on the basis of anecdotal evidence and a full decade of economic journalism) was speculation that the size of the underground economy was immensely greater than was acknowledged by Statistics Canada, and growing fast. It earned the author a free lunch and a stern dressing down from a high ranking official of Statistics Canada, demanding a retraction and an end to dangerous ruminations suggesting that Canada's national agency was missing a big chunk of what was going on in the country.

Many 'guesstimates' of the size of the Canadian underground economy (and of the consequent size of the loss of tax revenue) were provided in the following decade—all equally large, equally based on oblique measures, and equally quickly dismissed. One of the more recent studies by Giles and Tedds made use of more formidable econometric tools and brought them to bear on the still quite fuzzy reality of the underground economy (Giles and Tedds 2002). These results (still based on oblique gauges) suggested that the underground economy had grown from 3.5 percent of GDP in 1976 to 16 percent in 1995, and that the yearly loss of tax revenue had grown from some CA$ 2 billion in 1976 to CA$ 44 billion in 1995. One can easily imagine that these numbers have reached new heights in 2010.

The fact that earlier guesstimates had been merrily dismissed (cognitive dissonance galore!) has meant that this more-sophisticated study has also been dismissed just as merrily. The denial persists, and no serious policy action has been initiated to deal with the problem.

The difficulty in gaining an exact quantitative measure of disloyalty is not unlike the difficulty of gauging the size of the underground economy. This does not mean, however, that because it cannot be measured precisely, it does not exist.

To generate greater attention to these provisional soft conjectures about the rise in disloyalty in the federal public service, it might be useful to shed some light on the mechanisms underpinning such a drift toward disloyalty.

Analytical framework

In this section, we suggest a provisional map of how the forces at play that can be seen most clearly at work at the political–bureaucratic interface might operate on three key mechanisms—in order to unearth additional oblique evidence that disloyalty is being generated there.

Three mechanisms lie at the core of the framework we are using: **mechanism I**: the way in which a self-interested satisfier takes into account perceived social rewards and penalties generated by the context when deciding how to behave (Jones 1984); **mechanism II**: the way experiences with changes in the context lead to value change and act as loyalty filters, that is, experiences redirecting loyalties (Mesthene 1970; Akerlof 1984); and **mechanism III**: the way the impact of the reshuffling of loyalties is dramatically modified by the existence of exit/voice costs and opportunities and by group reactions to loyalty and disloyalty (Hirschman 1970; Levine and Moreland 2002).

These mechanisms underpin a plausible stylized tale that can be set out in the following way.

First, individuals make choices (on the basis of limited information and limited rationality), taking into account not only personal rewards and penalties but also perceived social rewards and penalties. Since the social context in this case depends a good deal on custom, tradition and ethos as it pertains to organizations and issue domains, and tends to generate what Cass Sunstein calls *collective conformism* (a tendency to stick to established patterns even as group members change), the environmental ethos and the organizational culture have a compounding effect (Sunstein 2003).

Second, shocks both from within and from without generate changes in both the environmental ethos and organizational culture (like changes in technology) from time to time, and these modify the choice options over time. As a result, choice behaviour changes, and changed choice behaviour (with appropriate lags) becomes conceptualized and habitualized as change in values. Such transformation acts as a 'loyalty filtre' that may change the mix of personal self-interest and group interest and may do so in either direction: either by increasing loyalty to self or group or tribe or institution, or by diminishing it.

Third, the impact of the change in the mix of 'loyalties' may, in turn, trigger the decision to exit the organization or to make more use of the 'voice' option to get the organization to modify a tradition or covenant. Depending on the ease and cost of exit, the effectiveness of voice, and the dynamics of group reaction to such actions, the pressure on the organization to modify the tradition will either decrease (as non-conformists leave) or increase (as the voice option generates an emergent activist public). At the same time, agents who choose not to exit because the costs are too high and not to exercise voice pressure to try to get creative reform may displace their main loyalty to the 'tribe' or to sub-groups with which they identify and become passively or actively disloyal to the organization and institution.

These three mechanisms act in a loop.

By way of illustration, assume the following stylized, hypothetical situation at the political-bureaucratic interface:

    (1) a dire global economic situation entails a high cost of exit (because of lack of equally 'cushy' work conditions elsewhere);

    (2) the breaking of the political-bureaucratic bargain; and

(3) a new minority (and quite different) government following years of dominance by another political party—and, as a result, the limiting of voice options because of mental prisons inherited from the past that become barriers to effective interaction with the new government with its different philosophy).

In these circumstances, one might well conjecture that the disloyalty of the senior bureaucrats would increase. The operation of a loyalty filtre might well reinforce the loyalty to the well-protected tribe of senior bureaucratic officials as opposed to the elected government and its institutions, resulting in active and passive disloyalty.

One might also conjecture that the disloyalty would materialize with different intensity in different issue domains depending upon:

(1) the convergence or divergence of the problems;
(2) the sharpness of the cleavages between older and newer views in each;
(3) the particularities of the senior officials and politicians in place; and
(4) the costs of exit and voice options in each.

In issue domains where the decentralization drive and the propensity to reduce state-centricity of the new government are likely to be most disturbing to the existing order, one would expect a much higher degree of disloyalty. In the same spirit, one would expect senior officials fully engrossed by the principles of the last government on these fronts to be more aggressively disloyal than those who are more operations and efficiency driven.

None of this would materialize brusquely or overnight.

One should keep in mind that, in the case of the federal public service, the long tradition of loyalty of the bureaucracy to the elected government (until, and for some notwithstanding, the breaking of the traditional bargain), and the large portion of government operations where contentious/divergent issues do not predominate, would lead one to conjecture that the percentage of aggressively disloyal senior public servants might not be very large.

To the extent, however, that perceived explicit disloyalty at the highest level is not punished (but rewarded by international postings, for example), and that disloyal senior bureaucrats are not clearly identified or identifiable, even as few as five percent of senior officials being disloyal is consequential. It most certainly would be enough to generate a climate of paranoia in the whole system, to entice the political branches (starting with a degree of natural suspicion anyway) to react negatively, and to corrupt the bureaucratic-political interface dramatically.

Disloyalty is growing: some conjectures

Certain observations would appear to indicate that these three mechanisms are indeed at work, and that they provide a plausible explanation for the pattern of behavior that is conjectured.

Some things to keep in mind

The experience of Paul Tellier seems to reveal that the loyalty of senior officials could be carried from one majority government to the next. Tellier was clearly associated by many with the Liberal Party in what appeared to be a more partisan way than is usual and yet could become the Clerk of Privy Council in 1985 for the Progressive Conservative government led by the Rt. Hon Brian Mulroney.

Effective loyalty filtres were to emerge in the 1990s. First in line was the Al-Mashat affair in which a comedy of errors led to the embarrassment of the Mulroney government and to the indictment of senior bureaucrats for lack of due diligence and lack of professionalism. Then came traumatic edicts arising in the wake of the fiscal crisis that have already been mentioned: the famous discussion paper, *The Way Ahead for the Public Service*, in the fall of 1994 that concluded that a career public service is no longer "necessary or affordable", the 1994–95 annual report of the Public Service Commission stating as a *fact* "that the implicit employment contract which guaranteed relative job security to an employee has been abrogated", and program review with its frozen compensation, etc. (Linquist and Paquet 2000; Paquet and Pigeon 2000). Massive reduction in personnel, an eight-year salary freeze, and scaling down in work conditions across the board took their toll. The economy nevertheless was thriving so that exit was not unduly costly; many of the disgruntled took their leave, and those left behind seemed to have served the government well.

Something dramatically different seems to have occurred in the last five years however, that suggests that a sharper rise in disloyalty has been taking place.

First, the government of the Rt. Hon. Stephen Harper arrived with a mindset quite different from the one that had dominated for the previous decade: his successive minority governments might have generated apprehension in many senior officials but might also have carried with it a sense that they might not have to (or ought not to) change their mindset too fast since the philosophy associated with the elected government might not prevail for long.

Second, while there has always been a protective belt around senior officials—they take care of their own—this 'corporatism' has become much more robust of late as the 'tribe' or the 'system' has come to regard itself as under threat. Both a greater sense of entitlement and a greater sense of self-preservation would appear to have developed in the tribe of senior officials. The Gomery inquiry has provided ample evidence of the new capacity for senior officials to take care of 'their own'.

Third, moral relativism has reached new heights in the last decade in Canada and elsewhere. Unsurprisingly then, the sense of entitlement at the highest level of the Canadian federal public service has also increased dramatically. This should not be generalized lightly and one must remain conscious that a vast majority of senior officials are still totally devoted to the public good. There have been however, some highly visible examples of the other sort. The famous line 'I am entitled to my entitlements' used by veteran politician David Dingwall in an appearance before a Parliamentary committee in 2005 in respect of severance pay he received when he resigned from the Royal Canadian Mint, or the abuses allowed to prevail unchecked for the longest time in cases such as the alleged extravagant spending and poor administrative oversight by George Radwanski before he resigned as Privacy Commissioner, or the closed culture of the RCMP are echoes of some erosion of the moral foundations on which the public service used to be built and of the formation of enclaves or self-referential tribes in the Canadian federal public service (Paquet 2007c).

Mechanisms at work

Looking at the three mechanisms (mentioned earlier) in action might allow the detection of subtle and yet significant changes that might hold clues about their operations as sources of increased disloyalty. The reader is invited to probe the learning loop that follows—the work of loyalty filters, the deflection of the impact of the new mix of loyalties toward disloyalty, and the development of a new conformism of disloyalty—in search of positive or negative support for our general hypothesis about the existence and increase in disloyalty in the public service. What follows are some illustrative points only of mechanisms II, III, and I.

Mesthene-Akerlof Type II mechanisms

Part of the shuffling of loyalties from the institution to personal and tribal priorities has also been the result of a strong appreciation of the relative importance of expertise, while democratic values and representative democracy have suffered some devaluation in public services including this one. This has been slowly developing since the 1970s, but never more so than in the recent past when credentialism would appear to have come to trump all other sources of legitimacies.

This has most certainly dramatically influenced hiring and promotion, and, as a result, accelerated the shift from institutional/ organizational loyalty to group/tribe/profession loyalty: as the status of elected officials has become downgraded and the expertise of the bureaucracy lionized, their relative influence on governance has changed accordingly. 'Tribe' in some cases has meant profession, but in the case of the very senior public servants, it has become the community of senior officials.

Slipping from a role of advisor to the politicians (including persuading reluctant politicians to adopt particular positions) into the role of managing them and arrogating the decision-making process is a very short step. The managerial class has obviously not hijacked the political process, but it has claimed an ever-greater place at the decision-making table and often served the government less than perfectly (more on this topic in chapter 11).

Levine-Moreland-Hirschman Type III mechanisms

The new mix of loyalties may take many forms depending on context and circumstances. The context in the last five years has altered the mix significantly and strengthened the possibilities for disloyalty. The compounding of the:

(1) sharp cleavage between the old and new policy directions;

(2) emerging sense in the tribe of senior federal bureaucrats that senior bureaucrats are better interpreters of the public interest than elected officials;

(3) temporariness of the minority governments;

(4) limited exit possibilities for senior bureaucrats in difficult economic times; and

(5) great tolerance for disloyalty to politicians by the top layer of the bureaucracy as well as by opinion moulders like columnists and other *magistrats de l'immédiat*

…has significantly eroded of the notion of 'burden of office'.

A meaningful minority of senior, middle-aged officials may have found themselves unable to serve the government loyally and yet unable to find an exit leading to an equally cushy job. This may well have opened the gate to (active or passive) disloyalty depending on the nature of the cleavages (actively with respect to agonistic issues, passively with respect to less agonistic ones, and through hibernation in still others) and depending upon the protection of the tribe and temperaments.

To the extent that group loyalties have grown significantly, and paranoia has developed between the politicians and the bureaucrats, a quasi-psychosis has undoubtedly developed that has persuaded many bureaucrats that the government is not interested in listening to their voice. The media frenzy, especially through opinion–moulding columnists, has likely contributed significantly to this deterioration by generating a whole folklore of half-truths that have served disgruntled bureaucrats well in rationalizing their soft disloyalties.

Jones Type I mechanisms

Two factors might be worth underlining in the recent development of broad social forces that have influenced both choice behavior and loyalties, and have impacted on the *ethos* and the organizational culture of the Canadian public service.

The evidence on moral relativism is quite widely spread. The decline of all the paraphernalia of underlying social values carried by religion, family and community are no longer in good currency. Even the very notion of public service has been redefined by the public choice literature as simply fuelled by self-interest.

One should not be surprised therefore, that the internalization of such a value system has led a substantial number of public servants to allow their own personal interests or the interests of the tribe to take precedence over what the tradition and custom of serving the public may have meant in the past. This is the new conformism.

The second point that has been less fully acknowledged is the growth of sub-group or tribal identity. We know that, with the decline of grand narratives in general, agents have turned more and more toward their community of practice as the unit to which they have loyalty. This has been recognized in different work milieu, but it has become a feature of the federal public service over the last while, at all levels. One may underline in particular the growth of the 'community of regulators' and other similar communities. Some federal public servants have come to regard communities as their main or principal anchor within the public service. Such enclaves have come to generate the recognized reference points and standards of behavior—particular organizational cultures—where corporatist tribal/professional sentiments trump democratic engagement.

Cumulative causation toward the neurotic state

Each element in the learning loop integrating these three mechanisms, however limited in scope, has a multiplier effect through that loop: the permission to be disloyal and the rationalization of such disloyal action as work done in the higher interests of the country can only snowball and generate some additional paranoia on the part of elected officials. Such paranoia can then be used to rationalize further disloyalty since it has been argued openly in some instances that the government in place does not echo 'fundamental Canadian values'. This is a pattern that could be observed even in the 1990s (see chapter 6), but the heightened tensions of late have undoubtedly accelerated the process.

A similar state of affairs has already reached some critical level in many democracies, and certain countries have recognized it. The United Kingdom, for example, recently felt it necessary to use a *Magna Carta*-type mechanism, approving a formal code enforced by the highest authorities on both sides—the Prime Minister and the Civil Service Commission—that requires ministers to respect the impartiality of the public service, and to give fair weight to their advice, and the civil service to set out the facts and relevant issues truthfully, correcting any errors as soon as possible and not knowingly misleading ministers, Parliament or others (Thomas 2009a: 51). This amounts to a vibrant reassertion of democratic values in circumstances in which they were losing their dominium.

One may legitimately wonder whether the present Canadian *insouciance* on this front (about the failings on both sides of the political-bureaucratic equation) is the result of much naivety, immense cognitive dissonance, reprehensible disingenuity, or worse.

In praise of anecdotal evidence

Many may grant some general plausibility to our argument but bemoan the fact that, before we can take action, we need to have better evidence. In a world that has become mesmerized by scientistic quantophrenic arguments, there seems to be little place left for the force of practical intelligence and judgment. Yet our daily life is fully inhabited by the use of rules of thumb, and attention paid to gut feelings is at the basis of our survival. Medical doctors and a multiplicity of professionals (including professional baseball or hockey players) take action, not on the basis of computation, but on the basis of a practical intelligence that enables them to amass a large amount of scattered information, and to form a plausible judgment that often they would find difficult to explain in detail or to translate into a protocol or an algorithm (Gladwell 2005; Gigerenzer 2007).

If strategists or designers waited until all their interventions had been scientifically vindicated by double blind testing, there is much that would never get done. Most often they are in the position of a backwoods mechanic who does not have all the spare parts available to her and must be satisfied with vicarious fiddling to get the vehicle back on the road (Gigerenzer 2001).

In human affairs, especially in the world of strategy, the information is never completely available and certain. Failing to act on the basis of imperfect and incomplete information may mean that much damage will ensue.

What a practical mindset would suggest is that one must grapple with 'evidence' wherever it is, and whatever form it might take. It cannot rely only on hard quantophrenic material evidence; it must take into account all the realities that have an impact on the issue at hand, and even put a premium on the best use of imagination and foresight in exploring what is in the process of emerging. It is the only way to be 'ecologically rational' (i.e., taking action that takes into account all the cues from the environment and fits these with what the environment calls for) (Paquet 2009b).

Evidence and cues exist at the present time about the existence and rising level of disloyalty. By itself this does not give any certitude about the source of the problem or the potential cures. It establishes nevertheless, that the problem is not a figment of someone's imagination. The current trend toward disengagement has been recorded by the longitudinal federal public service surveys that have noted a significant increase in the rationale for wanting to leave the public service as something due to conflict between personal and organizational values. The registered higher level of disengagement of late has been significant enough to generate some action at the Privy Council Office (PCO) level. The fact that even PCO is concerned may not persuade the radical skeptics that disloyalty is on the rise, but given the congenital cognitive dissonance of PCO, it must mean that their intelligence corroborates the sort of ethnographic material collected by interviews (like ours) and lends some support to our hypothesis.

In particular, the evidence of a shift in loyalty from the Canadian democracy to the community of practice is a matter of great consequence. It has been clearly perceived by astute observers of the Ottawa scene like the Hon. Hugh Segal that, as he put it, "the federal public service is about the federal government first, its institutions, prerogatives, [etc.]…and their protection" (Segal 2010: 99). Any political ethnographer familiar with the Ottawa scene knows it well. Yet it is only very rarely that one can observe a sleight of hand in official documents that indicates that the tribe is willing to take action to serve the tribe to the detriment of the citizenry. This has been the case in the perversion of the mandate of Service Canada (read more in chapter 11).

Most of the time, it is not only difficult but also quite delicate and perilous to expose disloyalty. The tribe can hit back with a vengeance. One of us can still remember the personal costs borne by Scott Gordon as a result of his drive to expose James Coyne's misdeeds some fifty years ago. This is a cautionary tale. Gordon's original letter denouncing Coyne was signed by twenty-nine economists, and the short book he wrote soon after demonstrated very effectively that there had been deception on the part of the Governor of the Bank of Canada (Gordon 1961).

But after this event, Gordon was marginalized and shunned by the federal bureaucracy. His part-time career as a mediator in public service affairs was brought to a halt, and he was explicitly ignored by a royal commission later struck on monetary affairs (even though he was one of the best known Canadian experts in this area). He was later to depart from Canada to pursue a most successful career in the United States.

Two cases brought to our attention recently may get the reader to reflect for a moment on the extent to which what is denounced here is fact or fiction.

The first one pertains to the explicit corporatist refusal by a cadre of federal public servants to carry out intelligence work and to provide advice to government on action to be taken. This position was argued on the grounds that, while the request was perfectly legal, they felt it was not their responsibility to do so, that it was in violation of Canadian values as they understood them, and that their role was to defend Canadians unconditionally and not to help the government determine if assistance is legitimate and warranted in any situation.

The second one is the *sortie* of retired diplomats in defence of their colleague whose testimony had been challenged by military and political officials in the debate about the transfer of Afghan detainees to the Afghan government. In such a delicate manner, it would appear that, despite the cautious language used, the tribe of elders chose to support a member of the tribe unconditionally and publicly even though their knowledge of the file was and is quite limited. It revealed their primary loyalty to the tribe.

In the face of such evidence, it would be *insouciance déréglée ou téméraire* (the definition of criminal negligence in the Criminal Code) not to pay attention.

Four clarifying vignettes

The fact that one does not have incontrovertible quantitative evidence of an increase in demonstrated disloyalty should not lead one to ignore the widespread toxic phenomenon, but equally, it should not lead one to overstate the case irresponsibly.

The following vignettes are designed to sharpen the focus of a needed inquiry into this phenomenon of increasing disloyalty and decreasing trust somewhat by looking at four epiphenomena that might help observers get a better sense of the different forms that distrust may take, and of the different degrees to which some form of confrontational dissent may or may not materialize as disloyalty, and as a result, be regarded as defensible or not.

Dissent is not disloyalty. Whistle blowing raises the problem of conflict of loyalties squarely, and failure to provide *affectio societatis* is a mild but toxic form of disloyalty. As for the myth of a state clergy that is congenitally loyal, and the spurious implications that disloyalty is logically impossible, this may be a clever subterfuge to avoid the question at hand, but it is built on untenable foundations.

The virtue of dissent

Our main argument may have left the impression that disloyalty is always a vice. Indeed, most of the time it is. But we need to take a moment to delimit, to a degree, the terrain of reprehensible disloyalty from the one of creative and justifiable dissent.

Dissent is not disloyalty.

Jones and Sunstein have shown that there is strong pressure to conform in most situations. Conformism is however not unlike free-riding: it benefits from the actions of others without adding anything (Sunstein 2003: 12). This is why real learning is unlikely to occur in an organization where everyone agrees with everyone else, and why well-functioning organizations and societies benefit from a wide range of views.

In the better old days, much of the work of a democracy was accomplished through a robust dialectic of the elected official and the expert bureaucrat. They both had legitimacy (representation and expertise) and it was felt that, through their dialogue and intense interaction, some workable governing would ensue. Canada has lived through such a period in the mid-20th century (see chapter 1). Dissent was often recorded between politicians and bureaucrats, but it was well understood that the views of the elected officials should prevail.

One of the most interesting developments of recent times (and one that explains the popularity of the word 'governance') is the significant erosion of the legitimacy of both politicians and bureaucrats. Bureaucrats no longer have the monopoly of moral and professional legitimacies of yesteryear. They are only one of the many expert voices. The same may be said about the electoral process: it does not automatically grant legitimacy to elected officials any longer (Rosanvallon 2008: 111ff). The governed have become involved directly in various ways, and have expressed their dissent in effective ways by constructing a true *contre-démocratie* (Rosanvallon 2006). The dissent of the governed has materialized in a more diffuse and less theatrical way than officialdom, but has become quite effective in shaping governance (Carter 1998; Angus 2001).

It is fascinating to observe however, that despite the immense broadening of the range of legitimate stakeholders, much of the stylized debate in political science and public administration remains focused on the old dual system of the dialectics of politicians and bureaucrats, as if it were still the focal point of governing. In fact, the whole governance *problématique* (claiming that producers of governance are many) has been shunned because it redefines the whole notion of the political to include many more actors and experts interacting in many more loci.

Even within this reductive contested arena of bureaucrats and politicians, there has been a shift in the rules of the game. Instead of negotiated compromises, with the politicians having the final say, a substantial element of the bureaucracy has begun to claim that its expertise, professionalism and disinterested character provides it with a stronger and more credible basis to provide a more legitimate definition of the public good than the one suggested by those churned out by the electoral process.

Disloyalty emerges when it becomes clear that some senior bureaucrats are unwilling to accept the final say going to the politicians, and when they are willing to pursue and promote their own version of what they presumed to be the public good actively and relentlessly, through passive or active sabotage. This entails not only dissent but a redefinition of their burden of office in such a way that the bureaucrats would appear not to feel compelled to dedicate their full creative attention to the realization of what the politicians want to pursue.

This may not mean active sabotage (even though in some cases it does), but often simply a tepid *pro forma* contribution in the search for the best possible way to effect a policy or decision with which they do not agree.

The dissent of the governed plays a crucial role in participatory democracy. It brings new actors on the political scene and:

> [I]t makes questionable what has previously not been questioned and thereby opens up large areas of social life to public discussion, decision and action…[and] expands the options discussed within the public sphere where decisions are made and thus alters and renews the arena of democratic decision-making (Angus 2001: 65–66).

This sort of social criticism generates the creative energy required by a healthy democracy. It triggers social movements that are in turn "the crucible for the emergent publics" (Ibid., 83).

Such dissent may be regarded as creative disloyalty toward establishment and institution. Graham Greene spoke in 1948 of "the virtue of disloyalty" (quoted by Holloway 2008: 1) in defining the role of artists and other stakeholders who do the most to help institutions adapt to the change and flux of time because they are the least loyal to them.

Obviously this cannot be interpreted as a plea for disloyalty without limits, something that would lead to anarchy and a world of anything goes. Any meaningful definition of burden of office entails a duty of loyalty, and the erosion of such duty (possibly unwittingly with the dilution of the rules in good currency) may be consequential. This is the reason why the decline of the duty of loyalty in corporate law has been bemoaned (J. R. Brown 2006–07). Loyalty is the intrapersonal analogue of obedience and it presumes that loyalty and obedience are agreed to from the start (Falkenberg 1988). So it may be more accurate to restate Graham Green's phrase as "the virtue of dissent" to ensure that there is no ambiguity.

Whistle-blowing

In many quarters, whistle blowing is celebrated disloyalty. In this case, there is not only dissent about what is acceptable and can be done, but action to denounce action that is purported to be violating well-understood, agreed-upon principles, even though such denunciation stands in violation of a duty of loyalty to one's superior.

Disloyalty to a superior is clearly warranted if the actions of the superior are in violation of the law or explicit regulation or endanger third parties—trading off loyalties to superiors against a loyalty to principles protecting the population or the organization from risks. No loyalty is absolute. The central question has to do with the nature of the trade-off. One should be careful, nevertheless, in defending the logic underlying whistle-blowing. If it were to serve as a reference, there would be no basis to argue for a duty of loyalty: it would be by definition contingent since it could always be overridden by a superior duty—a question of personal judgment for anyone that *en son âme et conscience* feels that what is done by a supervisor or minister is not in keeping with what he/she feels is best for the country.

This would amount to legitimizing all forms of disloyalty. Given the fact that current whistle-blowing policies guarantee that whistle-blowers will not be punished, there would appear to be no limit to the damage that can be inflicted except one's conscience. This may be immensely dangerous.

The only way to determine if whistle-blowing action is warranted is an *ex post* examination of the complaint to determine if indeed the denounced action is in violation of law and regulation. But this makes current law and regulation in its present form into something absolute, and presumes that a proactive denunciatory defence of law and regulation as they stand is the accepted norm. Again, this may be unduly restrictive.

This *malaise* is all the more important since whistle-blowing need not be inspired by high-ground feelings, but may have its source in spite or malice. It may also be based on false information or on an abusive interpretation of law and regulation, and create much personal irreparable damage by a party that is promised immunity to begin with if he/she comes forward with a denunciation.

It becomes clear that the *malaise* surrounding whistle-blowing (from all sides), and the fact that it is both celebrated as an act of courage and loyalty to the higher good, but also still considered as an act of disloyalty, makes such an act only evaluable in context. It may be disloyal or not depending on circumstances. The law has often determined that in certain circumstances (like crimes against children), those who are aware of what is going one and do not come forward may be charged. This is the logic behind the whole world of criminal negligence ("unsettling or rash lack of concern" as per the Criminal Code). Yet, it is far from clear under what conditions one can speak of "unsettling and rash lack of concern".

For good reasons, one does not find that a generalized celebration of 'ratting' or *délation* is in good currency. There is still a certain stigma attached to *délation per se*: it is only upon being satisfied that the loyalty to higher things fully legitimizes the disloyalty to lower things that comfort is regained.

Affectio societatis

Any form of organization is built on the assumption that those who choose to become associates have a will to engage and to contribute actively to the common work. In French law, this sort of spirit of collaboration has a name—*affectio societatis*. It is a most important element in corporate law: more or less capturing the fact that partners enter into a partnership in good faith with a will to associate and a commitment that is consequential. In French law, failure to demonstrate *affectio societatis* may lead to the dissolution of the partnership.

This presumption may give heartburn to quantophreniacs, but it has proved an important foundational aspect of French law, and has turned out to be more operational than it might first appear.

As a constitutive element of organizations, *affectio societatis* entails that active and creative contribution to the association or partnership is expected, is part of a postulated moral contract, and therefore is part of the burden of office of the associates. A delinquent associate (i.e., one failing to provide *affectio societatis*) is in breach of contract, and failing to live up to his burden of office. Consequently shirking is not only the source of X-inefficiency, but also a way of failing the test of *affectio societatis,* and a form of disloyalty that can have grave consequences.

This particular phenomenon triggers very interesting considerations. First, it underlines the fact that disloyalty may be the result not only of acts of commission but also of acts of omission. This is similar to failure to provide help to persons in difficulty or failure to provided professional defence to employees—it can be regarded as reprehensible. Second, it illustrates the fact dramatically that failure of engagement and commitment may be a form of disloyalty, whether or not it may result from shocks that have mitigated or attenuated the original commitment. Finally, it makes the point forcefully that the burden of office as a nexus of moral contracts may be difficult to define, but that its very existence may be sufficient to determine if there has been disloyalty: breaking a moral contract is disloyalty.

The myth of the state clergy

A most fascinating strategy to immunize state workers from being accused of disloyalty has been in good currency in public administration circles for quite a long time. It has, as the Hon. Hugh Segal suggests, taken the form of declaring state workers not as being concerned first with public administration and its privileges, but as mainly motivated by the public good, as being charged with different, higher-order and nobler tasks, and as having been chosen for those tasks on the basis of exceptional qualities enabling them to respond to this calling.

Jane Jacobs has stylized this Manichean view of the world very aptly in her book *Systems of Survival,* in which she contrasts the public and the private spheres as corresponding to two very distinct sorts of activities characterized by two syndromes: the guardian moral syndrome and the commercial moral syndrome (Jacobs 1992). In her world view, public sector employees are "guardians" of the public good and characterized in so doing as: being ostentatious, adhering to tradition, showing fortitude, being obedient, disciplined and loyal, but also (since nothing is perfect) as dispensing largesse, making rich use of leisure, taking vengeance, and deceiving for the sake of the task. This is contrasted with the lower-order world of private sector employees as "traders" engaged in commercial activities and characterized in so doing as: being honest, efficient, industrious and collaborative, respecting contracts, and being open to novelty and dissent for the sake of the task.

In the Jacobs-ian universe, those two worlds are not only contrasted but should remain entirely separate: public purpose and private gain are incompatible, and therefore should never mix for what would ensue then would be "monstrous hybrids".

Jacobs' book was on the desk of most Ottawa senior bureaucrats in the early 1990s. It provided the intellectual argumentation in support of the special status being claimed by public servants as a group of persons dedicated to the public good rather than being simply busy, like other workers, with private endeavours. This special status obviously called for special treatment because the public sphere was purported to be not only different in degree from the private sphere but also as different in kind.

This view of this world has had important impacts on Canadian political culture: it explains the visceral opposition to private sector presence in health care and to public–private partnerships, etc. It has also underpinned the view that not everyone is suited for these higher-order tasks: public sector employees are presented as chosen only because they have the exceptional qualities required to respond to this calling—for public service is a vocation not a job. Indeed, we are informed that the Treasury Board Secretariat is preparing a joint venture with public administration academics to defend this special status of the 'state clergy'.

For Jacobs, despite superficial similarities in the nature of the tasks carried out by employees of the public and private sectors, the differences are fundamental: public servants as embodiment of the Hegelian State *sortent de la cuisse de Jupiter*. In that view of the world, the expression 'disloyalty of public servants' is an oxymoron, a contradiction in terms. Public servants are the new state clergy and loyalty is consubstantial to their very being— loyalty to the pursuit of the public good, a task for which they are obviously much better suited one might be led to conclude than the non-descript bunch of individuals churned out by the electoral process.

We have not been very taken by Jane Jacobs' view of the world. It has always appeared to be extremely simplistic, naively Manichean, and perilously misleading: simplistic because it occludes civil society and reciprocity—this is not a two- but multi-party game; Manichean because it denies what governance studies have explored over the last decades—the richness and effectiveness of inter-sectoral collaboration; misleading because it provides unwarranted sanctimonious blessing to public sector activities *per se*. It is hardly surprising that this conceptualization has been seized by the bureaucracy as a gift from the gods. It fails miserably however, any test of reasonableness.

One of the many perverse unintended consequences of Jacobs' stylization is the fact that it has provided moral support for an anti-democratic push by the public managerial class to usurp the dominium of the elected officials, and a displacement of democratic values by professional/corporatist values in the ethical fabric of the Canadian federal public sector. Indeed, this has led to both democratic and professional values being conflated and confounded in the emerging version of the code of ethics of the Canadian federal public service, leading one to feel that the former are slowly *engulfed* by the latter. It is hardly surprising in these circumstances that the political-bureaucratic interface has been tilted.

The impact of these developments on the disloyalty debate is important. By strengthening the legitimacy of the bureaucracy (and professional values) significantly, and, as a result, significantly reducing the relative valence of the politicians (and thereby democratic values), the recent developments have contributed much to the attenuation and de-clawing of the notion of disloyalty. Bureaucratic judgment is slowly being allowed to openly challenge the legitimacy of the judgment of elected officials, and therefore allowing a hollowing out of the notion of disloyalty completely in its basic sense of requiring deference to democratic values as dominating.

In this new context, the shift from a dominance of democratic values to a dominance of professional values tends to reinforce the relative importance of the tribes within the public service, and to allow corporatist values to trump democratic ones. The rumoured process under way at the Treasury Board Secretariat to put even more emphasis on the missionary and exceptional nature of work in the public sphere, and to condone the Jacobsian view of the world anew is not innocent. It would aggravate the erosion of democratic values further, as well as deterring much experimentation with private–public–civic collaboration. The result would be to confer even more valence to *homo corporativus* in the federal public service.

Conclusion

This chapter had two main ambitions: to provide a philosophical map of what is meant by disloyalty, and to put forward the hypothesis that there has been an increase in disloyalty in the Canadian federal public service.

On the first front, we hope to have enriched the notion of disloyalty somewhat and to have extracted it from the closet of topics 'unsuitable for discussion'.

Whether this philosophical map will prove useful is, however, something that remains to be seen. Our test of this has a Schumacherian flavour. As Fritz Schumacher explained "mapmaking is an empirical art that employs a high degree of abstraction but nonetheless clings to reality" (Schumacher 1977: 7). Type I or so-called scientistic mapmakers have a basic principle: in case of doubt, leave it out. Type II pragmatic mapmakers (i.e., mapmakers of our sort) take a different approach; like Schumacher, they suggest turning this principle into its opposite, and working on the basis of the guiding principle: if in doubt, show it prominently.

The cost of this second approach is not that high since if something does not exist, someone will quickly denounce it and show it not to be true. It happens within days on Wikipedia. On the other hand, the benefits may be high. The logic is simple: if one limits oneself to what is true beyond doubt, one minimizes the risk of error, but at the same time one maximizes the risk of missing out on what might be most important (Ibid., 3). For instance, if you are drifting in a leisurely way down a river in a small boat, and there may be a 1,000-metre fall downstream, on which type of mapmaker would you like to be able to count?

On the second front, we are sure that most will complain that we have not provided the smoking gun, and that our 'demonstration' has failed to meet the standards of what has been famously called the 'interocular trauma test'—that is, generating findings that hit the researcher, the reader and the audience between the eyes. That much we concede.

Have we been able to persuade our audience that our conjectures have merit and deserve some attention through our work as backwoods mechanics? Only the reader can say!

CHAPTER 6

The Neurotic State·

*The political community must be able to distinguish between
disagreement with particular policies of the community and
disloyalty to the community itself.*

—Stephen L. Carter

One of the perplexing features of Canada's political scene over
the last several years is a dramatic, if silent, revolution in the
functioning of the federal state. Program review, alternative service
delivery and other such initiatives had a clear decentralization
and privatization thrust, while at the same time carrying a good
governance flavour (transparency, accountability, integrity).
Yet the net effect of these initiatives has been a phenomenal
re-concentration of power in central agencies and in the Prime
Minister's Office, and a shift toward a neurotic governance
regime. The former phenomenon has been carefully documented
and analyzed (Savoie 1999; Simpson 2001); we would like to
examine the latter.

A superficial examination of these issues has led some
observers to suggest that the re-concentration of effective power
at the center is the culprit: that it has generated the emergence
of the new bunker mentality, and transformed the federal public

---

* This chapter is co-authored with Luc Juillet.

service into an enterprise where dissent is being subtly suppressed and where disagreement has come to be regarded as a form of treason. But the causality also runs the other way. Mutual distrust between the citizenry and the government, as well as fear of the political consequences of the disclosure of critical information about government activities, contribute to a tightening of central controls. They breed organizational paranoia. One must look at the dynamics that have generated this emerging neurotic governance regime to help explain the reconcentration of power and other dysfunctions that have been noted in the recent past.

At the root of this dynamic is the growing distrust of government by the citizenry. This distrust has produced added pressure for more transparency and hard accountability at a time when the turbulent environment and the accelerated pace of change would appear to require the new governance regime to be more flexible and more decentralized, that is, calling for more discretion for the agents of the state, and softer forms of accountability (Juillet et al. 2001).

While this growing public distrust is not a phenomenon unique to Canada, the response to public distrust has been significantly sharper in Canada because the Office of the Prime Minister and some other central agencies have a much more formidable power base than similar agencies in other advanced democracies. In reality, we live not in a parliamentary democracy in Canada, but a world in which Cabinet acts as a mini sounding board for a prime minister and Parliament is ignored (Simpson 2001).

One important element of the Canadian response has been a sharp decline in the willingness of governments and bureaucrats to disclose information about their operations, as it became evident that information disclosed this way is often used to fuel attacks on the political and bureaucratic processes. This culture of secrecy in turn has led to greater distrust, and to more vehement requests for information, and so on. What has ensued is greater distrust on the part of the citizenry, and paranoia on the part of the state.

The main consequences of this vicious circle have been the rise of a new *raison d'État*, and the activation of a number of mechanisms that have corrupted public discourse and the governance regime. The culture of secrecy has hardened into a neurotic state, and the virus of paranoia has cascaded down the bureaucratic ladder.

Caught between distrust of the citizens and circling of the wagons by the Prime Minister's government, the federal public service has not only firmly sided with the government, but it has exacerbated the degree of paranoia.

In fact, as the information commissioner pointed out in a special report to Parliament in response to the then newly-elected Conservative government's discussion paper on access reform:

> [t]he current government's proposals are every bit as much a "bureaucrat's dream" as were those of the Chrétien government.... There is no more eloquent testimonial to the power of the forces of secrecy in government than the radical change they have wrought, in a few short weeks, to the Prime Minister's election promises for access reform (Reid 2006).

As a matter of consequence, the governed have become devoiced, their dissent generating retribution and rebuke, not only by politicians but also by faceless middle-ranked bureaucrats defending not so much the interests of the government as their own particular version of what the interests of the government are.

We would like to identify the symptoms of this silent revolution and track down the source of the neurosis; to document some of the forms it has taken; to look at this dynamic at work in the access-to-information files; and to hint at the implications it appears to hold in store for the federal public service, and for democracy in Canada.

The symptom: a new raison d'État

It is difficult to determine a precise date for the emergence of this neurotic syndrome. One may note however that this new dynamic was already in place in 1995 when explicit reference was made in official federal government documents to the "public interest" as having to be defined in the light of the need for "fulfilling federal obligations and interests". The French version was even more ominous *"remplir les obligations du gouvernement fédéral et en protéger les intérêts"* (Canada 1995).

This is not an entirely new phenomenon. There have in the past been a number of instances where action has been taken to devoice the government's critics, but by 2001 there had been a significant increase in the scale and importance of these efforts to suppress dissent, or to effect censorship by brandishing the phrase "contrary to the interests of the government".

This has been nothing short of an epistemological coup, through which the state declared that it had interests 'of its own' and that they should prevail over others. It was a change of kind more than degree. True, one had witnessed this sort of arrogance in the era of the Rt. Hon Pierre Trudeau, but perhaps because of the very self-assured intellectual arrogance on which it was built, it had never translated into the high degree of intimidation, exclusion and censorship observed in the era of the Rt. Hon. Jean Chrétien and subsequently.

In recent years, the new arrogance has been accompanied by a sense of insecurity that has led to much double-talk, dissimulation and deception. Autocratic intervention to suppress dissent has been routinely accompanied by sermons on openness, participation, citizen engagement, and the need to build a sensitive citizen-centred *modus operandi*. This mismatch between words and deeds has become a chronic feature of the new regime in many segments of the federal public service.

The pattern obviously does not apply to all agencies. Some departments and agencies have maintained a reasonable degree of effectiveness and integrity, and a good fit between words and deeds. Others have suffered from different styles of dysfunction as a result of history, circumstances and personalities. Most federal departments and agencies have been permeated by a certain *malaise*, ascribable to the fact that key central agencies, which are "*définisseurs de situation*" and have a major impact on the *modus operandi* of the whole system, have been fundamentally affected by this new mindset.

Whatever form the neurosis took, the result has been the discouragement of critical thinking about any aspect of the federal apparatus, processes and policies inside bureaucracy, and the emergence of a sort of self-censorship that prevented not only critical thinking, but as a matter of consequence, any meaningful social learning. (Hubbard and Paquet 2007c).

Canada has not become a police state, of course. All these interventions have been rather subtle: hypersensitivity, over concern with hidden motives, a sense of guarded and pervasive suspicion etc., all in response to the citizenry's true sense of a loss of confidence. But this *malaise* has transformed government's way of doing business.

It is easy to slip from this defensive stance to one in which the preservation of the operating system comes to be regarded as the central purpose of the governance regime (and its staunch defence, the dominant logic—la *raison d'État*). Indeed, it has occurred.

The distrust-paranoia vicious cycle

The idea of the *raison d'État* is that the state takes itself as it own end, and in so doing considers society as a means to this end (Millon-Delsol 1992). It rationalizes the use and abuse of power, and the resort to exceptional measures as a way to maintain control over the governance process because it is a pursuit that is regarded as pre-eminently important.

Checks and balances are usually in place to ensure that each sphere of the state remains within its own field of competence, and that the state does not encroach on the legitimate realm of the individual, of civil society, etc. To monitor, control, redress and sanction such trespassing, the agencies responsible for checks and balances must have the legal authority to deal with encroachment and corruption (O'Donnell 1998).

In many democracies, there has been a phenomenal erosion of this delicate balance over the past few years. In Canada, this problem has been aggravated by a number of idiosyncratic systems failures: the collapse of the fractured Conservative opposition for many years, the trivialization of the controls of the House of Commons, the Cabinet's becoming a focus group rather than a decision-making body, and the effective re-centralization of power in the hands of the Prime Minister and his advisors. The crisis of confidence is hardly surprising.

This crisis of confidence is apparent on several fronts. Firstly, there has been a remarkable drop in support for politicians as a group both in Canada and elsewhere (Pharr and Putnam 2000). A similar trend is observed in attitudes toward political parties (Carty et al. 2000). Canadians have also shown a declining level of trust in the executive and legislative branches of government as a whole. According to 1996 surveys, only 21 percent of Canadians trusted Parliament to represent them, a sharp decline of about 60 percent since the mid-1970s (Leduc 1995; Clarke et al. 1995).

This decline of trust in political authorities should not be confused with apathy toward politics. Disengagement from traditional avenues of political participation, such as political parties, has led to the growth of alternative forms of political engagement, which tend to be more grassroots-based and confrontational, *vis-à-vis* state agencies. It translates into a greater demand for information (Nevitte 2001). Recent comparative longitudinal studies of political attitudes in Western democracies have found a simultaneous decline in respect for government authority and a growth in support for democracy (Inglehart 2000).

This erosion of trust has many sources: the lack of accuracy and comprehensiveness of information about what government does, the changes in the ways in which public institutions are evaluated, and the deterioration in the performance of public institutions (ascribable either to declines in the capacity of political agents, or in the fidelity with which political agents defend citizens' interests) (Pharr and Putnam 2000: 22–26).

The difficulties of operating transparently in a political environment of distrust and criticism are further exacerbated when the media and opposition politicians use access-to-information provisions mainly as a tool to publicly embarrass the government. This has led to a number of paranoid reactions.[1]

The neurosis of the Canadian state

To study the emergence of this neurotic style in federal governance and the organizational dysfunctioning that it has generated, we used a simple framework proposed by Manfred Kets de Vries and Danny Miller. They examine the patterns of symptoms and dysfunction that appear to combine into syndromes of pathology, and the mechanisms through which neurotic styles and organizational behaviors would interact and lend support to one another (Kets de Vries and Miller 1984; Kets de Vries 2001).

Different styles of neurosis

Neurosis is a sort of dysfunction that generates affective and emotional problems but without disrupting the functioning of the organization. There are different styles of neurosis: paranoid, compulsive, dramatic, depressive, schizoid. Each has its own characteristics, dominant motivating fantasy and associated dangers. Table 6.1 borrowed from Kets de Vries and Miller, provides a broad characterization of these different styles.

Table 6.1   *Summary of the neurotic styles*

	Paranoid (suspicious)	Compulsive	Dramatic	Depressive	Schizoid (detached)
Characteristics	mistrust	perfectionism	self-dramatization	sense of guilt	non-involvement
	much info processing	rigid formal code	overcentralized	ritualism	internal focus
	hypersensitivity	focus on trivia	narcissism	helplessness	estrangement
	perceived threats	ritualized evaluation	2nd-tier lacking influence	unflexibility	self-imposed barriers to information
	centralized power	dogmatism	exploitativeness	bureaucracy	insufficient scanning of environment
Fantasy	I cannot really trust anybody; I had better be on my guard	I don't want be at the mercy of events I must control all things	I want to get attention from and impress people I am not good enough	It is hopeless to change the course of events in my offer	The world of reality does not offer any satisfaction so it is safer to remain distant

	Paranoid (suspicious)	Compulsive	Dramatic	Depressive	Schizoid (detached)
Culture	fear of attack	rigidity	idealizing	lacking initiative	insecurity
	intimidation	inward directed	hyperactive	decidophobia	conflict ridden
	uniformity	tightly focused	impulsive	lacking vigilance	indecisive
	reactive	obsessive	bold ventures	leadership vacuum	inconsistent
	conservative	non-adaptive	non participative	no sense of direction	narrow perspectives
	secretive	exhaustive evaluation	action for action's sake	lacking motivation	lacking warmth
Dangers	distorsion of reality	fear of making mistakes	overreaction to minor events	inhibition of action	bewilderment and aggressiveness
	defensive attitude	excessive reliance on rules	actions based on appearances	indecisiveness overly pessimistic	emotional isolation

Source: Adapted from Kets de Vries and Miller 1984: 24–25 and Kets de Vries 2001: 146–147.

All individuals have mildly dysfunctional neurotic traits, but certain dominant patterns of these traits betray a dominant neurotic style. Organizations also display such traits that permeate or colour the functioning of the organization and its organizational culture. While these organizational traits may emerge as a result of various environmental forces, or shared fantasies and myths developed through the history of the organization, they also depend to some extent on the personality and management style of the leader.

To psychoanalyze an organization, one must rely on interviews or some significant interaction with members of the organization, and the impressions, anecdotes and such data as ethnographic studies unearth. The results of such an investigation of the organizational fabric of a large concern like the federal state do not necessarily reveal a single dominant neurotic style. Many segments may indeed be associated with different styles.

For instance, Statistics Canada may be more readily associated with a compulsive style, while this need not be the case for the Privy Council Office (PCO). Some might associate Canadian Heritage with the dramatic style, Human Resources and Social Development Canada with the depressive style, Foreign Affairs Canada with the schizoid syndrome. Each of these hypotheses would require an extensive investigation to ascertain its validity.

Yet one may make the case that, over the past few years, as central agencies tightened their grip on the governance of the country, a particular neurotic style has permeated the whole system—as a result of signals and pressures emanating from the Privy Council Office. The results we have uncovered in our work suggest that the whole federal state has been permeated by a paranoid style of neurosis.

The full verification or falsification of this hypothesis would require much more space than is afforded for this chapter. However, there is enough scope for us to sketch briefly, and in a general way, the main features of the syndrome, to illustrate how this dynamic works, and what consequences one may expect.

Main features

The paranoid organization usually emerges in the face of a dynamic environment that requires continuous scanning to detect threats and challenges.

A first characteristic of this type of organization is its managers' focus on perpetual vigilance and preparedness for emergencies, and on controlling the internal operations to be able to make use of them. Indeed, the constant effort to 'uncover' organizational problems leads to tension and to an excessive sensitivity to any exposure to risk. This fosters a perceived need for constant readiness to counter threats.

A second organizational characteristic is the propensity to centralize power in the hands of top executives and their consultants. Those who feel threatened demand control over their subordinates. As they become distrustful and fearful, the locus of power shifts upward. This dynamic has an impact on junior executives, as key decision makers tend to direct their distrust externally, and demand the same sort of distrust to be shared by their subordinates. Indeed, not sharing the distrust becomes itself a source of distrust if and when an insider questions it. This quickly leads to insecurity and disenchantment among lower-tier executives because of the atmosphere of distrust.

A third characteristic is a great conservatism. Top executives cope but they do not have a concerted and integrated strategy. Muddling through and fear lead to a risk minimization strategy by default.

Dynamics at work

The crucial element at the core of the paranoid organization is the pattern of confused interpersonal relationships generated by core hostility. In leadership, it is a most destructive attitude. The boss sees his/her subordinates as malingerers and incompetents, and either tries to exert intensive control and personal supervision or takes an overtly aggressive style and destroys their career. This management pattern generates uncooperative behavior and further mistrust, suspicion and vindictiveness.

The consequences for decision making are important, as cognitive criteria are replaced by affected criteria in selecting alternatives. But they are most destructive for the organization as subordinates suffer from a constant *double-entendre*: they are asked to be frank and to express critical thinking, but are chastised as disloyal and treasonous when they do so.

This sort of neurosis and others mentioned in table 6.1 give rise to a number of common problems that Kets de Vries and Miller have identified: improper allocation of authority, out of line attitude to risk, inadequate organization structures, poor distribution of information, deficient calibre of executive talent (Kets de Vries and Miller 1984: 171–172).

The central challenge is working back from these symptoms to track down the source of these problems—and their underlying roots—in order to generate the requisite organizational therapy and find ways to implement it.

The central point about the neurotic state is that it is both difficult to reconstruct and almost certainly the result in good part of the unintended consequences of bad habits. This point has been forcefully made by Dietrich Dörner, whose analysis of "the logic of failure" reveals that in a dynamic system, crises do not emerge from the action of one major culprit, but from the cumulative effect of complexity, lack of transparency, and incomplete or incorrect understanding of the system: small mistakes, bad habits and certain mechanisms that catalyze the cumulative process (Dörner 1997).

These mechanisms are studied by political psychology but since many often work in contrary directions—as in the bandwagon effect and the underdog effect on voters. So they cannot be universally "applied to predict and control social events but...embod(y) a causal chain that is sufficiently general and precise to enable us to locate it in widely different settings".[2]

Access to information policy and the culture of paranoia

Recent debates about the rules regarding citizens' rights to have access to government information offer an interesting window on the dynamics at play within the federal bureaucracy, and illustrate the culture of paranoia in official Ottawa.

Over the past few years, the relationships between the federal government (politicians and bureaucrats) and the Information Commissioner have deteriorated. The implementation, interpretation and reform of access-to-information legislation have been bitterly debated by federal governments from the two major political parties. These developments conform in important ways to what one might expect from a paranoid organization.

The federal *Access to Information Act* was adopted in 1983 after decades of hesitation and debate. Since the adoption of an access to information law by the United States in 1966, there had been active proponents of similar measures in Canada. Gerald Baldwin (a Conservative member of Parliament), an early crusader of transparency in government, first introduced a private member's bill on access to information in 1969 and reintroduced it in subsequent sessions until 1974. It was almost to no avail, though the Trudeau government adopted limited official guidelines on information disclosure in 1973.

Canadians had to wait for the 1979 minority government of the Rt. Hon. Joe Clark to see the government table an access to information bill in Parliament. The Progressive Conservatives had promised an access to information law during the election campaign, and, upon taking power, introduced a bill that would have established a broad right of access to government records, a system to allow some exemptions and a review process to ensure they were appropriately used. Following the fall of Clark's government, the new Trudeau government reintroduced a modified version of the bill that became the *Access to Information Act* a few years later.

The act grants Canadians the right to access government records in any form, with some exceptions. Firstly, some classes of information, such as Cabinet records, are excluded from the ambit of the legislation. The act also allows for some exemptions. For example, section 14 provides for the discretionary withholding of documents regarding federal-provincial affairs when disclosure would run counter to public interest.

Importantly, the act also gives citizens the right to appeal to the Office of the Information Commissioner when they are not satisfied with the response given to their request. The Information Commissioner, an independent officer reporting to Parliament, can use extensive investigative powers to ensure that there has been appropriate compliance with the act. In cases where the use of exemptions is questioned, the Commissioner can review the requested document to determine whether they were legitimately exempted. However, while he/she can make recommendations, the Commissioner does not have the legal authority to force the disclosure of any records.

Over the years, the access to information legislation has been much criticized. On the one hand, members of Parliament, journalists, information commissioners, and citizens have all complained that the government is adopting an excessively broad interpretation of the rules for exemptions, and that delays in responding to access requests are unreasonable. On the other hand, the government and the public servants have complained that the demands are excessive, both extending to parts of the government's decision-making process that should remain confidential, and imposing an excessive burden on resources for compliance.

Since for quite a while the act simply served as a conduit for access to information that would "make the government squirm"(Simpson 2001: 57), the government and its public servants have become suspicious of requests, and have come to fear the consequences of information disclosure and transparency.

The symptoms

One of the most serious effects of the ensuing climate of distrust is the resulting change in the way that many civil servants work. In the interviews conducted for this project, several public servants have told us that they are increasingly reluctant to write down anything that could be construed as remotely controversial, since it might well make its way to the public domain through the access-to-information rules. One experienced manager with the Department of Fisheries and Oceans told us that, in the units where he worked, the unspoken rule had become: you don't write down anything important about issues that could become controversial. Another person spoke of someone who confided in her that she now worried about forgetting important things about her work because she was reluctant to take comprehensive notes during meetings.

This attitude appears to be fairly prevalent within the public service. The (now former) Information Commissioner noted that the attitude toward information management in the public service had truly become: "Why write it, when you can speak it? Why speak it when you can nod? Why nod, when you can wink?"(Ibid., 59). Many high-level committees in government, his office has found, have ceased the practices of "creating agendas, keeping minutes and tabling briefing notes and papers to assist discussion" (Canada 2000b: 22). In the words of Alasdair Roberts, it has come to a point where one may speak of a shadow government (A. Roberts 2000). This severe aversion to the risks of information disclosure has also led senior management and central agencies to tighten internal decision-making processes regarding disclosure.

The Prime Minister's Office (PMO) at the time of the Chrétien government also decided to contest the right of the Information Commissioner to review its records to determine whether it has grounds for refusing their disclosure. It claimed that the PMO falls outside the purview of the access-to-information law and became engaged in a series of fifteen lawsuits with the Commissioner's

Office to deny it the right to examine some requested documents concerning the Prime Minister's agenda.

Prime Minister Harper's government's approach has similarly been to assert in a public discussion paper that the right of access ought not to reach into the PMO or ministers' offices.

At the present time, interim Information Commissioner Suzanne Legeault has pointed out that she has not found a lack of will on the part of the present government to be transparent, while acknowledging that delays are becoming problematic (Canada 2010b).

Finally, another example of the desire of the government to keep a tight control over information disclosure issues is its reaction to the amendment of the *Access to Information Act* adopted in 1998. The amendment, which took the form of a private member's bill, added a subsection to the law that prohibits the destruction, concealment or falsification of records for the purpose of avoiding disclosure. In 1999, the Treasury Board Secretariat (TBS) published a new directive to departments, forbidding them to notify the Information Commissioner's Office about allegations of such violations of the access law. Instead, such matters were to be handled by deputy ministers themselves, who, following their own internal investigation, would decide whether to notify independent law enforcement agencies (Canada 2000b: 24).

The Information Commissioner's campaign

As could be expected, the former Information Commissioner (who served in this capacity from 1998–2006) responded sharply to the government's poor compliance with the letter and spirit of the access law in the recent past. However, in doing so, he adopted a confrontational approach that seems to have provided comfort to the government's and the civil servants' view that they were the object of sustained unreasonable attacks, and that they were generally considered as 'enemies' by the Commissioner and parts of the citizenry.

The confrontational approach of that Commissioner is well captured in his 1999–2000 report to Parliament. The first section of the report, entitled "Access—A Right Under Siege", began with the following statement:

> Last year, [...], the government was put on notice: There would be a "zero-tolerance" policy for late responses to access requests; a new, pro-openness approach to the administration of the Access Law would be expected and, most important, the full weight of the Commissioner's investigative powers would be brought to bear to achieve these goals (Ibid., 9).

These are uncharacteristically tough words for an officer of Parliament, whose authority to "put the government on notice" seems questionable at best. But the tone is indicative of the aggressive and uncompromising character of exchanges between the Commissioner's Office and the public service through most of his tenure. If the Information Commissioner has publicly complained that civil servants were "circling the wagons" as a result of his inquiries, he himself had clearly gone to war.

A Manichean language, pitting citizens against government, outsiders against insiders, is common in the documents penned by the Information Commissioner's Office dating from that period. "For too long, the whiners and complainers inside the system have had their causes taken up by TBS; it is the turn of the citizens on the outside and the access law to have the designated minister become their champion", the Commissioner wrote in his 1999-2000 report (Ibid., 14).

The report's practice of issuing annual 'report cards' to rate the performance of departments in responding to access to information requests in a timely fashion, while potentially serving as a useful vehicle of accountability, including praise when it was justified and offering to help bring about improvements in other cases, appears to have been just another illustration of the hard-nosed, confrontational approach of the Information Commissioner's Office during that era.

Under its grading scheme, any department failing to answer within the statutory deadline to 20 percent or more of the access requests that they receive is assigned an 'F'. While the Commissioner acknowledged that the Privy Council Office deserved to be praised for moving from an 'F' to an 'A' in just one year (by cutting the percentage of requests it answered outside the statutory deadline by 90 percent between 1998 and 1999), it nevertheless severely condemned it for leading an "attack upon the very foundation of the Commissioner's role" (Ibid., 9).

The tone and nature of these exchanges obviously affected the attitudes of some senior civil servants. Frustrated by a perceived lack of collaboration from senior bureaucrats, the Commissioner of the day resorted to issuing subpoenas to force deputy ministers to explain, on the record and under oath, the reasons for departmental delays in answering access to information requests. This aggressive use of investigative powers only comforted the senior bureaucracy in their view that the Commissioner's office was "out to get them". In memory of these encounters, one deputy minister, we were told by one interviewee, has had his subpoena framed and has installed it on the wall of his office.

The review process and the Bryden Committee

However, the former Information Commissioner was not alone in his battle with the former Liberal government and the public service on the issue of access to information. In June of 2001, a group of backbench members of Parliament, led by Liberal member John Bryden, took the highly unusual step of creating an unofficial ad hoc committee to study the reform of the access to information legislation. The creation of the committee, which was composed of members of Parliament from most parties, and was holding meetings within the parliamentary precinct, but which had not been mandated or created by Parliament, came about in direct response to the government's handling of the act's official review process.

In 2000, the government of the day finally decided that the time had come to make changes to the access-to-information rules. To study options and recommend specific changes, the then President of the Treasury Board Secretariat appointed a taskforce composed only of civil servants. While the taskforce created an advisory committee composed of outsiders, it nevertheless drew heavy criticism for being too close to the government and to the viewpoint of the public service.[3] Some members of Parliament, including John Bryden, were especially displeased by the limited role elected officials (who frequently use the access law) would get to play in the review process. Moreover, the taskforce, which received submissions and briefs from some stakeholders, was also condemned for not sufficiently consulting Canadians. The government, it was claimed by critics, was making sure that the review process would serve to curtail the scope of the legislation (Clark 2001a).

The Bryden Committee was meant to be a response to this process. Unlike the taskforce, the committee would consult more widely and work more independently from the government. However, as could be expected, the government at the time failed to collaborate with the independent-minded members, and it actively impaired its ability to conduct a full review by forbidding civil servants to appear before it (Ibid.; Clark 2001b). The government's official position was that, since the committee was not an official creation of Parliament, civil servants could be held liable for comments that they might make before it. Moreover, the Government House Leader argued, confusion might arise, which would be detrimental to the official review process, if civil servants' testimony was taken out of context, especially by the media (Lawton 2001).

While at the time, Bryden repeatedly tried to gain the collaboration of the Government House Leader and the Clerk of the Privy Council in this regard, he was thoroughly unsuccessful. Moreover, after having agreed to appear before the committee, officials from Crown corporations, such as NavCanada and Canada Post, decided to backtrack after seeing the government boycott the committee's work. As a result, the committee heard from advocacy groups and experts but was forced to table its report without the benefit of having talked to government officials. According to Bryden, some information experts also decided to abstain from participating in the committee's work for fear of reprisals and loss of government contracts (Jack 2001a). As a result, the committee's witness list was reduced by two-thirds, and two Liberal backbenchers decided to leave the committee (Jack 2001b).

The government's position and tactics only fuelled the fire of criticism by those who believed that it simply sought to control the scope of the act. Mike Gordon, chairman of Open Government Canada, a coalition of groups concerned about access to information, described the government's response in this way:

> This is an extremely hostile act by the cabinet and they are essentially putting the leash back on MPs. The [government] is saying that we, the cabinet, do not want to allow any public review; we want to control the Access Act and our little closed task force will be adequate to that effect (Ross 2001).

Some Liberal members of Parliament associated with the committee also used some unusually harsh language about the government. For example, Reg Alcock, then a Liberal backbencher, said that the Chrétien government had become blinkered and elitist over its years in power and displayed, like its bureaucrats, a natural desire to conceal information that might be embarrassing (Jack 2001a). Less surprisingly, the Opposition also used the opportunity to send a similar message. Grant McNally, a Democratic Representative Caucus member, is reported to have said: "There's a clear message there that the Prime Minister likes the culture of secrecy around the Access to Information Act. That should be a concern to all Canadians." (Jack 2001c; A. Roberts 2001a).

As we have pointed out, the election of a new Conservative government has not changed the scene much. In the *Federal Accountability Act* that received Royal Assent on December 12, 2006, changes were included that extended the reach of the legislation to include new institutions. The new Information Commissioner observed that some amendments required that previously-accessible records were to be kept secret unjustifiably and that the "special exemptions and exclusions designed for newly added institutions are unjustifiably broad" (Canada 2007a: chapter 1, 1–2/4).

Overall, debates about access to information suggest that a vicious dynamic is at play: the distrust of government leads citizens to aggressively seek disclosure, and to see in delays and exemptions clear signs of authoritarianism; in turn, citizens, members of Parliament, and the Information Commissioner publicly attack the government and the public service for failure to comply with the act. Mutual distrust and paranoia become natural reactions.

As a result, it seems unlikely that the interim Information Commissioner, by using a less confrontational and pessimistic tone and approach, can transform the tone of the debate on such a naturally contentious issue.

Consequences

The recent debates on access to information are symptomatic of a general organizational paranoia that has crystallized in some parts of the public service. One may reasonably ask what likely consequences can be expected from such a development.

There are at least three areas where there is cause for concern.

The first has to do with the capacity of the public service to truly become a learning organization and to contribute actively to social learning in Canada. For an organization to learn, information sharing, the tolerance of risks in seeking new ways of doing things, and the ability to openly discuss performance and past failures are essential. To the extent that an organizational culture of paranoia leads to a tightening of central controls over experimentation, as well as restrictions on the disclosure of information about considered options and past failures, organizational learning is stunted.

Secondly, in the new knowledge-based society, information is not only a public good, it is also a public resource. Some analysts have even talked about an "informational commons"(A. Roberts 2001b). While in earlier periods, information might reasonably have been rationed on a need-to-know basis without much consequence, in the new information society, access to information is a basic necessity. In this context, a culture of secrecy and adverse attitudes about information disclosure are tantamount to self-imposed restrictions on the availability to citizens of some of our most valuable resources. This can only dramatically weaken the capacity for citizen engagement.

Most importantly, perhaps, the culture of paranoia, fuelled by the adversarial dynamics surrounding access to government information, is threatening the health of our democracy. Democratic governments have to accept some responsibility for ensuring that their citizenry has access to the information required for their full, informed participation in governance processes. This is all the more important since the state is the largest repository of information in society, and often the only source of some unique data of great relevance for understanding our contemporary social and natural environment, and therefore needed for meaningful political participation by the citizenry.

Conclusion

The fast-paced nature of socio-economic change that creates the need for continual adaptation by public and private actors, the increase in relevant uncertainty, and a more critical citizenry that is distrustful of traditional political institutions and more skilful at opposition and challenge have combined to create major challenges for the effective governance of contemporary societies.

In looking for a response to these challenges, national states are tempted to turn inward and to attempt to regain greater control, and shield themselves from opposition and criticism, by depriving the citizenry of information about its internal decision making and operations.

Such a course of action has been characteristic of the Canadian response, but, given the phenomenal power of the state apparatus in Canada, the reaction has been stronger than elsewhere. It has generated a neurotic regime.

This disquisition is only meant to whet the reader's appetite and to suggest the heuristic power of an approach to organizational effectiveness that is based on neurotic styles. In this chapter, we have used a simple classification scheme to examine the dynamics that have led to this neurotic state. The neurosis has probably taken different forms in different segments of the Canadian state. But behind these diverse styles, one may detect a dominant flavour of neurosis—paranoia.

We have documented the tensions surrounding the interactions between stakeholders around the operations of the *Access to Information Act*. In this context, maximum openness is a sensible goal, provided that it is offset by operational principles seeking to ensure that the fundamental rights and basic interests of citizens are protected, and that the state preserves the ability to act effectively in the public interest. We have shown how paranoia has prevented the materialization of a workable set of arrangements.

While the access to information case is illustrative of this drift toward the neurotic state, it is not an oddity. The neurotic state hypothesis underpins a research program that attempts to make sense of a variety of instances that may otherwise be regarded as insignificant anomalies. In many other segments of the Canadian state, we have found other forms of neurosis that are not documented here. They have generated the same cumulative causation process leading to more secretiveness, decline in public trust, centralization, conservatism, lack of critical thinking, and failure for government to operate as a learning organization.

Nothing short of a cultural revolution can reverse the tendencies that underpin these different forms of neurosis. Democratic accountability and social learning will be best served by a widely shared culture of openness and transparency in government and the public service, and by the creation of a reasoned dialogue among public servants, politicians and citizens. Such a culture of openness and reasoned dialogue will not emerge unless we can restore greater trust in government.

Endnotes

[1] Public discourse has been sanitized, suspicion has come to prevail in a general way, and a garrison mentality has emerged in various segments of the federal public household. This has led to various whimsical knee-jerk reactions when any critical discussion of any initiative of the government has materialized—a decision by the authorities of the Canadian Centre for Management Development (now called the Canada School of Public Service) not to publish a series of studies on the general restructuring of government in the mid 1990s that it had funded and had been peer-reviewed and assessed as excellent even though not uncritical of government; the explicit control of the pulpit at the School by the top authorities and the development of an informal black list of persons not to be invited to lecture there; the sanitization of the content of courses to ensure that they are purged of any critical content and focus entirely on machinery of government issues; explicit censorship of *Optimum: The Journal of Public Management* by officials of Consulting and Audit Canada because of articles suggesting that the ill-fated Universal Classification System implementation process might be gender-biased, circa 2000 etc.—but it has most importantly translated into various forms of self-censorship and subservient behaviours, and a culture of courtesanship and deception in higher places.

[2] Jon Elster, *Political Psychology* (Cambridge, UK: Cambridge University Press, 1993): 5. Without describing the array of all such mechanisms that may be of use in our discussion, some may easily be used to illustrate our argument: tendency under pressure to apply an overdose of established measures, group think, tendency to ascribe to the other party the responsibility, symbolic and tactical reforms inflaming the opposition, cognitive dissonance, self reinforcement, etc.

[3] See, for example, Alasdair Roberts, "Reform of the Access to Information Act", *Working Paper*, Campbell Public Affairs Institute, Syracuse University, August 2001, 1-4; Ian Jack, "Liberals in 'clear conflict,' hearing told", *National Post*, 30 August 2001, A6.

CHAPTER 7

Fiscal Imbalance as Governance Failure

Fallacy isn't error, of course, but it can be treacherous.

—Thomas Schelling

Preamble

The first version of this paper was written in 2004, not as a vindication of the vertical fiscal imbalance hypothesis but as a critical comment on the disingenuity of the federal government (politicians and bureaucrats) in dealing with the issue. Recent federal-provincial transfers and the new financial circumstances of the federal government may have changed the nature of the imbalance (at least between the federal government and the provinces) but not the indictment of the federal government apparatus and its disingenuity up to the recent past in this file. The government of the Rt. Hon. Stephen Harper may or may not sway the dogmatic views of the bureaucracy on this issue.

Introduction

In a high-risk world of turbulence and rapid change, where the social needs may evolve rather rapidly, and the fiscal resources dry up or grow exponentially depending on international circumstances, the possibility of a mismatch between evolving fiscal responsibilities and statutorily defined fiscal resources at the different levels (federal, provincial, local) of governments in Canada is obvious.

The very existence of a well-established and permanent equalization payments program, and other forms of intergovernmental transfers designed to rebalance the fiscal equation, if and when the need arises, would appear to be the living proof that such is the case. In addition the chronic intrusions of the Canadian federal government into policy areas, falling clearly under provincial and local government jurisdictions (like post-secondary education and infrastructure), reveal that there are federal financial surpluses to allocate to these sorts of uses, and as a result provincial and local governments may not have been allocated a sufficiently large share of the limited fiscal resources to handle these needs themselves.

In the spring of 2002, this issue was raised starkly by the Séguin Commission, a study group created by the Parti Québécois Quebec government, under the chairmanship of Yves Séguin, a former (Liberal) Revenue Minister in Quebec. The Séguin Commission was struck to explore whether there were fiscal imbalances in the Canadian federation.

The Commission report (backed by carefully prepared projections by the Conference Board of Canada) concluded that indeed there was a fiscal imbalance that favoured the federal government. The official reaction of the Canadian federal government for some time afterwards was both brusque and outraged. Senior federal ministers and officials stated bluntly that the idea of a federal-provincial fiscal imbalance was a myth: not only did it not exist, it *could* not exist.

Our argument is that:

(1) the Canadian federal government (under the federal Liberal Party) has been quite disingenuous in denying the very possibility of a fiscal imbalance; while there may be legitimate differences of opinion about the size of such an imbalance, and about the sorts of remedies that might be

called for, there is no serious ground to claim that it is a logical impossibility in Canada; and

(2) fiscal imbalance is only one of many clear indicators of governance failure in Canada: that is, a *révélateur* of a good deal of disconcertation in the governing of Canadian affairs. Consequently, a permanent resolution of the problem requires more than a temporary reshuffling of the financial deck. It calls for a reform of the governance of the Canadian socio-technical federal system.

Fiscal federalism and the limits to fiscal predation

The economic logic underpinning federalism is that a multi-level governance structure may yield higher efficiency by assigning the different tasks involved in governing and managing the public household to the level of government that is able to do the job most effectively, most efficiently and most economically. It is on the basis of this logic that constitutions determine the different roles of the federal, regional and local governments, assign various responsibilities to them, and determine the fiscal resources to be allocated to each level to do these jobs. This allocation is often guided by a philosophy of subsidiarity that aims at devolving responsibilities to the lowest level of government (i.e., the one closest to the citizen) that can handle the task effectively, since needs may differ from place to place.

Fiscal federalism is the label used to refer to the wide array of processes and negotiated arrangements that define some workable sharing of resources and responsibilities among jurisdictions, and therefore a viable fiscal regime. This is a complex process haunted by considerable friction, disagreements, competing claims and political arithmetic.

The notion of fiscal imbalance or disequilibrium connotes the disparity between the legitimate revenues and expenditures of the different levels of government. It may be a horizontal imbalance between a large city and its suburbs, if the large city provides, without compensation, public-good-type services to the citizens of the suburbs. One may correct such disequilibrium through some financial contribution by the suburban government to the large city government. It may also be a vertical disequilibrium between the federal and provincial governments, or between the provincial and local governments. This is the case when fiscal resources are shared through pre-determined arrangements in such a way that a given level of government receives more than is required to dispatch its responsibilities, while another level receives less than is necessary. Fiscal resource transfers can repair this situation between surplus and deficit levels of government, or through a redistribution of governing responsibilities between levels of government, or both—through some changes in the rules or the basic arrangements underpinning the governance of the federation.

All levels of governments collect taxes, although they do not necessarily use the same basis to calculate them. Some taxes are collected on revenues or expenditures, others on the basis of property values only, still others on transactions, etc. But at the end of the day, the same citizen is imposed upon by these different schemes. This poses a serious coordination problem—a problem of governance—since one cannot continually add on new taxes or new levels of taxation separately, without generating repercussions on the whole fiscal regime, that is, on the ability and capacity of all levels of government to collect the revenue.

Whatever the source of the fiscal pressure (federal, provincial, local), the citizen, at first, complies with the request more or less willingly, having been persuaded more or less fully that it represents the price for the public goods and services that are supplied by the government in question. But as the fiscal burden rises as a result of all sorts of taxes, the citizen begins to feel some pressure, and rationally seeks ways to reduce such pressure through legitimate tax avoidance or illegal tax evasion.

The global impact of these various strategies is well known and has been captured in a stylized way by the Laffer curve, which defines the relationship between the effective tax rate and fiscal revenues of governments.

One can easily see in figure 7.1 that if the tax rate (on the vertical axis) is zero, the tax receipts by governments (on the horizontal axis) is also zero. One can easily also see that if the tax rate is 100 percent (i.e., if all income is taxed away), tax receipts are not likely to be different from zero, since no rational citizen would declare any income to such a predatory government. The whole economy would go underground.

Figure 7.1   *The Laffer curve*

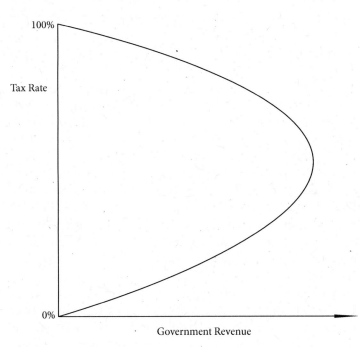

Between a tax rate of 0 and 100 percent, fiscal receipts by governments would grow at first as a larger portion of incomes is taxed away, but government revenues would peak in absolute terms as the citizens come to feel more pressed, and are led to indulge in more and more effective strategies of tax avoidance and evasion.

The Laffer curve may take different shapes depending on the fiscal mores and ethos of a country and may change from time to time.

This curve phenomenon poses a particularly difficult problem of governance in federal states, since the effective global tax rate depends on the compounded tax policies of the three or more (when there are regional governments) levels of government. The unilateral action of one level of government may impact on the tax receipts of other levels if the additional fiscal pressure generated by a new tax initiative at one level triggers more tax avoidance or evasion *in toto*. A government that increase taxes without taking into account what is already imposed on the citizenry by other levels of government may, indeed, generate an erosion of the tax base for everyone and trigger a drop in tax receipts for all levels of government.

This is not a theoretical nicety for academics. Recent studies would appear to indicate that Canada is in the critical zone of the Laffer curve: that is, in the zone where the tax receipts' reaction to changes in tax extraction rates is significant. David Giles and Lindsay Tedds have shown that there is a significant relationship between the effective tax rate and the growth of the underground economy in Canada. In the period 1976–1995, the effective global tax rate grew from around 30 percent to around 36 percent of GDP (gross domestic product), and this would appear to explain the growth of the underground economy—from an estimated 3.5 percent of GDP in 1976 to an estimated 16 percent in 1995 (Giles and Tedds 2002).

To gain a better appreciation of what this means, one may suggest that the CA$ 130 billions of income that were not declared in 1995 corresponds to the combined GDP of British Columbia and Saskatchewan. This would mean that while the estimated losses in government fiscal revenues ascribable to the underground economy were in the neighbourhood of a few billions of dollars in 1976, they might have been in the neighbourhood of CA$ 44 billions in 1995. An extrapolation would suggest that by 2006–2007, more than CA$ 60 billions might be lost by governments in tax receipts as a result of tax avoidance and evasion. Whatever the exact numbers, this has most certainly exacerbated the problems of tax sharing among the different levels of government.

As a result, one cannot presume that any level of government can raise the tax burden of its citizens in any way it chooses without having a potentially negative spill-over effect on the fiscal revenues of other levels of government. The doctrinaire position of some federal politicians and bureaucrats therefore—who state peremptorily that there cannot logically be any fiscal imbalance since all governments in deficit can always reduce it by raising new taxes—is not very persuasive.

If there is a structural fiscal imbalance, it is absolutely crucial that it be corrected via collaborative governance arrangements and fiscal concertation.

Many stakeholders (like the business community) nevertheless often react negatively to calls for fiscal concertation or fiscal reform, fearing that any new fiscal arrangements might simply provide an opportunity to raise taxes. This explains why much care must be taken, when discussing fiscal imbalance problems, to ensure that any solution being envisaged is not only arrived at collaboratively, but is shown to be demonstrably fiscally neutral with respect to the total tax burden. Otherwise, robust opposition may result from suggestions of even the most minor and reasonable repairs to the fiscal plumbing.

Séguin, Conference Board, Federation of Canadian Municipalities, Sgro and others

The Séguin Commission was created by the Quebec government in May 2001 and tabled its report in March 2002 (Séguin 2002).

It immediately generated a burst of interest in fiscal imbalance issues throughout Canada (Mintz and Smart 2002).

The federal-provincial fiscal imbalance

The Séguin Commission, in large part, based its fundamental finding—that there is a fiscal imbalance in Canada—on the analysis of the patterns of government revenues and expenditures in Canada, and on certain projections of revenues and expenditures of the different levels of government in Canada that had been prepared by the Conference Board of Canada. This was done originally for the federal and Quebec governments only, but, by the end of the summer of 2002, the Conference Board study had been extended to the rest of Canada (Conference Board of Canada 2002). At the core of its findings was a forecast of cumulative federal surpluses of over CA\$ 570 billion from 2001–2002 to 2019–2020, and of cumulative deficits for the provinces.

For the Séguin Commission, this fiscal imbalance has its origin in three main sources:

(1) the different dynamics of revenues and expenditures at the federal and provincial level—the provinces having responsibilities for sectors like education and health where the rate of growth of expenditures will be much higher than the rates of growth of financial needs in sectors for which the federal government is responsible;

(2) the volatile and capricious nature of federal transfers to the provinces, which have been routinely and unilaterally slashed by the federal government in response to its own priorities;

(3) the propensity of the federal government to intervene in provincial jurisdiction under the broad banner of its 'power to spend' where such interventions do much to make the fiscal imbalance less obvious because they tend to reduce the size of 'visible' federal surpluses through this kind of lavish spending.

The Séguin Commission identified important consequences of this fiscal imbalance: first, it prevents provinces from serving the citizens as well as they should; second, it introduces a higher degree of confusion in the decision-making process than is necessary; and three, much less efficiency and accountability ensue as a result.

To solve this fiscal imbalance problem, the Séguin Commission put forward a number of propositions: first, some immediate fiscal transfers to the provinces from the federal government (CA\$ 2–3 billions to Quebec, some CA\$ 8 billions for all the provinces) to help them meet their obligations; second, a redefinition of the sharing of fiscal resources: the replacement of the conditional Canadian Health and Social Transfers by unconditional transfer of income tax points or some other tax field like the GST; three, modification of the equalization payment scheme to limit the federal 'power to spend', modification of the rules for the calculation of the transfers, and making the negotiation of future adjustments to the scheme more transparent.

The federal/provincial/municipal fiscal imbalance

The Séguin Commission, and the subsequent studies of the Conference Board of Canada in the summer of 2002, focused exclusively on the federal-provincial fiscal imbalance, but many of the arguments presented by the Séguin Commission would appear to be equally valid for the provincial-local levels.

Even without the benefits of Conference Board-type nationwide financial projections for the provincial-local levels, some more limited projections made by the Conference Board of Canada based on the likely fiscal situation of Quebec municipalities (*Union des municipalités du Québec* 2003), but also a number of other empirical studies (Federation of Canadian Municipalities 2001, 2002; Burleton 2002), make a very strong case for the presumption that there is also a fiscal imbalance between the provincial and local levels of government.

Indeed, if one were to use the Quebec data as an indicator of the overall fiscal situation of the city-regions in Canada, the situation is quite alarming. It is surmised by that Conference Board study that, if no overhaul of the fiscal regime is engineered,

Quebec municipalities are likely to see their debt load triple over the next twenty years, and the property tax burden double over the next five years. It is not, therefore, just a problem of deficit in capital budgets and higher debt load as a result of the need to repair the deteriorated infrastructure, but also a problem of facing a deficit in financing basic operations. Such pressures would require phenomenal and destructive property tax increases in the present scheme of things.

The first source of this provincial-local fiscal imbalance has to do with the growing relative importance of cities as a source of the wealth of the nations and provinces in which they are located. Toronto represents over 40 percent of the GDP of Ontario; Halifax, Montreal and Vancouver, half the GDP of their respective provinces; Winnipeg and Calgary and Edmonton together, some two thirds of the GDP of Manitoba and Alberta respectively. These city-regions are the main locus of innovation and creativity in their respective provinces, and have seen their responsibilities increase without their being provided with the necessary resources to generate the requisite social capital in order to underpin the economic growth and social progress of their extending hinterland.

The second reason why fiscal imbalance may have worsened of late has to do with the relatively slow growth of the fiscal resources at the local level, as noted by the Federation of Canadian Municipalities and the TD Bank Financial Group: while local government revenues have grown by 14 percent in the period 1995–2001, provincial revenues have grown by 30 percent and the federal receipts by 38 percent.[1]

As a result, in Canada it can be agreed that city-regions' level of expenditures have not kept up with what would have been required to maintain competitiveness. It has been estimated by the Federation of Canadian Municipalities, for instance, that per capita local government expenditures (in US dollars) are less than US$ 800 in Canada, over US$ 1,600 in the US, and over US$ 2,100 in Europe. It is not too far off the mark to suggest that the local government pockets approximately one tenth of what the provincial and federal governments raise in taxes, even though the former have to provide essential services to a much greater degree.

The third reason—and why one might despair about the situation improving—is the immense reliance of local governments in Canada on property taxes. Some 55 percent of municipal revenues come from property taxes in Canada. In the United States, it is 21 percent. This sort of tax may be adequate to deal with services to property (police, fire protection, garbage collection, etc.), but as cities get burdened with much broader responsibilities related to education, immigrant integration, development and the like, it cannot underpin an adequate tax regime.

The Quebec study has shown that, in the last decade or so, property values have been relatively stagnant at a time when income or sales grew by close to 3 percent per year. Moreover, even when property values grow, the real asset value may not be realized and remains only a 'potential' asset value. Taxing it before value realization may generate extraordinary hardship for those on a fixed income. One must find ways therefore to finance these new 'urban expenditures' differently.

The plight of local government

However sharp the disagreements between the federal and provincial governments about the existence and extent of the fiscal imbalance between them, there is broad agreement about the difficult financial situation of cities. This agreement has prompted some action—action that has been hastened by the recent deep recession.

This alarming diagnosis was confirmed by the OECD (Organisation for Economic Co-operation and Development) examination of the Canadian case in its Territorial Reviews. The Sgro Report of the Prime Minister's Caucus Task Force on Urban Issues that reported in November 2002, while it focused on needs and carefully avoided the fiscal imbalance issue, built on the conclusion of the OECD report that a "new rationale for more federal involvement" in urban issues existed. It implicitly recognized that cities cannot meet the challenges of urban sustainability with the resources made available to them now and, therefore, that more resources need to be injected into solving urban problems. It argued for a cooperative and negotiated approach involving the three levels of government. The three sectors targeted by the Sgro Report as priorities were affordable housing, transportation and infrastructure. In each case, a national strategy is proposed that can only be realized through the massive transfer of resources toward urban priorities (OECD 2002; Sgro 2002).

The solution of transferring fiscal resources to cities is not, however, envisaged by Sgro or by the Ottawa-vetted OECD report. What was proposed instead was a redefinition of the roles of the different levels of government to match their present existing fiscal resources, and the negotiation of contract-type agreements (as suggested by the OECD) to provide the required resources to cities somewhat conditionally.

This is neither a surprising research result nor a surprising policy recommendation. Transfers from senior governments constitute only 19 percent of municipal government revenues in Canada, while it is 27 percent in the United States and 31 percent in Europe. In such circumstances, one might reasonably expect an urban strategy to recommend an increase of such transfers. In Canada however, neither the federal nor the provincial governments—given their centralized mindsets—would consider the possibility of transferring significant financial resources to cities, except in the form of conditional and tightly controlled grants.

Even though the Conference Board of Canada study for the *Union des municipalités du Québec* suggested that it might be necessary to transfer one quarter of the provincial value-added tax to the cities, speculations about the possibility of transferring income tax points or other significant tax fields to the local governments still appear fanciful and are not really on the radar screen.

Still, a loose arrangement of this sort (if somewhat capriciously interpreted) has been negotiated between Manitoba and the city of Winnipeg, and is firmly in place in Ohio, New York State and in Scandinavia. However, as the consolidation of cities into a smaller number of larger urban units proceeds, the plausibility of such transfers increases. An exemption from the GST for municipalities was confirmed in the March 23, 2004 budget. In addition, a transfer to municipalities of a portion of the federal tax on gasoline, to spend on infrastructure, was doubled (to CA$ 2 billion per year) and made permanent in the spring of 2009. This transfer, by way of federal-provincial agreement, includes additional provincial funding usually targeted specifically.

The sophistry of the Canadian federal government

Even though the presumption of some fiscal imbalance can be said to be strong, the Canadian federal government of the day reacted brusquely to the contention that there might be one in 2005. Indeed, the Department of Intergovernmental Affairs (at first) and then the Department of Finance denounced what they have called "the myth of fiscal imbalance". The official federal government position was that fiscal imbalance is at once technically impossible, empirically nonexistent, most improbable, and in any case adequately handled by the existing fiscal transfer mechanisms. This might best be labelled the 'Stéphane Dion argument'.

Such a semi-contradictory cascade of arguments, and the obvious sophistry enmeshed in it, might not appear to deserve much attention or analysis. It would be a mistake nevertheless, not to see it as a *révélateur* of both a state of mind that unfortunately has had a significant impact in all areas of public policy in Canada, and of the state of affairs in Canadian federalism.[2]

The Canadian federal government under the federal Liberal Party suffered from what, following Stephen Carter, one might label a "liberal constitutional" fixation that is both anti-democratic and anti-communautarian. This fixation is built on a model holding that "the central government...is more likely than anybody else to find the answers that are right" and holds the view that citizens' views are "irrelevant, except when they happen to be in support, in which case they are crucial" (Carter 1998). Unfortunately, decades of such behaviour at the federal level appear to have had a deleterious effect on the mindset of provincial governments that would appear, in many instances, to have fallen into the same trap. This led to a rather disingenuous handling of the fiscal imbalance issue by a series of ill-founded propositions (Paquet 2004a: chapter 7).

A tautological argument: fiscal imbalance is a technical impossibility

It has been argued that, supposedly, the imbalance is technically impossible because of the fact that provincial authorities always have the ability to restore their fiscal equilibrium either by reducing expenditures or by raising new taxes. The argument is tautological but wrong, since the assumption is false. One can reach this conclusion only by dogmatically ignoring the Laffer curve phenomenon, and by trivializing the demographic pressures of demand on social services that fall under the provincial and local jurisdictions.

A specious argument: fiscal imbalance is empirically non-existent

A second argument suggests that the fiscal surpluses at the federal level are minute, the federal debt load extremely heavy, the provincial deficits rather small, the pressure on provincial expenditures not that great, and that the decision of most provinces to reduce provincial taxes has led to self-inflicted deficits.

The federal Department of Finance argumentation to this effect builds on many questionable assumptions:

> (1) there is, for reasons of competitiveness, 'pressure' to reduce taxes at the federal level, while tax reduction is

only a matter of 'choice' at the provincial level, indicating (when this option is exercised) that "they (the provinces) believe that they have sufficient revenues to manage their spending pressures";

(2) a relative appreciation of the "needs" of the federal government is imperative (for "only the federal government can stand behind nationwide programs and standards") while those of the provinces have been de-prioritized by the 'choice' of reducing taxes;

(3) a statement of 'expectations' based entirely on the whims of the federal government: it being stated that the provinces have no reason to expect difficulties since resource transfers were promised for the 2000–2005 period; this does not acknowledge the experience of the last decade demonstrating considerable whimsicality.[3]

The "forecasts are unreliable" argument: fiscal imbalance as improbable

The federal Department of Finance systematically argued that the forecasts by the Conference Board that indicated important probable cumulative surplus at the federal level, and cumulative deficits at the provincial level, were unreliable. Consequently, it is argued, one could not build any argument for fiscal transfers from such forecasts. If it is true that there are margins of error in forecasts, and that one may legitimately argue with the absolute levels of surplus and deficits generated by such a forecasting machine, this hardly legitimizes regarding any forecast as pure fantasy.

The sum total of the arguments was that federal surpluses are not as large as is claimed, and that they are 'needed' for priority tasks, that the provinces have a sufficient margin of maneuverability to immediately effect corrections to their fiscal deficits, and that since cities need additional fiscal resources, the federal government might legitimately transfer resources to them directly through conditional grants or 'contracts'. The recent federal-provincial agreements have cautiously shifted the approach to a degree in this specific case.

A plea for distributed governance

Even though there may be differences of opinion about the nature, size and import of the vertical fiscal imbalance syndrome in Canada, there is broad agreement that it is not *un être de raison* and that no fiscal sleight of hand will suffice to correct the situation. The matter calls for governance reform.

Governance is effective coordination when power, resources and information are widely distributed. Fiscal imbalance is a simple indicator of both poor coordination and a high degree of disconcertion in the Canadian federation. Correcting such governance failure requires an understanding of the various sources of the disconcertion, a good knowledge of the principles and mechanisms of good governance that should guide reforms, a fair appreciation of the elusive way in which Canadians deal with governance issues, a sense of the very high cost of inaction on this front, and some insight into the sorts of mechanisms required to improve the governance of the federation.

Turbulent times

It is not difficult to understand why disconcertion has grown in Canada. As technological change, economic growth, and socio-cultural effervescence increased, all organizations (private, public and civic) were forced to adapt to the new circumstances that created the need for a heightened capacity for speed, flexibility and innovation. New forms of integration and coordination, new structures and tools, but also a whole new way of thinking have been required (Paquet 1998). Private, public and social concerns ceased to be drivers of people, and had to become "drivers of learning" (Wriston 1992: 119); learning organizations became based on new forms of alliances and partnerships rooted in more horizontal relationships and moral contracts (Paquet 1999a).

This dispersive revolution crystallized into new networks of business organizations, more subsidiarity-focused governments, and increasingly virtual, elective and malleable communities. Major governance challenges ensued: acquiring speed, flexibility, diffuseness and innovativeness while maintaining the necessary coordination, coherence and integrity.

These forces have been at work for some time, but their impact has been considerably heightened by the digital revolution that has materialized over the last while. Businesses, governments and communities have been confronted with a greater demand for participation as technology made it possible. Citizens have also become much more active partners in the governance process. This has redefined the public space and founded distributed governance regimes based on a wider variety of more fluid and always evolving communities (Tapscott and Agnew 1999).

It does not mean just the process of dispersion of power toward localized decision making within each sector: it also entails a dispersion of power over a wide variety of actors and groups within the economy, society and polity.

All this has triggered a paradoxical outcome: as globalization proceeds, economic integration increases, and the component parts of the system become more numerous. The central question is how to organize for faster learning. And it would appear that the game of learning is going to generate more innovation and speed if those components confronted with different local realities are empowered to take decisions on the spot. This is why globalization has led to localization of decision making, to the dispersion of power toward city-regions (Naisbitt 1994).

Fiscal federalism redux

The new imperatives of distributed governance are bringing back the old spirit of federalism, that is, the spirit of subsidiarity. Federalism was designed to ensure a division of labour among the private, public and civic sectors, and among levels of government based on the dual principles of efficiency and decision making as close as possible to the citizen. Indeed, the existence of multi-level governance provides an opportunity for higher-level decision-making only if the lower level processes prove incapable of handling these responsibilities efficiently.

This was the original spirit of the program review exercise as designed by the Privy Council Office in the 1990s. But this governance exercise quickly degenerated into a cash grab exercise (fundamentally corrupting the original purposes), when deficit and debt reduction became the categorical imperative. This shift away from the original governance objectives underpinned the enormous cuts in cash transfers that led to the dramatic recentralization of fiscal power.

This shift toward centralization was rationalized in the name of egalitarianism: if equality is the primary good, centralization is necessary, since in order to redistribute resources, one has first to bring them to the centre. This stands in sharp contrast to the new guiding philosophy of federalism and the new centrality of distributed governance and collaboration based on subsidiarity.

Despite the fundamental propensity of the federal government to centralize, and the opportunities provided by episodic scandals (and their dramatization by the Office of the Auditor-General) to rationalize a return to a command-and-control mentality, a drift from egalitarianism to subsidiarity is in progress. One may reasonably hypothesize that it is bound to lead to a fair amount of devolution, much more participation, and an increase in the efficiency, transparency and legitimacy of Canadian governance.

This hypothesis may appear somewhat weakened by the chill generated by the sponsorship scandal and other irregularities that have led federal governments to impose more robust controls. One should not however be mesmerized by such bursts of collective hysteria fed by imprudent generalizations, some irresponsible reporting, and an unwillingness by the then, new, Rt. Hon. Paul Martin government (under a cloud of suspicion for the activities of its predecessor) to challenge the Office of the Auditor-General for fear of electoral fallout. The structural forces at work in driving the process of devolution are broader and stronger than these episodes of control frenzy. However such episodes underline the fragile nature of public opinion in Canada on these matters, and the wisdom of Canadian reluctance to address the governance challenges through grand palavers that can easily be derailed by accidental events.

The elusive Canadian way

The evolution toward this new form of governance (likely to repair governance failures and, as a result, reduce fiscal imbalance) is not likely to emerge as a result of a *coup d'état*. Canadians do not manage societal change in such disruptive ways—which they see as divisive and likely to generate nothing but stalemate. So, despite the hot rhetorical style of their political leaders, Canadians have generally chosen a distinctively "cool style" of evolution. Indeed, over the last decades Canadians have defined their "distinctiveness" almost despite their leaders, and they have been quite effective at it. This distinctiveness has been characterized by expressions such as "a passion for bronze" (Kimon Valaskakis) or "slow adrenaline" (Pico Iyer).

Canadians' rejection of grand schemes has at times been deplored as *occasions manquées*. But Canadians, with their hefty dose of tolerance and apathy, are ironists, "never quite able to take themselves seriously because always aware that the terms in which they describe themselves are subject to change", and they spend much time worrying about the possibility of having been initiated into the wrong tribe, and taught to play the wrong language game (Rorty 1989: 73–75). Thus they prefer:

    (1)   understatement, irony and self-mockery in their rhetoric, and they most certainly resist being "branded" like cattle, or "bridged" in a crippling way in the face of liquid modernity (Putnam 2000); and

    (2)   a sort of pragmatism and ad hoc *bricolage* in their practice, and a gamble on a combination of plural, partial and limited identities even though it often actually increases the distances between them and their fellow Canadians— for this is Canadians' distinctiveness (Paquet 2003).

It is interesting to note that Canadians are often left, therefore, in a state of schizophrenia, and find themselves torn between their commitment to centralized state-run social justice and their conviction that genuine solidarities are local and community-based. In fact, it is another element of Canadian distinctiveness that Canadians have refused to choose: they want both the state-run social justice *à la* Medicare and the community-based solidarity.

One only has to look at the current Harper minority government's decision to explain its commitment to 'fixing the fiscal imbalance' through a combination of financial transfers and constraining the federal spending power to some extent to see a manifestation of this ambivalence.

The central question is whether the top-down or bottom-up federalism will prevail when choice is required. Our hypothesis is that bottom-up federalism will overcome in the long run.

The cost of inaction

The governance failures revealed by the fiscal imbalance are consequential. Inefficiency, poor accountability and poor stewardship are the result; the measurement of these costs is however, extremely difficult. Thus, many observers have ignored the costs of inaction on the governance front.

Inefficiencies of all sorts are quite obvious nevertheless. First, it is clear that local and provincial priority needs remain unmet while federal surpluses can and have been spent in areas where, according to the citizenry, priorities were less urgent. The waste involved in this misallocation is important. Second, this misalignment of resources and needs not only generates static allocative inefficiency, but also translates into a lessening of Canada's competitiveness. Fiscal imbalance itself generates a significant amount of waste of resources as the result of the haggling and pestering between deficit governments and surplus governments. But even more damage is generated by the degree of aloofness and irresponsibility that poor governance injects into the fiscal regime as the lines of accountability become frayed.

Incentives matter. Why should governments act responsibly as spenders if they do not have to collect their own taxes? A great deal of waste ensues when spending becomes disconnected from taxpayers' diligence and degenerates into a simple game of intergovernmental squabbling that the citizenry does not understand.

If provinces or municipalities that want to spend more money were asked to collect the taxes they see fit to finance the goods and services their voters tell them they want, the lines of accountability would be clearer. But as long as many of these governments are prevented from raising their own taxes, or destructive vertical intergovernmental tax competition leads to tax base erosion, then significant losses can be expected.

It is difficult to put a dollar figure on the costs of inaction in resolving these governance failures. However, if economists have learned anything in the debates surrounding the identification and attempts to measure x-efficiency (the effectiveness with which a given set of inputs are used to produce outputs), it is that the x-inefficiency generated by poor governance, faulty incentives and the lack of effort, or the amount of misguided effort it generates, and the amount of slack it produces in the system, is very significant indeed.

In empirical studies of x-inefficiency, it is quite clear that its x-inefficiency varies considerably from country to country, and from one organizational setting to another; however, it is not unusual to find waste factor of the order of 25 percent. Some order of magnitude for the efficiency gains that might obtain if the governance failures were eliminated might also be gauged from some of the outcomes of organizational re-engineering resulting from tackling unforeseen external competition or the removal of state protection. If the direct exact measurement of such x-efficiency gains from governance overhauling were still missing, oblique gauges of it would appear to confirm that they are significant (Leibenstein 1976).

It may appear quite extraordinary that a subject as arcane as federal-provincial relations could arouse such concern in the citizenry that it ranks just below health and above education. Compounded with the fact that a significant majority of citizens believe that provincial and local governments need more fiscal resource however, this clearly indicates that governance failure and fiscal imbalance have become issues of national concern, and that the citizens are unwilling to tolerate inaction.

Missing mechanisms

Whatever the malefits ascribable to governance failures (and to the fiscal imbalance that reveals them), they are not likely to be resolved easily. Nothing less than a significant effort to modify the Canadian governance regime will do, but, as we have indicated, this will have to proceed par *étapes* and somewhat obliquely because Canadians have no taste for tackling big issues in a frontal way.

This significantly constrains what any prime minister can do whether in a majority or minority situation in Parliament. To face the three major challenges of productivity stagnation, decline in public trust and the growing social disengagement, and the general disconcertation of the Canadian socio-political economy, a prime minister cannot count on any dramatic instant reframing of perspectives. The only tool available is putting in place some missing mechanisms capable of providing some of the needed repairs.

These mechanisms are of many sorts.

First, the new philosophy of governance requires public space for dialogue and deliberation: nothing less than genuine forums where such questions might be debated. Second, there must be the possibility of developing looser and fuzzier mechanisms of coordination, for rigid rules may not be the best way to do the job in a turbulent context. Third, such deliberation forums and moral contracts initiatives have to be built on the sound basis of cost-based pricing of public services, of workable competition, and on the recognition of the new centrality of soft and fuzzier accountabilities.

The first family of missing mechanisms that is required would provide spaces for dialogue and deliberation. The Council of the Federation may evolve in a helpful direction or (a more likely outcome) it may turn out to be a most unfortunate initiative and a major impediment to the creation of 'truly broad' spaces for deliberation.

What are required are loci for federal/provincial/local deliberations as a necessary tool for reducing the high degree of existing disconcertation. How can one hope to bring the three levels of government to concert (albeit on restricted issues or areas of concern) when there is no place for them to meet? Given the impossibility of corralling all parties for a sort of fiscal Meech Lake meeting, one would at least require the necessary forums for deliberations on issue-domains or families of concerns.

The second group of missing mechanisms that are of crucial importance are those pertaining to certain critical policy fields. Since there is no hope of being able to reduce disconcertation directly *in toto*: it must be negotiated in more limited and tractable forums. There are six broad fields in which such covenants are urgently needed:

(1) health and education where performance indicators show that the results are far from optimal and where the federal government should clearly agree to have a completely hands off stance in terms of dictating approaches, if the provinces agree to transform the governance of these two broad areas;

(2) macro-stability and social capital where the federal role is prominent and where an agreement must be reached that some support has to be forthcoming from other levels of government;

(3) cities and public administration (or the role of the state) where some form of partnership has to be struck.

The third family of missing mechanisms is very diffracted, and corresponds to the array of arrangements required for the socio-economy to function properly and for self-organization to proceed as well as it can.

This ranges from mechanisms for permanently keeping programs under review, as the Harper government is currently doing, to ways in which new mechanisms of consultation and negotiation will be put in place, to the reform of the House of Commons, to the use of some form of proportional representation in elections of the sort recently proposed by the Law Reform Commission, etc.

A detailed list of this third family of mechanisms would carry us beyond the confines of this chapter, but it should be clear that they are not disconnected from the fiscal imbalance issue. For instance, it is clear that a subsidiarity-inspired renewed program review might accomplish much to reshuffle the different responsibilities among government levels.

Conclusion

Our examination of the fiscal imbalance issue as a *révélateur* of governance failure does not lead to much optimism. It has led us to conclude that fiscal imbalance is not a simple problem of public finance plumbing. Only a critical examination of the governance regime of the country holds the promise of any meaningful rebalancing likely to underpin effective collaborative governance. Yet collaborative governance is a form of partnership, and any partnership entails a sort of power sharing that the stakeholders would appear to fear. This is why there is such a denial *vis-à-vis* the fiscal imbalance syndrome in some high places: admitting that the problem exists could only lead logically to rethinking the foundation of the federation.

We have underlined the reasons why fiscal imbalance still exists in Canada (despite being hidden behind the current financial recession-driven deficits at all levels), shown how it is a *révélateur* of some more fundamental disconcertation, recognized that Canadians have a characteristic way of dealing with governance issues, and suggested that it is through the creation of a multiplicity of missing mechanisms that we may hope to resolve the governance problem and its fiscal echo effect.

By identifying three families of missing mechanisms (forums for deliberation, moral contracts in certain key areas, and a multitude of arrangements to limit inefficiencies, improve accountabilities and promote citizen engagement) however, we have only pointed in a promising direction.

Endnotes

1 Even though there have been important transfers to municipalities, these (GST rebate and more recently, the gas tax fund) have really only partly bridged the gap.
2 As an aside, the current (Stephen Harper) minority government's recognition of the existence of a fiscal imbalance and a commitment to fix it, has resulted in a financial settlement contained in the 2007 federal budget and a 2007 Throne Speech that promises to legislatively constrain (but not to end) the federal spending power. The fundamental mismatch between revenue raising and responsibility in the federation however remains. What is clear is that even if the new Harper government has acknowledged the problem, the message has not yet permeated the federal bureaucracy for which the forty-year-long 'Stéphane Dion argument' appears to remain forcefully in place.
3 To bolster the argument that "provincial needs" are not really that pressing, former minister (and former Opposition Leader), Stéphane Dion (in many speeches and decks) used to point to the fact that health expenditures as a percentage of GDP have not grown over the last while. This argument makes little sense, since the results quoted were simply the result of the dramatic reductions in federal transfers to the provinces that have forced provinces to ration health services to their citizens (S. Dion "Les municipalités et le gouvernement fédéral." Allocution à la Fédération canadienne des municipalités, May 26, 2001; S. Dion "L'équilibre fiscal et les relations financières entre les gouvernements au Canada." Allocution au St James Club, March 13, 2002).

PART III

Repairs in Many Dimensions

The pathologies of governance illustrated earlier fairly present the state of distress of federal public administration in Canada: it is crippled by an antiquated system of beliefs, mental prisons, and bad habits that have generated neuroses and disfunctionalities, and a decline in the capacity to transform and to learn.

What is required is a refounding of public administration as a practice within a new philosophy of governance fit for the new networked order. The shift from 'Big G' top-down government to 'small g' distributed governance, from the welfare state to the strategic state, will entail a massive re-tooling, re-structuring and re-framing of public administration: a task that one cannot hope to map comprehensively in a few chapters. At best we can provide some indications of the sort of repairs that are possible and desirable.

In part III, we propose a five-way strategy not as a panacea but as a series of trails worth exploring.

The first way to refurbish public administration is to indulge in some *bricolage*, some re-tooling, some experimentation with new mechanisms of coordination. These new mechanisms have been experimented with at the service delivery level but only very timidly. The most ambitious version (Service Canada) has been all but explicitly sabotaged by the dynamic conservatism of the central senior managerial class. It is our view that one might be able to do much in this way to revamp the whole accountability regime, and to remove the blockages to collaborative governance.

The second family of repairs has an anti-Jacobs flavour. It has to do with the end of apartheid among the private, public and social sectors, and the highest and best use of new collaborative relationships among sectors. Public-private partnerships are used as a laboratory to show what is feasible on this front.

The third ensemble of repairs pertains to the structure of the public sector *per se*. We have used human resources for purposes of illustration, even though it is only one of the dimensions of interest. We suggest that the public service could usefully be partitioned into segments operating under different regimes and rules. This ought to provide an indication of the sort of disaggregation of public administration that would appear to be warranted.

The fourth approach generalizes the first three somewhat by exploring what could be accomplished by organizational redesign. We underline the need to adjust the architecture of public administration to fit the new more complex vocation and purposes of the public sector. The neglect of the design function and the fixation on 'plumbing' alone in the machinery of government has led to gross mishaps. We draw attention to the extraordinary importance of organizational design and to the need to give this function new prominence in public administration.

The fifth strategy goes one step further, and shows how the business of public administration cannot be retrofitted by simple patchwork using only the traditional cast of characters in place. To reframe public administration to make it fit with the new philosophy of collaborative governance will require introducing *new actors* operating much less in a top-down hierarchical mode and much more in a horizontal or transversal way through negotiation and mediation. The case of the ombudsman is used as an illustration of what might be accomplished by inserting such actors in the system as producers of governance: this insertion of new players is meant to modify the very fabric of the system and the nature of the regimes in place. It should be effective if the new actors can escape being tainted by the old autocratic public administration style.

The new philosophy of collaborative governance suggests that one must go well beyond repairs to the public administration system. The whole Boulding triangle, covering the full range of private, public and solidarity organizations and institutions, has to be recast and a whole new set of mixed organizations and institutions brought forth.

As for public governance *per se,* it will also have to be modified fundamentally to be able to play its new roles. The five types of interventions mentioned above do not exhaust the panoply of instruments that are available and will have to be used. Our only objective here has been to illustrate the range of interventions to be considered. To ensure that the reader is made aware of the true potentialities of these instruments; we have made reference in each case to the existing organizational setting. But to plug the black hole, the very notion of public administration must be recast, to be brought in line with the new imperatives of 'small g' distributed governance and of the new imperatives of G_2 within it.

Traditional public administration experts and their political science mentors are still in denial *vis-à-vis* this necessity. They still live in a 'Big G' government world; they still assume that someone must be in charge, and they still anchor their arguments in the mythical omniscient state with its anchor in shared values. They still insist on playing snakes and ladders on a board of GO. Governance is a word that sticks in their throat like an unwelcome chicken bone. To deflect attention from the challenge to the powerful that this implies, they are likely to interpret our five-way approach, not as an invitation to redesign the public household, but as simply making too much of the need to dust off the antiquated apparatus a bit. As a result, what we propose as a needed revolution in the mind may well be interpreted as nothing more than a call for minor plumbing repairs.

It is for this reason that we are pessimistic about the capacity of the traditional public administration enterprise to become part of the solution. The fundamentalism and dynamic conservatism of the public managerial class and of its academic brothers needs to be shaken off. The attacks on the conventional edifice have, nevertheless, to be pointed out enough so as not to be discarded as sheer utopia. Whether we have found the right register to generate a revolution in the mind of the traditional public administration tribe remains to be seen. Our strong sense is that *il est peu probable que la porte du changement puisse s'ouvrir de l'intérieur!* It may be however, that living in Ottawa for so long has coloured our judgment too much.

CHAPTER 8

Alternative Service Delivery: The Thin Edge of the Wedge

No one has "the answer", there is no blueprint...[it] will involve a process of public learning of a high order.

—Steven A. Rosell

Introduction

The federal government's mid-1990s agenda was dominated by program review, which was aimed at redefining the roles and responsibilities of government in light of extreme fiscal pressures. Its goals included putting the emphasis on core responsibilities and increasing service delivery efficiency.

One significant follow-on was the 1995 framework for alternate service delivery (ASD), issued by the Treasury Board Secretariat as a template to guide choices of delivery arrangements so as to provide more seamless and citizen-centred service, including organizational structures outside the public sector and cross-sectoral partnerships.

Alternative service delivery is a fuzzy expression.

First, it refers clinically to the fact that there often exists a variety of alternative ways to deliver a given program or service.

Second, it connotes a critical evaluation process through which one may explore the constellation of approaches available for the delivery of programs or services. The possibilities range from tinkering with quality service initiatives and re-engineering of existing processes, to partnering, contracting out, devolution and privatization (Lindquist and Sica 1995). Finally, it was a slogan (no longer in vogue) used to identify a policy initiative designed to promote the idea that an active search process would ensure that all programs would be delivered in the optimal way, in some unclear sense of the term (Canada 1995).

The 1995 ASD policy initiative tended to frame the public policy questions in a rather restrictive way: it presumed that the task at hand was well defined and that the range of alternative delivery instruments was well-specified. Consequently, the sole remaining problem was to ensure that the most technically efficient/economic stratagem was selected.

To some extent this early formulation trivialized the real-life complexity of policy problems that are usually rather ill-defined: the policy issue is often not well understood and cannot be easily collapsed into well-structured program tasks. Moreover, the range of plausible alternative delivery schemes may not be well-specified, so choosing the best delivery scheme is no simple task. In the public policy literature, such ill-structured problems are called "wicked problems": pertaining to issues in which goals either are not known or are very ambiguous, and in which the means-ends relationships are highly uncertain and poorly understood (Rittel and Webber 1973).

Except in rare cases where problems and issues, ends, means and means-ends relationships are well defined, it is not always possible to establish clearly even whether or not a program in existence or a delivery mechanism in place are effective responses to the basic governance questions that have led to their being set up in the first place. Consequently, it is not clear that one can meaningfully address the issue of the appropriate new roles and relationships that would emerge, if a preferred delivery scheme is adopted, without first exploring what are the basic questions to which the programs and the delivery mechanisms are supposed to respond.

This is quite important because just as program review quickly lost its vocation to redefine the role of government and took on a cost reduction focus, so the ASD initiative morphed from a broad 'choice-of-instrument' philosophy into something that was more about improving access and service performance using a traditional 'inside-out' view, with technology being regarded as a key driver for reducing costs.

While the term 'ASD initiative' has disappeared from the official 'lingo', the original philosophy for the federal approach thrives. Some significant strides were made on service improvements but limits were rapidly reached: the much more difficult task of service transformation had to be tackled.

Contextualizing the alternative program delivery debate amounts to exploring the general policy questions to which the debate has been trying to respond and to ascertaining what the dynamic social learning mechanism is that is likely to respond in a most effective way to the original concerns (Michael 1993; Lévy 1995).

This broader approach obviously complicates matters under discussion. But it has two important advantages. First, it raises the questions of governance and effectiveness explicitly, and ensures that the debate focuses on the dynamic and creative learning that is necessary, and is not restricted to static efficiency/economic dimensions. Second, it warns against an artificial and mechanical separation of the policy process into policy making, program design and service delivery phases. These phases are seen as integrally interconnected: the feedback loop among them and between the whole policy process and the basic governance questions are seen as non-separable components of the process of social learning (Vickers 1965).

The chapter proceeds through four stages.

First we present some general reflections on governance and on the six questions of program review that provide, in our view, a reasonable version of the basic governance questions needed for an analysis of alternative service delivery. Second, we sketch, in a few paragraphs, a very simple analytical framework to guide our analysis of the alternative service delivery debate: we stylize three worlds corresponding to the different ways in which the ASD problem is approached, and we show the centrality of dynamic social learning that helps in discriminating amongst them. Third, we discuss some key questions that appear either to plague the debate or constrain the way to its resolution, and we suggest some answers. Fourth, we identify the ways in which roles and relationships are likely to shift under different scenarios as the ASD debate proceeds.

The foundational questions

Governance is the process through which a society/economy/polity steers itself and provides effective coordination when power, resources and information are widely distributed.

Fifty years ago, in Canada, governance was debated in the language of management science. It was presumed that public, private and social organizations were strongly directed top-down by rulers who had a clear understanding of the environment, of its drift, of the inexorable rules of the game they had to put up with, and of the goals pursued by their own organization. The challenge was relatively simple: building on the well-defined goals of the organization and on the well-identified constraints, determine how could one design the control mechanisms most likely to get the organization where it wanted to go.

As the pace of change accelerated and the issues grew more complex however, organizations (private, public and social) came to be confronted more and more often with "wicked problems". To deal with these wicked problems moreover, a new way of thinking about governance was required.

When the ground is in motion, organizations can only govern themselves by learning both new goals and the means to reach them as they proceed, through tapping the knowledge of all the stakeholders, and through mobilizing and motivating them to invent ways out of their predicaments. This distributed and decentralized governance deprives the leader of the monopoly on the governing of the organization: for the organization to learn fast, everyone must take part in the conversation (Paquet 1992; Webber 1993; Piore 1995).

It cannot be presumed that this process of social learning will proceed organically and smoothly. Failures of all sorts are predictable as a result of transaction costs, uncertainty, ignorance and other impediments to effective coordination in real time. The role of the state in this new knowledge-based economy is most importantly to act as a catalyst of the social learning process. This can be done in a variety of ways: unblocking communication channels, providing motivation to participate more actively in the multilogue, supplying information, income and other resources to those temporarily impaired by socio-economic contingencies of one sort or other.

Government's involvement is usually embodied in 'programs', that is, stylized interventions based on specific rules of eligibility, participation and financing, structure of benefits, etc. The central questions that need to be raised continually about each of these programs have to do with six criteria:

(1) whether the program still serves a public interest;
(2) whether there is a legitimate role for government in it;
(3) whether it should be handled in whole or in part by the private sector or the voluntary sector, or by the federal, provincial or local governments, or by any other agency;
(4) whether it might be handled best by partnerships among any of the above;
(5) whether (if the program is worth maintaining) its efficiency might be improved; and
(6) whether, in any event, the country can afford it.

The answers to such questions allow the observer to determine not only whether the program that exists should be maintained, is reasonable, and its delivery scheme adequate, but also whether there are alternative program designs and more effective ways to deliver the service that might be envisaged.

Those were the very questions that program review raised in probing the adequacy of the Canadian governance system through an investigation of a large number of the federal government programs. While such an inquiry left much of the Canadian governance apparatus out (everything under the purview of the provincial and local authorities and all the private sector and social sector arrangements), it assumed implicitly a general philosophy of governance based on self-reliance and subsidiarity—a philosophy built on personal responsibility and on the provision of help on the basis of individual needs by the private sector, community groups or the level of government closest to the citizen and capable of providing help effectively (Paquet and Shepherd 1996).

Dynamic social learning

From the very beginning of the alternative program delivery debate, there has been a great chasm between those who have had the *de facto* tendency to focus on criterion #5 (is there a way to improve efficiency through a modification of the program delivery mechanism?) and those who have articulated more ambitious plans for rethinking the whole public policy process and have suggested a *de jure* definition of the ASD initiative as trying to meet criteria #1 to #6 as a whole.

The tension between these two interpretations has been a source of confusion. This has been due to a dual technocratic illusion: one leading many to argue that there exists one-best technical solution to all delivery problems; another leading many to suggest that ASD is a panacea and that it would be sufficient to modify the delivery mechanisms in order to reform the whole policy process. Both these illusions have stood in the way of a reasonable debate, for most of the time there is no one-best technical solution applicable across the board when dealing with complex issues and a very heterogeneous and diverse population, and it is most certainly not sufficient in most cases to tinker with delivery mechanisms to transform policies in need of repairs.

The public policy process is a complex social system made of three components: structure, technology and theory. The structure consists of the set of roles of and relations among members of the organization. The technology refers to the tools used by members of the organization. The theory is the view held by members about the process, its purposes, environment and future. These dimensions hang together and any change in one affects the others (Schön 1971).

The capacity to transform is a measure of the organizational learning of this social system, that is, the speed with which it is able to restructure, retool and reframe its theory of itself in order to enhance, in an evolutionary and dynamic way, its triple-E performance: effectiveness (doing the right thing), efficiency (doing it right) and economy (doing it economically).

A bias for technology tinkering

It is in the very nature of an ASD-type initiative to focus much less, if at all, on the rationale for the program or on the appropriateness of roles and relationships in the program *per se* than on the machinery of delivery. This focus can only lead to a bias toward tinkering with technology.

Such a focus is built on an implicit presumption that the structures and theory of governance are given or may be regarded as optimal in some sense. The alternative service delivery initiative is therefore (wittingly or not) an effort to bolster the existing institutional order as it stands by improving its efficiency. And even if and when it develops broader ambitions, the ASD scheme is geared to work mainly through the highest and best use of the technology of delivery.

Those who have chosen this road to reform would appear to have immunized many fundamental dimensions of the policy process from critical discussion, through assumptions about:

(a) the separability of policy formation, program design and delivery mechanism;

(b) the sacred nature of the Westminster model of government and the consequent assumption that accountability to the minister must remain untouched as the process is amended; and

(c) the presumption that explicit detailed contracts are not only necessary but sufficient to ensure that the policy intended by the senior executives (political and bureaucratic) will be carried out.

Three different worlds

To understand the central importance of these assumptions (that are not necessary but are in good currency), it may be useful to construct three different artificial worlds in which they are allowed to play a more or less central or important role. This allows one to see clearly to what extent the non-negotiability of these assumptions might modify considerably the ambit, significance and effectiveness of the experiment with ASD.

The *Aucoin world* is built on a strong version of these three assumptions. He does not suggest that they can be easily met but argues that, through explicit, transparent and detailed contracts, it is possible to modify delivery mechanisms without affecting the other stages of the policy process or eroding the executive authority on policy substance. Thus it is possible to preserve the Westminster model (Aucoin 1995, 1996).

For Aucoin, the stylization of the policy process into water-tight segments that may cohabit without true interaction (so that one may tinker with re-tooling without any significant impact on structures and theory) is not a dogma; it is more in the nature of a simplifying axiom. He recognizes that most modifications in the technology are bound to have some impact on the roles and relations in the organization and to shift ever so slightly the view that the organization or system has of itself. But these impacts are minimized in order to keep the Pandora's box closed shut. Different logics may then inhabit the different segments of the public policy process without inter-contamination.

In such a world, ASD is an important tool because it generates efficiency gains with very limited external 'malefits' on the rest of the public policy process: each segment inhabits more or less a separate facility so rationales, roles and responsibilities may remain relatively untouched even if the technology is modified.

The *Jacobs/Mintzberg world* is almost the exact obverse. It is built on an assumption of a seamless integrity of the public policy process. Its dominant logic is defined by Jane Jacobs as the 'guardian syndrome'. Jacobs uses the term syndrome to denote a set of interconnected symptoms and values that define a collection of precepts and morals (Jacobs 1992). A syndrome is the basis of a process through which people form perceptions, make judgments and, as a result, take a particular form of action. This 'guardian syndrome' is built on a set of values and a theory that call for structures and technologies that are fundamentally different from those flowing from the competing syndrome, the 'commercial syndrome' (Ibid.; Mintzberg 1996a). These are depicted in table 8.1

The guardian syndrome is associated with the characteristic traits such as the shunning of trading, exerting prowess, etc. Those working in the public sector or those familiar with the traditional connotations often attached to 'bureaucrats' will certainly recognize these parameters of the state sector. Alternatively, the commercial syndrome is characterized by a number of traits such as the shunning of force, easy collaboration with strangers and aliens, etc. The picture that results, then, is not unlike a form of the protestant work ethic that is commonly accredited as being one of the pillars that underpinned the development of capitalism.

Table 8.1   Characteristic traits of Jacobs' syndromes

The Commercial Syndrome	The Guardian Syndrome
Shun force	Shun trading
Come to voluntary agreements	Exert prowess
Be honest	Be obedient and disciplined
Collaborate easily with strangers & aliens	Adhere to tradition
Compete	Be loyal
Respect contracts	Respect hierarchy
Use initiative and enterprise	Take vengeance
Be open to innovativeness and novelty	Deceive for the sake of the task
Be efficient	Make rich use of leisure
Promote comfort and convenience	Be ostentatious
Dissent for the sake of the task	Dispense largesse
Invest for productive purposes	Be exclusive
Be industrious	Show fortitude
Be thrifty	Be fatalistic
Be optimistic	Treasure honour

The power of this cosmology is the clarity and force of its message: individuals operating in one syndrome cannot and should not be expected to act as if they reside in the other. As a result, the misunderstandings and perpetual conflict between private entrepreneurs and state officials become reducible to a stalemate with no solution. Indeed Jane Jacobs goes so far as stating that if and when the two syndromes are mixed, that is, when there is any effort to elicit a "mixed" way to institute anything, this can only produce "monstrous hybrids".

In this sort of world, ASD is a very much more restricted tool. The technology of delivery has to be in keeping with the theory and structure defined by the dominant logic. Any independent overhauling of the technology of delivery is likely to have major (and possibly perverse effects) on rationales, roles and relationships to ensure congruence. But since these are somewhat rigidly fixed, the result is that ASD has a rather limited scope.

In the *Schumpeter world*, the three assumptions and the general axiom that technology, structure and theory are tightly separated are relaxed in a fundamental way. In fact, the public policy process is neither completely modularized nor completely seamless. Rather it is made of strongly interactive segments (Schumpeter 1934). We enter the world of cross-border exchange, partnerships, compromises and collaboration among the private, public and not-for-profit sectors in which the roles and relationships can be and are modified as new delivery mechanisms are put in place (Paquet and Roy 1996).

Tinkering with technology in a Schumpeterian world is neither inconsequential for the governance process as in the Aucoin world, nor dangerous as in the Jacobs/Mintzberg world. The echo effects of new delivery mechanisms modify the nature of the roles and relationship, and even the very theory of what the system is about. We enter the world of innovations and creative destruction. ASD remains an indirect route to transform governance. Some may prefer more direct routes through restructuring (as program review tried to do) and more ambitious efforts yet, dealing directly with the theory through suggesting a new philosophy of governance (Bouchard 1992; Paquet 1994; Burelle 1995). But ASD remains a credible strategy. Indeed, in the Schumpeterian world, ASD is neither as innocent as Aucoin would like, nor as noxious as Jacobs/Mintzberg would warn. All depends on the way social learning unfolds.

Focus on social learning

The only way to ensure that a public policy system continues to learn new goals and new means as the circumstances change is to ensure that it is equipped with a dynamic capacity to transform. This is not nested in technology, structure or theory but in the dynamic interaction among them.

In this context, if we accept a Schumpeterian view of things, alternative service delivery must be seen as a contribution to the modification of a delicate cognitive and learning organization. This formulation focuses less on static allocation of chores among sectors and more on the effectiveness of dynamic evolutionary learning (Paquet 1992).

The public policy process learns faster as a decentralized network organization (delayered, participative, operating through a network of units sensitive to local circumstances) (Snow et al. 1992). This, in turn, requires an organizational structure that is dramatically different from the one in place in hierarchical bureaucracies.

Whether one is led by tinkering with technology of delivery to the redesign of the traditional organizations into circular organizations *à la* Ackoff/Mintzberg (Ackoff 1994; Mintzberg 1996b) or into spherical structures that rotate competent self-managing teams and other resources around a common knowledge base (Miles and Snow 1995), any such restructuring, triggered by a new delivery mechanism, is bound to be the source of some reframing.

For instance, the creation of a delivery mechanism more sensitive to local circumstances is bound to generate a greater recognition of the variety of needs, and to foster a reframing of the policy away from a focus on rights and standardized rules (defined centrally) to a focus on needs and tailor-made services (defined at the periphery). The interaction among the different phases of the policy process commands continuous inter-adjustments: this is what organizational learning is all about. So, if a new logic is introduced at the delivery phase, this will impact on the whole process. Modifications at the technology-structure level may lead to a reframing of the very meaning of the policy thrust, but they may also lead to blockages and policy messes (Mintzberg 1996a).

In a Schumpeterian world, the benchmarks in assessing the response to the basic governance question are effectiveness and social learning. The alternative service delivery initiative defines ways in which modifications in the technology can reshape roles and relations to ensure maximum learning at the individual and organizational levels. This was at the core of the Institute of Public Administration of Canada (IPAC)/KPMG project (Lenihan 1995) and the criticality of this focus has been confirmed in broad surveys of recent changes in delivery systems (Wright and Zussman 1996). Experimenting at the technology level is therefore potentially important, and this revolutionary potential of ASD must be acknowledged. It is equally important, however, not to overestimate the impact of technology tinkering.

First, through a strategy of containment, its echo effects on structure and theory may be sanitized. This might lead to an efficient system of the most ineffective sort. In the long run, such a strategy would undoubtedly reveal itself to be ineffectual but it might persist in any event on the sole basis of the power structure that underpins the policy process.

Second, it would be unwise not to entertain the possibility that the ASD strategy might unwittingly and unwisely maintain federal control on many programs that should be legitimately devolved to provincial and local governments. This could be done through engineering delivery mechanisms that will give the impression that a program is at arm's length from the federal government when in fact it will remain entirely under its spell. If this were to be the result once too often, the ASD initiative might come to be regarded as a simple decoy to avoid decentralization and not really as an initiative designed to modify the governance system through the technology route.

Third, the worst scenario might be the possibility of the creation of hybrid organizations designed explicitly as decoys and purporting to be decentralized, while maintaining power at the top. This could only lead to more conflicts in a federal system like ours.

Concerns

We have identified a few clusters of issues that need to be clarified before any sustained progress can be made in the social learning process that the alternative service delivery strategy underpins. Failing to do so runs the risk of restricting considerably the ambitions and successes of any broad-based service transformation exercise.

The policy formation/program design/service delivery process

The focus on effectiveness not only calls into question the generalized use of the same instrument or technology, it also puts some constraints on the nature of the social learning process. As public services become more and more tailor-made, and the needs have to be assessed more and more locally, the whole public policy process becomes much more difficult to partition into water-tight compartments. Outcomes are not incommensurable, but they are not easily evaluable according to the same formal criteria because of the different extent to which groups of citizens differ and may even value their right to participate in the elaboration of policies differently.

Indeed, the same general philosophy of governance may lead to programs and delivery mechanisms that are quite different from one zone to the next. To be effective, in a context as diverse as the Canadian scene, the public policy process is bound to become a series of local systems of public policy, loosely federated through a fishnet-type structure.

One may obviously design learning loops along the axis running from general policy directions and principles to precise delivery mechanisms in those local settings, but, to the extent that different logics preside over the arrangements in the different segments, the coordination problem is made more difficult. Consequently, lopping off the delivery system may well impair the social learning process in a serious way. On the other hand, hoping to write comprehensive and transparent contracts is unduly optimistic: the configurations of circumstances are so broad-ranging that one may at best count on some loose convention or "moral contract" defining in a most general way the underlying values to be taken into account in shaping the tailor-made program (Paquet 1991–92; Fairtlough 1994).

Severing the delivery mechanism from the public policy process in such circumstances would likely throw a wrench in the machine and generate massive coordination failures. Devolution of service delivery might even have the perverse effect of generating recentralization of the administrative process after the coordination or delivery failures have been exposed (Paquet and Shepherd 1996).

A way out of this quandary is to recognize the need to construct, in an informal manner, the necessary points of concertation, harmonization and co-decision that must exist in a circular organization to make it into a learning organization (Ackoff 1994; Burelle 1995; Mintzberg 1996b).

Such a learning organization is defined by an absence of ultimate authority and a certain circularity of power, through an ability for all to participate, and to make and implement decisions that affect only themselves. In an integrated social learning cycle, with value-creation (scanning, problem-solving, abstraction) and value-exploitation (diffusion, absorption, impacting), a process of creation, destruction and renewal of knowledge exists. These stages cannot easily be segmented without much loss to the learning process. Consequently, additional coordination costs may be the price to pay for alternative service delivery (Boisot 1995).

The accountability nexus

Over and above the blockages ascribable to ignoring effectiveness and social learning strategies are those pertaining to accountability. The Westminster model posits the linear accountability upward of the whole chain of command to the minister. This model is becoming less than perfectly satisfactory.

An effectiveness focus requires that the needs of the citizenry be the dominant factor; a circular organization of the sort that is at work in the social learning cycle diffuses the accountability even more widely to a large number of stakeholders. This generates a need for 360° accountability based on a multilogue among the stakeholders.

Bruce Stone has suggested that a multiplicity of conceptions of accountability are intermingled in modern Westminster systems and must be traded-off one against the other in real-life democracies (Stone 1995). These are depicted in table 8.2.

Table 8.2   Relationships within accounting systems

Type of system	Basis of relationship	Analogous relationship
Parliamentary control	Supervision/command	Superior/subordinate
Managerialism	Fiduciary/contract	Principal/agent
Judicial/Quasi-judicial reviews	Individual rights/ procedural obligations	Appellant/respondent
Constituency relations	Representation/ responsiveness	Constituent/representative
Market	Competition/ consumer sovereignty	Customer/entrepreneur

In the Aucoin world, the executive elites are able to maintain the hegemony of the old parliamentary control as the only legitimate dominant logic. Senior managers and bureaucrats have no difficulty in striking a power-sharing partnership with the parliamentarians who are members of the executive. The two logics of the parliamentary control and managerialism are in some way kindred spirits: they share the same top-down philosophy.

More difficult trade-offs are bound to be generated as new delivery mechanisms that are more sensitive to citizen's needs are developed. The new outside-in logic that underpins them cannot always be reconciled with the hegemonic views of parliamentarians and senior bureaucrats. This can only trigger a major rethinking of the very business the government is in, whether the initiators of these new mechanisms wish to recognize it or not. Moreover, social learning entails also alliances with a diversity of partners and relationships with them that are, of necessity, looser. Indeed, corporations and agencies shift more and more from ruling corporate governance to some sort of contractual governance that may take a diversity of forms: from explicit, detailed, written contracts to implicit, relational contracting, reinforced only with non-legalistic mechanisms of compliance (Kester 1992).

As the knowledge content of the relationship grows, the aversion to opportunistic behaviour is likely to decline: trust is therefore likely to become ever more important and to be necessary to underpin the capability to search for and share new knowledge. Trust increases the aversion to cheating that increases trust in turn: this is a self-reinforcing mechanism (Mody 1993).

But trust requires 360° accountability and this does not easily cohabit with the Westminster model.

In a Schumpeterian world, the complexity is bound to become so great and the mutual trust so important that coordination can be effected much better through clan-type uncodified information, shared worldviews and practices, and moral contracts generating the requisite virtuous circle of openness, trust, empowerment and commitment (Fairtlough 1994). One cannot readily see how detailed, explicit, market-type contracts might be able to do the job, for, as Gareth Morgan puts it:

> ...defining work responsibilities in a clear-cut manner has the
> advantage of letting everyone know what is expected of them.
> But it also lets them know what is not expected of them (Morgan
> 1986).

The ominous "federal obligations and interests" clause

Even if the philosophy of governance based on self-reliance and subsidiarity were taken as a legitimate interpretation of the program review philosophy, and the first issues raised above were clarified and resolved (so that effectiveness issues would be given central importance, the public policy process would be recognized as fairly tightly integrated, and a form of 360° accountability could be engineered), there would remain a fundamental block to the fullest use of the ASD initiative.

This has to do with the blanket clause that was presented in the principles set out to guide the ASD initiative that called for the "public interest" to be defined in the light of the requirement of the federal government "fulfilling federal obligations and interests" (Canada 1995: 8). The French version is even more explicit: "*remplir les obligations du gouvernement fédéral et en protéger les intérêts*". This echoed the centralized mindset of the day. By 2002, this written clause had disappeared, but the spirit lives on.

While a legitimate constraint to impose on the search for alternative delivery schemes, this most important element has a bearing on the definition of the "public interest" and would appear to put certain roles and relationships in a privileged category—to be protected at all costs from modification. This would permit any initiative to be disallowed if, *in the opinion of the federal government*, it prevents the government from fulfilling its obligations (which is open to various interpretations) or if it does not serve the interests of the federal government (which are by definition a matter on which the federal government cannot be second-guessed).

Depending on the sense given to this interpretative clause, one may envisage two scenarios: scenario one, rooted in a philosophy of governance based on self-reliance and subsidiarity (Burelle 1995) in which the power of this interpretative clause is extremely restricted and covers only statutory and legal commitments of the federal government; and scenario two, rooted in a much more centralized philosophy of governance based on egalitarianism and compulsive centralism in which this interpretative clause might be used to ensure the continuance of federal control (directly or indirectly) in the name of "elusive" federal interests (Hirsch 1976).

The same argument holds obviously at the provincial level in their relationship with districts, local governments, not-for-profit agencies etc. Different governments and different government departments may interpret such a clause in quite different ways. It is not so clear that the disappearance of the clause in the bureaucratic jargon in good currency means that the mindsets of central agencies and key senior bureaucrats have changed. To the extent that this mindset continues to prevail, it continues to shape current (and future) government's decisions, choices and actions more than any government knows. Thus one is forced to conclude that scenario two is the more plausible (Paquet and Roy 1995; Paquet and Shepherd 1996).

Shifting roles and relationships

Alternate service delivery has gained both visibility and legitimacy and will have a growing impact on Canada's governance.

Public policy is very much an evolutionary process in which different phases are co-mingled and interacting, this means that wittingly or not, ASDs (including the ASD initiative) have transformed roles, relationships and rationales here and elsewhere around the world and will continue to do so.

The central query is about the extent of those transformations. This will obviously depend upon three sets of realities:
1) . the nature of the world we live in,
2) the extent to which blockages and tension points will be dealt with effectively, and
3) the likelihood of scenario one or two dominating when it comes to protecting federal or provincial obligations and interests.

On the first point, an uneasy consensus would appear to be emerging. It is taking some distance from the Jacobs/Mintzberg fundamentalist position which suggests that reform is an all-or-nothing process, that the ASD initiative is bound to flounder, and that roles and relationships will evolve very little if at all. The consensus would appear to fall half way between the Schumpeter and Aucoin scenarios: it is widely recognized that, of the two, the Schumpeterian world is the more realistic stylization of what is the current state of affairs, and therefore that many roles and relationships will be fundamentally transformed over the next decade. This view is tempered significantly nevertheless, by the widely-accepted Aucoin argument that there can be cohabitation between different logics at the policy formation and program design, and at the service delivery stage, without the former being tainted by the latter. This helps to explain why there has been less concern than might have been expected about the significance of the role and relationship changes.

On the second point, it is unlikely that the first three blockages or tension points will be resolved by common agreement in the near future.

Effectiveness issues will continue to be avoided and efficiency issues favoured in public debates; the Aucoin position about the partitionability of the policy process is, if anything, gaining credibility in federal circles and is likely to fuel the interest in the ASD initiative; the accountability issue is likely to remain unresolved so we are likely to be locked in a *soft Westminster position*: accountability to the political and bureaucratic executive will continue to be hegemonic, and there will be multi-stakeholder consultations, but not 360° accountability. These unresolved issues will undoubtedly slow down the progress of the ASD initiative.

On the third point about the meaning of the "federal obligations and interests" clause (and clauses of the same sort at the provincial level), scenario two is likely to continue to prevail for the next few years. Undoubtedly, this will lead to much support for the preservation of a very high degree of centralization in Ottawa for all sorts of reasons, including the myth that standardized and centralized national social programs constitute the essential glue necessary to keep the country together (Banting 1996). While this myth is fundamentally groundless, it is nevertheless still an icon in Ottawa (Paquet 1996a; Richards 1996).

From this general diagnosis, one may surmise that some roles and responsibilities are likely to change in the Canadian governance system. These conjectured changes in roles and relationships remain rather tentative because much depends on the extent to which we have gauged the sensitivities, mental blocks and determination of the different actors well.

These ethnographic observations (and others) have influenced our conjectures on the evolution of roles and relationships as a result of the ASD approach.

At the macroscopic level

1) There will be a significant increase in the role of the private and the not-for-profit sectors in the Canadian governance system and a reduction of the formal role of the public sector, but there will not be a commensurate decline in the degree of control of the public sector.

2) There will be a significant increase in the number of alliances and partnerships between government and either the private or the volunteer sectors, but again without a significant decline in the degree of control of the public sector.

3) The ASD approach will slow down the process of devolution from the federal government to the provincial and local governments, as improved efficiency and greater closeness and sensitivity to the citizens in federal delivery schemes will provide arguments in favour of the federal government maintaining its presence and control through federally-coordinated or monitored agencies in a number of sectors where presently a case can be made that provincial governments and private or not-for-profit concerns could do a better job.

4) One may expect additional federal-provincial tensions to the extent that the federal government attempts to maintain national standards through federally-monitored agencies even though needs and preferences are not standardized across the land.

At the mesoscopic level

1) The governance structure of all sectors will be dramatically transformed as the stakeholders become more conscious

both of their relative vulnerability and of their undeniable power. The circular organization with 360° accountability will not be put in place in the short-run, but pressures in this direction will translate into a much greater degree of consultation and negotiation with a larger number of stakeholders.

2) One may expect an erosion of the absolute property rights approach of both private concerns (which had absolute rights to the whole surplus) and public concerns (which had the monopoly on public coercion). They will be forced through alliances to attenuate their rights and to negotiate arrangements for sharing power.

3) The whole notion of evaluation will be transformed in the public sector as the various types of accountabilities evolve and become legitimate. Different mixes of accountability rules will be imposed on different issue-domains. One may expect a growing power of the courts in the interpretation of the different covenants until some degree of trust has developed among partners. The Gomery effect has obviously slowed down this process in a remarkable and unfortunate way.

4) There will be the emergence of a multiplicity of new forums where the negotiation of the new local systems of innovation and the new local social bargaining will be carried out. Local authorities, community groups and the citizenry will acquire more say on certain features of the public policy programs.

At the microscopic level

1) A successful round of redefinitions of the delivery mechanisms for programs will reduce the power and significance of the federal Public Service Commission dramatically as a substantial portion of the public service activities will slip away from its authority.

2) Because of the difficulty in designing the mechanisms of coordination, harmonization and co-decision

making among the many stakeholders, the Treasury Board Secretariat and equivalent agencies will see their influence grow significantly as new horizontal policy fields emerge that will require some policing in the name of ultimate accountability. Standardization will increase balkanization, and there will be a swing of the pendulum toward recentralization in the name of efficiency and fairness.

3) The downsizing of the official public service will transform dramatically the relationships with unions as their memberships dwindle and their relative bargaining power declines.

Conclusion

In dealing with a complex system, it is always very difficult to find exactly what can be ascribed to a specific initiative. Usually, causality is plural and diffuse and one has to be particularly careful not to overstate the impact of one debate within a forum where many conversations are going on at the same time. But the ASD approach has acquired such a high profile and has brought about enough change already that one is almost forced to speculate about its impact. In fact, a tipping point in reform may already have been reached at the federal level.

The consequence of program review (and of the ASD initiative that it spawned) that has the greatest significance may well turn out to be the fact that it will have helped Canadians to understand the full possibility of reform in their governance system through the administrative route (Paquet 1996b).

This means that what is being learned in the trenches these days may serve us all well in the proximate future, as one of two scenarios unfolds.

Either the federal government will decide to go much further and faster along the devolution line. In this case, much that is being experimented with now will be of use. Or if devolution does not prevail, the breakdown of the country may well result, bringing about havoc, and a new wave of reflective fireplace chats about all the might-have-beens. But also, and more importantly, the practical resolution of difficult problems (that had been declared unsolvable) will be rediscovered in the various experimental responses generated by prototyping and serious play (but ignored) in earlier times.

Either way, the ASD approach will have played and will continue to play an important part in the rebalancing of 'government-as-usual' with innovative government.

CHAPTER 9

P3 and The "Porcupine Problem"

A number of porcupines huddled together for warmth on a cold
day in winter;
but as they began to prick one another with their quills, they were
obliged to disperse.
However the cold drove them together again...

—Arthur Schopenhauer

Introduction

In Schopenhauer's parable, the animals arrive at a solution by maintaining a safe distance from one another, and as a result, while their mutual need for warmth is only moderately satisfied, they do not get pricked.

In recent decades, the private, public and social/civic sectors have developed strategies of *rapprochement* and *concertation* in the name of greater efficiency, effectiveness and economy. Indeed, public-private partnerships (PPP or P3) have been shown to reduce administrative and operations costs by some 20 to 50 percent in public transportation projects (L. Roy 2003). In other areas, P3s have had mixed performances: great successes, mediocre results, and major failures.

It is therefore important to understand the causes and sources of such successes and failures, and to develop the basis for some protocols that would tend to increase the probability of positive outcomes. This is a tall order for a short chapter.

Public-private partnerships—be they bipartite or multipartite —clearly pose a porcupine problem that needs to be resolved somehow. The completely different logics and mechanics of coordination that underpin private, public and social organizations may, if properly harnessed, lead either to impressive synergies, innovation and higher productivity, or to a good deal of waste. To make the highest and best use of P3s, however, one must elicit the conditions for the best warmth/prickliness ratio.

Many have chosen to resolve the porcupine problem by walking away from it: vilifying the P3 process entirely, damning it as fundamentally *contre-nature*. Others have uncritically embraced this new form of mixed organization, and have been in denial *vis-à-vis* the substantial evidence that it has often failed miserably. A third group (to which we belong) has felt that the benefits of P3s can be substantial, but that they cannot be obtained unless certain conditions are met.

This chapter analyzes the porcupine problem posed by P3s, and suggests a workable set of conditions that promise some value adding, and as little prickling as possible: moderate warmth and safe distance.

Section 1 presents some basic economics and politics of the P3 process, some features of the different stages in that process, and a short primer on the centrality of well-executed contractual arrangements. Section 2 deals very briefly with the strong ideological opposition that has been mounted against such arrangements in some 'progressive' circles. Section 3 derives some lessons from our examination of a wide range of experiences in Canada and abroad, and suggests some levers that might be used to ensure a much greater probability of success for P3s. The conclusion tries to explain why the debates around P3s have been so unenlightening, and have developed such a fundamentalist tone.

The political economy and contractual nature of the P3 process

Governments cannot necessarily dispatch, solo, the complete range of tasks associated with the provision of all public or mixed public/private goods in the most effective, efficient and economical way. Many state monopolies have come under attack for their ineffectiveness, inefficiency and lack of innovativeness. Some forms of partnering with the private or social sectors have been shown to produce better results for taxpayers. As a result, reform-minded (and cash-strapped) governments have extended the concept of contracting out to a wider range of public activities, and significantly expanded the scope of the work done in partnership with other sectors (Bettignies and Ross 2004).

These partnerships are hybrid arrangements that have been quite varied in terms of the targeted results, the geographical terrain encompassed, and the range of rationales of their instigators (Vaillancourt Rosenau 2000). The public activities that are involved range widely as well: from infrastructure to the re-engineering of both 'clean' services (such as civil air navigation or revenue collection) and 'dirty' ones (e.g., water, sewage and energy), to experimenting with de-institutionalizing persons with intellectual disabilities, and increasing collaboration with the voluntary or cooperative sectors on a variety of fronts.

These arrangements have been designed to take maximum advantage of the relatively better performance, for certain tasks, of the different basic integrating mechanisms at work in the different sectors: *quid pro quo* exchange (market economy), coercion (polity), and gift or solidarity or reciprocity (community and society).

The first arrangement is based on price and non-price competition, and provides robust incentives likely to generate pressure for productivity and innovation, but may be plagued by opportunism and shirking, especially if the metering of the 'product' or of the final outcome is difficult. The coercive approach would appear to economize on coordination costs, but may lack the flexibility to adapt to local circumstances. The third family of arrangements is diffuse, and appears fragile, because it is heavily built on good will, but it may be most effective when trust is imperative, and the need to mobilize strong commitment matters a great deal.

P3s as a particular form of such institutional *metissage* can best be stylized from three complementary perspectives: first, as a mega-community process involving divergent interests and developing partnerships based on trust, in which parties may jointly pursue somewhat different objectives (Gerencser et al. 2006; Otazo 2006; Ramonjavelo et al. 2006); second, as a number of phased activities that go from the initial decision to enter into contractual relations with a partner or many partners, all the way through tender and evaluation, and selection of partners, designing, building and operating facilities (Carson 2002); third, as a contractual arrangement defining the role of each party to the partnership, their duties and responsibilities, their portion of the burden of risk and of the value-added generated, and the nature of the co-governance process (Kooiman 2003).

The first perspective draws attention to P3s as complex processes based on a mega-community—"a public sphere in which organizations and people deliberately join together around a compelling issue of mutual importance, following a set of practices and principles that will make it easier to achieve results" (Gerencser et al. 2006). This entails a requisite amount of both trust (institutional, inter-organizational, and interpersonal) and social capital.

In practice, Gerencser and others have identified four critical elements for a thriving mega-community:

(1) understanding the problems to be resolved, the necessary players and partners, and the ways in which they affect one another;

(2) the presence of partners in a listening, learning and understanding mode;

(3) designing and customizing of suitable cross-sector arrangements; and

(4) experiments, learning from them, and effective collective monitoring of progress.

People and groups potentially affected by, or involved in any P3, are by definition players in the mega community. For all of them, their interests in it (and views of it) will tend to be framed by the mindset that dominates the culture in good currency in the socio-economic context. Their opinions will evolve to some extent as time passes, and will change to a greater or lesser degree as a result of external influences.

Partners have quite different expectations. In the private sector, the main interest is the profitability likely to ensue if additional efficiency and effectiveness are value-adding through P3s. From the public sector point of view, even though the public good is readily invoked, bureaucrats, elected officials, political opposition, and the unionized public service may have diverse interests, and may not see things the same way. This is bound to have an impact on the nature of the negotiated contracts. The not-for-profit mindset is no more univocal. Board members, paid permanent staff and volunteers may pursue different objectives that will shape their direct involvement and choices in P3s.

The media also play a special kind of role as opinion-moulders, to the extent that they influence the frames of reference of both the mega-community and the particular actors, and help to shape their perspectives.

The second perspective relates to the different phases in the construction, negotiation, and management of P3s.

The simplest representation of the array of possible arrangements is the one suggested by the Canadian Council for Public-Private Partnerships (CCPPP), which co-relates the degree of involvement of private partners (but one may add easily social partners also) with the degree of risk they shoulder.

Figure 9.1   P3 risk versus private spectrum

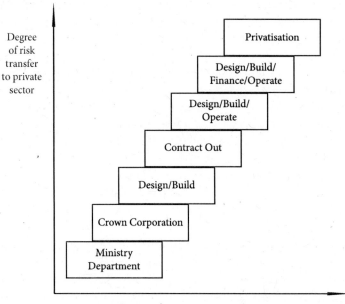

Source: The Canadian Council for Public-Private Partnerships.

This very linear and simplistic representation of the very complex P3 process has the merit of identifying a range of possibilities: from organizational arrangements where the participants are engaged in a minimal way as sheer suppliers of particular goods and services, to arrangements where the partners engage in the totality of the procurement and delivery of some public good or service, to arrangements through which the public sector completely relinquishes responsibility for the production and delivery of public services to independent private or social entities.

A more complete view would also take into account the broad social environment within which the key stakeholders are nested, the mega-community of stakeholders, and the different challenges each of the phases (from opting for P3s to the design/build/operate phase) brings forth: a high degree of understanding, trust and legitimacy in the mega-community, the choice of the right organizational form and of the right partners, the recognition that the different phases (choice of instrument, request for tenders, negotiation of the agreement, monitoring of the operations, etc.) may call for arrangements of different sorts, the right capacity to do and to learn, a rigorous management of the partnership, and some external evaluative framework capable of acting as a fail-safe mechanism (Aubert and Patry 2003).

A more complex representation might be that the P3 game is the combination of two sub-games.

The first is a *cognitive* game meant to provide the coordinating guidance likely to ensure as high a productivity quasi-rent as possible. This may take the form of either cost reduction and/or a better level of service. These results are meant to be achievable through a variety of ways: better incentive-reward systems and motivation, taking advantage of field experience, economies of scale, better risk management, more innovation, etc. This in turn generates a productivity quasi-rent—that is, a surplus ascribable to a more effective allocation of resources.

The second is a *distributive* game meant to generate the most fruitful way of sharing the proceeds among partners, so as to ensure the viability and resilience of the arrangement.

While waste upstream is often reduced through a robust competition amongst potential suppliers, at the time of request for tenders, this does little to determine how the quasi-rent will be allocated among the partners once the contract is signed, unless these issues are explicitly addressed in the contract. The looser the arrangements, the more possibility for opportunistic behaviour there will be and, therefore, the more trust will be required.

This struggle over the sharing of costs, risks and profits generates additional costs of renegotiation/bargaining if a contract is not 'complete'. And since complete contracts are often not feasible (because of all sorts of contingencies generating instability and uncertainty that are truly not predictable), there is a substantial possibility that these additional costs will become very heavy, and that the allocation of both risks and quasi-rents will in turn generate much unfairness and therefore much inefficiency.

Thus Scott Carson has underlined the importance of three important *ex ante* tests of viable P3s:

(1) value-added to all partners being quite visible in the early phases of the process, and the realization by all partners that mid-stream changes are always extremely costly;

(2) cost effectiveness of the time and resources used in the tendering and negotiation phases of the process;

(3) fairness in the distribution of the productivity quasi-rent and of the risks that can be expertly assessed by third parties (Carson 2002).

The third perspective focuses on the contractual arrangement *per se*. Its role is to ensure goodness of fit among a complex context, a diverse mega-community, intricate design-build operations, and an effective inquiry/monitoring/learning/dispute resolution system. The nature of the contractual arrangement is meant to ensure effective, transparent, fair, legitimate and creative co-governance.

The motivations for entering into P3s may be economic and financial, managerial or strategic. For example, it may be ascribable to the fact that the public sector can no longer adequately finance all public projects (Drummond 2006). It may also be that the public sector expects to realize significant cost efficiency measures. Or it may be an attempt to shift the risk burden away from the taxpayers to the private partners. It may also be a way to cope with expertise deficiencies. More recently, there has been a deeper intermingling of public, private and civic expertise to create P3s that are focused on creating or re-engineering complex, expensive, technologically-sophisticated systems (e.g., revenue collection across several government departments and agencies).

In any of these cases, the nature of the contractual arrangements calls for negotiations by very competent experts.

This has been the cornerstone for the successes of P3s in many countries: developing common objectives, clear delineation of inputs, risks and returns, precise definition of the responsibilities, authorities and risks, robust arrangements for risk shifting, strong and quick dispute resolution mechanisms, etc.

It entails a much stronger design, selection and contract negotiation apparatus on the part of public sector agencies, than that which is often in place. But when such expertise is in place, in an increasing number of complex cases, joint-solution procurement (enabling the collaborative design of a wider range of options, and proceeding in stages where the measured capacity and competence of possible partners is realistically assessed) is preferred over traditional procurement in which government determines the solution to a problem and provides vendors with detailed specifications.

With regard to the most complex of these arrangements (those involving the design, build and operation of major infrastructure— bricks and mortar, or technology-rich systems), the choice is not between the traditional approach and P3, but between P3 and deferring projects indefinitely, as a result of public financial and competence constraints. Since those projects are often large in scale, capital intensive, require technical capabilities that exceed public sector capabilities, and are usually attached to identifiable revenue streams, they are initiatives that are the most amenable to P3s. It is not surprising that they have been the most popular.

Such projects—especially the bricks and mortar kind—have acquired a good reputation from some studies, showing that they have been able to deliver an average saving of 17 percent as compared to conventionally procured public sector schemes (Burleton 2006: iii). An added advantage of such P3s is that the public sector partner is usually immunized against any cost overrun in the construction phase (since it has no responsibility for it) and often against cost overruns in the exploitation phase (since the revenue stream depends on the availability and use of the facilities).

Because of their long-term nature, their scope and sophistication, infrastructure projects are, however, vulnerable to miscalculations and to changes in the socio-technical context.

Consequently, contractual arrangements must ensure constant monitoring and evaluation of the process in order to detect any mishaps or flaws very quickly, and develop a protocol to ensure that differences of opinion can be resolved quickly. This is the foundation of effective social learning (Aubert and Patry 2005, Aubert et al. 2005).

Finally, there is a need to ensure that fail-safe mechanisms are in place in order to avoid sabotage in the form of frivolous delays engineered by parties to the agreement who hope to gain from delay tactics. Such failsafe mechanisms are meant to kick in when the usual protocols of dispute resolution fail, and if, in the view of dispassionate third parties, further delays in resolving the unresolved questions would endanger the project in significant ways. In such matters, the optimal amount of coercion in P3s is not zero.

The ideological opposition to P3s

However difficult it might be to forge the mega-community, to establish clearly and realistically that a quasi-rent really exists and can be captured, to develop the requisite capabilities and the appropriate policy and contractual instruments to do so, and to put in place the required monitoring/evaluation/learning mechanisms to allow the arrangements to be modified smoothly as circumstances and issues evolve—the major hindrance to making use of P3s is not of a technical nature: it has to do with the ideological opposition of the 'chattering classes' to such arrangements, an opposition that has been widely echoed in the media.

Even though it may be established that P3s might be economically and financially desirable—and might even provide a better quality and more responsive service—such arrangements remain highly suspect for citizens who have been brainwashed for half a century by a culture of entitlements generated by the 'welfare state'.

Two recent books are interesting *révélateurs* of the depth of ideological revulsion *vis-à-vis* P3s especially in Quebec (Boismenu et al. 2004; Rouillard et al. 2004). In both books, there is a rejection of the idea that the state might be regarded as simply "*un vulgaire prestateur de services*" (Rouillard et al. 2004: 86).

Indeed, a certain Hegelian-flavoured metaphysics haunts both books: the state (always spelled with a capital S) is regarded as the fundamental societal "organism" with moral purposes that transcend those of its individual citizens (Paquet 2005d).

Therefore, depending on the coefficient of Hegelianism harboured by the authors, tinkering with the state is perceived as less or more a case of *lèse-majesté*. For the soft Hegelians (Boismenu et al. 2004), there is more to the state than service provision, but this does not prevent one from legitimately seeking more efficiency and effectiveness in alternative non-state delivery systems. For the hard Hegelians (Rouillard et al. 2004), any tinkering with any aspect of the state sphere that may reduce its scope or ambit can only be regarded as an impoverishment of governance.

Both books (although to a different extent) are led to take a particularly critical aim at the P3 component of the Charest strategy for re-engineering the Quebec state.

In Gérard Boismenu's book, the tone is skeptical. It is fairly argued that "*la montagne a accouché d'une souris*" (Boismenu et al. 2004: 56). The authors' view might even be interpreted as not necessarily opposed to P3s, but rather unimpressed by the way in which the Charest government is going about this strategy. There is no denial that P3s, under the right conditions, might help solve many problems, even though it is felt that the Charest government may be too timid and that its top-down clumsiness might leave much scope for discontent and sabotage by the permanent public servants who are threatened by such arrangements.

In Christian Rouillard's book, the tone is acerbic. The opposition to P3s is fundamental. It is asserted in a peremptory way that none of the winning conditions exist, and that none of the promises in terms of gains in efficiency and effectiveness, accountability and quality assurance in the provision of public services can be realized. All this is "*un discours illusoire et insidieux*" (Rouillard et al. 2004: 108), "*une chimère*" (Ibid., 115). Nothing is proved or disproved here, nor is there any need to do so: we are in the world of dogma.

The attack by the Rouillard book on P3s in general is not entirely groundless. Indeed, P3s are not automatically a success. Some winning conditions are necessary for P3s to work, and these are not always in place. What makes the argument somewhat toxic is that the authors presume, without any proof, that such conditions can never be realized.

The ideological underpinnings of this position are clear: if one were to allow for the possibility of such collaborative governance, the very sacred nature of the state would be eroded, and its metaphysical dominium thereby questioned—an act of heresy that cannot be entertained.

Other critics are less strident (Flinders 2005). Their comments have to do with the fact that P3s might potentially tie the hands of future governments (e.g., by requiring future contractual payments), and thereby raise challenges of accountability, transparency and legitimacy.

With respect to accountability, there is no doubt that "[d]evolving authority over decision-making and public expenditure to non-elected partnerships creates the need for new and robust forms" of accountability (Ibid., 229) that may be more complex, more horizontal, and softer, and may appear less satisfactory for taxpayers.

Such concerns can be over-stated, however, and are easily repaired. Moreover, in the area of water and wastewater utilities, for example, credible observers have talked about "the myth of public sector accountability" in traditional arrangements, and said that "[w]hile municipal accountability may sound good in theory, it rarely works in practice" (Brubaker 2003: 24). There is no reason to believe that the genuine difficulties cannot be overcome by effective contracting and monitoring, together with third-party evaluation and adjudication in case of disagreements.

With respect to transparency imperatives, the concerns are clearly over-stated: optimal transparency is not necessarily maximal transparency (Juillet and Paquet 2002) and transparency concerns cannot be allowed to trump commercial confidentiality. Some information must be kept private for legitimate business reasons. It is a matter of balance that, in most cases, can also be resolved satisfactorily by effective contractual arrangements.

As for legitimacy, there is no reason to believe that effectively, reasonably and fairly negotiated partnership contracts cannot be defended in the court of public opinion. In fact, Canadians are already on board. The Canadian Council for Public-Private Partnerships reports that six of ten Canadians (and 55 percent of public service union workers) support P3s (CCPPP 2004). Of course, not surprisingly, there is a good deal of variation in the public support by region, and by type of service.

For example, support for P3s is estimated as significantly higher in Saskatchewan (three to one) than in Toronto (just over half), while it is estimated, understandably, to be lower in the field of water treatment in Ontario than elsewhere.

However ill founded the ideological opposition to P3s may be, this opposition has acquired legitimacy in labour unions and so-called 'progressive' and state-centric quarters. This has been especially strong in the recent debates in Quebec (Aubert and Patry 2005) and it has led governments, at all levels throughout the country, to shy away or pull back from such arrangements at the first sign of controversy (Burleton 2006).

P3s opponents have also focussed their attention on the fact that poor contractual arrangements have plagued many of the early exercises in P3, ascribable to incompetent negotiators (Mehra 2005). As a result, P3s have developed in Canada at a rate that is a great deal slower than has been the case in the United Kingdom or other European countries.

Lessons learned and winning conditions

In order to better categorize the root causes of the difficulties experienced by P3s (and consequently, to better gauge the families of prerequisites likely to be worth focusing on when attempting to ensure as high a probability of success as possible), we have stylized the overall P3 process in four modules sketched in figure 9.2.

Figure 9.2   *The P3 process as four modules*

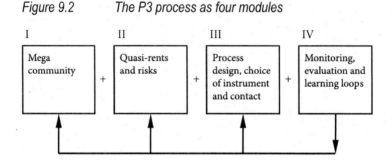

Module I pertains to the environment in which the P3 is embedded. It refers to the sort of sociological basis on which one can build: the level of trust and social capital that facilitates relationships among potential partners, the buy-in of the different stakeholders, the carrying capacity of the contextual institutions, as well as the ideological climate and the organizational culture that is present. It connotes the degree of connectivity and the organizational texture of the environment. Without a supportive infrastructure, the mega-community will not crystallize around reasonable potentialities, or will collapse with the first crisis or two.

This explains why relational capital is so crucial (especially at a time when potential partners, deciding whether or not to opt in, take into account things like reputation and other intangibles) and why venomous media reporting may poison the well and ruin the projects. It also underlines the need not only to obtain support from the mega-community at the time the project is launched, but also to maintain and sustain it with continuous action all through the P3 process.

Module II deals with the requirement for a credible gauge of the value-adding and of the nature of the risk-sharing involved in the collaborative arrangements. Even if it is not possible to foresee all the possible eventual situations that may materialize, one needs to be able to scope the project sufficiently well that the orders of magnitude involved are relatively credible. This sort of informational base must quickly come to complement and supplement the trust capital that has allowed the partnership discussion to emerge.

If the costs, value-adding and risks are not gauged in a reasonably accurate way, if the prospective sharing of these is not reasonably sound and perceived as fair, and if the complementary capabilities brought to the project by the different partners are not adequately recognized *ab ovo*, then again, the arrangement is unlikely to proceed very far or to be robust.

Module III relates to the refinement of the process design and the development of contractual arrangements (both formal and informal) that will embody the contours of suitable arrangements to the degree possible (but often with strategic penumbras penciled in). This entails not only the definition of the roles and responsibilities of all parties, but also the choice of instruments, and the array of contingency plans that will kick in, in certain eventualities.

Since there is no way to write a totally complete contract envisaging all the possible eventualities, nor to presume that the rules in place will apply unambiguously to all possible circumstances, a suitable contract requires the provision for effective and rapid modification protocols and dispute resolution machinery, and some fail-safe mechanisms when all else fails. Co-governance cannot work if such mechanisms are not in place, even though they may be rarely or never ever used.

Module IV focuses on the central importance of continuous monitoring, including by credible third parties, effective and intelligent evaluation, and the existence of mechanisms through which the collaborative organization will learn through revising not only its instrumentalities and means but also its objectives and broad orientation as the project proceeds, and experience reveals that the original plans might prove inadequate or less useful than had been originally anticipated either because of changes in the environment or in the project itself.

Indeed, this fourth module feeds into the other three, and constitutes the basis of the process of social learning.

Effective social learning is crucial to a successful P3. It would enable experience to feed into the mindset of the mega-community and allow the community to transform its views. It would lead to a more refined and credible view of both rents and risks, and therefore to revisions of the early estimates. And, it would allow modifications in the provisions of the contracts accordingly.

But this entails that there exist loci where the requisite discussions can be held.

One of the great weaknesses of the P3 process is both a poor understanding of the nature of such required discussions and deliberations, and the lack of the requisite places where such deliberations can be carried out. As a result, blockages quickly ensue, and viable P3s collapse for lack of safe places where the challenges generated by shocks in the environment or by unforeseen developments can be discussed, and appropriate adjustments be arrived at.

Some of this may take the form of dispute settlement or fail-safe mechanisms, but, in the main, deliberation sites must be provided on a continuous basis for the mega-community.

Unlike experts whose framework is solely technical, citizens and other members of the mega-community form opinions by integrating facts and values. P3s must presume that context and circumstances may change, and that there must be provision for people's views on tough issues to be aired and discussed, for reframing to occur, and for decisions to ensue.

Such discussions evolve through three stages—consciousness raising, reconciling proposed actions with basic values, and leaders deciding and acting to resolve the issue. A diagram that Yankelovich and Rosell have used is quite useful; see figure 9.3.

Of the three stages, Yankelovich and Rosell argue that the second is the hardest, being "driven less by information, and more by feelings, values and moral convictions" (Yankelovich and Rosell 2006) (one might add ideology), and one that people will avoid if they can. This suggests that finding effective ways to stimulate the mega-community's crystallization (with its interpersonal, inter-organizational and institutional trust base), and then sustain it, is not going to be easy. But ignoring this social learning challenge, and hoping that all dysfunctions will fix themselves organically, is a recipe for failure over the long haul.

Figure 9.3   The Yankelovich-Rosell social learning process

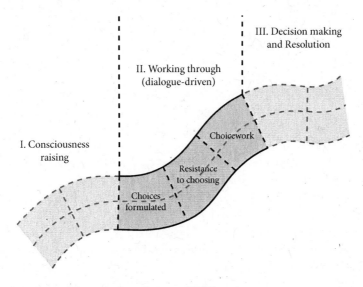

Source www.ViewpointLearning.com (2001).

If our analysis holds water, a number of modest general propositions would appear to be warranted. They do not provide the key to always-successful P3s, but they identify a number of important pressure points where effective action might be possible. One of the key differences between our list and the ones provided by other observers is that it gives more attention to context, communications and learning loops.

It has been our diagnosis that P3s have been wrongly interpreted as matters that can be handled solely through technical and legal strictures. The literature has failed to take note of the context of modern policy and regulatory development. As Carl Taylor has reminded us, the development of a policy or regulatory initiatives must meet four challenges: Is the proposal put forward technically feasible? Socially acceptable? Can it be implemented with the negotiated help of all the relevant and necessary partners? And is it socio-politically not too destabilizing? (C. A. Taylor 1997).

The undue concern with the conditions for technical and legal feasibility alone has led too many groups interested in P3s to ignore the other three challenges. This has proved disastrous in many cases.

From our point of view, the success of P3s obviously depends on sound technical feasibility and competent legal contracting, but the major sources of failure are elsewhere. The winning conditions and useful levers are mainly relational, and they require a most important capital of trust, and a most effective communication apparatus.

The eight modest general propositions that follow (two for each of the four modules identified above) are not presented as a panacea, but as a checklist that should be kept in mind. Failure on any of these fronts may be regarded as an omen of P3 failure to come.

Proposition I-a

P3s require an aggressive proactive and sustained communication strategy to ensure that all the stakeholders are fully informed and immunized against ideological sermoning.

This is the fundamental requirement to ensure the crystallization of the mega-community, and the nesting of the P3 in a network of supporting relationships. It is also a way to ensure the maintenance of the trust and social capital required for the P3 to thrive. Finally, it is the only way to counter effectively the toxic effect of the ideological and interest groups attacks on these better ways to dispatch public service.

Proposition I-b

P3s do not only require effective communications, but also active and creative negotiations to obtain and sustain the buy-in and active collaboration of all the key players in order to give some tonus to the mega-community

It is one thing to obtain the *nihil obstat* of stakeholders, and quite another to engage them actively in a process of collaboration. Unless one is able to mobilize the mega-community's capital of trust, and to negotiate the requisite moral contracts commensurate with a culture of collaboration, the P3s will not survive to the first mishaps. This means that more than legal guarantees are required: it entails the development of a robust culture that will help deal with the unforeseen.

Proposition II-a

P3s must be built on credible evaluations of the value-added by the collaborative agreement.

One of the fundamental weaknesses of any potential P3 is the unrealistic appraisal of what might reasonably be expected from the venture. Not only do unreasonable expectations poison the relationships, but they are condemned to generate resentment and lack of credibility as results materialize, and to erode significantly the legitimacy of the arrangement within the broader mega-community.

Proposition II-b

P3s must ensure a fair sharing of risks and profits.

The fair sharing of profits and risks is the foundation of P3s. Any arrangement based on unfairness can only breed distrust and disloyalty, as events reveal that the arrangement was based on deception. Whatever reason might have led one party to use stratagems to lure another party into a structurally unfair deal, it can only lead to a collapse of the deal, and to a long-term deterioration of relations.

Proposition III-a

P3s will not succeed if it turns out that the choice of instrument was poor or if the process and the contract capturing its spirit are poorly designed

There are important project design and legal dimensions to P3s. If a P3 is not an organizational form suitable for the task at hand, little can be done to salvage the project. In the same way, if neither the design of the project nor the legal contract is competently drawn up, P3s will crumble under their own weight.

Proposition III-b

P3s must be closely, expertly and flexibly managed.

Although the contract is the central instrument in a P3, there can never be a complete and perfect contract that has envisaged all possible contingencies. Consequently, the effective management of a P3 contract is extraordinarily important. Project management skills are therefore essential; otherwise the arrangement is bound to founder on a mountain of minute contentions that will bring it down.

Proposition IV-a

P3s must build in the provision for credible and effective continuous external evaluation.

Whatever care is put into developing the mega-community, in choosing the right partners and instruments, in nurturing these relationships, in designing the process and contract aptly and managing it well, little can be accomplished to ensure that the P3s are on course unless one has been careful to put in place mechanisms of continuous external evaluation. This monitoring system will provide the necessary feedback to identify any mishap early, and it will be essential if social learning is to prevail. Moreover, such sources of continuous external information and appraisals will also help in guaranteeing legitimacy for the P3s in dealing with the mega-community.

Proposition IV-b

P3s also require effective dispute resolution and fail-safe mechanisms.

Despite the immense care in defining the setting and in monitoring the progress of the P3 process, disputes are bound to arise. These disputes require some external reference point or source of evaluation that can be used to bring the different parties to settle their dispute, and if no settlement emerges, some fail-safe mechanism or arbiter must be envisaged that would be empowered to ordain some form of settlement.

Conclusion

The terrain of public-private-social partnerships is plagued by the multiple meanings of the partnership label, by ideological referents, and by the paucity of meaningful evaluation of the thousands of experiments carried out throughout the world (Vaillancourt Rosenau 2000; Marty et al. 2006). As a result, ideology and presumptions are having a field day.

Until such time as a richer conceptual framework is put in place, most of the case studies are simply too disparate to elicit a robust perspective on P3s. In dealing with P3s, we are still at a stage of development akin to the one stage where Biology 1 classified animals according to the number of their legs.

Although no canonical set of rules that would lead automatically to successful P3s is available yet, at least our provisional framework may help to identify what would appear to be the main sources of failure. This sort of pathology of organizational forms may not be inspiring but, in this field, as in many others, it provides a *point de départ* (Paquet 2004b).

Even if mixed institutions and organizations have blossomed, and if these blended institutions and organizations often perform better than pure ones, this is still not a view in good currency. The Canadian mindset would appear to be trapped in a time warp: ever since Jane Jacobs' book of 1992, the Ottawa clerisy has been mesmerized by the argument put forward in this book that any form of organizational *métissage* can only generate "monstrous hybrids" (Jacobs 1992).

This is a view that is entirely unwarranted.

But the *anti-métissage* theology still prevails in 'progressive' circles. Even if blurring and blending have now acquired intellectual credibility (Thacher and Rein 2004) and P3s are more and more widely used at all levels of governments (and with great success) all around the world, the view that P3s impoverish governance because it reduces the size of the state or corrupts any search for the public good remains in good currency.

Fortunately practice need not wait for theory or ideology to grant permission to act. One may therefore expect that the current wave of interest in using P3s will continue unabated, and that our modest general propositions (and those of others working in the field) may help to avoid a few disasters, although it may not completely resolve the 'porcupine problem'.

However, if our central argument about the importance of the mega-community is accepted, it becomes clear that this is where the battle against the fundamentalists will be won:

(1) by a better dissemination of information about the successes of P3s in a large number of terrains; and

(2) by an effort to persuade the mega-community that one does not need to have a theoretical answer before engaging in an experiment.

P3s may be one more case where, even if the problem remains intractable in theory, it can be resolved in situated policy practice (Schön and Rein 1994).

CHAPTER 10

The Myth of the Public Service as a Lump of Labour

... for appropriate regulation, the variety in the regulator must be equal or greater than the variety in the system being regulated.

—Ross Ashby's statement of the Ashby Law

Introduction

The 'lump of labour' fallacy is an old economic chestnut. It refers to the presumption that there is a fixed amount of work to be done in the world, so that any increase in the amount any worker does reduces the amount of work left to do, and thus the number of available jobs. As a result, the argument goes, automation leads to unemployment since it reduces the amount of work left. This is an idea economists have ridiculed for a long time, yet it resurfaces periodically under new garb. More recently, it has been embraced by the economically naive, arguing that more jobs can be created by reducing the length of the workweek.

This 'lump of labour' fallacy I (as we would call it) focuses on there being a fixed quantity of labour. There is, however, another equally toxic 'lump of labour' fallacy—the lump of labour fallacy II: that presumes that labour is qualitatively homogeneous, like a lump of butter, within different sectors.

According to this argument, all work is done by 'guardians' in the public sector and by 'traders' in the private sector, and there is a difference of kind between these types of work. This second fallacy is not in good currency in the private sector, where it is generally agreed that there is little merit in assuming that labour is homogeneous: nobody but the most ethereal theorist believes that there is such a thing as 'a labour market' where everyone is substitutable for any one else. This is not a useful way to describe what is, in reality, a complex and differentiated matrix of labour exchanges, where the entities exchanged have little commonality one with the other.

But the situation is different in the public sector where it is readily assumed by many observers that public sector employment has a different quality because it is public employment, and this lump of somewhat undifferentiated work has come to be associated with a higher calling, a heavier burden of office, and to be perceived as requiring greater protection and higher status than other types of work.

This fallacy has created very serious problems of adjustment in the real world of the segmented labour markets in the public sector. It has led naive observers to suggest that any reduction in the size of the lump of public sector employment (whatever type of public sector job might be eliminated) automatically entails an impoverishment of societal governance since 'public sector employment' cannot be eroded without undermining the 'sacred' work of the state.

What makes this particular level of public employment optimal is never examined, and what makes all public servants fundamentally and essentially different from other workers is never clearly explained either. It is simply readily assumed by many—inspired by the work of Jane Jacobs (1992)—that this is the case.

This presumed idiosyncrasy of public sector employment has now become one of the most important constraints on the evolution of governance in Canada: it has dramatically stalled the exploration of a whole array of collaborative arrangements between the private, public and social sectors (because these would be likely to erode the almost sacred basis of state employment) and has prevented serious efforts to modernize the public sector whenever it might entail fragmentation of the body of public servants that might be required to operate under different regimes.

As a result, any need felt for effective re-engineering of government into a more inclusive, more participative, more collaborative and more effective apparatus in today's world (through all sorts of means including public-private partnerships (PPPs or P3s) or other arrangements reducing the size of the formal state workforce) has been opposed because every public sector job has been consecrated as one of 'guardian' of the public good and/or of the fabric of society and therefore declared untouchable. While this might be regarded as a plausible negotiating position for public sector unions, it is hardly defendable intellectually. Nevertheless, it is an argument in good currency in certain ideological circles (Rouillard et al. 2006). All this has not prevented *de facto* the emergence of a wide variety of arrangements regulating different segments of employment in the public sector. But the very multitude of public sector labour unions has not eroded the overall view that there is such a thing as 'public service' and that problems experienced by 'the public service' should be dealt with as a whole. The history of reform initiatives proposed over the last fifty years has almost universally been trying to tackle the public service *in toto*, and this is the reason, we suggest, why they have all failed.

This chapter first sketches the evolution of the idea of an impartial and competent clerisy of public servants from the early part of the 20th century on in Canada; then, it identifies some of the challenges this view has had to weather over the last half century, and the crucial impasse that it has generated in the recent past; finally, it suggests that nothing less than a reframed view of public sector employment as essentially differentiated on the basis of a more realistic definition of 'burden of office' is necessary if one is to ensure a smooth continued evolution of Canadian governance.

In the beginning was a good idea

The idea of an independent, impartial, competent and well-trained collection of public sector employees for the core of the governing apparatus of any advanced democracy makes good sense. Key processes, like ensuring the supremacy of the rule of law, lie at the heart of the credibility of the governors in the eyes of the governed. The burden of office of core public servants is to ensure behaviour congruent with public trust.

The idea of such a "permanent career public service, recruited free from political or personal patronage on the sole basis of ability as revealed through…competitive examination" took hold in the 1870s in Britain for just this purpose (Hennessey 1996: 122).

The Canadian federal professional public service (PPS) was created in 1918–19, and its fundamental design remains essentially unchanged to this day. By 1918, political patronage, that was said to have been rampant in the civil service since long before Confederation, became widely regarded as "threatening to undermine the Liberal-Conservative coalition which had won the election of December 1917" (A. Roberts 1996: 6–7). As a result, significant reforms were undertaken, and the modern PPS was established.

Unfortunately, the design, borrowed by the Canadian federal government from the United States, resulted in overkill: what had been developed by consultants to deal with endemic corruption in the city of Chicago—something that had never actually existed on the same scale in Canada—was imported holus bolus into this country (Ibid.).

In this particular version of house cleaning, the important concepts of political impartiality and competency were assumed to be best secured through external controls and a great reliance on rules, as opposed to individual judgment. When it was proposed in this country, there were fierce arguments in the Canadian political community "about the wisdom of the proposed reforms" (Ibid., 8), but, in the end, "possibilities for less restrictive but equally effective merit reforms...[were] overlooked, and...a tired and distracted political executive...[was] finally gulled by American consultants of doubtful competence" (Ibid.).

The 1918–1919 reforms resulted in a rigid, hierarchical service: "1,729 standard classes of employees, further grouped into 34 occupational groups...Everything was categorized, everything arranged....Incredibly no distinction was made between routine tasks and intellectual or policy-making work." (Granatstein 1998: 25). As we will see, this proved to be the Achilles' heel of a flawed reform.

The results were not as effective as had been hoped: by the beginning of the 1930s, in Granatstein's words, the federal civil service was still "a swamp of patronage, a refuge for the inefficient and incompetent...some able public servants in the technical branches...and in more general areas...some senior public servants of ability...it was completely incapable of running the affairs of an aspiring nation....[T]he problem was one of organization and people" (Ibid., 23, 26–27).

As a result of World War II and the emergence of the 'welfare state', the PPS grew significantly from 46,000 in 1938–39, to 117,000 in 1946 (of which nearly three quarters were temporary), to as many as 275,000 by the mid 1970s and to about 250,000 today (including bureaucrats in agencies like Revenue Canada).

Significant attempts were made to ensure the efficiency and effectiveness of this growing administrative system: the 1961 Glassco Commission ('let the managers manage'), the 1979 Lambert Commission ('make the managers manage'), sometimes short-lived initiatives to enable better control, better management and/or better reporting to Parliament (like PPBS in the late 60s and PEMS a decade later), and the 1990 report of the PS2000 project. But the Auditor-General's 2001 Report is quoted as still pleading to managers "please...manage".[1]

The design put in place in 1918–19—"unwieldy and unnecessary" as it may have been, in the words of Roberts (A. Roberts 1996: 75)—has remained largely unchanged despite the recommendations of these various commissions. Even the 2003 *Human Resource Modernization Act*, which put most of the levers for managing human resources (HR) in the hands of deputy heads (directly or through a legislated bias towards delegation) has been referred to by experts as only "a modest step forward...not address(ing) current HR problems" effectively head on (Hubbard 2003).

Strains, stresses and denials

The challenges posed by the Great Depression and World War II led a powerful group of mandarins, as partners to the governments of the day, to reshape the contours of Canada's institutions and its place in the world. This activism led to an extraordinary growth in public sector employment both as a result of population growth and of the new entitlements to promised public goods generated by the new propulsive state.

As long as economic growth proceeded at high speed, 'Big G' government was able to deliver on its promises. But when the world economy began to slow down in the late 1960s, and when the oil price explosion brought it to a halt in the 1970s, a gap developed between what was expected by the citizenry from 'Big G' and what it could deliver. This fiscal crisis generated massive government deficits and high inflation.

Like other western democracies, Canada experienced a great unraveling of government credibility and fiscal capacity. This took its toll on the PPS. In the 1970s, to deal with rising costs of government and the public service, rising deficits, increasing tax burdens, and erosion of confidence in government, many countries veered to new public management (NPM) processes that put the accent on results, service to the public, delegation of authority, greater attention to cost and the quest for efficiency, adoption of private sector practices such as 'contracting out' and merit pay.

The response from the public sector management community was largely hostile. Denouncing the NPM initiatives became a new gospel in public administration circles. It was felt that public sector activities were essentially and fundamentally different from private sector activities, and not lending themselves to such 'rational' practices. In the words of Jane Jacobs, a vigorous missionary of this new faith, any attempt to mix "guardian" and "commercial" activities could only produce "monstrous hybrids" (Jacobs 1992). Jacobs' book became compulsory reading for federal bureaucrats in the 1990s: it provided the rationale for the *status quo*.

Those in denial *vis-à-vis* NPM found moral support in the fact that, despite waves of reforms, the long-standing ability to 'manage and administer' appeared to become problematic as evidenced by numerous fumbles (gun registry, sponsorship program, or the current, seeming inability to achieve promised savings in procurement, etc.).

Unfortunately, none of this appears to have eroded a basic faith in the existing arrangements. If anything, the language in good currency has become more vibrant. Basic concepts of political impartiality and competency have morphed into new weasel words—'non-partisanship' and 'merit'—and came to be elevated to almost sacramental status in discussions about the essential characteristics of public sector employment. It remains unclear whether the controls and rules aimed at giving substance to these new words have actually been either beneficial or realistic.

A dispassionate look at the rosy picture currently drawn of Canadian public administration (*à la* Gow 2004) suggests that the situation may not in fact be all that rosy (Hubbard and Paquet 2007a; Paquet 2007b).

Indeed the multiplicity of relatively recent initiatives—by the Clerk of Privy Council (the Deputy Minister (DM) Committee on the Renewal of the Public Service stewarded by Margaret Bloodworth), the Public Policy Forum's initiative under the guidance of former Deputy Minister Ian Green, and more recently the Prime Minister's blue-ribbon committee co-chaired by former senior Cabinet Minister David Emerson (and before him, Don Mazankowski) and former clerk of the Privy Council Paul Tellier—would appear to indicate that the PPS is still considered as badly in need of repair.

All the reform initiatives of the last few decades were to respond to the challenges generated by a broad transubstantiation of government that is in progress—blending government as a high-reliability organization and government as a deliberately innovative organization (Sabel 2004) to provide both security and nimbleness.

While the earlier reform efforts attempted to bring a burgeoning federal governing apparatus under better control, latter ones were truly experiments with different organizational arrangements (e.g., special operating agencies such as Revenue Canada with more HR flexibility, and the creation of new entities such as NAV CANADA).

The profound change involved however, not only the way things were done but also what was done. And it is still going on. This explains why no amount of effort at public service reform— however well intentioned—has been particularly effective. Reform of this latter kind requires taking a much deeper look at what the PPS is doing and should do, and no scheme can succeed until one key issue is tackled, debated and resolved.

That issue is the unstated assumption (that often many are not aware they are making) of *the illusion of totality,* built on a Jane Jacobs sense, that all the work done in the public sector is *sui generis* and fundamentally different from and qualitatively 'superior' to whatever is done in the rest of the socio-economy.

The illusion of totality and the futile search for the Holy Grail

To our way of thinking, the 'lump of labour fallacy II' is the major stumbling block on the road to meaningful reform. Not until it is recognized that: (1) public sector work is not, in all its components, different in kind from work done in other sectors; (2) public sector work is as heterogeneous as work in other sectors; (3) different sub-groups of public servants doing substantially different types of work should be operating under significantly different regimes—can one hope to reform the PPS in today's world.

This mythology stands in the way of really effective strategies for reform and renewal. Indeed, as we argued earlier, it has resulted in:

> a variety of idealized expectations and requirements from
> the central agencies that are unlikely to assist in the efficient
> delivery of the intended services...[that] emanate from utopian
> management frameworks that are being formalized and imposed
> on the whole of government (Clark and Swain 2005).

Yet this illusion of totality is staunchly defended despite clear indications that employees define themselves in quite different ways (e.g., as forming various communities of practice and labour unions). Consequently, the efforts at reform or renewal have been unduly focused on the search for the 'Big Solution'—the recipe that would apply across the board and at all levels, despite the fact that the personnel to whom these reforms are meant to apply experience extraordinarily different circumstances.

The very existence of the Public Service Commission (PSC) is an embodiment of this illusion of totality. Both the PSC and Treasury Board Secretariat (TBS) continue to dream of imposing a single regime on all federal public employees. One may recall the ill fated 'unified classification system' promoted by TBS in the late 1990s (a scheme that aimed at unifying the whole lump of public employment into a single classification scheme). As for the PSC, over the years its mandate has been narrowed and major chunks of the public service are now excluded from its direct scrutiny as a result of the creation of independent agencies. But even as the PSC's vocation appears to be tilting more and more toward an auditing role for certain aspects of human resource management, the focus remains on the PPS as a whole.

This illusion of totality survives because this assumption of the sacred 'homogenize-able' lump of public labour remains largely unstated. If it were made explicit, it would become obvious that the diagnoses and recipes in good currency suffer from the elephant and the blind men syndrome: each party approaching the problem in a partial way, and then generalizing from there to the whole of *the* public service. This has been the major flaw of the initiatives to reform the PPS for the last forty years.

Even today, the language used in dealing with reform efforts refers to *the* public service as a meaningful whole. This was true of the recent DM's committee, of the two-year study launched by the Public Policy Forum, and of Prime Minister Harper's "Advisory Committee on the Public Service".

The burden of office as principle of differentiation

If there is no magic bullet to solve the problems of the public service as a whole, the most effective way to tackle the PPS problem is to start with an X-ray of public sector employment in order to reveal its different sub-systems, to understand the significant differences in the burden of office of public servants in these different systems and the way in which different expectations apply to these different groups of public servants, so that one might be able to design different and tailor-made regimes likely to be the most effective governing mechanisms in each case.

In our view, a meaningful X-ray of the public sector would identify four concentric circles of differentiated public servants corresponding to different categories of people with different burdens of office and confronted with varying citizens' expectations.

At the core are the 'super-bureaucrats': this includes the true super-bureaucrats (like the governor of the Bank of Canada, Supreme Court judges, and the federal and provincial auditors general) who are intended to be 'above the fray'. They hold the offices charged with ultimate oversight function in matters pertaining to the fabric of our democratic society, and their protection from external pressures is usually extraordinary robust. This category also includes the uppermost senior bureaucrats (deputy ministers, associate deputy ministers and deputy heads), who are expected to be the highest order guardians of the integrity of key processes that lie at the heart of democracy.

The next ring corrals the 'guardians', a somewhat larger (but not very large) group of bureaucrats whose work underpins the fundamental policy and regulatory work of governments and may be said to do work as guardians of basic public values. Their work requires a great deal of independence and a capacity to resist pressures both from interest groups and political communities. It may be said that Canada designed its original PPS precisely to protect this category of bureaucrats through employment systems that ensure they can 'speak truth to power' and play the role of neutral implementer(s) of legislative policy (Savoie 2003).

The third ring is made of the 'professionals' proper and is a somewhat-larger group of persons whose work is important to the infrastructure of the state. Most of their work may be said to be akin to the work of any responsible professional in any sector. Many of the individuals who fall into this category may not need to be part of the public service at all. They may also work for crown corporations or for partners of governments and indeed may often find employment in the private or social sectors.

The fourth ring might be referred to as 'employees'. It is a much larger group of bureaucrats that may be on the public sector payroll, but often only for historical reasons. They primarily perform activities that are conducted routinely in other sectors, and therefore their functions and activities are not in any way inherently 'public sector' in nature (although they may be the contact point between the state and the citizen) and need not be performed by the professional public service.

So the human resources of the public sector are *de facto* fragmented into ensembles of personnel that are quite different in nature. Consequently there are good reasons to believe that not all the categories of personnel need to have the same regime of attachment to the public sector, or to remain attached to the public sector at all, and there are no reasons why they should be treated in an identical manner.

While the first two categories are fundamental pillars of the public service, the latter two categories cover personnel that, to varying degrees, are not dealing, in an essential way, with issues that demand the same degree of protection as that which is bestowed on the other two groups. These two sets of groups would appear to require quite different rules of the game and HR arrangements.

The partitioning of the traditional PPS in this fashion is set out in table 10.1. It provides a rough picture of the coverage and size of each category, but also of the burden of office of members of these different categories, and of the citizens' legitimate expectations about their work.

It should be clear that these categories are separated by porous boundaries that allow meritorious individuals to move though the ranks in the same manner that it is known to occur in other sectors, where a bank clerk might become a bank president. A brilliant professional may indeed be expected to graduate to core level employment, and even to the inner core, but he or she might also be allowed to thrive and progress as a professional throughout his or her career. Moreover, there would be of necessity some exceptions for personnel operating close to the inter-group boundaries: for instance, circumstances may demand that some support staff operating in support of inner core personnel be granted special status.

Table 10.1   *Human capital in the Canadian public service*

Higher	3) **Professionals**
	
	Main challenge:
	   Balance professional & political
	Main job:
	   Ideas, innovation & horizontality
	HR goal:
	   Learning (40,000)
		1) **Super-bureaucrats**
		
		Burden of office:
		   Safeguard fabric of society
		Main job:
		   Co-governing & enabling
		HR goal:
		   Commitment (< 500)

Uniqueness	4) **Employees**
	
	Main challenge:
	   Reliability & fairness
	Main job:
	   Productivity
	HR goal:
	   Responsiveness (185,000)
		2) **Guardians**
		
		Burden of office:
		   Loyalty
		Main job:
		   Stewardship & management
		HR goal:
		   Productivity (<10,000)

Value   Higher

Source: Adapted from Morris et al. 2005. The size of the PPS is estimated at about 250,000 (including separate agencies like Revenue Canada) in 2010.

This type of partitioning would appear to fit the present environment, and it constitutes a powerful argument against a one-size-fits-all approach. Such a partitioning of public sector employment identifies different types of human capital requiring different types of employment relations and regimes.

Group 1 represents core human capital, both highly unique and valuable. They are at the inner core and their employment relationships tend to be long term and focused on organizational commitment and trust. Group 2 represents human capital that is highly valuable but less unique. The employment relationship will tend to be relatively more focused on immediate performance and a results-based approach. Group 3 represents idiosyncratic human capital that has specialized knowledge and is not always easy to find in the market, but is most of the time readily available; it requires an employment relationship that is based on partnership that preserves some continuity over time. Group 4 may be regarded as ancillary human capital that is of less strategic value and not unique to the organization; the focus is more on compliance with preset rules, regulations and procedures (Morris et al. 2005).

In the heyday of the mandarins, the small size of the state, the deference to elites, and the relative paucity of technical specialists in government combined to enable a few "intelligent generalists" (as Granatstein calls them) to have an immense influence not only on the adoption of major policies but also on the way they could be implemented, despite a 'one-size-fits-all and rules-and-process-bound bureaucracy'. They could 'work around it'. Scheming virtuously was not only possible then, but it was expected and condoned at the very top, and a few people could engineer significant change.

The drift from top-down 'Big G' government to a more inclusive and horizontal 'small g' governance (as a result of the growing turbulence of the environment and of the greater variety and complexity of the socio-economic systems to be governed when no one is in charge) has transformed the governing process: more stakeholders with different interests and competencies have come to be involved in the stewardship of the socio-economy. A few 'intelligent generalists' (however imaginative or competent) can no longer as easily 'scheme virtuously' and have a huge impact on policy choices and/or ensure successful execution. The world is so complex and there are so many players: Ashby's law applies. Variety in the regulator has had to increase because of the greater variety in the system being regulated.

As a result, new units of management analysis (e.g., regions, categories of workers, issue domains) are of the essence as well as new units of policy analysis (e.g., city-regions, communities of practice). On the HR management front, very many different categories of public sector workers have crystallized and have received more or less formal recognition through unions or categories of types of employment.

Our crucial point is that central agencies and management boards of all sorts must take notice of this new context and change their perspectives accordingly. The sheer denial of the new complexity will not do, and top-down, one-size-fits-all mechanisms will no longer work.

Central agencies will have to allow for enough flexibility in organizational arrangements and work environments (e.g., work structure and work systems for HR, procurement, administration, finance, IT, etc.), while focusing on the ligatures that will be needed to knit together the quilt of organizational and institutional arrangements that have sprung to life (different institutional ecologies) into relatively coherent wholes in the name of efficiency, effectiveness, fairness and legitimacy.

Real challenges of innovative government in a 'small g' world

The need for a more innovative government requires a capacity for greater mass collaboration and coordination across and within jurisdictions and sectors, and that, in turn, entails the development of a variety of new skills and new approaches. It is our view that a finer-grained definition of public sector employment is likely to provide a better instrument to ensure both a more reliable and a more innovative government by putting in place a clearer definition of the burden of office of the different sub-groups and a sharper definition of their real accountability and their real jobs.

However, one cannot argue persuasively in favour of such a sub-division unless it can be demonstrated that:

(1) such a partitioning and the associated HR regimes will help ensure a better mix of reliability and innovation of the Canadian state;

(2) such a partitioning of public sector employment (and the associated HR regimes) is technically feasible, socially

acceptable, implementable, and not too politically destabilizing; and

(3) such a partitioning will accommodate the legitimate strategies of key actors like the Clerk of Privy Council and groups like the Public Policy Forum.

The new partitioning would help to make renewal real

Category 1: For the 'super bureaucrats', the main challenge is dedication to preserving the fabric of society. Their main work is to act as co-governors (to help decisions to be made directly or indirectly) and to 'enable' the implementation of whatever has been decided (in so far as governments have direct roles to play).

There is no simple way to guarantee such commitment and dedication. At the same time, it would be grossly naive to presume that they will materialize organically as a *grâce d'état*. There is a need to remind them of their engagements in the same manner as it is useful, at times, to remind officials and citizens of the *Magna Carta*. This could be done through a clear yet general letter of appointment, delineating the broad principles that should guide their action (in the light of the Constitution and other founding documents) in the case of uppermost super-bureaucrats, and providing more pointed details about the philosophy of the elected government, when dealing with other lower order super-bureaucrats like deputy ministers.

The federal lower order super-bureaucrats (deputy ministers and deputy heads) have been designated as accounting officers under the new *Accountability Act* and answerable to the appropriate committee of Parliament on certain matters. This makes them the new 'backstops' with respect to the reliability of key financial processes of the federal government.

For all super-bureaucrats, a combination of trust and competence is crucial. For some, it also entails a fundamental loyalty to the government in power. The need to work closely with the government of the day, straddling the political-bureaucratic interface and overcoming past loyalties and past commitments, is a daunting challenge. Indeed, disloyalty at this level is nothing less than an *abus de confiance* and a cardinal sin.

Category 2: For 'guardians', the biggest challenge is loyalty, and their main work is stewardship and management.

They are charged, in a general way, with ensuring that the wishes of the elected government (as expressed in policy directions) are carried out in a way consistent with the laws of the land. It is fair to say, nevertheless, that the intermediation role they must play (especially at the most senior levels) has not always been as easy as it might have been presumed to be. Loyalty may have come, in the minds of some guardians, to be synonymous with loyalty to the direction set by a federal political party that has dominated for long periods of time and/or to the institution of the PPS as opposed to the laws and rules of the land. While this sort of behaviour might be regarded as understandable, it is also reprehensible and may indeed erode the very foundation of the PPS system.

This group can be presumed to have taken an oath of loyalty, and to have agreed that such an oath weighs heavily in their burden of office. In such cases, letters of appointment would be yet a bit more precise (both on guiding principles and general directions favoured) so as to ensure as few *malentendus* as possible.

Since the guardians are the lynchpins in the implementation of the policy and regulatory work of the government (for they design the organizational arrangement, and adjust the work environment appropriately), they help scope out the value-added and the nature of the risk taking of the key players. To do this, they must build and sustain the necessary trust in the key players. As James O'Toole would put it, leaders must:

> provide the "glue" to cohere independent units in a world characterized by forces of entropy and fragmentation. Only one element has been identified as powerful enough to overcome these centripetal forces, and that is trust. And recent experience shows that such trust emanates from leadership based on shared purpose, shared vision and, especially shared values (O'Toole 1995–96: xvii).

Category 3: For 'professionals', the main challenge is the harmonization of professionalism with (legitimate) political orientations and directions.

It is the locus of policy implementation and the site of major risk-taking. Most policy directions can easily be perverted at this interface. Yet this is also where the greatest danger exists that rigidity will stunt social learning and prevent policies from evolving as they should, in the light of circumstances. Professionals must find a balance between the legitimate expectations of the government and the legitimate constraints imposed by their professionalism.

In group 3, the greatest number of ideas and the most significant degree of innovation is necessary. These persons are not simple employees and yet they cannot be expected to be dealt with as if they were in the inner sanctum of government policy-making nor charged with safeguarding key processes. Personalized letters to set out their main challenge could only lead to micro-management on a scale that would sterilize their work and suppress the degree of innovativeness required from these professionals.

One must therefore put in place an HR regime for professionals that provides the requisite respect for the margin of maneuverability they need, the constant upgrading of skills and capabilities they require, and the use of judgment in their day-to-day operations that is mandatory.

Category 4: For employees, the challenge is reliability and fairness in the dispatch of their relatively routine work in the public household. The work is similar to work done in other sectors and may be tied to projects or arrangements that span weeks, months or years. There is no reason such employees could not be treated in the same way as in other sectors where many more dimensions of the working conditions are open to collective bargaining. Indeed, ensuring comparability with other sectors so as to facilitate the requisite amount of mobility is crucial even though it may entail some erosion of unwarranted privileges. In fact, this may be overdue. This might even include the use of regional rates of pay so as not to unduly distort local labour markets.

In a world of mass collaboration however, one should be careful not to unduly sanitize all aspects of group 4 activities. This is especially crucial for public sector employees who interface with the public. Front-line public sector workers have social learning responsibilities for the public sector. They are the first ones to detect anomalies or ill-fitting applications of standard rules. Too often, in the command-and-control world of 'Big G', front-line workers allowed themselves at times to become tyrannical implementers and enforcers. In the 'small g' world, they are meant not only to be sensitive to local circumstances, but also to be enabled and required to ignite processes of revision and modification of rules that may have unfortunate unintended consequences.

In fact, over and above the usual incentive reward systems that can encourage such social-learning behaviour, one must also count on robust fail-safe mechanisms like ombudspersons capable of deterring tyrannical, unreasonable and abusive behavior that prevents effective mass collaboration in the governance regime.

Given the size of group 4 and the extraordinary variety of the functions allocated to its members, only system-wide approaches (with appropriate safeguards) can be effective. The existing regime may need to be modernized and reformed but, in some ways, it would continue to apply—even including the rather static position-based system that has been used from the beginning.

Private and social sector employees have developed a great sensitivity to clients over the years. This has been supported and rewarded by their employers. There is no reason why it could not be implemented in the public sector.

This new partitioning is workable

Despite the fact that the propensity to look at public sector employment as inherently 'different' *in toto* remains alive and well, the reality of public sector employment already recognizes important differences among the diverse groups of employees.

For example, the allocation of work to occupational groups does a rough job of distinguishing between different qualifications and capabilities, and the process of selection and promotion varies greatly from one class of employment to the other.

But the idea of reframing the approach to public sector employment by sharpening the boundaries of the separate segments (and entertaining the possibility of setting up different accountability and HR regimes for them) has been opposed on ideological and technical grounds.

Ideologically, this partitioning has been perceived as an attempt to lessen the 'higher nature' of state employment and is fought in principle by those who believe that the state (always spelled with a capital S) is regarded as the fundamental societal 'organism' with moral purposes that transcend those of its individual citizens as expressed in other sectors.

So, depending on the coefficient of Hegelianism, harboured by the different passionate observers, tinkering with the state is perceived as less or more a case of *lèse-majesté*. For the soft Hegelians, there is more to the state than service provision but this does not prevent one from legitimately seeking more efficiency and effectiveness in alternative non-state or mixed delivery systems. For the hard Hegelians, any tinkering with any aspect of the state sphere that may reduce its scope or ambit can only be regarded with suspicion. There is not much one can do against such fundamentalism, but it should be made clear that such a position does not hold much water except at a theological level.

Technically, this partitioning entails the design of an alternative to the sort of system that has been in place for the last century or more. As a result, the forces of inertia and the vested interests in the old ways have come into play, and it has been argued that an alternative approach would be too complicated and impractical. Yet, it is our view that such a plural approach to public sector employment is technically feasible, socially acceptable, implementable, and not too politically destabilizing.

As mentioned earlier, there is already some partitioning of the public sector employment in sub-groups that has emerged organically as a result of the process of union recognition and the crystallization of communities of practice. So there is no reason to believe that one could not negotiate the recognition of these new categories that have some basic integrity with existing unions or public servant organizations, with central agencies, with the PSC, and with parliamentarians.

It would most certainly prove to be socially acceptable to all but the hard Hegelians. One may anticipate that the sort of clarification of roles of the different groups of public servants that such partitioning would entail might help greatly in educating the citizenry about the exact differentiated role of the public servants. It might also help them to appreciate the many ways in which government serves its purposes, and to get taxpayers to understand the rationale for the sort of working conditions that need to be negotiated for the different categories. Indeed, there is reason to believe that this new approach would be welcome.

On the matter of implementability, it is clear that tough negotiations are to be expected with the existing unions and the professional organizations of all sorts that represent existing fragments of the public service, especially if the existing regimes are to be significantly modified. But it should not be as difficult as some opponents suggest. Already, the myth of permanent employment (*emploi à vie*) in the public sector has all but disappeared. So the bone of contention will be rooted much more in the different ways in which the different groups might be stewarded. And since some unions like PSAC (Public Service Alliance of Canada) and PIPS (Professional Institute of the Public Service of Canada) use collective bargaining quite differently and express quite different priorities, it should not be impossible to arrive at fair negotiated settlements that are quite different but that satisfy these groups.

The bottom line is that some of the present fracture lines have little merit and are largely the result of historical accidents. The possibility of rationalizing the partitioning of public sector employment somewhat differently to better reflect differences in the burden of office, if wisely negotiated with both employers' agencies and employees' representatives should not generate much political turmoil.

Will a refurbished public sector:

- with super-bureaucrats as co-governors and enablers focused on protecting the fabric of society and thinking about the future,
- with loyal guardians being entrusted with the protection of key processes,
- with professionals ensuring an implementation of policies in a creative and imaginative manner through balancing their professional and public servant values,
- and with employees becoming effective deliverers of services but with a sensitivity to local circumstances and to the mobilization of mass collaboration, meet the challenges we have identified in the earlier portions of the chapter?

Our answer to this is clearly yes.

However, our view is that this will not necessarily be forthcoming as a result of a single touch of a magic wand, but as a result of tinkering and *bricolage* within each of these categories aiming at tipping points.

Partitioning would make room for the new initiatives underway

What has been regarded as a plague of separate ongoing initiatives to tackle the 'public service problem' may turn out to be a blessing in disguise. The different approaches likely to be adopted by the many committees looking into the matter these days may indeed lead to a variety of complementary initiatives that may not have been planned this way, but may entail a broad process of transformation of the public service as we know it.

In speaking to members of APEX (the Association of Professional Executives of the Public Service of Canada) at its 2006 annual symposium, the then Clerk of the Privy Council and head of the public service, Kevin Lynch singled out five areas of focus for the PPS:

a) clarity around roles, responsibilities and accountabilities;
b) teamwork;
c) the quest for excellence;
d) leadership (matching people with work and meeting the renewal challenges); and
e) the capacity to plan and think for the future (facing the policy challenges).

A partitioned PPS along the lines we have suggested makes it more likely that efforts to focus in these five areas would be successful. The clarity around roles, responsibilities and accountabilities increases dramatically if the frame used is one that provides for the partitioning into four categories, thereby permitting the devising of quite different HR regimes that match the fundamental differences in challenges and main jobs of work.

Each of the other four—teamwork, excellence, leadership, and planning and thinking for the future—seems particularly relevant for one or the other of the four categories we propose.

Teamwork is clearly of central importance for the professionals in category 3 where horizontality is one of the main challenges. Excellence is needed across the board but is of particular importance for category 1, the group of co-governors of the country. Leadership is clearly a central task of the guardians of category 2 and its impact on the whole public service is phenomenal.

Finally, the capacity for planning and thinking for the future (facing the policy challenges) speaks both to the importance of the main challenge for the super-bureaucrats (especially the deputy ministers and associates) and to the need for paying attention to ensuring effective succession planning.

Partitioning the PPS into groups according to their burden of office may also help enhance the probability of success of some on-going HR renewal initiatives.

The government launched two initiatives in the recent past aimed at 'making renewal real': the establishment by the then Clerk, Kevin Lynch, of a deputy minister committee (led by Margaret Bloodworth) to deal with public service renewal and the establishment, by Prime Minister Harper, of an external advisory committee to himself and Lynch on its renewal and future development.

The efforts of these two groups were aimed primarily at renewal of category 1 and 2 (the core public service) and its feeder groups, paying attention in particular to recruitment, development and retention at those levels and the necessary HR tools to do so successfully.

Targeting the PPS core and allowing variety in HR regimes for different categories would seem to make the task somewhat more tractable.

The Public Policy Forum project was focused on four thematic areas: values-based leadership; ideas/innovative thinking; excellent management of people and money; and accountability and public trust.

These themes would appear to be most relevant for category 2 (which represents the nexus for matching people with work and setting the appropriate work environment) and category 3 (where what is prized is the idiosyncratic knowledge of professionals with their focus on innovation and learning and the importance of horizontal relationships and collaboration).

The new partitioning as enabler

We do not propose this partitioning as the 'magic bullet' to heal all ills of the PPS. But we do believe that our scheme is a useful prototype—something provisional that can probably be improved but might also serve as a basis for deliberation and as a powerful enabler of the necessary renewal.

The new partitioning with separate regimes for the four groups of public servants allows some of their central potentialities to blossom. It is conducive to new forms of complementarities and collaboration based on *stigmergy*—a method of communication in emergent systems in which individual actors or groups or parts of the system communicate with one another by modifying their local environment rather than through coercion and direct pressure (Wikipedia).

Group 1 is involved in a symbiotic co-governance with the political apparatus. An appropriate regime would focus on generating the requisite commitment to design governance arrangements likely to 'harmonize the drive to meet the objectives of the government and the constraints that must be respected if one is to maintain and protect the fabric of society'. Such a commitment commands a loyalty to both these imperatives that is not easy to maintain, and it is difficult to imagine fail-safe mechanisms that would be anything but the opprobrium of not honouring fundamental moral contracts.

While it is clear that some loyalty is due to the elected government by all public employees, it is a much more creative, supportive and active loyalty that is required in group 1. Indeed, in the case of uppermost super-bureaucrats, they are loyal by playing a role of checks and balances on the government. And while such loyalty may have been loosely presumed to emerge organically in the past, as a sort of *grâce d'état*, it is now clear that a moral contract needs to be explicitly negotiated, and that collegiality as a fail-safe mechanism may not suffice. The new regime might be able to provide the framework that, in large measure, is missing now.

Group 2's burden of office, if properly circumscribed, has to do with ensuring adaptation of the governance apparatus to circumstances. Freedom to adapt to variety has to be released by the regime developed for this group, confronting individuals with the challenge of harmonizing local preferences to overall values.

The complexity of this 'harmonization of the dominant governance design with the richness of circumstances' cannot be rigidly framed by linear rules and inflexible norms. The specific regime that must be put in place for this category needs to provide the basis for such *arbitrages*. It cannot allow for as much latitude as the one afforded to group 1, but it must provide the requisite margin of maneuverability if the right alignments and ligatures are to be put in place. At the present time, the essentially deliberative and dialogical nature of the activities of this group is not adequately reflected in what remains an unduly restrictive framework that does not make the highest and best use of the mind and imagination of the incumbents.

Group 3 is a world of communities of professionals facing a different world of trade-offs: the reconciliation, in communities of practice, of what is required by government decisions and choices, and the hard realities of what is technically feasible and socially acceptable from a professional point of view.

While new norms and codes are slowly emerging bottom-up and through transversal transfers of best practices, this group is quite ineffectively mobilized for the time being. Instead of being seen as the phalanx required to be on the front line every day and to translate the 'will' of the government into 'workable' practices (and consequently managing the interface where much of the social learning and the constant fine tuning of government's work is carried out), this group has too often been required to operate in an unthinking and mechanical way by unduly restrictive frames. The legal blinders imposed on them centrally have even often unintentionally inflicted a great deal of damage and costly unintended consequences. A new regime would help make the highest and best use of this extraordinary intellectual capital.

As for group 4, it is likely that a new regime that would allow collective bargaining to cover a much broader territory—as it does in other sectors—would not only serve them better, but would also allow for the development of more flexible and effective work arrangements.

Some may be skeptical about these new value-added frontiers that might emerge through the exploration of new HR regimes. Our own view is that it reveals a failure both of imagination and will. While it is not appropriate to flesh out detailed blueprints for each of these four regimes (others are better equipped to build on this prototype and to suggest workable schemes), it is crucial to ensure that dynamic conservatism, intellectual laziness, and institutional self interest are not allowed to trump experiments in the design of new and more value-adding HR regimes. This is the challenge this chapter wanted to put at the centre of current debates on the renaissance and renewal of the 'public service'.

Conclusion

As far back as 1983, one may find in the Auditor-General's report a chapter entitled "Constraints To Productive Management in The Public Service" that noted:

> ...one of our most troubling findings has been that many management problems persist in spite of efforts to overcome them....[primarily due to] the impact of political priorities on the management process, the degree of administrative procedures with which managers have to cope, and the disincentives to productive management that are characteristic of the public service....if some of these constraints were recognized and modified, and if a deliberate effort were made to establish an environment that encourages managers to achieve satisfactory results at reasonable costs, significant improvements could be made in achieving value for money (Canada 1983: 2.1, 2.4, 2.6).

This sort of cautious auditor's language does not dare to call for innovation, but it is clear that if the environment may be said to not even encourage satisfactory results, *a fortiori*, it does not encourage innovation. Much of it can be ascribed to the rigidity of the administrative systems and in particular to the *imperium* of the accounting regimen.

What is called for is a softening of the notion of accountability.

On this front, accounting professionals in the Auditor-General's Office, like their counterparts in the United States General Accounting Office, may indeed be said to have

> particular blinders...that may not permit...[them] to take the broader view of the tradeoffs associated with various formulations of...universalistic norms and prescriptions for accountability...sufficiently sensitive to various institutional contexts, public objectives and tradeoffs (Posner 2006: 73).

The hard-line financial accountability in good currency has deterred innovation. Yet today's fluid environment and the emergence of the strategic state call for new ways to 'satisfice'— to involve different kinds of people, with different skills, doing different kinds of things. This in turn requires different systems for effective 'management' since imagination and innovation are key drivers of this kind of work.

Such innovation and productivity-enhancing initiatives need to be nurtured and fostered through the freedom to follow one's hunches in thinking, testing and discussing. This kind of licence however, can best be experienced by public sector actors in the context of issue domains where the nature of the issue is well understood, and with a full appreciation that, depending on the nature of the burden of office, the latitudes availed to individual public servants may be greater or lesser than is currently the case.

The core public service would be expected to play its part, either safeguarding the fabric of society or protecting the integrity of key systems. They would not necessarily have a monopoly on the work itself: in this case in any advanced democracy, it would be the politicians at the end of the day who decide and are judged accordingly by the people.

But the core PPS would be expected to provide the basic infrastructure to ensure that such decisions can be made in the best interest of the country, and should be protected accordingly. And to the extent that representative democracy is enriched by a degree of participation by the citizenry, it is the role of the core public servants to ensure that the citizens are allowed to play this kind of governing role.

As for the non-core public sector employment, quite different rules might apply very effectively: lesser protection and privileges corresponding to their lesser burden of office. But in a truly refurbished public service, no one would be freed from some responsibility in the process of social learning and innovation. To those on the front line who may feel that their role is at times underestimated, we say that they are right. As Gilles Vigneault used to say in an old song *"c'est pas toujours le capitaine qui voit premier venir le vent"*. Consequently, the new HR regime must take this responsibility into account. This is not impossible; it has been successfully implemented in other sectors.

To expect a complete transformation of the public service overnight would be utopian. Yet there are reasons to believe that the present predicaments have triggered a genuine search for a series of effective responses to these problems. Our argument has been that attacking the problem *par morceaux* may be the most promising strategy.

Endnote

1 Quoted by then Clerk of the Privy Council Mel Cappe in an address to the ADM Forum, Ottawa, April 24–25, 2001.

CHAPTER 11

Design Challenges for the Strategic State: *Bricolage* and Sabotage

The idea of design involves inquiry into systems that do not yet exist.

—A. G. L. Romme

Introduction

Much re-engineering of the state is bound to occur as the welfare state is retrofitted and gradually replaced by a strategic state that is less focused on protection and redistribution and much more on productivity and innovation. This has led to the emergence of a multitude of new organizational forms that are not, strictly speaking, patterned on the traditional hierarchical departmental model. This has, in turn, created new challenges in the design of organizations that can ensure a requisite mix of reliability, accountability, nimbleness, exploration capability, innovation and creativity. Organizational design capability, nevertheless, is poorly instituted in the Canadian system.

Organizational design is most often inherited from tradition and history, or is the result of improvisation by the last batch of imperial newcomers, eager to inflict their footprint on the organization they have just recently joined. As a result, there is often not a good fit between the design, the mission and the context of the organization: neither the faceless forces of history nor the hastily drafted back-of-envelope organization charts ensure good design (Paquet 2007a).

So, concern about design surfaces, but the response is rarely adequate: the skimpiest of contours are sketched (as amateurishly as the last time the concern emerged) and the ensuing job of fleshing out the details is delegated to junior executives as part of what is called an implementation strategy. It is hardly surprising that what ensues is not of great significance: little more than tinkering with organization charts.

The major source of the problem is that this sort of architectural work requires a wholly different way of thinking. It is not (and cannot be) guided by the single-minded sort of logic that dominates science (the search for general knowledge and the subsequent test of its validity), but by an inquiry into systems that do not yet exist. The logic, in this latter case, is that of disclosing and crafting a new 'world', with the sole purpose of ascertaining if it works, and to ensure that it does (Romme 2003: 558).

In the first section of this chapter, we provide a conceptual framework, and we identify the particular challenges created by the emergence of a world in which nobody is in charge. In the second section, we sketch the many dimensions of the organizational design process. In the third section, we use this approach to examine two pathologies of governance recently observed on the federal scene in Canada: a case of *passive sabotage* (where fixation on an old and inadequate design in the face of new challenges has proved disastrous—nuclear safety) and a case of *active sabotage* (i.e., deliberate use of design to ensure failure—Service Canada). In conclusion, we suggest ways in which the organizational design function might be bolstered at the federal level in Canada, but we also underline the fact that this kind of function needs to be instituted as well within the federation, and that such mechanisms should be helpful not only in improving effective governance, but also in exposing the ugly face of sabotage early enough to prevent the worst outcomes.

Designing a living organization

Organization and organization design

An organization may be X-rayed as a mix of *people* (stakeholders of all sorts with their skills, talents, and responsibilities), *architecture* (relationships of all sorts defined by the organization charts and the like), *routines* (process, policies and procedures), and *culture* (shared values, beliefs, language, norms and mindsets) (J. Roberts 2004).

At any particular time, these components (people, architecture, routines and culture (PARC)) are assembled within organizations in various ways—bound together by ligatures making them into a more or less coherent whole. A shock disturbing any of these components (whether it originates within or without the organization, whether it modifies a physical or a symbolic dimension) triggers some realignment in all the other dimensions. So the organization continually evolves: more so and faster when the environment is turbulent.

Organizations are therefore assemblages that are constantly challenged (over-ground and underground) as a result of new circumstances, the action of new or transformed stakeholders, new emerging relationships, new procedures, or changes in the material or the symbolic order. The role of the organization designer is to intervene in real time in an existing assemblage to improve this four-dimensional configuration of the organization in a manner that generates better dynamic performance and resilience. This sort of intervention has to take into account the turbulence and evolution of the environment in which the organization operates, but also the limitations of such tweaking given imperfect knowledge and the profound uncertainty about what it will generate in terms of unintended consequences.

The core task of organizational design is to disclose new worlds. For organizations are worlds: they are a totality of interrelated pieces of *equipment* to carry out a specific task (such hammering in a nail); tasks that are undertaken for some *purpose* (like building a house); and the activities involved bestow those accomplishing them with *identities* (like being a carpenter) (Spinosa et al. 1997: 17). This is the sense in which one speaks of the world of medicine, business or academe.

However, there is more to organizations than the interconnection of equipment, purposes and identities. In talking about these new worlds, Spinosa and others use the word *style* to refer to the ways in which all the practices are coordinated and fit together in an organization. Style is what coordinates action, what makes certain kinds of activities and things matter.

In their study, Spinosa and others show how economic, social and political entrepreneurs are those who spot disharmonies between what seems to be the *rules* in good currency and what would appear to be the sort of *practice* likely to be effective. They detect anomalies. Those anomalies create puzzles. The reaction to puzzles by inattentive observers is often to ignore them, and pursue the on-going tasks. Entrepreneurs recognize instead that the anomalies are creating mysteries, and that what is called for are 'ways of understanding mysteries', the search for "guidelines for solving a mystery by organized exploration of possibilities" (Martin 2004: 7).

Tackling such an exploratory task can only be done by trial and error. This is the world of prototyping, experimentation, serious play and organizational design. Innovative and entrepreneurial persons in all areas (economic, political, social) become organizational designers and redefine the style of their organizations (Schrage 2000; Sabel 2004).

A significant handicap in this sort of endeavour is that this type of world-disclosing activity or inquiry—based on empathy (for one designs always for somebody else), on holistic problem-solving (looking for what works *in toto*), and prototyping (not waiting until one has the best solution, but starting with anything promising, prototyping it, getting feedback, playing with it, and learning in that way)—Tim Brown quoted in Martin 2004: 11—is not what higher education is organized to foster, and, as a result, the skills required are not necessarily cultivated and widely available (Paquet 2006a).

Successful design work in a world where nobody is in charge

One of the most important changes of this kind that has occurred over the last while in the institutional order, that defines the rules of the game in our democratic societies, is the drift from a world where some person or group could (legitimately or not) claim to be in charge, to a world where complexity, turbulence and surprises are so important that it cannot be argued persuasively that anybody is in charge (Cleveland 2002).

This has significantly increased the complexity of the design work necessary to keep the institutional order up to the challenges generated by such a turbulent environment. It has been argued that what is required is:

(1) a new vocabulary because critical description is crucial at the diagnostic phase;

(2) a new form of knowledge, a new type of exploratory activity and a new process of experimentalism-based creative thinking;

(3) a new type of competencies to do this work; and

(4) windows of opportunity to 'tinker' with the organization with a modicum of chances of success (i.e., at a time and in a way that prevents these efforts from being neutralized by the dynamic conservatism of those who benefit from the existing order).

This often calls for exceptional circumstances. Otherwise the pressures of those confronted with real and substantial losses in the short term will trump the timid actions of those hoping for uncertain future benefits from a new order.

However, this process will lead to nothing substantial unless one has been able to develop (5) a mental tool box of levers capable of guiding the work of crafting new organizations, usable in such design work. But, because organizational design is akin to creating a new world, none of the above will suffice unless the design process (6) truly discloses a coherent world (a body) and contributes to impart it with a style (a soul) that provides it with a sextant—focal points that underpin its being able to sustain effective coordination and change.

Given these conditions for successful design, it is hardly surprising that such work is eschewed, and that so many organizations are so poorly designed. It is much easier for governors and managers to focus their attention on less daunting tasks.

A sketch of the design process

The design process is difficult and elusive, very much like the pragmatic inquiry of professionals in their practice. But it must be anchored, at the very least, in a loose protocol if it is to serve as a launching pad for effective exploration.

The what: the Simons-type model as a possible template

Robert Simons has proposed a template based on four basic questions that one might reformulate in the following way:

(1) **Customer/stakeholder definition**

What are the best possible assemblages of meaningful primary stakeholders that would represent fully the range of effective partners, clients, etc. making up the broad unit structure?

(2) **Performance variables**

What are the most effective diagnostic control systems (the various mechanisms likely to monitor the organization best and to suggest ways to excite them)?

(3) **Creative tension resolution**

What are the best mechanisms to resolve the creative tensions between the frames of mind of the different layers and rings of partners in the organization and likely to catalyze interactive networks?

(4) **Commitment to others**

What are the mechanisms of shared responsibilities and commitment to others that will ensure some coherence for the organization and the requisite mix of reliability and innovation?

The answers to these questions are meant to help define the four basic dimensions of the Simons framework:

(1) the span of control (who should decide?);
(2) the span of accountability (trade-offs in performance measures when it comes to rendering of accounts);
(3) the span of influence (the full nature of the interactions and the degree of mobilization they entail); and
(4) the span of support (the full range of shared responsibilities).

Simons suggests that proper alignment for the organization requires that the spans of control (hard) and support (soft) on the supply side of resources be adequate to meet the obligations imposed by the spans of accountability (hard) and influence (soft) on the demand side of resources (Simons 2005)

The how: experimentalism and serious play in a dynamic world

At the source of the process leading to the constant adaptation of the organizational design, when nobody is in charge, is the dual capacity of allowing:

(1) as many stakeholders as possible who detect an anomaly to initiate remedial action, and
(2) such action to proceed experimentally even though the remedial action is not perfect, on the basis of a strong belief that mass collaboration will help improve it and thereby find a faster way to the next best (always temporary) solution.

This calls for a drift toward open source governance (i.e., a form of governance that enables each partner, as much as possible, to have access to the 'code' and to 'tinker' freely with the way the system works within certain well-accepted constraints)

(Sabel 2001); and a priority to 'serious play' (i.e., a premium on experimentation with imperfect prototypes one might be able to improve by retooling, restructuring and reframing innovatively and productively) (Schrage 2000).

By partitioning the overall terrain into issue-domains and communities of meaning or communities of fate (i.e., assemblages of people united in their common concern for shared problems or a shared passion for a topic or set of issues), it is possible to identify a large number of sub-games—each requiring a specific treatment. Each issue-domain (health, education, environment, etc.) and even some sub-issue domains (like mental health), being multifaceted and somewhat different must be dealt with on an *ad hoc* basis (in the way a sculptor facing blocks of stone of different texture must deal with each block differently), with a view to allowing the design of its own stewardship to emerge.

This open system takes into account the people with a substantial stake in the issue-domain, the resources available and the culture in place, and allows experiments to shape the required mix of principles and norms, of rules and decision-making procedures likely to promote the preferred mix of efficiency, resilience and learning. A template likely to be of use everywhere may not be available yet, but it does not mean that a workable one cannot be elicited here and now.

However, it is not sufficient to ensure open access, one must also ensure that the appropriate motivations are nurtured so that all meaningful stakeholders are willing and able to engage in 'serious play' (i.e., become truly producers of governance through tinkering with the governance apparatus within certain limits). This in turn requires that a modicum of mass collaboration and trust prevail (Tapscott and Williams 2006), and calls for a reconfiguration of governance, taking the communities of meaning seriously. Such an approach may not only suggest that very different arrangements are likely to emerge from place to place, but also would underline the importance of regarding any such arrangement as essentially temporary: the ground is in motion and diversity is likely to acquire new faces, so different patterns of organizational design are likely to emerge. Consequently, good governance would require that any formal or binding arrangement be revisited, played with, and adjusted to take into account the evolving diversity of circumstances. It would open the door to the design of more complex and innovative arrangements likely to deal more effectively with deep diversity (Paquet 2008e).

Prototyping would appear to be the main activity underpinning 'serious play':

- identifying some top requirements as quickly as possible;
- putting in place a quick-and-dirty provisional medium of co-development;
- allowing as many interested parties as exist to get involved as partners in improving the arrangement;
- encouraging iterative prototyping; and
- encouraging all, through playing with prototypes, to get a better understanding of the problems, of their priorities and of themselves (Schrage 2000: 199ff).

The purpose of the exercise is to create a dialogue (creative interaction) between people and prototypes. This may be more important than creating dialogue between people alone. It is predicated on a culture of active participation that would need to be nurtured. The sort of democratization of design that ensues, and the sort of playfulness and adventure that is required for 'serious play' with prototypes, are essential for the process to succeed, and they apply equally well to narrow or broad organizational concerns.

The wherewithal: tripartite *bricolage*

In the beginning is the anomaly noted by a stakeholder that points to an aspect of the performance of the organization that would appear to be much below legitimate expectations. This calls for *bricolage* (i.e., tinkering with the ways the organization operates, or with certain of its structural features, or with the definition of the purposes of the organization—re-tooling, re-structuring or re-framing will be the labels used for such *bricolage*).

As Donald Schön explained, any social system (and organizations are social systems) contains technology, structure and theory:

> the structure is the set of roles and relations among individual members. The theory consists of the views held within the social system about its purposes, its operations, its environment and its future. Both reflect, and in turn influence, the prevailing technology of the system. These dimensions all hang together so that any change in one produces change in the others (Schön 1971: 33).

Obviously the law of least effort entices stakeholders to tinker with technology and operations first, for it is likely to be easier (e.g., generate least resistance, take less time, and involve fewer people) than if one were to fiddle with the structure or to question the purpose of the organization. Yet often, most efforts to correct anomalies often quickly become a mix of the three sorts of *bricolage*.

Continuous trial and error leads to experimentation with different prototypes that embody different degrees of retooling, restructuring and reframing. Indeed, minor retooling often triggers a cascade of effects that end up, over time, with major reframing. However there is no guarantee. In other cases, blockages at one of these levels may be powerful enough to derail the whole process of repairs that has been triggered by the original anomalies, and organizational decline may ensue.

Finally, the nature of the anomalies and the severity of their impact may trigger different approaches to the required repairs. The inertia of the organization and the degree of cognitive dissonance may well mean inattention to the early warning signals, and significant denial of difficulties even in the face of very poor performance. This often makes minor *bricolage* less likely, and allows organizational decline to proceed unhampered until some threshold is reached when action is finally seen as mandatory. In such cases, instant major overhaul is often the only option.

In a mega-system like the state apparatus of a modern industrialized socio-economy, the potential for inattention to anomalies and neglect of repairs is very high, especially if there is no agency charged with the responsibility of oversight of the adequacy of the organizational infrastructure, of detection of anomalies requiring repairs, and of the conduct of repairs when needed.

In the Canadian federal government, following a 2007 restructuring of the Privy Council Office (PCO), the 'machinery of government' apparatus is described as follows:

> [it] provides advice and supports the Prime Minister on matters related to…[the Prime Minister's] prerogative and responsibilities as the overall manager of Canada's system of Cabinet government…supply[ing] advice on matters relating to:
>
> • The structure, organization and functioning of government;
> • The organization of Cabinet and its committees;
> • Ministerial mandates and responsibilities;
> • Transitions from government to government;
> • Ethics and accountability issues [consistent with Westminster-style government]; and
> • The role of the Crown, the Governor General and Government House, as well as issues related to honours policy (Canada 2010a).

These are part of the responsibilities of a deputy secretary, grouped with legislation and house planning as well as formal legal advice to the Prime Minister and others in the PCO portfolio. It does not seem to give priority to monitoring the state of the organizational infrastructure in a continuous and particularly careful way, and appears prone to be inattentive to any anomaly that does not generate a crisis.

To the sort of inattention or neglect that this seems to imply, one must add the possibility of active resistance of officials (in private, public and social organizations) to any profound change, and even more so when what is involved constitutes nothing less than "a challenge to the psychological comfort of the powerful" (O'Toole 1995–96: 238).

The massive redesign of many organizations and institutions as a result the drift from 'Big G' government to 'small g' governance (from the welfare state to the strategic state) in some cases (like Canada) has generated forceful resistance within the technocracy (often emboldened by an ambivalent citizenry not eager to lose state protection) to new deals that would call for a lower valence for the state, more inter-sector partnerships, and more mass collaboration—all initiatives that have been seen as reducing the power of the powerful including, especially, the upper levels of the bureaucracy in place, and implying a greater personal responsibility for the citizenry.

In a context inhabited by neglect of organizational design issues, badly equipped capacity-wise to deal aptly and seriously with such issues, and plagued with powerful defensive technocracies, superficial tinkering with organization charts is often administratively expedient even though it is hardly a recipe for wise design.

When crises boil over, technological pathologies and a few minor structural defects are corrected, but when the cultures of organizations are indicted (when what is involved is nothing less than a need to rethink and reframe the notion of the business the organization is in, the theory of what the organization is about), the forces of inertia, self-interest, or fear often succeed in stopping any profound transformation. By a sleight of hand that amounts to nothing more than a modification of some superficial rules of the game or a slight exercise of musical chairs for the officials in the top ranks of the sick organization, the pretense that the problem has been resolved quickly gets accredited.

Even when particular committees of inquiry or mandate review forums draw attention to the need for a more fundamental transformation at the level of theory and organizational culture, those matters are readily dismissed as fuzzy and too elusive to be tractable, and there is little will either within the organization or at the oversight or monitoring agency level to insist on those foundational dimensions being dealt with on the pretense that such endeavors are too complex, take too much time, and are rarely successful. Such rationalizations force these foundational issues off the table (Paquet 2004c; Paquet 2006b; Paquet 2007c).

As a result, most initiatives that are carried out under the general rubric of organizational design are merely tinkering with innocuous technological features (as open annual meetings and the like) or superficial structural features or organization charts without ever attempting to resolve the admittedly more difficult and obviously more important problem of the reconciliation of the different frames of reference and of the trans-substantiation of the organizational culture or theory of what the organization is about. The rationale is that it is easier to start with easy moves, but it is hardly persuasive when this entails never going beyond that stage.

Indeed, one of the most important occluded factors in the study of organizational design is the capacity for sabotage by groups with a vested interest in the *status quo*. These occluded forces are often so important that some wise transformation experts, like Albert Hirschman, have suggested that no reform is likely to succeed unless it comes as a total surprise, and acts as a thunderbolt. This may be unduly pessimistic. Much can probably be done, despite the countervailing forces, but only if the saboteurs are exposed (be they passive or active) and if corrosive critical thinking is allowed to openly question their rearguard action as sabotage.

The best way to illustrate the significance of organizational design may be to expose some failures that can be ascribed either to deliberate design sabotage or to a nonchalant attitude that allowed poor organizational design to survive.

Such active or passive sabotage can easily do much damage, especially when there is no one monitoring the scene, when the forces of denial are powerful, and when there is little in place that might serve as fail-safe mechanisms.

The all-too-easy world of sabotage

The design process sketched in the last sections suggests the basic elements of effective design and redesign. Such an ideal of continuing dynamic adjustment is rarely observed in the real world. There are always weaknesses that survive at different pressure points in the process.

One may identify four major sources of design failures:

(1) the six preconditions not being in place;
(2) the Simons conditions being unmet: the what;
(3) poor social learning through prototyping and serious play failing: the how; and
(4) the failure of going beyond the superficial in the tripartite *bricolage*: the wherewithal.

The first major source explains why organizational design is not well done in general. It can only be repaired by a fundamental change in the mindset and a massive investment (intellectual and financial) in this type of work. While it must be held responsible for much of poor or whimsical design everywhere, it is difficult to ascribe particular failures to this general disease.

Nothing but full recognition of the centrality of this long-term function, and its being embedded formally in the institutional architecture will ensure that the work is done. In the absence of such embeddedness, it may be said that there will be no continuous monitoring and evaluation of organizational design, and that it is hardly surprising that the what, the how and the wherewithal of good organizational design is not what it should be.

The other three sources are more proximate, one might say. They point to particular actions that might have prevented observed failures or might have triggered them.

In the next section, we briefly describe the background, the issue and observed blockages in two recent files, and we point to significant design failures and equally important inaction when repairs were in order. In each case, the Simons conditions were not met, social learning was stunted, and critical reflections about the philosophy of the organization did not occur.

Two vignettes

Canadian Nuclear Safety Commission

Background

The independent Atomic Energy Control Board (AECB) was established in 1946 to control and supervise the development, application and peaceful uses of nuclear energy in Canada, as well as to participate in an international measure of control. From the beginning, the AECB was given regulatory powers aimed at encouraging and facilitating research and investigations as well as developing, controlling, supervising and licensing the production, application and use of atomic energy. The possibility existed from the beginning for a company to be established. Atomic Energy of Canada Limited (AECL) was established in 1952 with no mandate specified for it in legislation (Canada 2007b).

Canada quickly became a world leader in this sector—creating multi-purpose research reactors from scratch, and enabling the first Cobalt-60 treatment for cancer in the world in Victoria, BC in 1961; together with AECL, Ontario Hydro and General Electric, a commercial power generator (CANDU) was brought forth in 1962.

Nevertheless, the passage of time has changed the landscape. In the twenty years between 1974 and 1994, several reviews took place, including one by Parliament, two ministerial reviews and other studies (Canada 1994b). The 1994 Auditor-General's report enumerated key changes that had transformed the context since AECL's inception—federal regulatory reform, cost recovery (with the consequence that regulatees wanted more say), more age-related failures of reactors, increasing citizen concerns over the environment, environmental assessment requirements, etc.— noting that stricter procedures were being required and that judicial review of regulatory inspections and enforcement was increasingly being invoked (Ibid).

A refurbished regulatory apparatus was put in place—the Canadian Nuclear Safety Commission (CNSC) through legislation that received Royal Assent in 1997, and came into effect in 2000. The new apparatus was designed to split regulatory powers from concerns about research and development as well as marketing, and provided for a much more detailed and prescriptive approach to regulating. The CNSC was directed by the authorizing legislation to regulate:

> the use of nuclear energy and materials to protect (to a
> reasonable level and in a manner consistent with Canada's
> international obligations) health, safety and the environment...
> [as well as] to respect Canada's international commitments on the
> peaceful use of nuclear power (Canada 1997b).

This was (and is) to be done through regulations that must be vetted by the Governor in Council. The CNSC has the authority to exempt any activity, person, class of person or quantity of nuclear substance, temporarily or permanently, from the application of the governing legislation, in accordance with regulations. The CNSC also conducts legislated environmental assessments, and implements non-proliferation provisions of nuclear cooperation agreements between Canada and its nuclear trading partners, and Canada's bilateral agreements with the International Atomic Energy Agency (IAEA) on nuclear safeguards verification.

The CNSC is a "court of record" (as per the Act), whose president may establish panels of commission members and decides if they should act as the commission (except with respect to regulations and bylaw making), but has no voting privileges except in case of a tie. It operates with 800 employees and a budget of CA$ 90 million (Canada 2009).

The Minister of Natural Resources Canada has the authority to issue binding directives to CNSC "on broad policy matters with respect to the objects of the Commission" (Canada 1997a). In effect, CNSC is part of the minister's portfolio. Nevertheless, because it is an independent quasi-judicial administrative tribunal, the responsible minister and any other minister (e.g., those whose responsibilities are affected by it) are expected to follow centrally issued advice in dealings with it. That advice states:

> [T]he nature of the relationship between a Minister and an administrative tribunal with independent decision-making or quasi-judicial functions is a particularly sensitive issue.... Ministers and Secretaries of State shall not intervene, or appear to intervene, on behalf of any person or entity, with quasi-judicial tribunals, on any matter before them that requires a decision in their quasi-judicial capacity, unless authorized by law (Canada 2007c).

The change in the nuclear industry has broadened and deepened since the Auditor-General's 1994 report.

On one hand, it has become an increasingly sensitive industry worldwide for several reasons, including those related to aging facilities as well as fears related to security, health and the environment. Aging nuclear power generating facilities are raising questions of replacement choices and decommissioning costs. Security fears related to proliferation together with the rise of state and non-state terrorism, as well as growing health and environmental concerns including waste management, are also increasing in importance as time passes. (For example, some strongly safety-minded experts call for a design of a nuclear reactor that ensures the probability of an accident causing harm to a member of the public who is outside a nuclear facility is less that one in a million in one year. In 1990, with various upgrades, an accident at a key AECL research reactor for world medical isotope production, that was built in 1957, was conjectured by critics as likely to be in the range of one in 10,000. The probability of an accident today is, of course, much lower.

On the other hand, peaceful uses continue to grow in nature and scope: the world has begun to take a hard look at its dependency on oil and to look at nuclear energy as an alternative; medical applications of nuclear technology blossom, and agricultural applications emerge.

AECL was created to further peaceful uses of nuclear energy based on heavy-water technology. Significantly subsidized (with estimates in the billions) but operationally profitable and commercially oriented, it remains deeply embedded in Canada's nuclear research efforts. It has stimulated and launched successful commercial ventures in both medical and power generation worldwide, currently accounting for the production of raw material for half of the world's medical isotopes.

Nevertheless, with its reliance on longstanding heavy-water technology, AECL is argued by some to be destined to become a lightweight player. Ottawa-based corporation MDS Nordion is a dominant player in nuclear medicine and relies to a large degree on AECL as a major supplier.

By the very nature of its business, AECL is one of CNSC's important regulatees.

Several federal ministers together with their policy departments have a significant interest in this industry, including those concerned with the environment, health, international affairs and national security, as well as the two that are currently represented on AECL's board of directors (Industry Canada and Natural Resources Canada) by their deputy ministers.

Issues

Recent difficulties involving an extended shutdown of a 50-year old AECL research reactor that produces more than half of the world's medical isotope spiraled, over a few weeks (from the initial reactor shut down in mid November 2007 to its restart in mid-December 2007), into an international crisis in which a hasty legislative override of CSNC was used to authorize the restart of the reactor.

The president of CNSC was removed from her post (but kept on as a member of the Commission), accused by the Prime Minister of needlessly endangering the lives of Canadians, and the minister responsible for Natural Resources Canada asked her in a letter to provide reasons why she should not be fired (*National Post* 2007). In response, she sued the federal government over what she saw as an unfair dismissal (Dalrymple 2008), and resigned in September 2008. The chairman of AECL's Board of Directors resigned in December 2007, after just over a year in the job.

The longer-term consequences of this shutdown crisis for Canada, for AECL and for MDS Nordion may well turn out to be significant. Canada's leading medical journal put it this way:

> [W]hy is something as important as the world's medical isotope supply dependent on a half-century old reactor? Will coordination with Europe be improved to guard against future shortages? How long will it be before the United States starts making its own isotopes? (*Canadian Medical Association Journal* 2008).

The difficulties have been exacerbated by an announcement by AECL of the abandonment, for cost reasons, of its decade long plan to replace the reactor with two modern ones dedicated to medical isotope production.

The inability of AECL to meet its longstanding commitment to its important customer MDS Nordion (to successfully bring modern replacement reactors on stream) as well as the inability of CNSC and AECL (until recently) to reach an agreement on a process for some kind of pre-project design review of the latter's new flagship project (an advanced CANDU reactor) could only translate into a significant disadvantage for AECL in its marketing efforts to domestic and foreign governments, as well as for its marketability— should the government wish to pursue the full or partial privatization of AECL.

Blockages

While there would appear to exist some levers in the law to deal with unexpected situations when CNSC and AECL might not be in agreement (such as the possibility for the minister of Natural Resources Canada to provide binding directives, and Governor in Council vetting of regulations proposed by the CNSC), it is not at all clear that these mechanisms are adequate to deal smoothly with broader public interest trade-offs. The aim of the underpinning legislation is, *inter alia*, to limit the risks to national security, the health and safety of persons and the environment that go with the development, production and use of nuclear energy and substances to a reasonable degree, and in a way consistent with international obligations.

While the wording may allow for a little flexibility of interpretation, the former President of CNSC—who held the post from 2001 to very early 2008—signaled that as she saw it, the agency's regulatory regime was "the most modern in the world, separating health and safety from economic and political interests" (Canada 2007d). For her, the authors were told, protection of domestic markets (something Canada's competitors seem to find a way to do) was irrelevant.

At the same time, the admonition to ministers and secretaries of state to treat quasi-judicial bodies sensitively and specifically to refrain from intervening or being seen to intervene on behalf of an entity on any matter that requires a decision in their quasi-judicial capacity, appears to preclude any minister with a legitimate policy interest from doing or being seen to do anything to push for creative approaches being applied by the CNSC. Similar admonitions would apply to policy deputy ministers; those who are also board members for AECL might feel doubly hamstrung. Even the Clerk of the Privy Council might be anxious to avoid any perception of inappropriate interference.

The main levers for dealing with necessary discussions and trade-offs in the public interest by the different stakeholders are therefore ineffective because the barriers erected to safeguard CNSC's independence prevent them from being used in a timely-enough fashion if an unexpected crisis arises. This leaves CNSC's governance *de facto* to itself thereby placing over-reliance, some might say, on the perspectives of a few individuals without sufficient built-in checks and balances (i.e., embedded loops for social learning) to ensure that other points of view are given adequate attention.

The joint CNSC/AECL 'lessons learned' exercise—carried out by the Talisman International LLC as a result of the fiasco—reported in June 2008. Given a narrow mandate, Talisman concluded that:

> [T]he overarching root cause of the...extended outage in late 2007 was due to a CNSC and AECL set of processes which were "expert based" not "process based". The prevalent culture of informality was considered a significant and fundamental flaw in both organizations' methods of operation, and contributed to a series of misunderstandings regarding reactor plant safety system upgrade status, AECL licensing commitments, and CSNC regulatory requirements and license conditions...[I]n summary the Talisman team believes that improved communications, clear license conditions, and a mutual understanding of plant status and outstanding licensing and inspection issues, along with improved inspector training and enforcement and in-house legal staff, would help prevent the misunderstandings which led to the extended outage in late 2007 (AECL 2008).

Service Canada

Background

In 1989, the then Clerk of Privy Council, Paul Tellier, was the driving force behind PS2000, the first administrative review at the federal level in Canada to designate 'quality of service to the public' as an overarching goal of public management (O'Neal 1994).

In 1993, connectivity to the Internet moved to centre stage at Industry Canada as a Director General, in charge of a relatively obscure function, was able to get backing for an approach that evolved into a major 'branding' effort that, by 1999, was announced in the Speech from the Throne as an objective "to be known as ... [the government that was] most connected to citizens" (Canada 1999). To reach this objective of being most connected to citizens and businesses, the government proposed the GOL initiative (Government On-Line GOL (1999–2006)) as a project that was ultimately allocated CA$ 880 million in new money over six years, and that was built around two principles:

grouping information and services around client's needs and priorities, and partnering within the federal government as well as with other governments to cluster services in order to better serve the public.[1] At the same time as the GOL initiative was launched, a three-year Service Canada pilot project was brought forth, including the two existing channels of communication (the Canada website and a 1-800 line).

As well, Service Canada involved a federally driven integrated front door for information and services comprised of Service Canada access centres located in different federal departments and agencies, co-located in federal and provincial departments, or located in municipal organizations, and in non-governmental agencies (Canada 2006b). By 2004–2005, the network (SII) operated at 76 locations.

In 1997, the then Clerk of Privy Council, Jocelyne Bourgon, who saw service to the public as a key goal for federal public sector/service reform, gave full support to the recommendation of a federal-provincial-municipal public service managers conference that had expressed a strong interest in learning about the main drivers of service quality improvement, and launched the Citizens First survey of 1998—an initiative that was celebrated as "leading edge" in the service quality community (Accenture 2006: 48).

The three-year Service Canada pilot project was extended in 2002 with a view to developing a single window strategy based on a three-way partnership of Treasury Board Secretariat (policy and coordination), Communications Canada (website and 1-800 number), and Human Resources Development Canada (HRDC) (which had its own federal social services delivery network and was given responsibility to manage the integrated front door Service Canada network for the system as a whole). A committee of Directors General was charged with the coordination work. This committee reported to a Deputy Minister level committee and each Deputy Minister in turn reported to his or her minister.

By 2004–2005, HRDC's own network had become 320 (in-person) Human Resources centres, operated a little differently across the country as needed, plus mail services. HRDC had been split into two departments and both networks were located in one part of the former department, while telephone and Internet services were located in the other. In 2005, the government announced in its budget that one of the two new departments was to become the foundation of the new government of Canada network.

In this way, the three objectives—citizen-centred service delivery, e-Government, and on-going service delivery of a range of federal social programs by one department—came together organizationally in 2005 when Service Canada was launched as a stand-alone entity combining delivery networks (i.e., SII plus social services). The deputy head was also named associate Deputy Minister for one of the 'policy' departments that had been part of the 'old' HRDC, and became responsible for providing corporate services for the two 'policy' departments (HRSD (Human Resources Social Development) and HRDC) as well as for itself.

Service Canada, the new (integrated) backbone, opened its doors in September 2005. In its first annual report in 2005–2006, Service Canada described its mandate this way:

> To improve services for Canadians by working with partners
> to provide access to the full range of government services and
> benefits that Canadians want and need in person, by telephone,
> Internet or mail (Canada 2005a).

The spirit of entrepreneurialism and serious play that had been engendered by spinning Service Canada off into a separate entity was clear in its words that year.

It was also clear in its actions that included the introduction of a performance scorecard, establishing an office for client satisfaction, entering partnerships with other governments (e.g., registration of births in Ontario), having its executives spend four days a year at the front line, and using service offerings themselves to see how they work (Ibid., 26–28).

In early 2006, Service Canada was moved back closer to the two policy departments (which were merged back into one that is called HRSDC (Human Resources and Social Development Canada)). The Deputy Minister of Service Canada was required to report to the departmental Deputy Minister and, as a result, its corporate services were no longer shared with *separate* entities, but shared within the same departmental (i.e., HRSDC) 'skin'. Reports on its plans and accomplishments (including the 2005–2006 Annual Report) became part of HRSDC's reports.

In June 2008, Service Canada's website described its purpose:

> Service Canada is about improving the delivery of government services…offer[ing]…single window access to a wide range of Government of Canada programs and services for citizens (Canada 2008b).

Issues

Since 2000, the global company Accenture has been issuing highly regarded annual reports on the progress of 22 national governments (including Canada) in their journey toward citizen-centred service delivery. Their four-pillar model (citizen-centred, cross-government, multi-channel, proactively communicated service) sets out goals, key challenges, and service implications in four stages (see table 11.1).

Table 11.1   *The Accenture model*

Stage Factor	1- Establishing eGoverment	2 - Using eGovernment	3 - Embracing the four pillars	4 - Building the trust
Goals	• Number of services on line	• High percentage of citizens and business uptake	• Services cross-channel and cross-government - one stop / end-to-end	• Citizens trust their government implicitly
Key challenges	• Internet capability	• Citizen outreach • Citizen uptake	• Cross-government collaboration • Service integration	• Content of services
Service implications	• Service availability	• Service delivery	• Service value	• Service trust

Source: Extracted from and lightly modified, Accenture 2006: 6.

Canada scored very well from the beginning (2000) with the combination of GOL and SII. In particular, Canada's vision of streamlined service delivery (for individuals and for businesses collaboratively across jurisdictions, and later for federal corporate services) was seen as one of the most far-reaching and inspirational in the world (Accenture 2007: 87), and Canada has been lauded for "being ahead of the curve for years" (Accenture 2006: 45).

In fact, by the 2006 report, Canada (along with the United States) was ranked as one of the two trendsetters based on its performance "although still working on connecting vision to implementation in Service Canada" (Ibid., 46).

Accenture observed in its 2007 report, however, that Canada was nudged out of its first place ranking by Singapore (by a little), mostly because of how citizens perceive their performance in terms of service availability, delivery, value and trust. It reported that:

[C]itizens are clearly seeing a gap between the government's promise and its practice…in terms of…"citizens voice" alone, Canada ranked 9th out of 22 countries…[and] less than half of the respondents believe service has improved compared to three years ago, a greater number think it has stayed the same or in fact, gotten worse (Accenture 2007: 87).

In fact, Canada was listed as a country in danger of losing momentum (Ibid.).

Blockages

Virtually from Service Canada's inception as a stand-alone entity, problems began to emerge with the main policy departments (formerly HRDC) both with respect to the policy-service delivery linkage as well as with the shared corporate services.

'Service delivery' is an issue-domain in its own right that requires policy choices and decisions to be made. By its very nature it cuts across other issue-domains (e.g., labour market or aging), both within and across jurisdictions, and as such, demands integration at the political level.

It is still treated nevertheless, as just one of a raft of management issues, and it is without either a designated spokesperson at the Cabinet table or one who can hold Service Canada properly accountable to the government of the day for progress towards the public pan-Canadian goal of service to the citizens *and* service integration, taking into account the expectations generated by earlier pronouncements.

The very entrepreneurialism of Service Canada as a separate organization was directed to improving services to Canadians. This citizen-focused service delivery goal, encompassing all levels of government, could not but be strongly constrained (and be bound to lose out) to the goal of federal service delivery integration and efficiency, when Service Canada was required to share corporate services, in effect, with an important federal department (or two in its 'split' mode) that was meant to be only one of its partners.

This shared corporate services partnership, involving very unequal players in terms both of 'clout' and of 'size', could only lead to the commitment to federal government program delivery improvement *trumping* the much broader objective of providing the best possible access to the full range of government services that Canadians want and need.

Without political direction as a counterweight, the earliest opportunity to tame Service Canada and bury it back into HRSDC (and to redefine its role much more narrowly as to serve only the federal government) seems to have been too attractive to senior central bureaucrats to let pass by.

Design failures

These two files would warrant a much more detailed treatment than that which is possible in the context of a short chapter. Moreover, much in these files is still not available for external scrutiny. So we are forced to provide nothing more than a short statement about organization design flaws, and a tentative identification of what would appear to be the main sources of the problems.

The Canadian Nuclear Safety Commission (CNSC) case

The fundamental issue in this case is the failure to have seen *ab ovo* the need to devise (and put in place) satisfactory and workable ways to:

(1) debate, discuss and integrate different legitimate perspectives (expert versus policy, security versus social and economic dimensions);

(2) to do so smoothly (in a different but timely manner, as the context changes); and

(3) to have satisfactory fail-safe mechanisms in place in case of stalemate.

It is our view that the organizational failure was quite predictable, and that the process was *passively sabotaged* by a gross neglect of the scrutiny required by the precautionary principle at the time of designing the new regulatory framework for CNSC.

The Simons conditions were not met, and, as a result, the social learning engine was prevented from going into action, and the tripartite *bricolage* proved impossible.

The Simons equation was clearly out of balance. The spans of control and support on the supply side proved unable to meet the requirements of accountability and influence on the demand side. An unduly restrictive mandate that *precluded* consideration of social and economic impacts meant that the weight was entirely on security-focused control without due consideration of the commitments to others. Although there is a real need for safeguarding (and being seen to safeguard) a regulatory agency from undue political interference, this does not obviate the need to take into account the full range of stakeholders who are best able to serve partners and clients in considering organizational design. In this case, the range was obviously truncated so that some (e.g., those dealing with legitimate citizen/client concerns related to R & D, economic growth and Canada's reputation in the hunt for alternate power generation) were excluded. Moreover, there was no margin of maneuverability as a result of the unduly narrow definition of performance, and of the absence of any viable conflict resolution mechanism with the demand side.

A modicum of prudence and design competence would have led to a refusal of such an overly prescriptive mandate for the CNSC, of such a fundamentalist focus on security as an absolute, of the exclusion of social and economic considerations altogether in final decisions, and of the consequent insularization of the CNSC from its life world context.

Trade-offs must be made between legitimate public policy objectives such as risk to environment (and even health) versus risks to the country's ability and legitimacy to contribute to a field, be it with research and development or selling and using its own high quality products at home and abroad for worthy causes.

In an advanced democracy like Canada's, these kinds of trade-offs need to be brought to the Cabinet table—something that was *de facto* not possible. The unduly narrow definition of stakeholders and of acceptable performance variables was a major flaw leaving too much to the diktats of experts.

Another element dictated by a modicum of prudence and design competence would have been the provision for forums where differences of opinions might be legitimately discussed. In this case, the quasi-taboo attached to any effort to make other viewpoints available to the CNSC constitutes a major design flaw. And the Talisman recommendation about improving communication does not address this fundamental problem.

Finally, the legal setting has provided no fail-safe mechanism in the case of irresolvable differences of opinion, except ministerial or parliamentary directives, that can only kick in when there is a full-blown crisis—not only an apprehended crisis. A less flawed design would have not only provided for legitimate forums for discussions, but also for processes of conflict resolution.

These flaws were an important source of the fiasco of 2007.

These design flaws prevented any possible social learning, and closed the door to any possible *bricolage* (retooling, restructuring or reframing). Unless the legal framework is amended, the on-going necessary conversations (temporarily made possible by the post parliamentary decision *glasnost*) may not be capable of being carried out except in a paralegal way without a true *perestroika*. As a result, little or no innovation can be anticipated.

The potential for informal exchanges at a time when informality has been damned as the main source of the problem by Talisman (even in a narrow way) is very limited. It is more likely that CNSC experts with strong views, reinforced by an international body (IAEA), that is worried exclusively about global proliferation, security, environmental and health concerns and sees Canada's CNSC as a 'poster child', will be unmoved by any argument echoing a different perspective.

The Service Canada case

The fundamental issue in this case is the power struggle between those in the technocracy, who put a priority on serving the citizen well and those who see their job as improving the functioning of the federal government taken by itself (and not incidentally, the functioning of the federal bureaucracy). In this case, the latter group clearly saw Service Canada as undermining the basis of the federal government and its bureaucracy by working collaboratively with other governments, and thereby opening the door to possibilities that the new packages of services might come to be seen as better delivered by other levels of government. The spectre of subsidiarity was seen as almost around the corner. Especially in the world of human resources and social development where the federal authority is widely contested, any weakening of the base of federal operations could be seen by the federal technocracy as a threat. As a result, serving the federal machine came to trump serving the citizen well.

As opposed to the CNSC case where neglect of the importance of good organizational design led to passively sabotaging a very important and complex regulatory process, the case of Service Canada looks like one of *active sabotage*. The redirection of the Service Canada initiative away from its original mandate in 1999 appears to be a deliberate effort to tame and neuter an initiative that was, in the process of better serving the citizen, seen as disserving the federal bureaucracy.

The consequence of failure in this case is not a life-threatening crisis likely to trigger some overt corrective action, but something much more insidious. The consequence may well be the slow abandonment (at least at the federal level) of international leadership around citizen-centred service delivery (even though the drum-beating rhetoric about it may continue), the resurgence of the sort of mindless and insensitive 'rationalizations' of the sort that has led to the closing of post offices and the disappearance of the federal presence and service wickets locally, or to the centralization of taxation offices that has drastically eliminated any possibility of face-to-face interaction with tax collectors regionally. Increased distance between federal bureaucrats and citizens can only increase the level of cynicism about government's ability to serve them well. With it, one may speculate on the increase in the exasperation of elected public officials at the federal level with the ability of the public service (as its main administrative partner) to do its job well.

In this case, the failure has little to do with neglect or error, but it has a lot to do with organizational behavior in a bureaucracy and the principal–agent problem.

Important trade-offs are made at the Cabinet table in this case between:

(a) improving service to individual citizens and businesses (over a broad range of activities) through collaboration among governments and sectors; and

(b) improving service to them by one government and/or one or two key federal departments and agencies, as they are made in the case of major procurement decisions that have domestic and foreign policy implications.

Asking the minister responsible for those one or two federal departments to trade-off the benefits for his/her units against the benefits of the Canadian citizens from a much larger initiative is bound to pose problems and is probably unreasonable. This is the reason why Australia has created a ministerial post to ensure that the interests of the broader initiative would be defended at the Cabinet level and that appropriate accountability for such a broader initiative would be in place. Pushing the trade-off down to the level uppermost bureaucracy (i.e., the deputy minister of one department of which Service Canada had become one part in 2005), as happened in the second stage of the evolution described above, made the situation even more unworkable.

Having no way to have the trade-offs made at the Cabinet table allows those bureaucrats with their own objectives (such as, at their worst, bigger budgets, more prestige, more discretionary resources to indulge in amenities of all sorts, etc.) to advance their own version of what the priority should be: in this case, the self-serving objective of the federal government infrastructure *trumped* the interests of the Canadian citizens and businesses.

It has been shown in the past that even a super-bureau like the Bank of Canada might be led to pursue objectives that did not

412

appear to be the same as those of the government or those that the best interests of the citizenry may dictate.[2]

Bureaus have a capacity to pursue their own objectives independent of the government to some degree. Our hypothesis is that such may be the case in the Service Canada events. 'Prestige-survival-power' might be said to have trumped the 'public interest' as the citizen would see it. The fact that, in so doing, the bureaucracy has also been led to punish success, adds to the gravity of the indictment (Hubbard and Paquet, see chapter 3 of this book).

More important perhaps is the reasonable conjecture that the Service Canada experience may not be unique. How many creative and successful federal initiatives to better serve Canadian citizens are scuttled in the name of the prestige survival of the federal technocracy? How would we know? The question is all the more important as cases that might be construed as active sabotage are infinitely more costly and reprehensible than the trivial abuses of a head of agency circumnavigating to his destinations in the most roundabout way just to fatten his personal air miles account, yet the former actions are infinitely less visible in the absence of any oversight of organizational design than the petty abuses likely to be picked up by internal auditors.

One may therefore infer from the information available that the derailed design came to be clearly out of line with what the Simons conditions would suggest—that prototyping, serious play and experimentation were clearly sabotaged and social learning consequently stunted—and that tinkering with organization charts came to be used as a decoy to hide a deliberate effort to modify the philosophy of Service Canada away from its original vocation of serving Canadian citizens at large better, to the immensely reduced task of serving the integration of services of the Canadian federal government.

As to the question of what sort of organizational design might have succeeded in preventing such slippage, there is no simple and absolute answer. One may easily envisage a variety of schemes (independent agency, department, but also horizontal political mechanisms to bring clusters of ministers together, etc.) that would have ensured that the original direction would have been maintained. Therefore, a separate minister is not the only thinkable solution. The experience of various other countries has shown that a wide range of mechanisms may accomplish this sort of task (Roy and Langford 2008).

Conclusion

It is difficult to underestimate the toxic effect of organizational design failures (whether they are the result of passive or active sabotage) and as a result, it is difficult to overestimate the benefits that might flow from a greater attention to organizational design in the private, public and social sectors.

Yet this trail has not been as fully explored as it should have been, and much of what one might call *pathologies of governance* must be properly ascribed to these flaws. Such a possibility is all the more probable because of the fact that cumulative social learning on this front has turned out to be less effective than it should be. Design inquiry is so often left to practitioners and management consultants, that, as a result, "the body of design knowledge appears to be fragmented and dispersed"—much more so than in other bodies of knowledge (Romme 2003: 569). The time may be ripe for a revolution! As Chalmers Johnson would put it, "multiple dysfunctions plus elite intransigence cause revolution" (Johnson 1964: 22).

The question is: what should the revolution entail?

It might take three forms.

First, what is required is a better and fuller appreciation of the organizational design function, and the development of the required competencies to ensure that *ex ante* proper advice is sought and obtained about the sort of architecture required for effective performance. This applies both at the level of individual organization (e.g., department or agency) and centrally (e.g., the federal government as a whole).

It is mindless to ask intelligent and well-trained personnel to operate in organizational settings that can only lead them to be predictably irrational and therefore to render the organization dysfunctional.

Second, what is required is an oversight function 'in real time' to monitor organizational performance. This sort of *veille organisationnelle* and organizational vigilance (again both at the individual organization and 'central' levels) should be as important as the sort of monitoring that is in good currency for human and financial resources. It should not be an audit function that would best be performed *ex post* and might fall into the bailiwick of the Office of the Auditor-General, but as an activity designed to detect any sign of malfunctioning (as soon as possible), it being understood that organizational design is always somewhat experimental. Moreover, this *veille* should be of central import in social learning by highlighting successes that might deserve more attention and might lead to imitation elsewhere, by detecting early warning signals of problems so as to be able to draw attention to repairs before a crisis occurs, and by questioning organizational redesign that would appear to make no sense or worse still, be toxic.

Third, what is required is that the Office of the Auditor-General, instead of being allowed to creep into policy matters, be directed to pay more attention to organizational matters. This might lead to *ex post* in depth evaluation of major organizational disasters like the assignment of massive operational tasks to agencies having little or no operational experience and capability as seems to have happened in the gun registry file.

These three initiatives are also listed by order of priority, with the autopsy phase obviously being given a lesser priority in a world that emphasizes the importance of social learning.

These macroscopic changes cannot however replace the need to ensure that greater attention is paid in all departments and agencies to matters of organizational design and organizational performance. Nor can it replace the need to ensure, at the local level, that the requisite failsafe mechanisms are in place to ensure that blockages and sabotages are not allowed to prevail.

Anticipating that something awful may ensue from a flawed design is marvelous when one can, but it cannot suffice, because, capacity for anticipation is as problematic as capacity to design perfect apparatuses right from the start. One must accept the inevitability of prototyping and experimenting on this front, and work at ensuring that learning loops are going to be as short and fast as possible. Indeed, even this may be too optimistic. One may have to be satisfied to prevent harm.

Promoting good things and working at reducing bad things may look the same on the surface, but, at the operational level, they are quite different:

> [S]crutinizing the harms themselves, and discovering their dynamics and dependencies, leads to the possibility of sabotage. Cleverly conceived acts of sabotage, exploiting identified vulnerabilities of the object under attack, can be not only effective, but extremely resource-efficient too (Sparrow 2008: 27).

Preventing harm, experimenting, learning as fast as one can along the way would appear to be the best we can hope for. This is the only way to harness complexity. The word "harness" is quite apt here: it conveys "a perspective that is not explanatory but active—seeking to improve but without being able to fully control" (Axelrod and Cohen 2000: xvi). In the world of organizational design, it may be the only way to go.

Endnotes

1 unpan1.un.org/intradoc/groups/public/documents/UNPAN/ UNPAN023528.pdf [accessed August 6, 2008]. The federal investments were for: online service improvements (130 most-used services in 34 departments and agencies); strategic infrastructure (privacy protection including a secure channel); service improvements (service quality

and standards as well as obligatory measurement and improvements); communication and measurement; and public servants' readiness to make the highest and best use of these new channels.

2 K. Acheson and J. F. Chant 1973: 637–655. An earlier case (and a more juicy one) is exposed in Gordon, 1961. The personal costs borne by Gordon as a result of his drive to expose Coyne's misdemeanor is a cautionary tale; see chapter 5 of this book.

CHAPTER 12

Ombuds as Producers of Governance

Je laisse à d'autres le soin d'inquiéter, de terroriser et de continuer
de tout confondre.

—René Magritte

Preamble

This is a think piece. It is not meant to provide a definitive answer to the question of how justice will be ensured, how the role of ombuds and other less formal agents should evolve, and how ombudsing and other forms of less formal agents of justice might differ from place to place. On such matters, practitioners should have the final say. This paper aims only to provoke reflection on this question, with a view to breaking out of the box of conventional thinking.

The chapter deals with two separate problems: the need to broaden first, the concept of justice and second, the role of ombudsperson in this new territory.

The first part is an examination of the problem of access to justice in a world that is becoming more diverse, complex and turbulent. It has been argued explicitly in the last decade that the formal justice system may not serve the community well, and that a more distributed, multiple-access, and open-source system of justice should be put in place.

The second part argues for a more creative role for ombuds and for seeking to enlarge the portfolio of governance mechanisms by factoring in ombuds as producers of governance, and particularly important agents of the governance of justice through their mediation work.

The judgment of wider courts

The expression 'wider courts' may not be elegant, but it serves to draw attention to the fact that the notion of access to justice does not connote only access to the courts and to the formal legal apparatus. The problem was raised in the year 2000 in a symposium organized by Justice Canada entitled, "Expanding Horizons: Rethinking Access to Justice in Canada", an invitation by the legal establishment to use lateral thinking in developing strategies for better ways to provide access to justice for Canadians.

At that Justice Canada meeting, many experts acknowledged the acuteness of the problem: a 'message of anxiety' on the part of Justice Turpel-Lafond with regard to the way the justice system treats Aboriginal groups; a 'message of disconnection' between the formal system of lawyers and courts, and the real living law of everyday interaction from Roderick Macdonald, and a plea for more opportunities for citizens to participate more fully in the lawmaking process; and a 'message of denunciation' by philosopher Jacques Dufresne, who claimed that the formal judicial institution, the fortress, is "preventing the normal carrying out of justice, as well as being the source of injustice because of the lack of preventive justice, and who argued for a *justice douce*" (Paquet 2000).

Whether what is needed is more prevention, better connection, or more restorative justice or something else, it was noted that there were already alternative processes providing justice outside the formal system, and there was a need for more of them, and of a more ambitious sort.

419

New mechanisms for a paradoxical world

The search for new mechanisms for access to justice has emerged from the diversity of contexts, principles and circumstances. But if one-size-fits-all would appear not to be satisfactory, it has been felt that there is a need (in the name of fairness) for some agreement on some 'basic principles'—a sort of *Magna Carta*— that would guide the exploration and the shape of new initiatives, and some focus on *"local justice"*—an effort to work at the level of the different groups, disputes, issues, etc. where one can expect to fine-tune better practices, rather than through broad-ranging accords (Elster 1992).

Finding workable arrangements may not be easy in our paradoxical world (L. L. Fuller 2001).

Two paradoxes need to be resolved:
(1) the one pitting local justice against substantive equality; and
(2) the one pitting inclusion and participation in the justice process against representative democracy.

'Equal but different' would appear to be the foundation of the new flexible system based on local justice and the acceptance that there might be various windows giving access to justice. The way to resolve these paradoxes is an agreement on principles at the meta-level: general principles defining the corridor of acceptable differences and permissible variety. This is a challenge for jurists to generate such foundational meta-solutions.

The inclusion of the citizen more directly upstream through alternative avenues to the formal legal process or downstream in the case of restorative law indeed challenges the democratic method of choosing officials and allowing them to take decisions for the collectivity. These new ways short-circuit what is regarded as due process, and can be seen as derailing normal ways. As a result, this will require a major re-interpretation of the very notion of representative democracy, and represents another significant challenge for jurists.

In the short run, nothing less than a *Magna Carta* of basic principles will be required as a guide to the necessary exploration: what the corridor of permissible variations is within the corridor of justice. What is also required is much more experimentation and a better knowledge of what has worked or not.

In the longer run, first, what one might hope for is a refurbishment of our philosophy of justice that might well be rooted in what Amartya Sen has put at the centre of the whole process of social, economic and political development—the freedom from different servitudes or the elimination of 'unfreedoms' due to the lack of political margins of maneuverability, of social opportunities, of economic possibilities, and of transparency and security guarantees. Second, one has to strive for the establishment of a "distributed and open-source justice system"—a system where justice is available in a variety of forms, from a variety of sources, and through a variety of channels so as to ensure the citizen true access to justice (Sen 1999).

But this cannot be tackled at a general level. Too many forces of dynamic conservatism are at work to maintain the *status quo*. The problem must be tackled in an experimental way by developing segmented experiments using existing tools or instruments that are promising but have been under-used and under-developed. This is the road of least resistance: experimentation in many loci according to different ways of widening the 'existing courts' through experimentation designed not only to open new trails but to establish new ways of producing governance. One such front that is among the most promising is the 'burden of office' of ombudspersons as producers of governance.

Ombuds as producers of governance

Fifty years ago, the very word ombudsman and the institution attached to it meant nothing to most people outside of Scandinavia. Now it is common currency in some one hundred countries. The main reason for this phenomenal growth has been the growth of big government, and the consequent need for someone to protect the citizen from any unfair decisions of 'Big G' government. The same rationale has been generalized to the private and social sectors, where potentates were also felt to require a watchdog. Ombudsing activities have contributed significantly to remedying the damages caused by the abusive powers of agents of these diverse potentates.

But in recent times, the context has changed: decentralized organizations have become the new world of work, so governing systems have become more complex, and the problems of coordination more 'wicked'. Most issues faced by citizens are now the results of a multiplicity of interwoven multi-sectoral forces, agents, groups and organizations more or less consciously shaping the context in concert (Gregory and Giddings 2000). We have moved in all sectors from 'Big G' government to 'small g' governance—from a world of command-and-control to a world of coordinate-and-cultivate (Paquet 1999a, 2005a; Malone 2004).

The crucial question has to do with the changing role of the ombudsperson in this new world: that is, a world where no one is completely in charge; where abuse emerges not from a single source but from a constellation of actors from all sectors, each of whom have a piece of the information, of the power and of the resources; where the source of abuse is diffuse, polycentric and may be systemic; where consensus is often unattainable; where conflict resolution can only be arrived at by creative compromise, negotiation and organization redesign; where issues need clarification, bargaining needs to be more effective, and new arrangements need to be experimented and played with; and when the modern democratic ethos seems to encourage failure to confront and political correctness, and therefore to discourage creative conflict, at a time when creative conflict resolution is becoming crucially important in our bargaining society (Johansen 1979).

Our argument is that, in this new context where there are multiple principals and multiple right-holders (Grandori 2004), it is no longer sufficient for the ombuds to act as a shield: to assuage individual mistreatments, and to try to poke at elusive scapegoats.

One must also, and more importantly, work to attenuate the malefits of what can only be called systemic governance failures caused by multiple forces by dealing explicitly with their systemic sources. This does not reduce the importance of protecting widows and orphans, and of ensuring that individual wounds are taken care of, but it underlines that the burden of office of ombuds goes beyond these duties. What is required is the capacity to detect governance flaws at the origin of these mishaps, and to help launch the process that will ensure that the governance apparatus will be appropriately repaired. The trigger may still be personal damage and complaints, but the answer can no longer be only personal reparation; it must also entail eliciting what might be a plausible and reasonable appreciation of the nature of the dysfunction, and some promising organizational redesign and architectural repairs to the governance apparatus.

The independence, accessibility, informality, cheapness and speed of the ombudsing process, together with the powers of investigation (inquiry may be a better word), and some form of statutory base of operation—all these features make ombudsing better suited to appreciate the new fluid realities, and better prepared to deal with governance failures than the more traditional legal (more rigid) and political (less reliable) processes. This explains why the ombudsing process would appear to be an instrument of choice in the 'small g' governance world.

But all institutions are mortgaged to their past. Righting the wrongs done to citizens by public authorities or by other potentates through obtaining reparation, case by case, by way of meek interventions, has long been the main focus of ombuds' activities. This may explain why (at least, it is our contention as an external observer from the mezzanine), in general, the ombuds have often been slow—like other official corps—to recognize the shift from 'Big G' to 'small g', and therefore have failed, in many cases, to acknowledge the new important challenges facing them (like becoming a producer of governance), and have not taken the necessary steps to transform the nature of their capabilities, practice and culture so as to prepare them to perform such a task well (Paquet 2007c).

In the rest of this chapter, we will first sketch the features of the new environment faced by ombuds, underline the new importance of the pathologies of governance at the root of the mishaps they observe daily, surmise that there have been costs attached to the reluctance to delve into these pathologies as forcefully as one might like, and reflect on the inefficiency of the ombuds process as a result of it. Second, because this state of affairs suggests that some effort at reinventing the burden of office of ombuds is in order, we propose what needs to be done and in what way, in aid of making bargaining less inefficient, rationality more ecological, and experimentation more likely. We argue furthermore that this is a road worth travelling. Some guideposts for this voyage are provided.

'Fragmegration'

We live in an era when the ground is in motion, and ongoing interacting economic, financial, technological, social, political and legal change is the key driver. Turbulence is the outcome of this mix of interacting transformational forces. Rosenau has proposed a label to convey the basic nature of this new epoch, "fragmegration". It draws attention to the joint dynamics of centralization and decentralization, of localizing and globalizing, of fragmentation and integration, that are unleashed in this new world (Rosenau 2003).

Networked ecologies of governance

This is an era of organization-breaking, of weak and failed states, of distributed stewardship: the nation-state and other potentates are losing their dominance. This does not mean that nations disappear or states vanish. But rather that the state is less prominent, and is called upon to play some new, different, and somewhat attenuated roles. Organizational refurbishing is therefore most important (Fukuyama 2004). The institutional tsunami in progress has not yet, however, fully revealed its outcome—the shape of the new type of public sector *en émergence*, for instance.

One thing is certain, however: the boundaries between the private, public and social (civic) spheres—that have never been well-defined either conceptually or statistically—do not correspond to a rigid frontier. In the world of governance, they are becoming a wavering and evolving zone of fracture between subsets of organizations and institutions that are characterized by different integrating mechanisms (Paquet 1996–97). Power, resources, and information are being distributed increasingly widely throughout the terrain of private, public and civic organizations. One of the main challenges for societal governance is to engineer the requisite coordination through "networked ecologies of governance" (Paquet 1995).

This new fluid institutional reality is made up of three generic ensembles of organizations, dominated by different integrating mechanisms—*quid pro quo* exchange (market economy), coercion (polity), and gift or solidarity or reciprocity (community and society). Kenneth Boulding used a simple triangle as a mapping device—with each of these families of integrating mechanisms in its purest form at one of the apexes, and all the inner territory representing organizations and institutions embodying different mixes of these integrative mechanisms (Boulding 1970).

There has been a tendency for the new socio-economy to trigger the development of an ever larger number of 'mixed' institutions, blending these different mechanisms to some extent (e.g., market-based public regulation, public-private-social partnering, corporate social responsibility etc.) in order to provide the necessary signposts and orientation maps in a new confused and confusing world. This has translated into a much denser filling of the Boulding triangle: mixed institutions capable of providing the basis for mediation, cooperation, harmonization, *concertation*, and even co-decisions involving agents or organizations from the three sectors (Laurent and Paquet 1998). One can stylize this development via a series of emerging concentric circles within which there are different degrees of "institutional and organizational métissage" (Hubbard and Paquet 2002). This is depicted in figure 12.1.

Figure 12.1   *The adapted Boulding triangle*

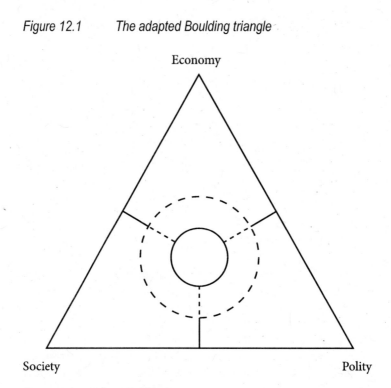

Economy

Society   Polity

Source: Adapted from Boulding 1970.

At any one time, a more or less integrated governance pattern coheres people, architecture, routines and cultures into an arrangement that generates good performance. Such a coherent pattern is rarely unique and permanent as circumstances evolve. Two centrally important characteristics of this process of co-evolution (of the system and its environment) and joint evolution (economy, society, polity) are 'resilience' (the capacity for the economy-polity-society nexus to spring back undamaged from the pressure or shock emerging from the environment, through some slight rearrangements that do not modify the nature of the overall system), and 'learning' (the capacity to improve current performance, as a result of experience, through a redefinition of the overall objectives; and a modification of behaviour and structures as a result of new circumstances).

These characteristics are in creative tension, since resilience calls for preservation, while learning means change. They must be kept in balance. Managing this tension well demands a capacity to switch to a greater or lesser dependence on one family of integrative mechanisms or another as circumstances change. To cope with an environment that is turbulent and generates surprises, organizations and societies must use their environment strategically in much the same way as the surfer uses the wave to adapt more quickly. This calls for non-centralization for two reasons.

First, because the game of learning is going to generate more innovation, if component parts of a system, when confronted with local challenges, are empowered to take decisions on the spot (Naisbitt 1994). In fact, the best learning experience in this kind of world can be effected through highly decentralized and flexible teams, woven by moral contracts and reciprocal obligations, negotiated in the context of evolving partnerships (Lester and Piore 2004).

Second, because, faced with this type of turbulent environment, organizations can only govern themselves effectively by experimenting, by becoming capable of learning both what their goals are, and the means to reach them *as they proceed*. To do so, everyone must take part in the 'conversation', and bring forward each bit of knowledge and wisdom that each person has, that has a bearing on the issue (Piore 1995).

This is a world in which creative mediation is required, not only to do remedial work for the maligned party, but ever more importantly to contribute creatively to identifying the coordination failures at the core of the governance mishaps, and to suggest the sort of organization redesign necessary to prevent such occurrences. The ombuds is ideally located to do this work and to become a genuine producer of governance.

Coordination: the optimal amount of confrontation is not zero

The passage from a command-and-control, hierarchical, someone-in-charge pattern of governance to a more horizontal, collaborative no-one-fully-in-charge pattern obviously entails major coordination challenges. Governance is often defined as effective coordination when power, resources and information are vastly distributed in many different hands.

While there has been a tendency to search for coordination through shared values and consensus, and to presume that such conciliation might emerge by 'immaculate conception', this is a somewhat naive and romantic point of view. Effective coordination does not emerge organically or without tension, except in some rare cases. Most of the time, agents and groups have quite different views of the good, and one cannot avoid confrontation in the process of mediation. Indeed, confrontation is a healthy first step in any process of change, and a steady diet of conflicts somewhat happily resolved is more likely to generate trust and better coordination (Hirschman 1995) than the distillation of *consensus mous* (i.e., vague and empty agreements).

This latter route, *consensus mous,* built on a congenital failure to confront, is most likely to generate resentment, misunderstanding and frustration, and to destroy the social capital of trust. One may easily presume that there is something like a quantity theory of angst in any organization or social system (in the way Will Self suggested that there is a quantity theory of insanity in them (Self 1991), and that if one suppresses much of it in the open, it is bound to re-emerge in other loci of the organization. So there is a great danger that, in failing to confront as a result of excessive civility or political correctness, ombuds may simply shift the problem to elsewhere in the organization.

A long tradition of soft mediation, however, has made confrontation somewhat unnatural for many ombuds. Indeed, there has even been a palpable culture of fear to confront, and a reluctance to proceed confrontationally with inquiries (a Deweyan word much preferable to the police-sounding word 'investigations') aiming at revealing unwarranted assumptions, reprehensible routines, and deep-rooted dysfunctions of organizations.

It is easy to understand why people fear to confront. One naturally fears rejection, ridicule, or potential embarrassment. Indeed, there is a social stigma attached to bullies, or persons regarded as rude, because, like Erasmus, they dare to call a fig a fig and a spade a spade. And this fear to confront is bound to grow when confrontation in a governance context is tantamount to a questioning of many of the parties responsible for or connected with the organizational dysfunction, and not just one.

The result of this failure to confront is more often than not a degeneracy of the inquiry into an irrational commitment to find a 'quiet resolution at all costs', and the consequent development of *langue de bois* and *langue de cotton*—meaningless discourses aimed at making the problem disappear rather than trying to identify its source clearly, and dealing with it frontally.

Failure to confront entails some form of complicity with and encouragement of improprieties and it is quite destructive. It ensures that bad situations endure, and that social learning is stunted. It might be defended as expedient in terms of costs of transaction in the short term, but the opportunity costs of such an approach in the long run are enormous, because it allows the root causes of the mishaps to remain unrevealed and the governance repairs left undone. In a social context where political correctness has become a new civic religion, meek ombudsmanship lacks an appetite to proceed beyond the surface issues to the roots of the problems.

Inefficiency of bargaining

Underlining the crucial importance of conflict does not deny that conflict needs to be contained and resolved if it is to generate social learning. This can be done in various ways. But to contain and resolve conflicts, one must understand—as Geoffrey Vickers so aptly says—that "human conflict is an exercise in communication" (Vickers 1973: 146). The challenge is therefore to find the conditions, which favour dialogue and deliberation if we want resolution and containment of conflict.

It is naive to hope that such containment will arise as a mechanical result of the restraints and assurances of membership: as the result of an objective appreciation of the common situation, of an objective assessment of the expectations of others, and of an objective gauge of what individuals have learned to expect of themselves as members of the organization or society. This postulates an unbounded omniscience and a pattern of loyalty and mutual trust among the disputants that are unlikely to materialize in a world where not all disputants are hyper-rational, and where they have different notions of the good, and multiple incompatible loyalties (Ibid., 148).

This explains the temptation to confront the issues head on (when one is forced to) by mimicking the game playing of the courts, and it is equally naive. Wallowing in the futile search for a wholly unattainable consensus, on the basis of hard juridical principles, simply kills the urge to craft creative political compromises in response to conflicts at the very time when such creative ombudsing is what is needed.

As Frank Ankersmit put it:

> ...much if not all that is, (from a political point of view) new, unexpected, unforeseen, and unforeseeable will initially present itself in terms of interests not in terms of rights and legal cases. Sometimes it is only thanks to the existence of conflicts that we may become aware that something is awry and needs to be remedied (Ankersmit 2002: 43).

The search for "compromises stimulates political creativity, consensus kills it" (Ibid., 39). So, provocatively, Ankersmit argues for "principled unprincipledness" as a way to achieve peaceful coexistence in a society deeply divided on principles (Ibid., 28). Ankersmit's discussion is consequential for ombuds for it debunks the seductiveness of the juridical model: he reminds his readers that a society attempting to settle, juridically, issues that are essentially political "may be expected to blind itself to its most urgent problems" (Ibid., 43).

The inescapable road between the equally dead-endish organic emergence of consensus and juridical adjudication is bargaining. In the new world of 'small g' governance, there has been an increasing role for bargaining. But bargaining as a process is particularly diffuse, unstructured and inefficient, as a result of "the lack of convincing equilibrium solutions and...the incentives concerning the presentation of claims and the exploitation of power positions" (Johansen 1979: 515). There is always imperfect information, and incentives to supply biased information. So bargaining is often an inefficient procedure that wastes resources in the process, and fails to realize the potential gains (Ibid., 519). Ombuds can do a lot to attenuate this governance failure.

The ensuing challenges for the ombuds: some hypothetical ways forward

Ombudsmanship is an old and venerable profession, and over the last few centuries it has been value-adding. But in the new 'small g' world, the reduction of the burden of office of ombuds to curative personalized case work or to quasi-juridical adjudication, can only lead to a trivialization of the ombuds' work through becoming either: (1) totally ineffective as a mediation process, and incapable of creatively eradicating the sources of mishaps or even being interested in doing so; or (2) a mechanical process not unlike human rights commissions—claiming to speak for those who cannot speak for themselves but *de facto* agreeing to become the uncritical defenders of the indefensible by accepting all claims as equally valid, putting them in a garb of rights, and as a result, becoming the source of problems rather than of solutions.

In both cases, the credibility of the ombuds is under threat.

The only way out of this quandary is to employ greater depth in the inquiry process: accepting the need to tackle the issues *revealed* by the cases head on with an explicit intention to unearth and expose the source of the problem, and to become the architect of better governance arrangements capable of eradicating the causes of the difficulties.

What needs to be done

This entails the ombuds becoming less passive and more active, more of an *animateur* than a moderator, a master of critical thinking, yearning to smoke out the symptoms of dysfunction and capable of tracking down their sources and causes in a confrontational way if necessary. The core concern of ombuds should be to force both the plaintiff and the organization to face assumptions they may not be aware they are making, to contribute, through the ombudsing process, to the emergence of a *super-vision* (Innerarity 2006: 194) that defines and clarifies the nature of the problem in a manner that makes all parties see things that they are unwilling or unable to see by themselves— thereby teaching both the plaintiff and the organization the value of conflict.

To do so requires the ombuds to be troublemakers, persons who from the very beginning ask permission to confront, and are allowed to scheme virtuously in order to help the organization evolve (Paquet 2009a). This is the only way for ombuds to avoid being totally absorbed in the particular complaint and its idiosyncrasies, and to get at the core of the underlying issues— what one might regard as the nature of 'what the complaint reveals'. This *révélateur* dimension is what should guide the inquiry.

It might reveal nothing more than the emptiness of the charge against the organization: the misconception of a misguided complainant who has confused his/her preferences with a right or a wrong. But it may also reveal a major flaw in the governance of the organization. This revelatory work requires confronting both parties in order to generate an escape from the mental prisons that prevent both parties from seeing the issue in its totality.

Such bringing forth of a new awareness and a new frame of reference is unlikely to emerge without much critical thinking and some confrontation. Indeed, if mediation were to ban such confrontation, it would flounder and (most of the time) be incapable of accomplishing anything but myopic and expedient obfuscation—even if the parties were happy with it. In a culture and ethos that loathes confrontation and discourages it, ombudsmanship may find it difficult to generate this sort of value-added. But if it is not done however, the usefulness of the ombuds is certainly likely to be questioned.

In what way

It is quite presumptuous for laypeople to suggest to professionals how to do their work. So it should be clear that this is not what is intended here. Our intent is only to draw attention to 'the perils of focusing on the particulars of cases, without an appreciation of the context'. One can become absorbed in the minutiae and details of the idiosyncratic event, as in a black hole. Escaping from this black hole is the central challenge. This can only be accomplished by bringing both the future and the past to bear on the issue: the shadow of the future impact of the sort of resolution of the issue under consideration, and the forces of inertia buried in the history of the organization that must be considered to understand what the 'real' and fundamental sources of the difficulties have been.

This is difficult work.

On the prospective side, one wants to ensure that the future is not merrily discounted as pliable, the future impact of the impending decision being disregarded in an irresponsible way. *Catastrophisme éclairé* is the name given by Jean-Pierre Dupuy to the effort to escape from this myopic and triumphalist belief that any unfortunate future consequence can be ignored because it can be corrected in due time (Dupuy 2002). Making the consequences of an impending decision stark and inexorable has an extraordinarily sound impact on the generation of the *super-vision*.

On the retrospective side, one must decipher how some inexorability has become grafted onto the organization's experience. What one is after is an historical comprehension of the dynamics of the situation. This calls for a process of reconstruction of the past that has been illustrated by Jean-Marc Ferry using a novel by Arturo Pèrez-Reverte (*The Flanders Panel*). This novel is developed around a painting showing a seigneur and a knight playing chess in full view of the chessboard—a painting produced two years after the death of the knight—on which the painter has inscribed "Who has taken the knight?" A restoration artist secures the help of a chess master to reconstruct to game from the positions of the pieces on the board in the painting. Through a process of elimination of impossible moves, the chess master logically reconstructs the game, and comes to the conclusion that the black queen has taken the knight (Ferry 1996).

This dual operation—making the inexorabilities of the future more visible, and of reconstructing the processes that have generated the crisis—is crucial if one is to identify what is centrally important for the issue to be resolved and what it requires in terms of modification to the governance arrangements.

In aid of what? Efficient bargaining, ecological rationality and experimentalism

The new turbulent context and the new world of work generate a need for evolving arrangements if collaborative governance is to succeed. But such arrangements are unlikely to emerge unless:

(1) the inefficiency of bargaining is corrected;
(2) some standards of ecological rationality (reasonableness, speed, specifics of the domain and matching the context) are ensured in the deliberations carried out; and
(3) the requisite amount of experimentation is initiated and underwritten, by agents like ombuds who have the opportunity and the capacity to do so.

The ombuds are, through inquiries, able to correct the problems of incomplete and distorted information, of escalation of threats and the like. Indeed, this is one of his/her fundamental contributions to the development of the *super-vision* that will allow all parties to see things they could not or would not see by themselves.

The ombuds are also, through mediation and negotiation, able to guide the process of discussion, not with the view of finding the 'optimal' general solution to domain-general problems, but rather of arriving at a plausible domain-specific resolution that meets the minimal requirements of both passing the test of reasonableness and matching the circumstances and environment.

At the risk of hurting the sensitivity of ombuds, we would compare them (using an analogy proposed by Gerd Gigerenzer to explain ecological rationality) to the backwoods mechanic who:

> has no general-purpose tool nor all spare parts available to him. He must fiddle with various imperfect and short-range tools, a process known as 'vicarious functioning'...He will have to try one thing, and if it does not work, another one, and with step-by-step adjustments will produce serviceable solutions to almost any problem with just the things at hand (Gigerenzer 2001: 43).

In so doing, the ombuds have ample opportunities to experiment. Their mandates vary considerably, and often remain relatively more fluid and open than those of other organizational agents. At the same time, their function has both moral authority and legitimacy, and office holders like these are held in high social esteem. The office and office holders are also better equipped than most other officials to inquire in a bold fashion, and to suggest creative ways of dealing with the issues at hand. This is immensely more promising than the two alternative avenues that have tended to be in good currency of late: quasi-judiciarization and empty talks aimed at problem-elimination.

As we have hinted at earlier, ombuds have much to lose by becoming too closely associated with the formal justice system, and its propensity to fall into the Manichean habit of seeing everything in black and white, in terms of guilt or innocence, and not at all in terms of organizational redesign and social architecture. Equally the role has much to lose by becoming known as the locus, where problems are simply dissolved, made to disappear, and/or drowned in a sea of talk.

The third way between judiciarizing on the one hand and sanitizing palavers on the other focuses on the exploitation of the reconstructive work as a launching pad for the exploration of novel solutions by experimentation: prudent new ways to experiment with new collaborative mechanisms, and to improve the capacity for social learning. This calls for the ombuds to play a key role in smoothing the process of collaborative governance through:

(1) the bringing forth of contingent moral contracts as a way of making the relationships involved in collaborative governance less intangible; and

(2) the learning-by-doing and doing-by-learning through which these moral contracts are continually modified as problem-handling reveals the need to do so.

Ombudsing is the business of generating collaborative governance. Collaboration is always contingent: it is built on the tentative premise 'I will if you will', and it does not crystallize instantaneously—it develops in stages. After a period of frustration, when it becomes obvious that one cannot do whatever has to be done alone, a period of experimentation driven by cost-benefit considerations becomes possible. In the second stage, building relations and close monitoring are the order of the day; tentative examination of joint action take place. In the third stage, increased confidence prevails, organizational memory is built, and the possibility of extending the scope of collaboration is envisaged. Demanding formal arrangements prematurely kills confidence. What is required is the development of loose, flexible and non-legally-enforceable instruments in the nature of moral contracts (e.g., memoranda of understanding, and the like).

These modifiable moral contracts (Paquet 1992) serve many purposes. First, they embody some mechanisms of coordination, some bases for defining agreed-upon representations, some grounds for justification, and some elements to help shape interpretation when some is needed. Second, they serve as a way to anchor, ever so loosely, the basis for monitoring and sanctioning as a foundation for social learning.

Moral contracts and conventions are deliberately elusive and flexible because they need both to serve as guideposts only as long as certain circumstances prevail, and to evolve as circumstances change. They make for reflexive governance—governance that constantly calls into question its own foundations in the light of changing circumstances, triggers constant problem re-definition as experience is accumulated, and even a re-configuration of the very approach to governance. This kind of governance does not pertain only to the process of self-steering, self-regulation, or self-organization, but it aims at disclosing the process of continual self-renewal and self-creation of the organization (Voβ et al 2006: 4; Paquet 2005b: chapter V; Paquet 2009a).

By what means? Prototyping and serious play

This is obviously a risky operation as one is entering *terra incognita*, but it would appear to be a risk worth taking, because it provides mediation with a creative and forward-looking edge.

For the time being, there is a vacuum in the whole area of organizational design: little time is spent on it, and, when it is done, it is often a job performed with extraordinary incompetence because of the poor understanding of the process of prototyping, and serious play with prototypes that are at the core of social learning (Paquet 2007c).

The ombuds accumulates a great deal of experience through the normal activities of responding to complaints, probing different terrains, and experiencing dysfunctions of different sorts. It is possible, through such experience (and those of colleagues worldwide) to identify the characteristics of various issue-domains, of the different communities of meaning or communities of fate (i.e., assemblages of people united in their common concern for shared problems, or a shared passion for a topic or set of issues). This is enough to develop a capacity to come up with idiosyncratic workable prototypes to deal with new situations at hand.

A general template likely to be of use across the board may not be available yet, but it does not mean that a workable one cannot be elicited in the face of precise issues (Sabel 2001, 2004).

As we mentioned earlier—but it is worth repeating—prototyping would appear to be the main activity underpinning social learning:

- identifying some top requirements as quickly as possible;
- putting in place a provisional medium of co-development;
- allowing as many interested parties as possible to get involved as partners in improving the arrangement;
- encouraging iterative prototyping; and
- thereby encouraging all, through serious play with prototypes, to get a better understanding of the problems, of their priorities, and of themselves (Schrage 2000: 199ff).

The purpose of the exercise is to create a dialogue (creative interaction) between people and prototypes. This may be more important than creating a dialogue between people alone. It is predicated on a culture of active participation that would need to be nurtured. The sort of playfulness and adventure that is required for serious play with prototypes is essential for the process to succeed (March 1988; Paquet 2009b: 159ff).

One should not underestimate nevertheless, the great deal of reluctance to experiment, to innovate, and to play with prototypes that inhabits most organizations and institutions. Most organizations have considerable capital invested in routine: any transformation is bound to expropriate the privileged positions or advantages of a number of parties. As a result, change is too often seen as a zero-sum game, where everyone presumes that the only possible gains will be to the detriment of other parties. It is easy to understand as a result, why the dice are loaded against change. Very often the potential gains as a result of change remain only potentialities, while the losses are mostly obvious and measurable. What is required is for ombuds to become agents dedicated to breaking out of this mental prison, and to transform the view of change from a zero-sum game into a positive-sum one.

This opens the way to collaborative exploration and, through experimentalism, rekindles a new form of dynamic solidarity and the emergence of "experimentalist accountability" (Sabel 2001: 142), through mechanisms of performance monitoring, comparative benchmarking, the pooled experiences of diverse and often rivalrous groups, and practical deliberations focused on the need to respond to urgent problems that call for the mobilizing of some discovery procedure (Ibid.).

Conclusion

For the wide-ranging family of ombuds around the world (from the one-person office already under threat, to well-established offices with a robust mandate), this invitation to subversion, and to the production of governance, is bound to be received quite differently. Some will gauge the gamble too ambitious and dangerous; others will simply state that they are already engaged in this sort of business. Our suggestions are threatening to some and superfluous to others. The central reason for arguing in favour of such action by ombuds at this time is that there is a lack of agents of change engaged in such work in the new world of 'small g' governance. There is also a goodness of fit between the ombuds and this sort of job.

This shift of the profession's centre of gravity very carefully for, without adequate preparation, an overly aggressive stance or an imprudent incursion into this new realm of activities, could be disastrous.

The charge must be led by the more robust agencies, after careful development of their capacities as social engineers. Following that, the executive development activities, and the R&D of the professional bodies of ombuds must be altered in such a way as to help the smaller offices to gain enough capacity to enter this realm of activities with some confidence. Finally, there must be a broad-based communications strategy to prepare partners and clients to accept this broader role. In particular, there will be a need to explain that this in no way threatens the conventional role of ombuds, but rather, bolsters and strengthens it by providing much additional value-added.

The Forum of Canadian Ombudsman could provide the basis for the cumulative collective intelligence and collective memory that is bound to emerge from these experiments: the experiments recorded, and their success or failures acknowledged. This would soon help all ombuds to have access to a pool of innovative experimental technologies of collaboration that have been prototyped and played with around the globe. Not all of those experiments will be exportable outside of their cultural ethos, but the very process of sharing knowledge about these experiments should inspire imaginative playing with prototypes experimented with elsewhere. In practice, humans learn by refining and extending prototypes: a child learns the word bird (by being exposed, say, to a robin) and learns to identify other non-prototypical birds by adding flats and sharps to the basic prototype. In the same way, organizational design prototypes may be imaginatively extended to be of use in quite different and changing *milieux* (M. Johnson 1993; Paquet 2005a: chapter VII).

This transubstantiation of the ombuds entails nothing less than a change in paradigm. Consequently, it is bound to require a revolution in the mind of practitioners: what is proposed is a change in the nature of the ombudsing business as fundamental as the revolution that carried biology from the time when animals were classified by the number of legs, to the world of DNA. For biology, this transition took a long time; in the case of ombuds, what is proposed is that it be attempted in one generation, that is, a few decades.

For governance aficionados, the game is worth the candle. It remains to be seen if professional ombuds will agree.

Some may regard this sort of facilitation and education mission on the road to collaborative governance as a mission impossible. They have a point. Sigmund Freud used to say that there were three impossible professions: to educate, to cure, and to govern, because they require the collaboration, and the complicity of those who are supposed to be on the receiving end of the professional work. One cannot educate without explaining, cure by simple application of recipes, or govern by decree. It can only work as processes of co-production (Innerarity 2006: 193).

Ombuds nevertheless, have no choice.

Ombudsing is clearly also an impossible profession. Its contribution to collaborative governance cannot be anything less than accompanying the participants in a process of discovery in which they might be able to conjure up new perspectives and identify directions that they were unable to see before. This professional work must start, as Saul Alinsky put it, from where the world is, as it is, not as we would like it to be, working inside the system, getting people to "let go of the past and chance the future", and take a new step. This must happen notwithstanding the difficulty that this is likely to represent—as Alinsky observed— "Dostoevsky said that taking a new step is what people fear most" (Alinsky 1972: xix).

Governance and Beyond

If you only have a hammer, everything looks like a nail.

—Anon

The two authors of this book have spent *in toto* some fifty years, directly and indirectly, working in and on public administration. This should amount to sufficient evidence of our commitment to the public household. So our indictment of the poverty of public administration at the federal level in Canada should not be interpreted as a facile mockery or a form of treason. Our intent has been to draw attention to important governance challenges unmet as well as to some provisional diagnoses about the sources of the present difficulties.

Our somewhat stark overall diagnosis has been arrived at in four stages.

First, we have briefly sketched the forces that have led to a general transformation of the public administration enterprise over the last while:

(1) the drift from 'Big G' government to 'small g' governance;

(2) the concurrent transformation of government from G_1 processes emphasizing reliability, to G_2 processes emphasizing innovation; and

442

(3) the ways in which the realities of public administration have slowly been perverted by a process of fictionalization of real politico-administrative processes, and then of enforcement of those fictions that has driven public administrators to engage a large portion of their energies in responding to the demands of an artificial, self-centered administrative apparatus rather than focusing on meeting real societal demands and needs.

Second, we have provided a broad historical sketch of the evolution of the spirit of public administration at the federal level in Canada, and a conceptual framework to help probe the more recent evolution of the public administration apparatus in the direction of a more open-source, inclusive, collaborative and autopoietic system.

The underlying trends ('Big G' to 'small g', G_1 to G_2, the evolution of the relationships between politicians and bureaucrats, decentralization, movement toward open-source federalism, etc.) were acknowledged, along the way, as having been bucked by a formidable dynamic conservatism on the part of both academics and practitioners (including taking refuge in the dialectics between reality and fiction) that has not stalled these processes completely, but has slowed them down significantly.

Third, we have reviewed a variety of pathologies that have ensued. Some of the illustrations were obtained from direct conversations with senior executives of the Canadian federal public service over the last few years; others were revealed by the study of certain policy files. The array of bad habits that appeared to have come to be in good currency would be sufficient to trigger concern. The policy files examined have shown that those bad habits have translated into pathologies of governance. These vignettes re-enforced the plausibility of our black hole analogy.

Fourth, we have reviewed a number of recent files where governance failures had been noted. The issue-domains dealt with remain somewhat selective, but our probing has provided not only damaging evidence about the current state of affairs, but also some suggestions about potential repairs. So the black hole exists, but all is not doomed.

Canadian public administration seems to be in distress, but this has not stopped the bulk of the administrative machine continuing to provide basic services reasonably well for now. Indeed, this is the good news: the routine functions of public administration acting as a kind of 'organic automatic pilot' have continued to provide services in a reasonable way overall. What has failed to a significant extent is action that would appear to require agency, as when the automatic pilot must be shut down, and human piloting is required anew. These latter functions depend a good deal on effective political-bureaucratic collaboration, and are showing signs of strain. The negative echo effect on regulation and service delivery is also beginning to be visible.

We hinted, in passing, earlier in this volume at some initiatives that would appear to deserve some attention. In the rest of the conclusion, acknowledging that any system is a mix of theory, structure and technology (*à la* Schön), we identify the broad directions of the general strategy of repairs that would appear to be needed at these three levels, if the growth of the black hole is to be stunted.

At the philosophical level

Chapter 2 has suggested that what is required is nothing less than a revolution in our belief systems, in our philosophy of governance, and in our notion of what business the federal public administration apparatus is in. For the time being the Canadian public administration is paralyzed by mental prisons and the idolatry of too many sacred cows. These 'boxed-in perspectives' (Westminster, egalitarianism, etc.) prevent the 'system' from even envisaging alternative avenues because of a self-imposed prohibition against indulging in any critical thinking about too many of these assumptions about our governance system.

Two of the most important elements in this panoply of taboos are the refusal to question the assumption of the immaculate conception of the public service and the presumption that misalignment between the priorities of the legitimately elected officials and the interests (personal or tribal) of the public servants is a logical impossibility in Ottawa.

As a result, the sheer invocation of iconic Westminster has, for generations, been used to prevent any serious discussion of the need to work actively at reconciling the dual legitimacies of the elected official and the expert bureaucrats. Assuming naively that no misalignment is possible has allowed the development of a most extraordinary chasm between this fiction and reality, and therefore has increased the possibility of much disloyalty being experienced. Bureaucratic disloyalty, while being sanctimoniously denied, has developed to the point where it is, at times, self-righteously celebrated in the open by individuals in the managerial class (and by their academic and media acolytes) as a welcome corrective to the wishes of elected officials who have come to be regarded in certain quarters as unreliable (and even illegitimate) definers of the public interest.

The fact that, in certain files, the public administration apparatus has been able to sabotage efforts to better serve the public (when it threatened to weaken its own dominium and its hold on centralized power), as we showed in chapter 10, is a cautionary tale, and an indication of the extent to which the Westminster system may have been turned on its head.

The self-interested motivations of the managerial class as well as its claim at times to be a more reliable interpreter of the public interest than elected politicians, have come to raise even more serious questions as a result of recent developments showing senior federal civil servants clearly associating themselves with political parties rather than with governments, and their junior colleagues following suit through the politicization of their unions.

This maelstrom is in need of re-foundation on a sounder and clearer basis. For example, elected politicians can now reasonably and legitimately be concerned about the loyalty of a fraction of the senior bureaucracy. Although this fraction may be small, when one does not know for sure who those disloyal public servants are, it can lead to generalized paranoia, to administrative dysfunctions, and to governance failures. Nothing less than a re-foundation of our philosophy of governance will suffice.

Canada is not alone in encountering difficulties at the political-bureaucratic interface. The United Kingdom recently felt it necessary to approve a formal code enforced by the highest authorities on both sides, the Prime Minister and the Civil Service Commission, requiring ministers to respect the impartiality of the public service, and to give fair weight to their advice, and requiring the civil service to set out the facts and relevant issues truthfully, and to correct any errors as soon as possible and not knowingly mislead ministers, Parliament or others (Thomas 2009a: 51). Nevertheless, one is forced to wonder whether the present Canadian insouciance on this front (about the failings on both sides of the political-bureaucratic equation) is the result of much naivety, immense cognitive dissonance, reprehensible disingenuity or worse.

At the structural level

Along the way we have made numerous suggestions about structural changes, and we have indicted, in particular, the extraordinary weakness of the organizational design function in Canadian federal public administration. The amateurish and whimsical way in which this function is dispatched is at the source of many dysfunctions.

The Kafkaesque story of the human resources management process with its multiple *ad hoc* readjustments (in contradictory directions) in the name of some gospel of 'streamlining' is a pathetic illustration of a fundamental failure of the organizational design function inside the federal public service to keep the system aligned with the evolving external challenges. The same may be said of the calamitous mandate design of oversight bodies (e.g., in the nuclear energy sector).

This disastrous organizational design performance is ascribable at least in part to the self-serving ethos of the Canadian upper federal bureaucracy, but it is also due as well in part to the criminal neglect of the organizational design function as a central governance tool, and to a federal public administration system that would appear to systematically shun innovation and to be wedded to the *status quo*.

The list of organizational design mishaps over the last decades would be enlightening.

It should be clear however that the growth in size of the public administration systems has generated immense dis-economies of scale, and that this has led to such systems becoming less and less easily governable. Such negative scale effects are responsible for part of the problem. The fragmentation of the administrative systems in smaller units (as subsidiarity prevails) is likely to have positive effects.

At the levels of mechanisms

The blockages at the philosophical and structural levels cannot but stultify the capacity to make the highest and best use of all the available mechanisms to ensure effective, efficient and economical delivery of public goods and services to the citizens. While there were times when the Canadian federal bureaucracy could be said to have been boldly innovative in the search for new ways to serve better the citizens, the stubborn determination to avoid re-examining the political-bureaucratic interface critically in light of modern realities has taken its toll in the recent past.

What is not *verboten* as a result of mental prisons within the bureaucracy (as well as the executive and the legislature) would appear to be deterred by a commitment to risk aversion. To the extent that innovation at the mechanisms level is likely to be devised within the bureaucracy, one senses that instead of being in aid of better coordination, much that is accomplished amounts to boutique adjustments to the electronic plumbing aimed at changing everything at the surface level (or seem to do so) in order that nothing changes (although it seems to do so)—the principle of *di Lampedusa* generalized (Wallerstein 1998: 85)

Requiem for critical thinking

One of the most important findings from our series of breakfast meetings with samples of senior public servants (public servants who were particularly keen to serve as well as they could) has been the impact of the various forces hinted at above on critical thinking. One could not escape the strong feeling that it had become systematically discouraged. As we mentioned in chapter 3, in the last 15 years, any form of criticism (however mild and constructive) has come too often to be considered as a form of treason. As a result, a majority of executives have chosen to avoid critical thinking completely, and to withdraw into the 'technical' aspects of their work—to 'hibernate' as some called it—seeing no merit in engaging in discussions that would lead nowhere and could only get them into trouble.

The general quality of intra public service conversations would also appear, as a result, to have declined in part as a result of both this internal self-censorship and the very high degree of political correctness that has come to prevail over the years. We were told that the 'real' conversations are more likely to be carried out in the washroom than in the boardroom these days. Indeed, many participants remarked on the much less effective social learning than is desirable that has ensued.

Consequently, one could only conclude that there is little hope that revolution or reform of the Canadian federal public administration will come from within.

Invitation to subversion

And yet, change of necessity must come in great part to be accommodated from within. So we are inexorably led to an invitation to subversion: aiming the spotlight at a number of 'mental prisons' about aspects of governing and at 'pathologies' in our ways of governing ourselves with a view to exposing their toxic nature.

This exercise in critical thinking on our part may appear to be quite a naive undertaking. Family and friends will tell you with much condescension that 'everyone knows that rational disquisitions about the madness of our times are quite ineffective'. When the attention span of both the officials and their political sparring partners is measured in media-clips units, smart-alecky barbs become the new currency, and the impact of any critical deconstructions is quite short-lived...until the next cheap shot.

Yet in the face of a public discourse plagued with uncritical thinking, what is one to do if, like Magritte, one detests resignation?

One major lesson drawn from our diverse forays has been that one has to take the mores of the day seriously (with its five-second, dim-witted clip pronouncements and the sanctimony of ill-founded opinions propagated through the media), and to surf on them. In a social context where there are more stand-up comics than public intellectuals, debunking bunk frontally with a modicum of chance to be successful entails doing it in a humorous way: so that what the colonized mind will occlude or reject, laughter or smile might concede.

Humour (and its relatives, satire and irony) would appear to be the way. Humour is defined by Arthur Koestler as the simultaneous perception of a situation in two self-consistent but mutually incompatible frames of reference, in two different wavelengths.[1] This may have been the message of an editorial in the *Globe & Mail* on June 15, 2000, entitled "A call to irony". Canadians ignored it at the time. A decade later, it may be a message worth restating with greater probability that it might suffice to awaken emergent publics and to create the social movement that seems necessary to plug the black hole of public administration.

In the whole discourse that we have carried out in this volume, we hope to have succeeded in injecting at times a whiff of humour and irony in what was a long indictment of what

449

some Canadian scholars and practitioners, with missionary zeal, continue to regard as a superior model of public administration—one that they proudly invite the world to merrily adopt. Indeed it has become official policy in higher circles to propagandize the 'model' and to suppress any evidence that it might not be working that well.

We may have been unduly paralyzed by our *bonnes manières* in attacking this propaganda machine. We know that it is not sufficient to denounce the Canadian model of public administration by reporting as Mazankowski-Tellier did (and we quoted them in the introduction) that the Canadian federal government pay system costs 15 times more per employee to operate than the industry standard. In Canada, this statement had no impact. One would have to crank up the level of irreverence quite a bit if one is to have an impact.

What is required in Canada is not dry humour or slight deprecation in the manner of Aristophanes: Canadians perversely enjoy such failure of respect or courtesy for their ways as an opportunity to display their worldliness. What would appear to be required is the caustic and acerbic treatment of a Diogenes—another Athenian of the same period but one immensely more hard-hitting and irreverent than Aristophanes—to denounce the grotesqueness of our ways. And yet, it would be so un-Canadian! The caustic aphorisms of a Canadian Diogenes would be discarded too readily as 'over the top'.

So we end up with a quandary: we need a Diogenes (who is likely to be ostracized and ignored) so we may have to settle for an Aristophanes (who is bound to be ineffective in generating deep critical thinking). This explains why we are not hopeful...but we have hope, and why we may be led to much more irreverence in the future...but not too much—much more biting irony although not sarcasm. Indeed, this may be the promising road.

Endnote

1　Koestler illustrates his point by reproducing part of a dialogue in a film by Claude Berri: "Sir, I would like to ask your daughter's hand…Why not? You have already had the rest". In this dialogue, "hand" is first used in its metaphorical frame of reference and then suddenly in a bodily context. In this sort of endeavour, irony is a satirist's most effective weapon: "it pretends to accept the opponents' ways of reasoning in order to expose their implicit absurdity or viciousness" (Koestler 1978: 112–114).

The Sabotage of Harms

> *Scrutinizing the harms themselves,*
> *and discovering their dynamics and dependencies*
> *leads to the possibility of sabotage.*
>
> —Malcolm K. Sparrow

Subversion of the Diogenes or the Aristophanes variety is meant to exploit identified vulnerabilities of the object under attack. If one can unveil the dynamics of harms that are derailing public administration in different issue-domains, one may identify points of vulnerability and act on them in ways that may suffice to sabotage some of the processes. This requires analysis and imagination (Sparrow 2008).

It might prove quite effective to launch such a subversive campaign by identifying some of the harmful forces at work preventing the unfolding of 'small g' governance. Our broad objective in this book has been to argue for an open-source public administration that would be free from the strictures we have identified above. This remains a legitimate prime mover to action. But these acts of construction might be helpfully complemented by acts of destruction directed at the dynamics of particular processes that may be said to be toxic.

Most of the dynamics of harms may be said to be issue-domain-specific, and therefore might not be cross-sectorally relevant. But some more general forces may be said to be important enough in their toxicity to affect many sectors. So we thought we might leave the reader with some sense of what might be the sort of processes we have observed that would appear to deserve particular attention for those interested in becoming *saboteurs of harms.*

These processes were identified as a side-benefit of some discussions with senior executives of the Canadian public service as we were bringing this volume to completion. They should not be regarded as a comprehensive review of the general harm–generating processes in play, but as only a sample that most certainly floated to the top of our agenda as a result of our conversations.

Five sources of harms

The drift from spiritual anchors, to democratic values, to guilds' interests

There has been a tectonic transformation of the moral order at the foundation of the social order of advanced democratic societies in the recent past, and this has transformed their public administration. At the core of it is the emergence of a form of extreme secularism and exclusive humanism that has accompanied the growth of scientism (Charles Taylor 2007).

These waves have put the individual at the center of the world, rejected the former spiritual or sacred character of political and social structures like marriage, family, community, public service, etc., and weakened considerably (and in many cases dissolved) the set of constraints and standards in which the social order was embedded, shaping the social order.

This erosion of the externally generated moral order was supposed to be replaced by a new civil theology that was meant to provide underpinning values for modern man without any need to rely or call on the religious or the spiritual: new guideposts generated by democracy. It is fair to say that such a civil theology succeeded for a while in providing guideposts in the construction of the social order. In western democracies, democratic values were readily invoked as dominant ones meant to give significance and meaning to socio–political institutions. This civil theology has now begun to give signs of slowly being eroded as democratic values are fading out of mind for the vast majority of citizens and officials, and being displaced by loyalties to smaller communities of meaning such as professions.

This two-step shift from an anchoring in the spiritual realm to an anchoring in civil theology, and from a sort of civil theology to an anchoring in tribal and community groupings has had a significant impact on the process through which the public administration is shaped.

Citizens and officials as producers of governance have come to hold little faith in anything transcendent, be it spiritual or civic. Spiritual values and democratic values have been serially derided, and opportunism has come to be regarded as the norm. Interestingly, this is the very moment when public service personnel found it opportune to pull a rather interesting stunt—to begin to anoint the 'public service' as morally superior. Expert unelected officials have hinted that they are probably better suited to define the public interest than the more or less legitimate elected officials.

This presumption is already permeating the new code of ethics of Canadian federal public servants. The new version of this code (still a work in progress as of the spring of 2010) would seem to tend to submerge democratic values in the mass of professional values, expertise and managerial virtues that are supposed to emerge organically as a *grâce d'état* for the bureaucracy. This manoeuver can only feed the impression that we are a very small step away from representing the public service as deserving to be regarded as morally superior by definition. The fact that the idea raised no red flags in senior circles for months is scary.

Jane Jacobs has already written the gospel codifying this new faith by declaring public servants to be guardians—special persons never to be confused or even associated with merchants

(Jacobs 1992). This theoretical construct is now used by some to legitimize the raising of the bureaucrats to the status of a special enlightened elite—a managerial class better equipped to ascertain what the public good means than elected officials who are mostly persons without such qualities.

This bizarre drift in the federal public service—from spiritual values to democratic values to tribal interests as guideposts—has been an echo effect of the same *débordement* in modern society: a reaction to hyper-turbulence that has led to the creation of enclaves as a strategy of survival, and toward a loyalty to enclaves and tribal groups that has not attracted the attention it deserves. So what has been observed in public administration has echoed, in part, the changes in the ambient society.

Homo corporativus is heralded as the new unit of analysis: it takes action, primarily, that promotes its own tribal interest. It is therefore more likely to breathe disloyalty toward political leaders to the extent that the managerial class has persuaded itself that it knows best. Indeed as we noted earlier in this volume, we have recently been made aware of a whole cadre of specialized bureaucrats that has collectively come to refuse to execute the orders of the elected government even though the action that was called for neither called for unlawful action nor violated any so-called basic values: it simply did not agree with their self-defined notion of their burden of office.

There is a scent of 1968 in the air. However, it is not the result of powerless youth and civil society demanding to be heard, but the managerial class trying its hand at nothing less than a *coup d'état*.

The shift from a culture of duty to a culture of entitlements

The transformation in the extended order discussed above has been accentuated on the Canadian scene by a dramatic cultural change that has impacted the whole country, in all of its spheres, and can be seen very starkly in the Canadian federal public service.

455

What has been labelled as the rights revolution has entailed the gradual replacement of the culture of duty by a culture of entitlements. This sort of perversion has been dramatically recorded in the evolution of the Charter of Rights and Freedoms: originally designed to protect the citizen from the encroachment of their governments on their life, but seized by the citizenry as an instrument to secure entitlements from the state.

This shift is not unnatural. Many moral contracts with the public service have been rescinded or broken unilaterally by the government in power over the last two decades. The broken bargain between the politicians and the senior bureaucrats as echoed in the Al Mashat affair, along with a several-year wage restraint and significant workforce reductions, has had reverberations throughout the whole public service. It resulted in a cascade of disengagement and even in declarations in 1995 that what had been defined heretofore as intense loyalty could be construed to be an unhealthy form of co-dependency (Paquet and Pigeon 2000; Paquet 2010).

Many bureaucrats ceased to define their work primarily as a mission and sought protection from politicians and higher order bureaucrats in their labour unions, which soon began to take increasingly 'political' public positions—eventually openly calling for the election of certain candidates and opposing specific political parties, in effect, making a mockery of the notion of a non-partisan public service. There was no outcry of outrage internally or at large.

Even though program review in the 1990s weakened the presumption of 'jobs for life' at all levels a little, the relatively generous financial and fringe benefits that had emerged from collective bargaining (and that triggered similar benefits for non-unionized staff), accompanied by still significant job security and quite generous pensions, have persisted. All the while, the 'quo' for this 'quid'—the sense of duty to both citizens and governments of the day—has continued to erode.

The bravado statement mentioned earlier, "I am entitled to my entitlements", of the former head of the Royal Canadian

Mint, David Dingwall, to a Parliamentary Committee at the end of 2005, epitomizes the mindset. 'Clockers and climbers' have become well-known colloquialisms to refer to those who provide only a minimal amount of mental energy and service and leave their creativity at home, and those who approached the public service as no different from private service—becoming ruthless careerists and being somewhat encouraged to do so by the ethos of the new public management that, *sotto voce*, has celebrated the ways of the private sector since the 1970s.

In this new complex, adaptive system—open, dynamic, continually challenged by a turbulent environment, etc.—a new *systemic relational stewardship* is required if one is to feed a meaningful on-going direction-finding process (Painter-Moreland 2008) but, at the very moment, when this has become a *sine qua non*, the governance regime would appear to be breaking down into enclaves of guilds that are more self-serving than servants of the public interest. So paradoxically, it is at the very time that the bureaucracy would appear to cease to be a community of persons dedicated to the resilience of the public household and to the welfare of the citizen, that it has felt legitimized in claiming a greater voice in the public governance of the country.

The increase in disloyalty

The notion of loyalty is usually associated with the honouring of a moral contract, with living up to the legitimate expectations of those one is interacting with, of those who have put their trust in us. It is worth reiterating that disloyalty is, therefore, a breach of trust.

In our complex world, multiple moral contracts are over-layered on a network of heterarchical relationships, encompassing a variety of dimensions. According to circumstances that are ever changing, and to levels of knowledge and competencies that are varied and imperfect, the legitimacies of the claims of the different parties to the moral contracts differ and evolve. In this world, the multiple loyalties may be starkly incompatible.

In such context, blind loyalty and chronic disloyalty *vis-à-vis* any other party on one particular issue (without some appreciation of the complexities of the situation, and some critical thinking about the ordering or priorities of the different loyalties) are equally problematic. Moral pluralism prevails, so a balance of claims must be reached that allows no absolute over-ridingness by any claim or value (Kekes 1993). This zone of uncertainty is a fertile terrain for disloyalty.

As we mentioned earlier, the growing acuteness of differences of opinion is often due to the fact that issues under discussion are now more often than before *not* raising 'convergent problems' (for which the multiplicity of diverse responses offered tend cumulatively and gradually through time to converge toward an agreed-upon response or consensus) but rather 'divergent problems' (for which the more the problem is clarified, the more divergent and irreconcilable the points of view become).

In the face of divergent problems, there is an ever greater possibility of different stakeholders reasonably defending incompatible approaches, and therefore more scope for dissent (which may be desirable), but also for the possibility of disloyalty of one sort or another (which may be less so). In the many-dimensional world of governance (where 360° loyalties are likely to be difficult if not impossible to reconcile), divergent problems are the rule rather than the exception.

The more convergent the problems, and the more fully integrated and mature the community of practice, the sharper is the definition of the burden of office, and the easier it is to identify disloyalty. The more divergent the problem and the more diffuse and anomic the community of practice, the fuzzier is the burden of office, and the more difficult it will be to identify disloyalty.

There has been growing evidence in the recent past that the divergent nature of problems and the rise of ruthless careerism have generated a greater degree of passive and active disloyalty of federal bureaucrats to the duly elected government of the day, along with a greater degree of sophistication in defending one's own disloyal behaviour. The reference to the higher good in the name of which one may choose to ignore the primacy of democratic values has crept subtly into the narrative of bureaucrats: it has been argued with great seriousness that one cannot talk of disloyalty when a bureaucrat does not loyally serve the government of the day because he/she has a different notion of the public interest of the citizenry!

The barriers to stewardship

Collaborative governance, that is necessary when power, resources and information are widely distributed, calls for a form of collective stewardship, what Mollie Painter-Morland has labelled a new systemic relational stewardship capable of feeding a meaningful, organic ongoing, direction-finding process (Painter-Morland 2009). Yet any attempt to denounce the artificiality of the mystical notion of leadership and to replace it by a more practical notion of stewardship has proved very difficult. It has much to do with what has been perceived as the insurmountable barriers on the road to collaborative governance. These barriers are both cultural and psychological.

The cultural ones are ascribable to some fifty years of welfare statism during which citizens have come to acquire a dramatic dependency on the state, and have often lost their capacity to take care of their own affairs. This sort of voluntary servitude and the accompanying culture of entitlements have been toxic—leading citizens to expect that any problems they face can be unloaded onto the state apparatus. Over time, citizens have come to lose the confidence that they are able to handle their problems themselves (collectively and/or individually).

This has now contaminated the psyche of the citizenry. Peter Block mentions simulations run by Joel Henning in which three teams were asked to role-play three different styles of stewardship: team 1 was asked to role-play a high-control patriarchal style; team 2 to deal with a case of artificial and cosmetic empowerment; and team 3 to role-play a genuine exercise of participation and collaborative governance (Block 1998).

The first two teams felt manipulated and controlled, and were full of resentment and cynicism. What was most surprising however was the debriefing of team 3. Faced with the difficult task of collaborative governance, the prospects of real participation and accountability for an unpredictable tomorrow, and the human costs of collaboration, patriarchy began to appear better and better to team 3. To a certain extent, the culture of dependency has become so ingrained in our DNA, that we do not seem to have any longer the energy and the willingness to build collaborative stewardship. The clarity and simplicity of 'command and control' make it irresistible, and choosing this easy route of voluntary servitude allows one to postpone the struggle over real, shared accountability.

A certain sense of cultural/psychological despair was palpable in our conversations with senior officials in the fall of 2009. Intellectually, they recognized that they were producers of governance and that collaborative governance was the superior approach, but they seemed to share the fate of modern citizens who had been diagnosed more than 150 years ago by Proudhon as congenitally suffering from *"la paresse des masses" and "le préjugé gouvernemental"*—the unwillingness of the citizenry to get involved as producers of governance because it is too difficult and requires too much effort, and the consequent propensity to lean automatically in the direction of government and to demand that it take care of the problems (Proudhon 1850–51).

What was already toxic in 1850 has been dramatically amplified by years of welfare statism and a dis-habituation of the citizen to take care of himself. This sense of disempowerment has now permeated the mid-ranked public service: a majority of the professional managers (EXs) with whom we had discussions—whom we would regard as immensely more engaged and courageous than the average—gave signs of discouragement in the face of the task that would be imposed by the search for collaborative stewardship.

Breaking these cultural and psychological barriers—a sense of helplessness that generates much harm—will prove a daunting task. Something as massively important as the generational renewal, anticipated for the next decade or so, may be required to generate the requisite energy and willingness to overcome these barriers.

The painful drift from internal coherence to ecological fit

The traditional paradigm in public administration and political science is focused on a very narrow notion of rationality: instrumental rationality, the Weberian *Zweickrationalität*. This is a notion of technical rationality reduced to the calculation of means to reach some ends. This is the notion of rationality on which Weber constructed his analyses of bureaucracy (Weber 1968).

But in order for this notion to be useful, there must be an agreement on the objectives or ends to be pursued. In the complex world of collaborative governance, objectives are confused and conflictual. This limits considerably the usefulness of instrumental rationality.

Governance—by multiplying the number of stakeholders—imposes a new complexity to rationality. One is forced to deal with rationality differently: 'relational rationality' emerging from the interactions and deliberations among the different actors becomes a much more relevant concept. This entails a shift from a fixation on 'sheer means-ends internal coherence' toward an interest for 'external coherence', between the strategy pursued and the environment, or what has been called "ecological rationality" (Gigerenzer 2001).

Our discussions with senior officials in the fall of 2009 were significantly impaired by the hegemony of instrumental rationality on their reasoning. It proved to be a crippling reference in their back of the mind: a fixation on assuming both clarity of objectives and stability of preferences.

Being ecologically rational entails quite a different benchmark: it gauges a strategy not by its internal consistency on the basis of unrealistic assumptions, but by its adequacy in fitting pragmatically with the evolving environment.

The difficulty in orchestrating a reasoned discussion is ascribable to the fact that instrumental rationality is of little use in the face of an unpredictable tomorrow, and that there is no simple mechanical answer to the question of the best fit between strategy and an evolving environment. To increase the chances of being reasonably effective, participants have to rid themselves of the narrow strictures of instrumental rationality, and to adopt the stance of a backwoods mechanic who does not have all spare parts available to him/her and must fiddle with various imperfect and short-range tools—a process of vicarious functioning, of trial-and-error to produce a serviceable solution with the things at hand. It is no wonder that traditional bureaucrats and public administration academics are somewhat disoriented by this new context, and often reluctant to enter such a risky and demanding pathway. This kind of reluctance brings them to cling to the old *manière de voir*: even if it is ineffective, it has clarity and simplicity.

The only way to be ecologically rational is to experiment by elimination of misfits in search of goodness of fit. It is akin to the work of a designer in search of some kind of harmony between two intangibles: a form, which has not yet been designed, and a context that cannot be properly and fully described since it is still evolving. (Alexander 1964; Gilles and Paquet 1989).

A plea for the sabotage of harms as the next step

The enlightening insight of Malcolm Sparrow—that one must distinguish between promoting the general good and addressing specific harms, and that at times it is crucial to shift the focus from one to the other—is worth remembering in closing. Our main purpose throughout this book has been to keep our eyes on the need to refurbish our socio-political and economic system by making it into as much of an open-source system as one can. We have made this case a number of times in this book. But we have also tried to show how one has to expect major obstacles on this road: dynamic conservatisms of all sorts that explain why, despite numerous attempts at reform, there would appear to be no practical, workable and implementable global solutions available at this time.

The same may be said about the black hole of public administration. There is no blueprint or roadmap available to get us out of the hole and into the sort of ideal democratic governance apparatus that John Dewey celebrated all through his life. So we have been keeping our eyes on the ultimate objective; but along the way, we have also tried to deal with blockages of all sorts that seemed to stand in the way of progress. These local repairs were not meant to replace the broad roadmap, but to help clear the road ahead of real and imaginary obstacles.

At the end of our journey, Malcolm Sparrow may have conferred some order on our *travails*. The construction work to refurbish our democratic governance and a sensible public administration is the long-run objective; in the short run, one may have to focus on clearing the way, by removing many sources of harms, many local obstacles and specific barriers to the pursuit of the long-run evolving objective, so as to allow the most promising experiments and explorations to be developed as fully as possible, or at least not to be derailed or prevented by the defenders of the *status quo*.

Fighting fire with fire, sabotage with sabotage, is meaningful, however, only if one has been able to establish firmly that progress is not impeded because of the inherent limits to integrative strategies and collaborative governance—as too expansive, too threatening, and blocked by the fundamental inability of members to cooperate—but by deep cultural and psychological reasons or ideological mental prisons that prevent analysts from seeing the meaningful patterns through the mess of dots on the screen.

Much in this book has been dedicated to persuading the reader that collaborative governance is not unworkable. This being established, the best way to proceed, while the organizational apparatus likely to produce collaborative governance is being painfully constructed, is to open a second front of activities: a sabotaging attack on those cultural, psychological and ideological blinders at the source of key blockages on the road to collaborative governance.

Acknowledgements

Although they have been modified substantially a number of times, segments of several chapters have been drawn from previously published papers:

Hubbard, Ruth and Gilles Paquet 2008. "Clerk as Révélateur: A Panoramic View." In *Searching for Leadership: Secretaries to Cabinet in Canada*, ed. Patrice Dutil. Toronto, ON: Institute of Public Administration of Canada, 85–120.

Hubbard, Ruth and Gilles Paquet 2010. "Toward an Autopoietic Federalism." In *The Case for Decentralized Federalism*, eds. Ruth Hubbard and Gilles Paquet. Ottawa: The University of Ottawa Press, 159–203.

Hubbard, Ruth and Gilles Paquet 2007. "Cat's Cradling: APEX Forums on Wicked Problems." *optimumonline* [electronic journal]. www.optimumonline.ca, 37: 2: 12–18 [accessed June 7, 2010].

Hubbard, Ruth and Gilles Paquet 2008. "Cat's Eyes: Intelligent Work Versus Preverse Incentives – APEX Forums on Wicked Problems." *optimumonline* [electronic journal] www.optimumonline.ca, 38: 3: 1–22 [accessed June 7, 2010].

Hubbard, Ruth and Gilles Paquet 2009. "Not in the catbird seat: Pathologies of Governance" *optimumonline* [electronic journal]. www.optimumonline.ca, 39: 2: 11–20 [accessed June 7, 2010].

Hubbard, Ruth and Gilles Paquet 2009. "The Unwisdom of Cats." *optimumonline* [electronic journal] www.optimumonline.ca, 39: 4: 52–66 [accessed June 7, 2010].

Paquet, Gilles 2009. "Quantophrenia." *optimumonline* [electronic journal]. www.optimumonline.ca, 39: 1: 14–27 [accessed on June 7, 2010].

Paquet, Gilles 2010. "Disloyalty." *optimumonline* [electronic journal]. www.optimumonline.ca, 40: 1: 23–47 [accessed on June 7, 2010].

Juillet, Luc and Gilles Paquet 2002. "The Neurotic State." In *How Ottawa Spends 2002-3. The Security Aftermath and National Priorities*, ed. G. B. Doern. Don Mills, ON: Oxford University Press, 69–87.

Paquet, Gilles 2004. "Fiscal Imbalance as Governance Failure." In *How Ottawa Spends 2004-2005: Mandate Change in the Paul Martin Era*, ed. G. B. Doern. Montreal, QC and Kingston, ON: McGill-Queen's University Press, 25–45.

Paquet, Gilles 1997. "Alternative Program Delivery: Transforming the Practices of Governance," In *Alternative Service Delivery: Sharing Governance in Canada*, eds. R. Ford and D. R. Zussman. Toronto: Institute of Public Administration of Canada/KPMG, 31–58.

Hubbard, Ruth and Gilles Paquet 2007. "Public-Private Partnership and The 'Porcupine' Problem." In *How Ottawa Spends 2007-08, The Harper Conservatives- Climate of Change*, ed. G. B. Doern. Montreal, QC and Kingston, ON: McGill-Queen's University Press, 254–272.

Hubbard, Ruth and Gilles Paquet 2007. "The Myth of the Public Service as a Lump of 'Guardians'" *optimumonline* [electronic journal]. www.optimumonline.ca, 37: 1: 9–26.

Hubbard, Ruth and Gilles Paquet 2009. "Design Challenges for the Strategic State: Bricolage and Sabotage." In *How Ottawa Spends 2009-10*, ed. A. M. Maslove. Montreal, QC and Kingston, ON: McGill-Queen's University Press, 89–114.

Paquet, Gilles 2000. "The Judgment of Wider Courts." In *Expanding Horizons: Rethinking Access to Justice in Canada.* Ottawa: Department of Justice, 80–88.

Paquet, Gilles 2009. "Ombudspersons as Producers of Governance," *optimumonline* [electronic journal]. [www.optimumonline.ca, 39: 3: 6–20 [accessed June 7, 2010].

Bibliography

Accenture 2006. *Building the Trust*. Available at:
www.accenture.com/Global/Services/By_Industry/Government_
and_Public_Service/PS_Global/R_and_I/BuildingtheTrustES.
htm [accessed August 8, 2009].

Accenture 2007. *Delivering on the Promise*. Available at:
www.accenture.com/Global/Services/By_Industry/
Government_and_Public_Service/PS_Global/R_and_I/
DeliveringonthePromise.htm [accessed August 8, 2009].

Acheson, K. and J. F. Chant 1973. "Bureaucratic Theory and the
Choice of Central Bank Goals: The Case of the Bank of Canada."
Journal of Money, Credit and Banking, 5: 2: 637–655.

Ackoff, Russell L. 1994. *The Democratic Corporation*. New York:
Oxford University Press.

Agamben, Giorgio 2003. *État d'exception*. Paris: Seuil.

Akerlof, George A. 1984. *An Economic Theorist's Book of Tales*.
Cambridge, UK: Cambridge University Press.

Alexander, Christopher 1964. *Notes Toward a Synthesis of Form*.
Cambridge, MA: Harvard University Press.

Alinsky, Saul D. 1972. *Rules for Radicals*. New York: Vintage Books.

Anderson, Walter T. 2001. *All Connected Now*. Boulder, CO:
Westview Press.

Andreski, Stanislav 1974. *Social Sciences as Sorcery*.
Harmondsworth, UK: Penguin.

Angus, Ian 2001. *Emergent Publics*. Winnipeg, MB: Arbeiter Ring
Publishing.

Ankersmit, Frank R. 2002. "Representational Democracy – An Aesthetic Approach to Conflict and Compromise." *Common Knowledge*, 8: 1: 24–46.

Argyris, Chris and Donald A. Schön 1978. *Organizational Learning: A Theory of Action Perspective*. Reading, MA: Addison-Wesley.

Ashby, W. Ross 1956. *Introduction to Cybernetics*. London, UK: Chapman & Hall.

Ashby, W. Ross 1960. *Design for a Brain*. London, UK: Chapman & Hall.

Atomic Energy of Canada Limited 2008. "National Research Universal Reactor Safety Systems Upgrade and the Canadian Nuclear Safety Commission's Licensing and Oversight Process." *A Lessons Learned Report* by Talisman International, LLC, June (Available on the websites of AECL and the CNSC).

Aubert, Benoît A. and Michel Patry 2003 (December 8). "Dix conditions de succès pour des partenariats public-privé." *La Presse*.

Aubert, Benoît A. and Michel Patry 2005. "Les partenariats public-privé: le long et tortueux chemin du Québec." *optimumonline* [electronic journal]. www.optimumonline.ca , 35: 4: 68–74 [consulted June 7, 2010].

Aubert, Benoît A. et al. 2005 (February 23). *Synthèse critiques d'expériences de partenariats public-privé*. Montreal : Centre interuniversitaire de recherché en analyse des organisations (CIRANO).

Aucoin, Peter 1995. "Canadian Public Management Reform - A Comparative Westminster Perspective." (mimeo).

Aucoin, Peter 1996. *The New Public Management: Canada in Comparative Perspective*. Montreal: Institute for Research on Public Policy.

Axelrod, Robert and Michael D. Cohen 2000. *Harnessing Complexity*. New York: The Free Press.

Balls, Herbert B. 1970. "New Techniques in Government Budgeting: Planning, Programming, and Budgeting in Canada." *Public Administration*, 48: 3: 289–305.

Banting, Keith G. 1996. "Notes for Comments to the Deputy Minister's Luncheon." Ottawa, January 5.

Banting, Keith G. et al 2007. *Open Federalism: Interpretations, Significance*. Kingston, ON: Institute of Intergovernmental Relations.

Barnard, Chester 1938. *The Functions of the Executive*. Cambridge, MA: Harvard University Press.

Becker, Theodore L. 1991. *Quantum Politics*. New York: Praeger.

Benkler, Yochai 2006. *The Wealth of Networks*. New Haven, CN: Yale University Press.

Bennis, Warren 1976a. "Have we gone overboard on the 'right to know'?" *Saturday Review*, June 3, 18–21.

Bennis, Warren 1976b. *The Unconscious Conspiracy*. New York: AMACOM.

Bettignies, Jean-Étienne de and Thomas W. Ross 2004. "The Economics of Public-Private Partnerships." *Canadian Public Policy*, 30: 2: 135–154.

Blattberg, Charles 2004. *Et si nous dansions?* Montreal, QC and Kingston, ON: McGill-Queen's University Press.

Bliss, Michael 2004. *The Right Honourable Men*. Toronto: Harper Collins.

Block, Peter 1998. "As Goes the Follower; So Goes the Leader." *News for a Change*, July.

Boismenu, Gérard et al. 2004. *Ambitions libérales et écueils politiques – Réalisations et promesses du gouvernement Charest*. Outremont, QC: Athéna Editions.

Boisot, Max H. 1995. *Information Space – A Framework for Learning in Organizations, Institutions and Culture*. London, UK: Routledge.

Bouchard, Benoît 1992 (December). *Canadian Paper on New Orientations for Social Policy*. Paris: OECD.

Boulding, Kenneth E. 1970. *A Primer on Social Dynamics*. New York: The Free Press.

Bourgon, Jocelyne 2007. "Responsive, Responsible and Respected Government: Towards a New Public Administration Theory." *International Review of Public Administration*, 73: 1: 7–26.

Bradwell, Peter and Richard Reeves 2008. *Network Citizens*. London, UK: Demos.

Braun, Dietmar 2008. "Making Federalism More Efficient: A Comparative Assessment." *Acta Politica*, 43: 4–25.

Brewer, Gene A. et al. 2000. "Individual Conceptions of Public Service Motivation." *Public Administration Review*, 60: 3: 254–264.

Brown, David W. 1995. *When Strangers Cooperate*. New York: The Free Press.

Brown, J. Robert Jr. 2006-07. "Disloyalty without Limits: Independent Directors and the Elimination of the Duty of Loyalty." *Kentucky Law Journal*, 95: 1: 53–105.

Brubaker, Elizabeth 2003. "Revisiting Water and Wastewater Privatization." A study prepared for the Government of Ontario Panel on the Role of Government, and presented at the *Public Goals, Private Means Research Colloquium*, Faculty of Law, University of Toronto, October 3.

Burelle, André 1995. *Le mal canadien*. Montreal, QC: Fides.

Burelle, André 2005. *Pierre Elliott Trudeau*. Montreal, QC: Fides.

Burleton, Derek. 2002. *A choice between investing in Canada's cities or disinvesting in Canada's future*. Toronto, ON: Toronto-Dominion Bank, April 22.

Burleton, Derek 2006. "Creating the Winning Conditions for Public-Private Partnerships (P3s) in Canada." *TD Economics Special Report*, June 22.

Canada 1983. Office of the Auditor General. "Constraints to Productive Management in the Public Service." *Auditor General of Canada Report*. Ottawa: Office of the Auditor General, chapter 2. www.oag-bvg.ca.

Canada 1994a. "The Way Ahead For The Public Service." Discussion paper produced for the *Directors of Personnel Conference*, Cornwall, ON, October 4-6.

Canada 1994b. Auditor General of Canada. *Auditor General of Canada Report*. Ottawa: Auditor General of Canada, chapter 15: 7.

Canada 1995. Treasury Board Secretariat. *Framework for Alternative Program Delivery*. Ottawa: Treasury Board Secretariat.

Canada 1997a. *Nuclear Safety and Control Act* 1997, c. 9 19. (1).

Canada 1997b. Canadian Nuclear Safety Commission. *An Overview*. Ottawa: Canadian Nuclear Safety Commission. www.nuclearsafety.gc.ca/eng/resource/publications/CNSC_0748/CNSC_0748.cfm [accessed April 15, 2008].

Canada 1999. Privy Council Office. *Speech from the Throne to Open the Thirty Sixth Parliament of Canada*. Ottawa: Privy Council Office. www.pco-bcp.gc.ca [accessed July 22, 2008].

Canada 2000a. Justice Canada. *Expanding Horizons: Rethinking Access to Justice in Canada*. Ottawa: Justice Canada.

Canada 2000b. Office of the Information Commissioner of Canada. *Annual Report 1999–2000*. Ottawa: Office of the Information Commissioner of Canada.

Canada 2005a. Service Canada. *Service Canada Annual Report 2005-06*. Ottawa: Service Canada, chapter 8.

Canada 2005b. Treasury Board Secretariat. *Management Accountability Framework*. Ottawa: Treasury Board Secretariat. www.tbs-sct.ca/maf-crg/documents/booklet-livret/booklet-livret-eng.asp.

Canada 2006a. Office of the Prime Minister. *Speech from the Throne*. Ottawa: Office of the Prime Minister.

Canada 2006b. Treasury Board Secretariat. (www.tbs-sct.gc.ca/rma/
eppi-ibdrp/hrdb-rhbd/archive/sc-sc/descryption_e.asp[accessed
March 6, 2008].

Canada 2006c. Treasury Board Secretariat. *Key Leadership
Competencies*. Ottawa: Public Service Human Resources
Management Agency of Canada and the Public Service
Commission. www.tbs-sct.gc.ca/tal/kcl/intro-eng.asp [accessed
May 6, 2010].

Canada 2007a. Office of the Information Commissioner of Canada.
Annual Report 2006–07. Ottawa: Office of the Information
Commissioner of Canada.

Canada 2007b. Auditor General of Canada. *Special Examination
Report*. Ottawa: Office of the Auditor General, September 5.

Canada 2007c. Privy Council Office. *A Guide for Minister and
Secretaries of State*. Ottawa: Privy Council Office, chapter 14: 68.

Canada 2007d. Treasury Board Secretariat. www.tbs-cst.gc.ca/dpr-
rmr/2006-2007/inst/csn01-eng.asp [accessed December 6, 2008].

Canada 2007e. Office of the Prime Minister. *Speech from the Throne*.
Ottawa: Office of the Prime Minister.

Canada 2008a. Prime Minister's Advisory Committee on the Public
Service. *Pursuing a High Performance Public Service*. Second
Report to the Prime Minister. Ottawa: Prime Minister's Advisory
Committee on the Public Service, February.

Canada 2008b. Service Canada. Service Canada website. www.
servicecanada.gc.ca/en/about/index.shtml [accessed March 6,
2008].

Canada 2009. Canadian Nuclear Safety Commission. *2008-2009
Report on Priorities and Plans*. Ottawa: Canadian Nuclear Safety
Commission.

Canada 2010a. Privy Council Office. www.pco-bcp.gc.ca/index.
asp?lang=eng&page=information &sub=publications&doc=Role
/role2010_e.htm#7.2 [accessed May 13, 2010].

Canada 2010b. Testimony to the Standing Committee on Access to Information, Privacy and Ethic. Ottawa: Government of Canada, April 29, 2010.

Canadian Medical Association Journal 2008. www.cmaj.ca/cgi/content/full/178/5/536 [accessed November 6, 2008].

Carson, Scott 2002. "Establishing Public-Private Partnerships: Three Tests of a Good Process." A paper presented at the *International Applied Business Research Conference*, Puerto Vallarta, March.

Carter, Stephen L. 1998. *The Dissent of the Governed*. Cambridge, MA: Harvard University Press.

Carty, R. Kenneth et al. 2000. *Rebuilding Canadian Party Politics*. Vancouver, BC: University of British Columbia Press.

Canadian Council on Public Private Partnerships 2004. "The People Speak on P3: A National Survey on Attitudes to Public-Private Partnerships." A survey conducted by Environics Research Group for The Canadian Council on Public-Private Partnerships, November 22.

Chait, Richard P. et al. 2005. *Governance as Leadership*. Hoboken, NJ: Wiley & Sons.

Charney, Nicholas and Mike Mangulabnan 2008. *Scheming Virtuously: A Handbook for Public Servants*. www.cpsrenewal.ca.

Chwe, Michael S. W. 2001. *Rational Ritual*. Princeton, NJ: Princeton University Press.

Clark, Ian 2001a (August 7). "Ottawa Blocks MPs' Access to Civil Servants: Will Not Let Them Appear Before Openness Committee." *National Post*, A1.

Clark, Ian 2001b. (August 8) "Critics Blast Silencing of Civil Servants: Openness Committee: Boudria's Refusal to Allow Testimony Called Undemocratic." *National Post*, A6.

Clark, Ian and Harry Swain 2005. "Distinguishing the Real from the Surreal in Management Reform: Suggestions for Beleaguered Administrators in the Government of Canada." *Canadian Public Administration*, 48: 4: 453–476.

Clarke, Harold D. et al. 1995. *Absent Mandate*. Toronto, ON: Gage.

Cleveland, Harlan 2002. *Nobody in Charge*. San Francisco, CA: Jossey-Bass.

Conference Board of Canada 2002. *Projections des équilibres financiers des gouvernements du Canada et du Québec*. Ottawa: Conference Board of Canada.

Cotler, Irwin 2004 (June 16). " The Charter is Here to Stay." *Ottawa Citizen*.

Culbert, Samuel A. 2008 (October 20). "Get Rid of the Performance Review!" *The Wall Street Journal*, R4.

Dalrymple, Tobin 2008 (May 19). "Nuclear Safety Watchdog Names New President." *Ottawa Citizen*.

Delsol, Chantal 2005. "Le nouveau despotisme." *Géopolitique*, 89: 25–28.

Dion, Stéphane 2001. "Les municipalités et le gouvernement federal." Speech delivered to the Federation of Canadian Municipalities, May 26.

Dion, Stéphane 2002. "L'équilibre fiscal et les relations financières entre les gouvernements au Canada."Speech at the St James Club, Montreal, March 13.

Dorner, Dietrich 1997. *The Logic of Failure*. Reading, MA: Addison-Wesley.

Dror, Yehezkel 1997. "Delta-type Senior Civil Service for the 21st Century." *International Review of Administrative Sciences*, 63: 1: 7–23.

Dror, Yehezkel 1999. "Beyond Uncertainty: Facing the Inconceivable." *Technological Forecasting and Social Change*, 62: 151–153.

Drummond, Don 2006. "The P3-rebuilt City." *National Post*, July 26.

Durkheim, Emile 1895. *Les règles de la méthode sociologique*. Paris: Flammarion (reprinted 1988).

Dupuy, Jean-Pierre 2002. *Pour un catastrophisme éclairé*. Paris: Seuil.

Dutil, Patrice 2003. Interview with David Good at the Institute of Public Administration of Canada, www.ipac.ca/Publications_ InterviewDavidGood [accessed on August 11, 2009].

Elliott, Mark 2006. "Stigmergic Collaboration: The Evolution of Group Work." *M/C Journal* 9: 2, [electronic journal]. http:// journal.media-culture.org.au/0605/03-elliott.php [accessed August 8, 2008].

Elster, Jon 1992. *Local Justice*. New York: Russell Sage Foundation.

Elster, Jon 1993. *Political Psychology*. Cambridge, UK: Cambridge University Press.

Emery, Fred E. and Eric L. Trist 1965. "The Causal Texture of Organizational Environment." *Human Relations,* 18: 21–32.

Ewin, Robert E. 1993. "Corporate Loyalty: Its Objects and Its Grounds." *Journal of Business Ethics*, 12: 387–396.

Fairtlough, Gerard 1994. *Creative Compartments*. London, UK: Praeger.

Fairtlough, Gerard 2005. *The Three Ways of Getting Things Done*. Dorset, UK: The Triarchy Press.

Falkenberg, Gabriel 1988. "Insincerity and Disloyalty." *Argumentation*, 2: 89–97.

Federation of Canadian Municipalities 2001. *Fast Facts on Canada's Urban Regions*. Ottawa: Federation of Canadian Municipalities.

Federation of Canadian Municipalities 2002. *Will Canadian Cities Compete?* Ottawa: Federation of Canadian Municipalities.

Ferry, Jean-Marc 1996. *L' éthique reconstructive*. Paris: Les Éditions du Cerf.

Flinders, Matthew 2005. "The Politics of Public-Private Partnerships." *The British Journal of Politics and International Relations*, 7: 2: 215–239.

Ford, Richard and David R. Zussman, eds. 1997. *Alternative Service Delivery: Sharing Governance in Canada.* Toronto: KPMG/ Institute of Public Administration of Canada (IPAC).

Franks, C. E. S. (Ned) 2005. Testimony from Proceedings of the Standing Committee on National Finance of Canada. Ottawa: Government of Canada, June 7.

Frederickson, H. George 2005. "Whatever happened to public administration? Governance, governance, everywhere." In *The Oxford Handbook of Public Management,* eds. E. Ferlie et al. Oxford, UK: Oxford University Press, 282–304.

Friedmann, John and George Abonyi 1976. "Social Learning: A Model for Policy Research." *Environment and Planning,* A: 8: 927–940.

Fukuyama, Francis 2004. *State-Building.* Ithaca, NY: Cornell University Press.

Fuller, Lon L. 2001. *The Principles of Social Order.* Portland, OR: Hart Publishing.

Fuller, Steve 2005. *The Intellectual.* Cambridge, UK: iconbooks.

Gallie, Walter B. 1964. *Philosophy and the Historical Understanding.* London, UK: Chatto & Windus.

Gardner, Howard et al. 2001. *Good Work.* New York: Basic Books.

Garud, Raghu et al., eds. 2003. *Managing in the Modular Age.* Oxford, UK: Blackwell Publishing.

Gerencser, Mark et al. 2006. "The Mega-community Manifesto." *Strategy + Business* [electronic journal]. August 16. www. strategy-business.com

Gibson, James J. 1982. "A Preliminary Description and Classification of Affordances." In *Reasons for Realism,* eds. E. S. Reed and R. Jones. Hillsdale, NJ: Lawrence Erlbaum & Associates, 403–406.

Gigerenzer, Gerd 2001. "The Adaptive Toolbox." In *Bounded Rationality – The Adaptive Toolbox,* eds. G. Gigerenzer and R. Selten. Cambridge, MA: The MIT Press, 37–50.

Gigerenzer, Gerd 2007. *Gut Feelings – The Intelligence of the Unconscious*. New York: Viking.

Gigerenzer, Gerd 2008. *Rationality for Mortals*. Oxford, UK: Oxford University Press.

Giles, David E. A. and Lindsey M. Tedds 2002. *Taxes and the Canadian Underground Economy*. Toronto: Canadian Tax Foundation.

Gilles, Willem and G. Paquet 1989. "On Delta Knowledge." In *Edging toward the Year 2000*, eds. G. Paquet and M. von Zur Muehlen. Ottawa: Canadian Federation of Deans of Management and Administrative Studies, 15–30.

Gintis, Herbert et al. 2005. *Moral Sentiments and Material Interests*. Cambridge, MA: The MIT Press.

Gladwell, Malcolm 2000. *The Tipping Point*. New York: Little, Brown & Company.

Gladwell, Malcolm 2005. *Blink*. New York: Little, Brown & Company.

Goldsmith, Stephen and William D. Eggers 2004. *Governing by Networks*. Washington, DC: Brookings Institution Press.

Gordon, H. Scott 1961. *The Economists Versus The Bank of Canada*. Toronto, ON: The Ryerson Press.

Gow, J. Iain. 2004. *A Canadian Model of Public Administration?* Ottawa: Canada School of Public Service.

Granatstein, Jack L. 1998. *The Ottawa Men: The Civil Service Mandarins, 1935-1957*. Toronto, ON: University of Toronto Press.

Grandori, Anna, ed. 2004. *Corporate Governance and Firm Organization*. Oxford, UK: Oxford University Press.

Green, Ian 2007. "The Public Service and Trust." In *5 Trends That Are Transforming Government*. Ottawa: Public Policy Forum and Accenture, www.ppforum.ca/publications/5-trends-are-transforming-government, 18–26 [accessed August 28, 2009].

Gregory, Roy and Philip Giddings, eds. 2000. *Righting Wrongs – The Ombudsman in Six Continents*. Amsterdam, Netherlands: IOS Press.

Guéhenno, Jean-Marie 1993. *La fin de la démocratie*. Paris: Flammarion.

Hardin, Herschel 1974. *A Nation Unaware*. Vancouver, BC: J.J. Douglas.

Hardin, Russell, ed. 2004. *Distrust*. New York: Russel Sage Foundation.

Heath, Joseph 2003. *The Myth of Shared Values in Canada*. Ottawa: Canadian Centre for Management Development.

Hennessey, Peter 1996. *The Hidden Wiring: Unearthing the British Constitution*. London: Indigo.

Hine, Virginia H.1977. "The Basic Paradigm of a Future Socio-Cultural System." *World Issues*, April/May: 19–22.

Hirsch, Fred 1976. *Social Limits to Growth*. Cambridge, MA: Harvard University Press.

Hirschman, Albert O. 1967. *Development Projects Observed*. Washington, DC: Brookings Institution.

Hirschman, Albert O. 1970. *Exit, Voice and Loyalty – Responses to Decline in Firms, Organizations and States*. Cambridge, MA: Harvard University Press.

Hirschman, Albert O. 1995. *A Propensity to Self-Subversion*. Cambridge, MA: Harvard University Press.

Hock, Dee 1999. *Birth of the Chaordic Age*. San Francisco, CA: Berrett-Koehler Publishers.

Hodgetts, John E. 2007. "Royal Commissions: Personal Reflections." *Canadian Public Administration*, 50: 4.

Hofstede, Geert 2001. *Culture's Consequences: Comparing Values, Behaviors, Institutions, and Organizations Across Nations*. Thousand Oaks, CA: Sage Publications. Also at www.geert-hofstede.com [accessed May 5, 2010].

Holland, John H. 1995. *Hidden Order*. Reading, MA: Addison-Wesley.

Holloway, Richard 2008 (May 9). "Creative Disloyalty." *Scottish Arts Council.*

Horibe, Frances 2001. *Creating the Innovation Culture*. New York: John Wiley & Sons.

Hoskin, Keith 1996. "The 'awful idea of accountability': inscribing people into the measurement of objects." In *Accountability: Power, Ethos and The Technologies of Managing*, eds. R. Munro and J. Mouritsen. London, UK: International Thomson Business Press, 265–282.

Hubbard, Ruth 1995 (May 14). "A Vision of the Future." *Ottawa Citizen*, A2.

Hubbard, Ruth 2003. "Public Service Modernization: Fixing the Cart May Not Suffice." *optimumonline* [electronic journal]. www.optimumonline.ca, 33: 2: 8–15 [accessed June 7, 2010].

Hubbard, Ruth 2009. *Profession: Public Servant*. Ottawa: Invenire.

Hubbard, Ruth and Gilles Paquet 2002. "Ecologies of Governance and Institutional Metissage." *optimumonline* [electronic journal]. www.optimumonline.ca, 32: 4: 25–34 [accessed June 7, 2010].

Hubbard, Ruth and Gilles Paquet 2005. "Betting on Mechanisms: The New Frontier for Federalism." *optimumonline* [electronic journal]. www.optimumonline.ca, 35: 1: 2–25 [accessed June 7, 2010].

Hubbard, Ruth and Gilles Paquet 2007a. *Gomery's Blinders and Canadian Federalism*. Ottawa: The University of Ottawa Press.

Hubbard, Ruth and Gilles Paquet 2007b. "The Governance of Solidarity: An Exploratory Essay." *optimumonline* [electronic journal]. www.optimumonline.ca, 37: 4: 2–22 [accessed June 7, 2010].

Hubbard, Ruth and Gilles Paquet 2007c. "Cat's Cradling: APEX Forums on Wicked Problems." *optimumonline* [electronic journal]. www.optimumonline.ca, 37: 2: 12–18 [accessed June 7, 2010].

Hubbard, Ruth and Gilles Paquet 2009. "Design Challenges for the Strategic State: Bricolage and Sabotage." In *How Ottawa Spends 2009-10*, ed. A. M. Maslove. Montreal, QC and Kingston, ON: McGill-Queen's University Press, 89–114.

Hughes, Jeff and Jonathan Weiss 2007. "Simple Rules for Making Alliances Work." *Harvard Business Review*, 85: 11: 122–131.

Ignatieff, Michael 2001. *Human Rights as Politics and Idolatry.* Princeton, NJ: Princeton University Press.

Inglehart, Ronald 2000. "Postmodernization Erodes Respect for Authority but Increases Support for Democracy." In *Critical Citizens,* ed. Pippa Norris. Oxford, UK: Oxford University Press, 236–256.

Innerarity, Daniel 2006. *La démocratie sans l'État – Essai sur la gouvernement des sociétés complexes.* Paris: Climats.

Ivison, John 2008 (January 9). "Maybe It's Lunn Who Should Go". *National Post*, www.nationalpost.com/news/canada/story.html?id=228794 [accessed April 15, 2008].

Jack, Ian 2001a (August 20). "Pressure From Top Stalls Hearings: Boudria's Silencing of Civil Servants Sends a Message: 'Fear of Political Repercussions' Blamed as Witnesses Cancel on Access Committee." *National Post*, A1. Check title of article.

Jack, Ian 2001b (August 28). "'Defiant' Backbencher To Go Ahead With Report: MPs To Call For Reform of Access to Information Act." *National Post*, A6.

Jack, Ian 2001c (August 29). "Five of Eight Liberals on Committee Miss Hearing." *National Post*, A6.

Jack, Ian 2001d (August 30). "Liberals in 'Clear Conflict,' Hearing Told." *National Post*, A6.

Jacobs, Jane 1992. *Systems of Survival.* New York: Vintage Books.

Johansen, Leif 1979. "The Bargaining Society and the Inefficiency of Bargaining." *Kyklos*, 32: 3: 497–522.

Johnson, Chalmers 1964. *Revolution and the Social System.* Stanford, CA: Hoover Institution.

Johnson, Mark 1993. *Moral Imagination*. Chicago, IL: The University of Chicago Press.

Jones, Stephen R. G. 1984. *The Economics of Conformism*. Oxford, UK: Blackwell.

Juillet, Luc et al. 2001. "Gouvernance collaborative, imputabilités douces et contrats moraux: un cadre d'analyse." *Gouvernance,* 1: 4: 85–95.

Juillet, Luc and Gilles Paquet 2002. "The Neurotic State." In *How Ottawa Spends 2002-3. The Security Aftermath and National Priorities*, ed. G. B. Doern. Don Mills, ON: Oxford University Press, 69–87.

Kahneman, Daniel and Amos Tversky 1979. "Prospect Theory: An Analysis of Decision under Risk." *Econometrica*, XLVII: 263–291.

Keen, Peter G. W. 1999. "Transforming Intellectual Property into Intellectual Capital: Competing in the Trust Economy." In *Capital for Our Times*, ed. N. Imperato. Stanford, CA: Hoover Institution Press, 3–35.

Kekes, John 1993. *The Morality of Pluralism*. Princeton, NJ: Princeton University Press.

Kekes, John 2003. *The Illusions of Egalitarianism*. Ithaca, NY: Cornell University Press.

Keller, Simon 2007. *The Limits of Loyalty*. Cambridge, UK: Cambridge University Press.

Kester, W. Carl 1992. "Industrial Groups as Systems of Contractual Governance." *Oxford Review of Economic Policy*, 8: 3: 24–44.

Kets de Vries, Manfred F. R. 2001. *The Leadership Mystique*. London/New York: Financial Times/Prentice Hall.

Kets de Vries, Manfred F. R. and Danny Miller 1984. *The Neurotic Organization*. San Francisco, CA: Jossey-Bass Publishers.

Koestler, Arthur 1978. *Janus: A Summing Up*. London, UK: Picador.

Kohlberg, Lawrence 1981. *The Philosophy of Moral Development*. New York: Harper & Row.

Kooiman, Jan 2003. *Governing as Governance*. London, UK: Sage.

Kumon, Shumpei 1992. "Japan as a Network Society." In *The Political Economy of Japan,* volume 3, eds. S. Kumon and H. Rosovsky. Stanford, CA: Stanford University Press, 109–141.

Kymlicka, Will 1998. *Finding Our Way.* Toronto, ON: Oxford University Press.

Lacouture, Jean 2005. *Éloge du Secret.* Bruxelles: Éditions Labor.

Ladeur, Karl-H. ed. 2004. *Public Governance in the Age of Globalization.* Aldershot, UK: Ashgate.

Lakoff, George 2009. *The Political Mind.* New York: Penguin Books.

Laliberté, Jean 2009. *Les fonctionnaires.* Quebec, QC: Septentrion.

Laurent, Paul and Gilles Paquet 1998. *Epistémologie et économie de la relation: coordination et gouvernance distribuée.* Lyon/Paris: Vrin.

Lave, Jean and Etienne Wenger 1991. *Situated Learning: Legitimate Peripheral Participation.* Cambridge, UK: Cambridge University Press.

Lawlor, Maryann 2006. "Collaborative Technologies Demand Deep Change." *SIGNAL Magazine*, May.

Lawton, Valerie 2001 (August 13). "Bureaucrats crucial to hearings: Bryden." *The Hamilton Spectator*, A02.

Leduc, Larry 1995. "Citizens' Revenge." In *Politics: Canada,* 8th edition, eds. Paul Fox and Graham White. Toronto, ON: McGraw Hill Ryerson.

Le Grand, Julian 2003. *Motivation, Agency, and Public Policy.* Oxford, UK: Oxford University Press.

Leibenstein, Harvey 1976. *Beyond Economic Man.* Cambridge, MA: Harvard University Press.

Leibenstein, Harvey 1978. *General X-Efficiency Theory and Economic Development.* Oxford, UK: Oxford University Press.

Leibenstein, Harvey 1987. *Inside the Firm.* Cambridge, MA: Harvard University Press.

Leishman, Rory 2006. *Against Judicial Activism.* Toronto, ON: The University of Toronto Press.

Lenihan, Donald G. 1995. "A Framework of Questions for Alternative Service Delivery." (mimeo).

Lenihan, Donald et al. 2007. *Progressive Governance for Canadians: What you Need to Know*. Ottawa, ON: Crossing Boundaries.

Lester, Richard K. and Michael J. Piore 2004. *Innovation – The Missing Dimension*. Cambridge, MA: Harvard University Press.

Levant, Ezra 2009. *Shakedown*. Toronto, ON: McClelland & Stewart.

Levine, John M. and Richard I. Moreland 2002. "Group Reactions to Loyalty and Disloyalty." *Group Cohesion, Trust and Solidarity*, 19: 203–228.

Lévy, Pierre 1995. *Qu'est-ce que le virtuel?* Paris: Editions La Découverte.

Lindquist, Evert and T. Sica 1995. *Canadian Governments and the Search for Alternative Program Delivery and Financing: A Preliminary Survey*. Toronto, ON: KPMG/Institute of Public Administration of Canada.

Lindquist, Evert and Gilles Paquet 2000. "Government Restructuring and the Federal Public Service: The Search for a New Cosmology." In *Government Restructuring and Career Public Services in Canada*, ed. E. Lindquist. Toronto, ON: Institute of Public Administration of Canada, 71–111.

Malone, Thomas W. 2004. *The Future of Work*. Boston, MA: Harvard Business School Press.

March, James G. 1988. "The Technology of Foolishness." In *Decisions and Organizations*, J. G. March. Oxford, UK: Basil Blackwell, 253–265.

Martin, Roger 2004. "The Design of Business." *Rotman Management*, winter.

Marty, Frederic et al. 2006. *Les partenariats public-privé*. Paris: La Découverte.

Mazankowski, Don and Paul Tellier et al. 2009. "Achieving Results: Accountability and Action." *Third Report of the Prime Minister's Advisory Committee on the Public Service*. Ottawa: the Prime Minister's Advisory Committee on the Public Service. Available at www.pco-bcp.ca [accessed August 28, 2009].

McCann, Joseph E. and John Selsky 1984. "Hyperturbulence and the Emergence of Type 5 Environment." *Academy of Management Review*, 9: 460–470.

McCarthy, Helen et al., eds. 2004. *Network Logic*. London, UK: Demos.

McCormack, Lee 2008. *Institutional Foundations for Performance Budgeting: The Case of the Government of Canada*. Ottawa: Canadian Comprehensive Auditing Foundation.

Mehra, Natalie 2005. "Flawed, Failed, Abandoned 100 P3s: Canadian & International Evidence." Toronto, ON: Ontario Health Coalition. www.ontariohealthcoalition.ca.

Mesthene, Emmanuel G. 1970. *Technical Change*. New York: Mentor Books.

Metcalfe, Les 1998. "Flexible Integration in and after the Amsterdam Treaty." In *Coping with Flexibility and Legitimacy after Amsterdam*, eds. M. den Boer, A. Guggenbühl and S. Vanhoonacker. Maastricht: European Institute of Public Administration, 11–30.

Michael, Donald N. 1980. *The New Competence: The Organization As A Learning System*. San Francisco, CA: Values and Lifestyles Program.

Michael, Donald N. 1993. "Governing by Learning: Boundaries, Myths and Metaphors." *Futures*, Jan/Feb: 81–89.

Migué, Jean-Luc 1994. "The Balkanization of the Canadian Economy: A Legacy of Federal Policy." In *Provincial Trade Wars: Why the Blockade Must End*, ed. F. Palda. Vancouver, BC: Fraser Institute, 107–130.

Miles, Raymond E. and Charles C. Snow 1995. "The New Network Firm: A Spherical Structure Built on a Human Investment Philosophy." *Organizational Dynamics*, 23: 5–18.

Millon-Delsol, Chantal 1992. *L'État subsidiaire.* Paris: Presses Universitaires de France.

Mintz, Jack and Michael Smart 2002 (March 23). "Why Quebec's Tax Point Transfers are a Good Idea." *The National Post.*

Mintzberg, Henry 1996a. "Managing Government, Governing Management." *Harvard Business Review*, 74: 3: 75–83.

Mintzberg, Henry 1996b. "Musings on Management." *Harvard Business Review*, 74: 4: 61–67.

Mody, Ashoka 1993. "Learning Through Alliances." *Journal of Economic Behavior and Organization*, 20: 151–170.

Montpetit, Eric 2007. *Le fédéralisme d'ouverture.* Quebec, QC: Septentrion.

Morgan, Gareth 1986. *Images of Organization.* San Francisco, CA: Sage Publications.

Morris, Shad S. et al. 2005. "An Architectural Approach to Managing Knowledge Stocks and Flows: Implications for Reinventing the HR Function." Working Paper Series. Ithaca, NY: Cornell University, School of Industrial and Labour Relations, Center for Advanced Human Resource Studies.

Mulgan, Geoff 1997. *Connexity.* Boston, MA: Harvard Business School Press.

Naisbitt, John 1994. *Global Paradox.* New York: Morrow.

National Post. www.nationalpost.com/news/canada/story. html?id=228794. [accessed April 15, 2008].

Nevitte, Neill 2001. "Citizens' Values, Information and Democratic Life." *Report to the Access to Information Review Task Force.* Ottawa: Government of Canada.

Noer, David M. 1993. Healing the Wounds. San Francisco, CA: Jossey-Bass.

Norman, Donald A. 1999. "Affordances, Conventions and Design." *Interactions*, 6: 3: 38–43.

Norman, Donald A. 2007. *The Design of Future Things*. New York: Basic Books.

O'Donnell, Guillermo 1998. "Horizontal Accountability in New Democracies." *Journal of Democracy*, 9: 3: 112–126.

OECD (Organisation for Economic Co-operation and Development) 2002. *Organisation for Economic Co-operation and Development Territorial Reviews*. Paris: OECD.

OECD 2005. *Modernizing Government: The Way Forward*. Paris: OECD.

O'Neal, Brian 1994. *Reorganizing Government: New Approaches to Public Service Reform*. Ottawa: Public Works and Government Services Canada. http://dsp-psd.tpsgc.gc.ca/Collection-R/LoPBdP/bp375-e.htm [accessed August 28, 2008].

O'Neill, Onora 2002. *A Question of Trust*. Cambridge, UK: Cambridge University Press.

Otazo, Karen 2006. "On Trust and Culture." *Strategy + Business* [electronic journal]. August 28. www.strategy-business.com.

O'Toole, James 1995–96. *Leading Change*. San Francisco, CA: Jossey-Bass. [paperback edition published in 1996].

Painter-Morland, Mollie 2008. *Business Ethics As Practice: Ethics As Everyday Business of Business*. Cambridge, UK: Cambridge University Press.

Painter-Morland, Mollie 2009. "Leadership in Complex Adaptive Systems." *Rotman Magazine,* fall: 99–102.

Paquet, Gilles 1977. "Federalism as Social Technology." *Options: Conference on the Future of the Canadian Federation*, Toronto: The University of Toronto Press, 281–302.

Paquet, Gilles 1989. "The Underground Economy." *Policy Options*, 10: 1: 3–6.

Paquet, Gilles 1991–92. "Betting on Moral Contracts." *Optimum, The Journal on Public Sector Management*, 22: 3: 45–53.

Paquet, Gilles 1992. "The Strategic State." In *Finding Common Ground*, ed. J. Chrétien. Hull, QC: Voyageur Publishing, 85–101.

Paquet, Gilles 1994. "Re-inventing Governance." *Opinion Canada*, 2: 2: 1–5.

Paquet, Gilles 1995. "Institutional Evolution in an Information Age." In *Technology, Information and Public Policy, The Bell Canada Papers on Economic and Public Policy,* Third edition. T.J. Courchene. Kingston, ON: John Deutsch Institute for the Study of Economic Policy, 197–229.

Paquet, Gilles 1996a. "Gouvernance distribuée et habitus centralisateur. " *Mémoires de la Société royale du Canada*, séries VI: 6: 425–439.

Paquet, Gilles 1996b. "The Downtrodden Administrative Route." *Inroads*, 5:117–121.

Paquet, Gilles 1996–97. "The Strategic State." *Ciencia Ergo Sum*, 3: 3: 1996: 257–261 (Part 1); 4: 1: 1997: 28–34 (Part 2); 4: 2: 1997: 148–154 (Part 3).

Paquet, Gilles 1997. "Alternative Program Delivery: Transforming the Practices of Governance," In *Alternative Service Delivery: Sharing Governance in Canada*, eds. R. Ford and D. R. Zussman. Toronto: Institute of Public Administration of Canada/KPMG, 31–58.

Paquet, Gilles 1998. "Canada as a Disconcerted Learning Economy: A Governance Challenge." *Transactions of the Royal Society of Canada*, Series VI: VIII: 69–98.

Paquet, Gilles 1999a. *Governance Through Social Learning.* Ottawa: University of Ottawa Press.

Paquet, Gilles 1999b. "Innovations in Governance in Canada." *Optimum, The Journal of Public Sector Management*, 29: 2-3: 71–81.

Paquet, Gilles 2000. "The Judgment of Wider Courts." Proceedings of the Symposium *Expanding Horizons: Rethinking Access to Justice in Canada.* Ottawa: Department of Justice, 80–88.

Paquet, Gilles 2001a. "P3 Governance: A Power Game without a Master." *Summit: The Business of Public Sector Procurement,* winter: 8–9.

Paquet, Gilles 2001b. "Smart Communities and the Geo-governance of Social Learning." *optimumonline* [electronic journal]. www.optimumonline.ca, 31: 2: 33–50 [access June 7, 2010].

Paquet, Gilles 2003. "Toward a Baroque Governance in 21st Century Canada." In *The Canadian Distinctiveness into the XXIst Century,* eds. C. Gaffield and K. L. Gould. Ottawa: University of Ottawa Press, 59–88.

Paquet, Gilles 2004a. "Fiscal Imbalance as Governance Failure." In *How Ottawa Spends 2004-2005: Mandate Change in the Paul Martin Era,* ed. G. B. Doern. Montreal, QC and Kingston, ON: McGill-Queen's University Press, 25–45.

Paquet, Gilles 2004b. *Pathologies de gouvernance.* Montreal: Liber.

Paquet, Gilles 2004c. "Gouvernance et déconcertation." *optimumonline* [electronic journal]. www.optimumonline.ca, 34: 4: 18–46 [accessed on June 7, 2010].

Paquet, Gilles 2005a. *The New Geo-Governance: A Baroque Approach.* Ottawa: The University of Ottawa Press.

Paquet, Gilles 2005b. *Gouvernance : une invitation à la subversion.* Montreal: Liber.

Paquet, Gilles 2005c. "Gomery as Glasnost." *The Literary Review of Canada,* 13: 7: 12–15.

Paquet, Gilles 2005d. "Jean Charest's First 500 days: Two Anamorphoses." *Policy Options,* 26: 09: 73–75.

Paquet, Gilles 2006a. "Savoirs, Savoir-faire, Savoir-être : in praise of professional wroughting and wrighting." A thinkpiece for *Campus 2020 – An Inquiry into the Future of British Columbia's Post Secondary Education System.* www.campus2020.ca/EN/think_pieces/.

Paquet, Gilles et al. 2006b. *The National Capital Commission: Charting a New Course*. Ottawa: Report of the NCC Mandate Review Panel, December.

Paquet, Gilles 2007a. "Organization Design as Governance's Achilles' Heel." www.governancia.com, 1: 3: 2007e: 1–11.

Paquet, Gilles 2007b. "Letting The Cat out of Gow's Bag." *optimumonline* [electronic journal]. www.optimumonline.ca, 37: 4: 45–49 [accessed on June 7, 2010].

Paquet, Gilles 2007c. Background paper prepared for the Task Force on Governance and Cultural Change in the RCMP, Ottawa.

Paquet, Gilles 2008a. *Gouvernance: mode d'emploi*. Montreal: Liber.

Paquet, Gilles 2008b. "Superbureaucrats and counter-democracy." *Canadian Government Executive,* June, 14–15.

Paquet, Gilles 2008c. "A Plea for Intelligent Accountability." *Financial Management Institute Journal*, 19: 2: 9–14

Paquet, Gilles 2008d. "Governance as Stewardship." *optimumonline* [electronic journal]. www.optimumonline.ca, 38: 4: 14–27 [accessed on June 7, 2010].

Paquet, Gilles 2008e. *Deep Cultural Diversity*. Ottawa: The University of Ottawa Press.

Paquet, Gilles 2008f. "Stéphane Dion: source ou symptôme du malaise?" *Options politiques*, 29: 5: 36–40.

Paquet, Gilles 2009a. *Scheming Virtuously: The Road to Collaborative Governance*. Ottawa: Invenire Books.

Paquet, Gilles 2009b. *Crippling Epistemologies and Governance Failures*. Ottawa: The University of Ottawa Press.

Paquet, Gilles 2009c. "Quantophrenia." *optimumonline* [electronic journal]. www.optimumonline.ca, 39: 1: 14–27 [accessed on June 7, 2010].

Paquet, Gilles 2009d. "Gouvernance publique : $(G \rightarrow g) \cap (G_1 \rightarrow G_2)$." *optimumonline* [electronic journal]. www.optimumonline.ca, 39: 4: 17–34 [accessed on June 7, 2010].

Paquet, Gilles 2010. "Disloyalty." *optimumonline* [electronic journal]. www.optimumonline.ca, 40: 1: 23–47 [accessed on June 7, 2010].

Paquet, Gilles and Lise Pigeon 2000. "In Search of a New Covenant." In *Government Restructuring and the Future of Career Public Service in Canada*, ed. E. Lindquist. Toronto: Institute of Public Administration of Canada, 475–498.

Paquet, Gilles and Jeffrey Roy 1995. "Prosperity Through Networks: The Small Business Strategy That Might Have Been." In *How Ottawa Spends 1995*, ed. S. Phillips. Ottawa: Carleton University Press, 137–158.

Paquet, Gilles and Jeffrey Roy 1996. *Competition, Cooperation and Co-Evolution: Business-Government-Society Relations in Canada* (version III). Ottawa: PRIME documents.

Paquet, Gilles and Robert Shepherd 1996. "The Program Review Process: A Deconstruction." In *How Ottawa Spends 1996-97 – Life Under the Knife*, ed. G. Swimmer. Ottawa: Carleton University Press, 39–72.

Parker, Simon and Niamh Gallagher 2007. *The Collaborative State*. London, UK: Demos.

Parr, John et al. 2002. *The Practice of Stewardship*. Denver, CO: Alliance for Regional Stewardship.

Pharr, Susan and Robert D. Putnam, eds. 2000. *Disaffected Democracies*. Princeton, NJ: Princeton University Press.

Piore, Michael J. 1995. *Beyond Individualism*. Cambridge, MA: Harvard University Press.

Posner, Paul L. 2006. "Accountability Institutions and the Policy Process: The United States Experience." *OECD Journal of Budgeting*, 5: 3: 71–96.

Priest, Lisa 2009 (January 15). "Simple checklists save lives in the operating room." *The Globe & Mail*, A-4.

Proudhon, Pierre-Joseph 1850–51. *Confessions d'un révolutionnaire*. Paris: Garnier Frères/Vrin.

Public Policy Forum 2008. "Canada's Public Service in the 21st Century Destination: Excellence." www.ppforum.ca [accessed August 28, 2009].

Putnam, Robert D. 1993. *Making Democracy Work*. Princeton, NJ: Princeton University Press.

Putnam, Robert D. 2000. *Bowling Alone: The Collapse and Revival of American Community*. New York: Simon & Schuster.

Ramonjavelo, V. et al. 2006. "Une assise au développement des PPP: la confiance institutionnelle, interorganisationnelle, et inter-personnelle." *Canadian Public Administration*, 49: 3: 350–374.

Rao, Huggy and Robert Sutton 2008. "The Ergonomics of Innovation." *The McKinsey Quarterly*, September 17.

Raymond, Eric. S. 2001. *The Cathedral and The Bazaar*. Sebastopol, CA: O'Reilly.

Reid, John 2006. "Response to the Report of the Access to Information Task Force." Office of The Information Commissioner Reports. Ottawa: Office of The Information Commissioner. http://Blog.Privacylawyer.Ca/2006_4_01.html [accessed May 9, 2010].

Rhodes, R.A.W. and John Wanna 2007. "The Limits to Public Value, or Rescuing Responsible Government from the Platonic Guardians." *The Australian Journal of Public Administration*, 66: 4: 406–421.

Richards, John 1996. "The Case Against National Standards." *Policy Options*, 17: 5: 3–7.

Rittel, H. W. J. and M. M. Webber 1973. "Dilemmas in a General Theory of Planning." *Policy Sciences*, 4: 155–169.

Roberts, Alasdair 1996. *So-Called Experts: How American Consultants Remade the Canadian Civil Service, 1918-21*. Toronto: Institute of Public Administration, monograph no. 18.

Roberts, Alasdair 2000. "Protecting Your Right to Information." Speech to the *Founding Conference of Open Government Canada*, Toronto, March 11.

Roberts, Alasdair 2001a (October 18). "The Department of Secrets: The Chrétien Cabinet is Using Fears of Terrorism to Further Restrict Public Access to Information." *The Ottawa Citizen*, A19.

Roberts, Alasdair 2001b. "The Informational Commons At Risk." In *The Market and the Public Domain: Global Governance and the Asymmetry of Power*, ed. Daniel Drache. London, UK: Routledge, 175–201.

Roberts, Alasdair 2001c. "Reform of the Access to Information Act." Working Paper. Syracuse, NY: Campbell Public Affairs Institute, Syracuse University, August.

Roberts, John 2004. *The Modern Firm*. Oxford, UK: Oxford University Press.

Robertson, Gordon 2001. *Memoirs of a Very Civil Servant*, Toronto: University of Toronto (originally published in 2000 and reprinted in 2001).

Romme, A. Georges L. 2003. "Making a Difference: Organization as Design." *Organization Science*, 14: 5: 558–573.

Romzek, Barbara S. and Melvin J. Dubnik 1987. "Accountability in the Public Sector: Lessons from the Challenger Tragedy." *Public Administration Review*, 47: 227–236.

Rorty, Richard 1989. *Contingency, Irony and Solidarity*. Cambridge, UK: Cambridge University Press.

Rosenau, James N. 2003. *Distant Proximities*. Princeton, NJ: Princeton University Press.

Rosanvallon, Pierre 2006. *La contre-démocratie*. Paris: Seuil.

Rosanvallon, Pierre 2008. *La légitimité démocratique*. Paris: Seuil.

Ross, Jen 2001 (August 11). "House Leader Slams Access Act Overhaul: Boudria Warns 'Ad Hoc Group' Review to be 'Incomplete and Unsatisfactory'." *The Ottawa Citizen*, A3.

Ross, Malcolm, ed. 1954. *Our Sense of Identity*. Toronto, ON: The Ryerson Press.

Rouillard, Christian et al. 2004. *La réingénierie de l'État – Vers un appauvrissement de la gouvernance québécoise*. Quebec: Les Presses de l'Université Laval.

Rouillard, Christian et al. 2006. *Reengineering the State*. Ottawa: The University of Ottawa Press.

Roy, Louise 2003 (December 7). "Crise des transports publics: des alternatives pour sortir du cercle vicieux." *La Presse*.

Roy, Jeffrey and John Langford 2008. *Integrating Service Delivery Across Levels of Government: Case Studies of Canada and Other Countries*. Washington, DC: IBM Center for the Business of Government.

Rynor, Becky 2009 (July 14). "Rising Workplace Disloyalty 'No Big Surprise': Expert." *The Ottawa Citizen*.

Sabel, Charles F. 2001. "A Quiet Revolution of Democratic Governance: Towards Democratic Experimentalism." In *Governance in the 21ˢᵗ Century*. Paris: OECD, 121–148.

Sabel, Charles F. 2004. "Beyond Principal-Agent Governance: Experimnentalist Organizations, Learning and Accountability." In *De Staat van de Democratie. Democratie Voorbij de Staat. WRR Verkenning 3*, eds. E. Engelen and M. Sie Dhian Ho. Amsterdam, Netherlands: Amsterdam University Press, 173–195.

Sacconi, Lorenzo 2000. *The Social Contract of the Firm*. Heidelberg: Springer-Verlag.

Safire, William 1994 (September 26). "The New Disloyalty." *New York Times*.

Saveri, Andrea et al. 2005. *Technologies of Cooperation*. Palo Alto, CA: Institute for the Future.

Saveri, Andrea et al. 2008. "Technologies of Cooperation: A Socio-Technical Framework for Robust 4G." *Technology and Society Magazine IEEE*, summer: 11–23.

Savoie, Donald J. 1999. *Governing from the Centre*. Toronto, ON: University of Toronto Press.

Savoie, Donald J. 2003. *Breaking the Bargain*. Toronto, ON: University of Toronto Press.

Savoie, Donald J. 2008. *Court Government and the Collapse of Accountability in Canada and the United Kingdom*. Toronto, ON: University of Toronto Press.

Schnapper, Dominique 2002. *La démocratie providentielle*. Paris: Gallimard.

Schön, Donald A. 1971. *Beyond the Stable State*. New York: Norton.

Schön, Donald A. 1983. *The Reflective Practitioner*. New York: Basic Books.

Schön, Donald A. 1995. "Causality and Causal Inference in the Study of Organizations." In *Rethinking Knowledge*, eds. R.F. Goodman and W.R. Fisher. Albany, NY: State University of New York Press, 69–101.

Schön, Donald A. and Martin Rein 1994. *Frame Reflection*. New York: Basic Books.

Schopenhauer, Arthur 1851/1964. *The Pessimist's Handbook*. Lincoln, NB: The University of Nebraska Press.

Schrage, Michael 2000. *Serious Play*. Boston, MA: Harvard Business School.

Schrage, Michael 2008. "The Metric behind the Slogan." *Strategy & Business*, December 2: 1–3.

Schumacher, E. Fritz 1977. *A Guide for the Perplexed*. New York: Harper & Row.

Schumpeter, Joseph A. 1934. *The Theory of Economic Development*. Cambridge, UK: Harvard University Press.

Segal, Hugh D. 2010. "Beyond Centralization: How To Liberate Federalism?" In *The Case For Decentralized Federalism*, eds. R. Hubbard and G. Paquet. Ottawa: University of Ottawa Press, 93–115.

Séguin, Yves 2002. *Pour un nouveau partage des moyens financiers au Canada*. Ottawa: Rapport de la Commission sur le déséquilibre fiscal.

Self, Will 1991. *The Quantity Theory of Insanity*. London, UK: Bloomsbury.

Sen, Amartya 1999. *Development as Freedom*. New York: Knopf.

Senge, Peter M. 1990. *The Fifth Discipline*. New York: Doubleday.

Sgro, Judy 2002. "Canada's Urban Strategy – A Vison for the 21st Century." *Prime Minister's Caucus Task Force on Urban Issues*. Ottawa: Office of the Prime Minister, November.

Shapiro, Andrea 2003. *Creating Contagious Commitment – Applying the Tipping Point to Organizational Change*. Hillsborough, NC: Strategy Perspective.

Shirky, Clay 2008. *Here Comes Everybody*. New York: The Penguin Press.

Shore, Cris 2008. "Audit Culture and Illiberal Governance." *Anthropology Theory*, 8: 3: 278–298.

Sibley, Robert 2009 (April 11). "Never Mind the Economy, It's the Trust Deficit." *The Ottawa Citizen*.

Simon, Herbert A. 1947. *Administrative Behavior*. New York: Macmillan.

Simons, Robert 2005. *Levers of Organization Design*. Boston, MA: Harvard Business School Press.

Simpson, Jeffrey 2001. *The Friendly Dictatorship*. Toronto, ON: McClelland & Stewart.

Smith, Janet R. and Carl A. Taylor, eds. 1996. *Strengthening Policy Capacity*. Ottawa: Canadian Centre for Management Development.

Snow, Charles et al. 1992. "Managing 21st Century Network Organizations." *Organizational Dynamics*, 20: 5–20.

Sorokin, Pieter A. 1956. *Fads and Foibles in Modern Sociology and Related Sciences*. Chicago, IL: Henry Regnery.

Sparrow, Malcolm K. 2008. *The Character of Harms*. Cambridge, UK: Cambridge University Press.

Spinosa, Charles et al. 1997. *Disclosing New Worlds*. Cambridge, MA: The MIT Press.

Stein, Janice G. 2006. "Canada by Mondrian: Networked Federalism in an Era of Globalization." In *Canada by Picasso – The Faces of Federalism*, eds. R. Gibbins et al. Ottawa: The Conference Board of Canada, 15–58.

Stone, Bruce 1995. "Administrative Accountability in the 'Westminster' Democracies: Towards a New Conceptual Framework." *Governance*, 8: 4: 505–526.

Stratos Inc. 2003. *Building Confidence: Corporate Sustainability Reporting in Canada*. Ottawa.

Sue, Roger 2003. *La société civile face au pouvoir*. Paris: Presses de Science Po.

Sullivan, Helen and Chris Skelcher 2002. *Working Across Boundaries*. New York: Palgrave Macmillan.

Sunstein, Cass R. 2003. *Why Societies Need Dissent*. Cambridge, MA: Harvard University Press.

Sunstein, Cass R. 2005. *Laws of Fear*. Cambridge, UK: Cambridge University Press.

Sunstein, Cass R. 2006. *Infotopia*. Oxford, UK: Oxford University Press.

Surowiecki, James 2004. *The Wisdom of Crowds*. New York: Doubleday.

Taleb, Nassim Nicholas 2007. *The Black Swan*. New York: Random House.

Tapscott, Don and David Agnew 1999. "Governance in the Digital Economy." *Finance & Development*, 36: 4: 34–37.

Tapscott, Don and Anthony D. Williams 2006. *Wikinomics: How Mass Collaboration Changes Everything*. New York: Portfolio.

Taylor, Carl A. 1997. "The ACIDD Test: A Framework for Policy Planning and Decision-Making." *Optimum, the Journal of Public Sector Management*, 27: 4: 53–62.

Taylor, Charles 2007. *A Secular Age*. Cambridge, MA: Harvard University Press.

Thacher, David and Martin Rein 2004. "Managing Value Conflict in Public Policy." *Governance,* 17: 4: 457–486.

Thaler, Richard H. and Cass R. Sunstein 2008. *Nudge.* New Haven, CN: Yale University Press.

Thomas, Paul G. 2008. "Political-Administrative Interface in Canada's Public Sector." *optimumonline* [electronic journal]. www.optimumonline.ca, 38: 2: 21–29.

Thomas, Paul G. 2009a. *Who Is Getting the Message? Communications at the Centre of Government.* Ottawa: Research Study for the Oliphant Commission.

Thomas, Paul G. 2009b. "When the Machinery of Government Breaks down…" *optimumonline* [electronic journal]. www.optimumonline.ca, 39: 4: 43–50.

Thuderoz, Christian et al. 1999. *La confiance.* Paris: Gaëtan Morin.

Tocqueville, Alexis de (1840) 1961. *De la démocratie en Amérique.* Paris: Gallimard

Tussman, Joseph 1989. *The Burden of Office.* Vancouver, BC: Talonbooks.

Union des municipalités du Québec 2003. *La situation fiscale des municipalités québécoises.* Recherche conjointe de l'UMQ et du Conference Board du Canada, May.

Vaillancourt Rosenau, Pauline, ed. 2000. *Public-Private Policy Partnerships.* Cambridge, MA: The MIT Press.

van Hooft, Stan 2006. *Understanding Virtue Ethics.* Chesham, UK: Acumen.

Vickers, Geoffrey 1965. *The Art of Judgment.* London, UK: Methuen.

Vickers, Geoffrey 1973. *Making Institutions Work.* New York: Wiley.

Vickers, Geoffrey 1983. *Human Systems are Different.* London, UK: Harper & Row.

Voß, Jan-Peter et al., eds. 2006. *Reflexive Governance for Sustainable Development.* Cheltenham, UK: Edward Elgar.

Wahl, Andrew 2005. "Culture Shock: A Survey of Canadian Executives Reveals that Corporate Culture is in Need of Improvement." *Canadian Business Magazine*, October: 10–23.

Wallerstein, Immanuel 1998. *Utopistics – or, Historical Choices of the Twenty-first Century*. New York: The New Press.

Webber, Alan M. 1993. "What's So New About the New Economy?" *Harvard Business Review*, 71: 1: 24–42.

Weber, Max 1968. *Economy and Society*. New York: Bedminster Press.

Weick, Karl E. and Richard L. Daft 1984. "Toward a model of organizations as interpretation systems." *The Academy of Management Review*, 9: 2: 284–295.

Weinberger, David 2007. "The Folly of Accountabalism." *Harvard Business Review*, 85: 2: 54.

Wenger, Etienne 1998. *Communities of Practice*. Cambridge, UK: Cambridge University Press.

Wenger, Etienne et al. 2002. *Cultivating Communities of Practice*. Boston, MA: Harvard Business School Press.

Womack, John 1969. *Zapata and the Mexican Revolution*. New York: Knopf.

Wright, David and David R. Zussman 1996. "Review and Analysis of Recent Changes in the Delivery of Government Services." *Report to the Deputy Ministers Task Force on Service Delivery Models*. Ottawa: Government of Canada.

Wriston, Walter B. 1992. *The Twilight of Sovereignty*. New York: Scribner's

Yankelovich, Daniel and Steven Rosell 2001. www.ViewpointLearning.com.

Yankelovich, Daniel and Steven Rosell 2006. www.ViewpointLearning.com/about/model.shtml [accessed May 14, 2010].

Index

Accenture, 405–407

"Access - A Right Under Siege," 269

Access to information, 109, 254–255, 259, 265–274, 275

Access to Information Act, 265–266, 268, 275

Accountability
access-to-information and, 269–270

Accountability Act, xi, 6, 368
burden of office and, 223–224
collective intelligence and, 79
distrust and, 254–255
effectiveness and, 321–323, 326, 328, 329, 342

Federal Accountability Act, xi, 272–273, 368
intelligent, 139, 140–141, 148, 150
post-Gomery, 13–14
public service and, 131, 164, 181, 191, 367, 376, 379–380, 412, 460
quantophrenia and, 170–171
Simons conditions and, 388, 409
tax policy and, 296–297
uniformity and, 210
Westminster and, 91–92, 206, 313–314, 321, 326
See also Management accountability framework

Ackoff, Russell, 318

Adoption, of complex adaptive system, 68

Advisory Committee on the Public Service, xi, 147, 271, 362, 376

AECB. *See* Atomic Energy Control Board

AECL. *See* Atomic Energy of Canada Limited

Affectio societatis, 243, 247–248

Affordances, 213–216

Agreement on Internal Trade, 91

Akerlof, George, 236–237

Alcock, Reg, 272

Alinsky, Saul, 441

Al-Mashat affair, 54, 234, 456

Alternate service delivery (ASD)
concerns, 320–323
defined, 307–310
foundation questions, 310–312
"obligations and interests" clause, 323–325, 326
roles and relationships, 325–329
social learning and, 309, 312, 317–319, 329–330
technology and, 312–317

Anderson, Walter, 20

Ankersmit, Frank, 430–431

APEX. *See* Association of Professional Executives of the Public Service of Canada

Argyris, Chris, 36

Aristophanes, 450, 452

ASD. *See* Alternate service delivery

Ashby's law, 63, 353, 366

Association of Professional Executives of the Public Service of Canada (APEX)
on accountability, 140–141
on cities, 175–176, 177
conclusions of, 134–136, 165–166, 181–182, 194, 196–198
on confrontation, 154–155
on corporate culture, 123–124

Governance Series Publications

27. Ruth Hubbard and Gilles Paquet (eds.) 2010
    The Case for Decentralized Federalism
26. Gordon DiGiacomo and Maryantonett Flumian (eds.) 2010
    The Case for Centralized Federalism
25. Patrice Dutil, Cosmo Howard, John Langford and Jeffrey Roy
    2010
    The Service State: Rhetoric, Reality and Promise
24. Ruth Hubbard and Gilles Paquet 2010
    The Black Hole of Public Administration
23. Michael Small 2009
    The Forgotten Peace – Mediation at Niagara Falls, 1914
22. Gilles Paquet 2009
    *Crippling Epistemologies and Governance Failures – A Plea for
    Experimentalism*
21. O. P. Dwivedi, Timothy Mau, and Byron Sheldrick 2009
    *The Evolving Physiology of Government – Canadian Public
    Administration in Transition*
20. Caroline Andrews, Ruth Hubbard, and Jeffrey Roy (eds.) 2009
    Gilles Paquet – Homo Hereticus
19. Luc Juillet and Ken Rasmussen 2008
    *Defending a Contested Ideal – Merit and the Public Service
    Commission: 1908–2008*
18. Luc Juillet et Ken Rasmussen 2008
    *À la défense d'un idéal contesté – le principe de mérite et la CFP,
    1908–2008*
17. Gilles Paquet 2008
    Deep Cultural Diversity – A Governance Challenge
16. Paul Schafer 2008
    *Revolution or Renaissance – Making the Transition from an
    Economic Age to a Cultural Age*
15. Gilles Paquet 2008
    *Tableau d'avancement – petite ethnographie interprétative d'un
    certain Canada français*